APEC AND THE CONSTRUCTION OF PACIFIC RIM REGIONALISM

The distinctive regional grouping that is APEC (Asia-Pacific Economic Cooperation) has become the leading forum for government collaboration in the Asia-Pacific since its foundation in 1989. Comprising twenty-one diverse member states from the region, including the world's three largest economies (China, Japan and the United States), APEC has a broad agenda that embraces trade liberalization, trade facilitation and economic co-operation. It is unique in taking a non-discriminatory approach to liberalization based on the principle of open regionalism. This book uses APEC to ask incisive questions about collaboration in general and regionalism in particular, in addition to analysing APEC's activities and objectives, successes and failures. The book addresses issues of central concern to students of international political economy and international relations, and is also relevant to more general discussions about Asia-Pacific cooperation. It makes a major contribution to a broader understanding of the forces of regionalism and globalization at the beginning of the twenty-first century.

John Ravenhill holds the Chair of Politics at the University of Edinburgh. He was formerly Head of the Department of International Relations of the Research School of Pacific and Asian Studies at the Australian National University. His books include *The Asian Financial Crisis and the Architecture of Global Finance* (2000) (edited with Greg Noble) and *The Political Economy of East Asia* (1995).

Dedication

In memory of my parents, Frederick William George Ravenhill, and Kathleen Irene Ravenhill (née *Mabbott*)

CAMBRIDGE ASIA–PACIFIC STUDIES

Cambridge Asia–Pacific Studies aims to provide a focus and forum for scholarly work on the Asia–Pacific region as a whole, and its component sub-regions, namely Northeast Asia, Southeast Asia and the Pacific Islands. The series is produced in association with the Research School of Pacific and Asian Studies at the Australian National University and the Australian Institute of International Affairs.

R. Gerard Ward and Elizabeth Kingdon (eds) *Land, Custom and Practice in the South Pacific*
0 521 47289 X hardback

Stephanie Lawson *Tradition Versus Democracy in the South Pacific*
0 521 49638 1 hardback

Walter Hatch and Kozo Yamamura *Asia in Japan's Embrace*
0 521 56176 0 hardback 0 521 56515 4 paperback

Alasdair Bowie and Daniel Unger *The Politics of Open Economies: Indonesia, Malaysia, the Philippines and Thailand*
0 521 58343 8 hardback 0 521 58683 6 paperback

David Kelly and Anthony Reid (eds) *Asian Freedoms*
0 521 62035 X hardback 0 521 63757 0 paperback

Danny Unger *Building Social Capital in Thailand*
0 521 63058 4 hardback 0 521 63931 X paperback

Yongnian Zheng *Discovering Chinese Nationalism in China: Modernization, Identity, and International Relations*
0 521 64180 2 hardback 0 521 64590 5 paperback

Doh C. Shin *Mass Politics and Culture in Democratizing Korea*
0 521 65146 8 hardback 0 521 65823 3 paperback

John A. Mathews and Dong-Sung Cho *Tiger Technology: The Creation of a Semiconductor Industry in East Asia*
0 521 66269 9 hardback

Samuel S. Kim (ed.) *Korea's Globalization*
0 521 77272 9 hardback 0 521 77559 0 paperback

Gregory W. Noble and John Ravenhill (eds) *The Asian Financial Crisis and the Architecture of Global Finance*
0 521 79091 3 hardback 0 521 79422 6 paperback

Peter Dauvergne *Loggers and Degradation in the Asia-Pacific: Corporations and Environmental Management*
0 521 80661 5 hardback 0 521 00134 X paperback

Anthony J. Langlois *The Politics of Justice and Human Rights: Southeast Asia and Universalist Theory*
0 521 80785 9 hardback 0 521 00347 4 paperback

Alan Dupont, *East Asia Imperilled: Transnational Challenges to Security*
0 521 81153 8 hardback 0 521 01015 2 paperback

William T. Tow, *Asia-Pacific Strategic Relations: Seeking Convergent Security*
0 521 80790 5 hardback 0 521 00368 7 paperback

APEC AND THE CONSTRUCTION OF PACIFIC RIM REGIONALISM

JOHN RAVENHILL
University of Edinburgh

CAMBRIDGE
UNIVERSITY PRESS

PUBLISHED BY THE PRESS SYNDICATE OF THE UNIVERSITY OF CAMBRIDGE
The Pitt Building, Trumpington Street, Cambridge, United Kingdom

CAMBRIDGE UNIVERSITY PRESS
The Edinburgh Building, Cambridge CB2 2RU, UK
40 West 20th Street, New York, NY 10011–4211, USA
10 Stamford Road, Oakleigh, VIC 3166, Australia
Ruiz de Alarcón 13, 28014 Madrid, Spain
Dock House, The Waterfront, Cape Town 8001, South Africa

http://www.cambridge.org

First published 2001

Printed in Singapore by Green Giant Press

Typeface New Baskerville (*Adobe*) 10/12 pt. *System* QuarkXPress® [PK]

A catalogue record for this book is available from the British Library

National Library of Australia Cataloguing in Publication data
Ravenhill, John.
APEC and the construction of Pacific Rim regionalism.
Bibliography.
Includes index.
ISBN 0 521 66094 7.
ISBN 0 521 66797 6 (pbk.).
1. Asia Pacific Economic Cooperation (Organization).
2. Regionalism – Pacific Area.
I. Title. (Series: Cambridge Asia-Pacific studies).
337.15

ISBN 0 521 66094 7 hardback
ISBN 0 521 66797 6 paperback

Contents

Tables and Figures

Tables

Figures

Acknowledgements

As is so often the case, this project took far longer to complete than originally anticipated. It was placed on the backburner while other matters intervened – administrative responsibilities while I was head of department, the Asian financial crises, which drew me into another major project that required more immediate action, and a move across continents that saw my files disappearing into storage for longer than expected. For all concerned, not least the long-suffering editors at Cambridge University Press, the delays in producing this book were frustrating. In the end, however, they proved advantageous because they afforded me an opportunity to review APEC's evolution over a longer period of time than would otherwise have been possible, and, in particular, to take account of the impact of the financial crises on regionalism in East Asia.

Conversations with numerous officials and academics involved in the process of constructing Asia-Pacific collaboration aided my research for this book. There are too many to thank individually in these pages and, because many of the individuals would not wish, at least publicly, to be associated with some of the judgements expressed in this book, I will preserve their anonymity. I am very happy to acknowledge publicly, however, the very helpful comments received from colleagues who read some or all of the manuscript in one or more of its drafts: Peter Dauvergne, Ernie Haas, Natasha Hamilton-Hart, Greg Noble, and Jim Richardson. The three anonymous readers for Cambridge University Press similarly provided constructive ideas. That I have not been able to follow every suggestion that readers have made certainly does not mean that they were not influential in causing me to pause and rethink the presentation of various arguments.

I completed most of the writing for this book while I was in the Department of International Relations, Research School of Pacific and Asian

Studies, at the Australian National University. This was a particularly difficult time for Australian universities, buffeted by an unsympathetic government and inept management. The excellence of colleagues within the department, however, made it a stimulating and enjoyable working environment.

I owe a significant debt to those who have assisted me in the preparation of this manuscript, in particular to Robin Ward, who tracked down numerous obscure references, cleaned up the manuscript before its submission, and prepared the index with her customary skill and efficiency. As this was Robin's last major project before retirement from the ANU, this is an appropriate opportunity for me to record a collective thank-you from all those in the Department who benefited from her assistance over a period of more than three decades. David Sullivan assisted in collecting materials in the early stages of research; Mary-Lou Hickey tracked down one missing reference at the end.

At Cambridge University Press, a special vote of thanks to the Commissioning Editor, Phillipa McGuinness, with whom I have had the pleasure of working on the Cambridge Asia-Pacific Studies series for several years. I was pleased to have submitted the final manuscript during Phillipa's last month with the Press, a small consolation, I hope, for her frustration with earlier delays. Paul Watt, the Editorial Controller, was very patient when events contrived to disrupt his production schedule. Venetia Somerset, the copyeditor, helped clarify the presentation of some arguments.

As always, my biggest debt is to my partner and best friend, Stefa Wirga. She has tolerated with patience and humour the inevitable disruptions to her life and the extra burdens that a major project like this one have imposed, and has provided the encouragement and inspiration to help me see the project through.

Abbreviations

ABAC	APEC Business Advisory Council
ACP	African, Caribbean and Pacific group
ADB	Asian Development Bank
AFR	*Australian Financial Review*
AFTA	ASEAN Free Trade Area
ANU	Australian National University
APEC	Asia-Pacific Economic Cooperation
APIAN	APEC International Assessment Network
ARF	ASEAN Regional Forum
ASEAN	Association of Southeast Asian Nations
ASEM	Asia–Europe Meeting
AUSPECC	Australian Pacific Economic Cooperation Committee
DFAT	Department of Foreign Affairs and Trade (Australia)
DSMs	dispute settlement mechanisms
EAEC	East Asian Economic Caucus
EAEG	East Asian Economic Group
ECAFE	Economic Commission for Asia and the Far East (UN)
ECOTECH	Economic and Technical Cooperation
EEC	European Economic Community
EPG	Eminent Persons Group
ESC	ECOTECH subcommittee (APEC)
ESCAP	Economic and Social Commission for Asia and the Pacific (UN)/Economic Commission for Asia and the Far East
EU	European Union
EVSL	Early Voluntary Sectoral Liberalization
FDI	foreign direct investment
FEER	*Far Eastern Economic Review*
GATT	General Agreement on Tariffs and Trade

GDP	gross domestic product
GNP	gross national product
IAPs	individual action plans
ILO	International Labor Organization
IMF	International Monetary Fund
MFN	most-favoured-nation
MITI	Ministry of International Trade and Industry (Japan)
MOFA	Ministry of Foreign Affairs (Japan)
NAFTA	North American Free Trade Area
NATO	North Atlantic Treaty Organization
NBIP	Non-Binding Investment Principles
NGOs	non-government organizations
NICs	newly industrializing countries
NTBs	non-tariff barriers
OECD	Organization for Economic Cooperation and Development
OPEC	Organization of Petroleum Exporting Countries
OPTAD	Organization for Pacific Trade and Development
PAFTA	Pacific Free Trade Area
PAFTAD	Pacific Trade and Development Conference
PBEC	Pacific Basin Economic Council
PECC	Pacific Economic Cooperation Council (formerly Pacific Economic Cooperation Conference)
SEATO	South-East Asia Treaty Organization
SOM	Senior Officials Meeting
TEP	Transatlantic Economic Partnership
TRIMs	Trade-Related Investment Measures
UNCTAD	United Nations Conference on Trade and Development
WTO	World Trade Organization

Introduction

The Asia-Pacific Economic Cooperation (APEC) grouping was hailed by C. Fred Bergsten (1994), the prominent American economist, as 'potentially the most far-reaching trade agreement in history'. Even discounting Bergsten's hyperbole, APEC has made remarkable progress as an institution since its establishment in 1989. It has graduated from a ministerial-level gathering of twelve countries to an institution that stages annual summits of 'Economic Leaders' of its twenty-one members.[1]

> The founding members of APEC were the (then) six member states of ASEAN (Brunei, Indonesia, Malaysia, the Philippines, Singapore and Thailand) plus Australia, Canada, Japan, New Zealand, South Korea, and the United States. The 'three Chinas' (Hong Kong, the People's Republic of China, and Taiwan) were admitted in 1991. Mexico and Papua New Guinea joined in 1993, Chile in the following year. Peru, Russia and Vietnam were admitted at the Vancouver Leaders' Meeting in 1997, to take effect at the Kuala Lumpur Leaders' Meeting in 1998.

APEC has established a permanent Secretariat. APEC's ministerial working groups hold more than thirty meetings each year. Its members committed themselves to the goal of establishing free trade in the region by the year 2010 for developed economies and 2020 for less developed economies. The Seoul Ministerial Meeting in 1991 adopted the following statement of objectives:

- to sustain the growth and development of the region for the common good of its peoples and, in this way, to contribute to the growth and development of the world economy;

- to enhance the positive gains, both for the region and the world economy, resulting from increasing economic interdependence, to include encouraging the flow of goods, services, capital, and technology;
- to develop and strengthen the open multilateral trading system in the interest of the Asia-Pacific and all other economies; and
- to reduce barriers to trade in goods and services among participants in a manner consistent with GATT principles, where applicable, and without detriment to other economies. (http://www.apecsec.org.sg/virtualib/minismtg/mtgmin91.html)

APEC also launched a program ('economic and technical cooperation' or ECOTECH in APEC parlance) aimed at building the economic capacity of its less developed members; by the end of APEC's first decade more than 200 projects were running under its auspices.

APEC has evolved rapidly in a region historically regarded as suffering an 'institutional deficit'. It links the world's three largest economies (China, Japan and the United States) and many of the world's most rapidly growing economies. APEC member economies account for more than 55 per cent of global production and over 45 per cent of global trade. Intra-APEC trade alone accounts for more than a third of the global total. Following the decision at the Vancouver Leaders' Meeting in 1997 to admit Russia, APEC includes three of the five permanent members of the United Nations Security Council, the three principal adversaries in the Cold War. APEC embraces economies characterized by unusual diversity in levels of development by the standards of other regional cooperative schemes. Its members are similarly heterogeneous in cultures and political systems.

Moreover, APEC's approach to economic cooperation is unique among contemporary regional economic groupings. Unlike the European Union (EU) or the North American Free Trade Area (NAFTA), it has adopted a non-discriminatory approach to trade liberalization, an approach its members term 'open regionalism'. Because APEC will extend trade concessions to members and non-members alike on a most-favoured-nation (MFN) basis, its method of trade liberalization is arguably more consistent with economic theory than the free-trade areas or customs unions conventionally seen within the General Agreement on Tariffs and Trade (GATT) and the World Trade Organization (WTO) (Aggarwal 1993). Unlike other regional agreements, APEC has eschewed legally binding agreements. Trade liberalization is to occur voluntarily, with individual member economies allowed discretion in deciding how much flexibility they will exercise in meeting the goal of free trade by the year 2020.

APEC therefore holds considerable interest and poses a number of puzzles for students of international political economy. Even though a large number of studies of APEC were completed in its first decade (reflected in the length of the list of references for this book), few attempted to examine APEC in the context of questions that preoccupy students of international relations. This book attempts to fill this gap. It seeks to establish what the international relations literature on collaboration tells us about APEC and the reasons for its performance, and, vice versa, what implications APEC has for theorizing about collaboration in general and regionalism in particular. It is organized around a series of questions drawn from the literature on international collaboration. Readers seeking a chronological account of APEC may therefore be frustrated (although Appendix I provides a chronology of major developments in APEC), as may those expecting a study organized according to the principal areas of APEC's cooperation. The book does provide a comprehensive evaluation of APEC's activities but in several parts, organized around questions about the reasons for APEC's institutional design and effectiveness.

The book addresses four main sets of questions. The first relates to APEC's establishment in 1989. Why did the APEC initiative succeed when proposals for institutionalized Asia-Pacific regional economic collaboration over the previous quarter-century had failed to generate agreement among potential members? To what extent can the success of the 1989 initiative be attributed to changes in global structures – military, economic or ideational – or to changes in economic and political structures at the domestic level? What was the role of ideas and intellectual leadership in forging a successful outcome? To what extent was APEC part of a broader trend towards regionalism in the global economy?

A second set of questions relates to institutional design and evolution: the organizational form that APEC has taken, its approach to economic cooperation, and the impact that these have had on APEC's effectiveness over its first decade. For, after being launched with high expectations, reflected in the Bergsten quote in the opening sentence of this introduction, significant disillusionment with the capacity of the grouping to realize its stated objectives had set in by the end of its first decade. For instance, in January 2001, Bergsten (2001) was telling a very different story, suggesting that APEC's various efforts at trade liberalization were 'dead in the water'.

Why did APEC member economies choose to pursue 'open regionalism' rather than a discriminatory free-trade area? Why did they choose an approach that has avoided the creation of a strong regional secretariat? What are the advantages and disadvantages of open regionalism from the perspective of building an organization committed to collaboration in support of regional or global economic liberalization? What are the benefits and costs of eschewing a strong independent secretariat and relying instead on the capacity of national governments and private organizations to support collaborative activities? What does APEC tell us about the prospects for and difficulties of constructing a regional organization based on consensual decision-making, the so-called 'Asian Way', as opposed to the more legalistic or 'Cartesian' approach favoured by Western governments? How effective are other means, such as the peer pressure on which APEC relies, of attempting to ensure compliance with international obligations in the absence of sanctions?

A third set of questions is derived from constructivist approaches, which focus on the issue of identity in international politics. Initially, it seemed that APEC had triumphed in the contest of regional definition, vanquishing the alternative East Asian definition of the region proposed by Malaysian Prime Minister Mahathir. Again, however, matters changed significantly over APEC's first decade: by the turn of the century, as discussed in Chapter 5, East Asian governments were looking to their own regional organization rather than to APEC as a principal means of promoting collaboration. To what extent has APEC itself had an impact on the way in which states conceive of their identity, and has membership of the institution thereby influenced the way in which members perceive how they may best pursue their interests?

A fourth set of questions refers to the relationship between regionalism and multilateralism. Has APEC been a 'building block' or a 'stumbling block' in the process of global trade liberalization? To what extent have negotiations within APEC helped or hindered liberalization efforts in other trade forums? What does APEC's experience tell us about the advantages and problems associated with sectoral approaches to trade liberalization?

APEC is *sui generis*. For the student of international political economy, its uniqueness poses problems: how generalizable are any conclusions reached from a study of this unique institution? Having only a small number of observations is a classic research design problem (King et al. 1994). This study uses two methods to address this problem. First, in examining the evolution of intergovernmental collaboration in the Asia-Pacific, culminating in APEC's successful launch in 1989, multiple observations of the same variables are possible. The institution established in 1989 bore a close resemblance to proposals for an Organization for Pacific Trade and Development, first put forward in the 1970s. What variables changed over two decades so that repeated failure turned into eventual success?

Second, although APEC itself may be unique, it is an example of a broader genus – regional collaboration – and, at a more comprehensive level still, of inter-state cooperation in the global system. Questions posed in this book about the APEC experience are derived from these broader literatures and applied in the spirit of the method of 'structured, focused comparison' that Alexander George (1979) advocates.

Chapter 1 of this book reviews the literatures on collaboration and on regionalism and identifies questions which then inform the case studies of APEC's establishment (Chapter 2) and its institutionalization (Chapter 3). Chapter 4 begins with an examination of the main propositions that can be derived from the literature on how international regimes can affect governments' calculations of their interests and conceptions of their identity. It then examines the extent to which APEC's rules and procedures limit its capacity to shape members' behaviour. It includes case studies of two sets of negotiations – on investment principles, and on proposals for early liberalization in a selection of industrial sectors – that had a profound affect on how members regarded APEC's effectiveness as an instrument for pursuing their interests. The book concludes in Chapter 5 with an examination of APEC's record in its main areas of activity, seeking to explain its effectiveness by reference to the propositions derived from reviews of relevant theoretical literature in the earlier chapters, and looks at the implications of the first decade of collaboration in APEC for our understanding of regionalism.

CHAPTER 1

The Construction of Regional Intergovernmental Collaboration

When ministers of foreign affairs and trade from twelve countries met in Canberra in November 1989 they created the first regional intergovernmental organization to span the Pacific Rim.[1] The meeting introduced the term 'Asia-Pacific' to the lexicon of international relations. The creation of the APEC grouping appeared to provide further support for the idea that the 'Pacific Century' was about to dawn (Linder 1986; Coker 1988; Segal 1990).

APEC's formation was another indication that regional economic integration was back in vogue at the end of the twentieth century. Contracting parties notified GATT of thirty new regional agreements between 1990 and 1994 alone. Unlike APEC, however, these agreements sought exemption from GATT's MFN requirement. APEC's 'open regionalism' – the practice of making trade concessions available to member and non-member economies alike – is unique among the many regional economic agreements in effect in the global economy.[2] The growth of regionalism accelerated in the second half of the 1990s when the World Trade Organization received notification of an additional ninety agreements covering trade in goods or services (WTO 2001). By the end of the 1990s, only three of the 139 member economies of GATT's successor, the WTO – Hong Kong, Japan and South Korea – were not participants in a discriminatory regional trading arrangement (and the Japanese and Korean governments announced in 1999 that they would explore the possibilities of establishing a free-trade area between the two economies).[3] Around 40 per cent of the world's trade was conducted within these discriminatory regional groupings (WTO 1999, Chart II.3).

Regional trade agreements are part of the broader phenomenon of *regionalism*: the construction of intergovernmental collaboration on a geographically restricted basis.[4] The renewed enthusiasm for regional collaboration since the mid-1980s has embraced not only trade but also other issue areas, especially security. In the Asia-Pacific region, APEC has its counterpart in the security sphere in the ASEAN Regional Forum (ARF), created in 1994.[5]

The second chapter of this book looks at the reasons why APEC came into being in 1989 after several previous unsuccessful attempts at establishing an intergovernmental regional institution in the Asia-Pacific. Before focusing on the APEC case, I review in the present chapter the theoretical literature on regional collaboration to see what insights it provides for understanding why states agreed to the establishment of an intergovernmental institution in the Asia-Pacific at this time. In particular, this chapter addresses the question: what explains the new enthusiasm of governments for seeking regional solutions to their problems? In turn, this question breaks down into two components: why collaborate, and why collaborate on a regional basis?

Why Collaborate?

At one level, the question of why governments choose to collaborate is answered simply. Governments collaborate because it is their perception that they cannot achieve their goals at an acceptable cost through unilateral action, and because they believe that they can do so more effectively through cooperation with others. The emphasis on the inadequacy of unilateral action immediately raises questions when applied to the trade field. For neo-classical economic theory, the pursuit of trade liberalization through regional arrangements is a second-best option – for most economies, unilateral liberalization on a non-discriminatory basis would achieve superior results. Few governments are able to change their terms of trade through the imposition of tariffs (Whalley 1985: 23). The only exceptions are large economies, which might benefit either from using their size to extract concessions from their competitors or from applying optimal tariffs on imports. For others, the optimal policy is to remove their tariff barriers. Why then do governments pursue regional arrangements that involve them in costly negotiations, which achieve results inferior to those that economic theory suggests they might have obtained through unilateral action?

As unilateralism is at the heart of APEC's approach to trade liberalization, I examine this question in detail in Chapter 4. At this point, a couple of summary observations will suffice. Trade liberalization on a regional basis may help governments overcome domestic political economy obstacles to liberalization if it induces expectations of reciprocity, and it may also increase the magnitude of overall gains if other economies are persuaded to join the process. Second, although trade liberalization may be a principal means through which regional collaboration is realized, it may not be the only or even the primary goal of cooperation. Other economic objectives, such as technical cooperation and the promotion of the development of relatively backward parts of a region, or non-economic objectives, may figure prominently in governments' calculations or indeed be their primary motive for collaboration.

Governments are self-interested actors. To explain the resurgence of regionalism in the last part of the twentieth century requires an enquiry into factors responsible for changing the way governments perceive their interests and/or the best means of pursuing those interests. Much of international relations theorizing takes states' interests as given, a convenient assumption that makes for parsimony in explanation. Parsimony may not be a virtue, however, in attempting to explain a phenomenon as complex as governments' propensity to engage in regional collaboration.[6] An eclectic approach, to borrow Dunning's (1977) terminology, is needed to provide a comprehensive explanation of governments' changing interests in regionalism. In particular, it needs to be an approach that identifies the links between developments at the level of the international system and those occurring domestically. A complex interplay of factors, in which numerous feedback loops are present, drives changes in governments' perceptions of their interests.

Take, for instance, the growth of interdependence among states, which is a systemic factor (Ruggie 1983) but one that inevitably has domestic repercussions. The growth of interdependence may increase governments' desire to cooperate by making them more conscious of the transactions costs that impair economic interactions. It may also have a direct impact on the domestic political economy equation by fostering a new international division of labour that brings about a transformation of the domestic economic structure. In addition, a growth in interdependence is likely to open the way for new ideas to influence governments' calculations of where their interests lie and how they might best be pursued.

No single theoretical approach has a monopoly in explaining governments' changing interest in collaboration. In pursuit of an eclectic approach, the next part of this chapter examines arguments, derived from various theoretical perspectives, about the factors that have an impact on governments' choices on whether to engage in regional collaboration. While recognizing the importance of cross-cutting forces and multiple feedback loops that link the two levels, I divide these factors into two categories: those providing the systemic context in which governments operate, and those specific to the domestic economic and political systems.

The Systemic Context

Under this heading, I review arguments that focus on the distribution of power, on interdependence, on contagion, on knowledge, and on leadership.

The distribution of power

Regional arrangements are nested within a systemic structure of economic and political power, institutions and rules (Aggarwal 1985). Military alliances, moreover, have been closely associated historically with the willingness of states to enter into relations that deepen their economic interdependence with one another (Mansfield and Bronson 1997). The break-up of the Soviet Union, for instance, was a prerequisite for many of the new regional agreements formed in the 1990s. The distribution of power within the system and the shape of alliances will inevitably have some impact on governments' interest in regional collaboration. Beyond this commonplace point, theorizing on the relationship between regionalism and the distribution of power in the international system provides few generalizations that withstand empirical testing. Furthermore, the literature is characterized by hypotheses that are often mutually contradictory.

Some theorists (e.g. Deutsch et al. 1957; Russett 1967) have argued that the presence of a hegemonic power is necessary if regionalism is to succeed because a hegemon alone has the means and the incentive to supply the collective goods that will induce smaller states to enter into collaboration in a regional arrangement. Two strands of economic literature suggest, however, that the interests of a dominant economy may lie not in underwriting the collective good of economic openness but rather in promoting closure. The theory of optimal tariffs posits that large economies (alone) may benefit from restricting imports to exploit their dominant position in world markets.[7] A rational approach for a hegemon therefore may be to restrict rather than promote free trade. In a similar vein, variants of strategic trade theory suggest that large states may have an interest in economic closure to guarantee their home markets to domestic producers. Such closure enables them to exploit economies of scale and scope, and to gain 'first-mover' advantages.[8] Moreover, a hegemonic power may be able to maximize its leverage through a network of bilateral relations (a 'hub-and-spokes' approach as adopted by Nazi Germany in the 1930s; see Hirschman 1945) rather than by underwriting a multilateral or regional cooperative regime. As Ruggie (1982) has argued, it is not just hegemony that counts in the shaping of economic policy but the objectives of the government of the hegemonic state and the means chosen to pursue them. Hegemons will not necessarily be enlightened despots. A hub-and-spokes approach was the preferred US policy towards the countries of the Pacific from the end of the Second World War until the late 1980s.

Mattli (1999: 56) restates the importance of a dominant power for regionalism, arguing that 'successful integration requires the presence of an undisputed leader among the group of countries seeking closer ties'. A dominant state can establish a focal point for resolving coordination questions, and it may have the will and capacity to be a 'regional paymaster' whose side payments help resolve distributional disputes. He finds strong support for this argument in Germany's role in the European Union. It is clear, however, that at the very least the presence of a dominant power is not in itself sufficient to ensure a successful outcome to integrative efforts, and indeed can actually hamper them – as is evident in one of his own case studies. Attempts to create a Pan-American commercial union in the early 1890s foundered, Mattli argues, 'primarily because of growing resistance to American hegemony in Latin America' (1999: 131). The gap between what other states perceive as acceptable leadership or as unacceptable imperialism may be slight.

Moreover, it is questionable whether the European experience really does substantiate the argument that a hegemon is required to achieve success in constructing regionalism. Whether Germany has played the role of hegemon in European integration is a matter of dispute among EU specialists. Compare, for instance, Mattli's argument with Moravcsik's (1998: 498) conclusion that propositions about hegemonic stability are 'obviously misplaced in the EC context':

> When compared to the postwar United States and Japan in the Far East, Germany in Europe is small *vis-à-vis* its neighbors. As a relatively influential state with moderately pro-European preferences and a large domestic market, Germany made concessions, ideologically motivated in part, that contributed to European integration, yet there is little evidence that Germany's size or concessions were decisive. It might plausibly be argued that Germany, as the swing state between Britain and France, played a critical role; its decisions were particularly decisive for the future of Europe, yet this has little to do with hegemonic power.

An alternative structuralist explanation suggests that smaller powers will seek a regional arrangement with a hegemon not primarily because of the collective goods the hegemon can supply but because they hope that a regional institution will enable them to constrain the hegemon's freedom of action – an approach sometimes termed 'regional entrapment'. For others, the presence of a hegemon is important in the formation of regionalism because it will drive smaller states not to 'bandwagon' with it but rather to form a regional grouping in an attempt to balance against it. For still others, regionalism results not from hegemonic domination but from a process of hegemonic decline.[9] Smaller countries in this situation have a greater incentive to collaborate (with one another and with the former hegemon) as the behaviour of the dominant country becomes increasingly unpredictable because it is no longer able or willing to provide collective goods as it has in the past. (For an application of this argument to the Asia-Pacific region, see Crone 1993.) Proponents of each of these hypotheses can point to at least one historical instance where the growth of regionalism appears to support their arguments.

Still other mutually contradictory arguments are available on the relationship between relative capabilities and the prospects for regional collaboration. Regional arrangements offer an opportunity for a larger power to use its disproportionate resources to push reluctant smaller partners into 'deeper' integration than can be achieved in global negotiations (Haggard 1995). On the other hand, smaller states are all too aware of their vulnerabilities in negotiations in regional forums: a rich history exists of economically stronger states using regional arrangements to reinforce the dependence of weaker parties (see Hirschman 1945). They may be less willing to enter into them, or determined to limit the range of issues on the agenda, precisely because they fear they will be subject to greater pressure than would occur in a global forum. This caution has characterized the approach of weaker states in the APEC relationship: Soesastro (1994b: 50) notes, for example, that the developing economy members of APEC opposed suggestions that the grouping should go beyond the Uruguay Round agreements because they felt more vulnerable to pressure from larger countries in APEC than they did within the WTO.

Besides the problem of contradictory hypotheses, a major difficulty with arguments about the relationship between the overall power structure and collaboration is that changes that occur at the systemic level – especially hegemonic ascendancy and decline – do so infrequently and slowly. The evolution of the overall power structure, therefore, as Young and Osherenko (1993a) argue with respect to international regimes, is seldom a good predictor of changes in international collaboration, which occur much more frequently. Moreover, even if a stronger empirical fit between hegemony and economic cooperation at the systemic level was established, the relevance of such arguments for *regionalism* is questionable. The theory of hegemonic stability is a systemic theory, which cannot be transposed automatically to a regional subsystem. The behaviour of a 'regional hegemon' is likely to be affected by whether the benefits of the collective goods it provides can be partially 'privatized' by confining them to other states within the region (Lake 1993). As we will see, this question of preventing outsiders from free-riding on regional economic cooperation has been particularly problematic within APEC for the US government.

Interdependence

Interdependence is an attribute of both the international system as a whole and the relationships between two or more of its component units. The systemic feature of growing interdependence translates into an increasing openness of domestic economies (usually defined as a rise in the ratio of exports plus imports to gross domestic product [GDP]). The idea that interdependence can lead to more demand for collaboration between governments has long been an article of faith for many economists and political scientists. Cooper (1968: 10) states the proposition most baldly in asserting that the increasing sensitivity of economic events in one country to what is happening in its trading partners 'will compel a higher degree of economic cooperation'. Many would reject the *inevitability* of a cooperative outcome that Cooper's statement implies, since it is possible that interdependence, especially when manifested in asymmetrical relationships, will also generate conflict (Hirschman 1945; Waltz 1970; Kroll 1993).[10] Nonetheless, the functionalist premises of this argument are at the core of liberal approaches to international economic collaboration.

Interdependence increases the costs generated by lack of coordination among national policies. It exposes and can intensify the transactions costs involved in international exchange. It also renders the domestic economy more vulnerable to shocks ('externalities') emanating from partners who, consciously or not, may be exporting the costs of structural adjustment. The greater the interdependence of national economies, the more costly it will be for states to pursue policies that are out of line with those of their principal trading partners. A classic example was the Mitterand government's pursuit of expansionary policies in the early 1980s at a time when other industrialized economies were pursuing more cautious macroeconomic policies. Policy coordination can help reduce the transactions costs of managing interdependence, a central argument of the literature on international regimes (Keohane 1984). It may also help reduce the uncertainties of interdependent relationships by affording some control over the externalities generated by the behaviour of economic partners (Aggarwal 1993). Policy coordination can determine how states share the burden of structural adjustment across national boundaries.

Interdependence may affect the prospects for inter-state collaboration in another way: by changing states' perceptions of their identity as well as their interests. The early work on security communities by Karl Deutsch and his collaborators pioneered this argument. Deutsch and his colleagues (1957) suggest that increased communication among states may lead to a new sense of community. They see this as 'a matter of mutual sympathy and loyalties; of "we-feeling", trust, and mutual consideration; of partial identification in terms of self-images and interests; of mutually successful predictions of behavior, and of cooperative action in accordance with it ...' (reproduced in Deutsch et al. 1966: 17). This quotation identifies several links between interdependence, identity and behaviour that other authors have subsequently explored. For example, the importance of identity in determining states' interests and the way in which they interact with one another is a central theme of constructivist approaches (Wendt 1994). Growing interdependence, Wendt suggests, may change the 'intersubjective knowledge' that defines identities such that a new 'transnational community of interest' emerges. Similarly, in exploring the idea of 'empathetic' interdependence, Keohane (1984: 123) suggests that increased interactions may create a new sense of solidarity. This may encourage states to espouse a new concern for their partners' welfare that goes beyond narrow conceptions of domestic self-interest.[11]

The more sophisticated economic approaches recognize that states' responses to growing interdependence are ultimately a 'political question' (Cooper 1968: 12). For an understanding of these political dynamics, one has to move beyond the systemic level to examine how increased exchanges affect coalitions within the domestic political system. This approach was the central thrust of neo-functionalist theories of integration (Haas 1958). With growing interdependence, key actors in influential interest groups as well as in political parties recognize that national solutions to problems are increasingly ineffective, and lobby for increased intergovernmental collaboration. They engage in the building of both domestic and transnational coalitions, and transfer their attention away from the national towards the intergovernmental level.[12] Moreover, interdependence may increase uncertainty, which in turn provides openings for new knowledge and opportunities for relevant expert communities to play an enhanced role in policy-making.

Increased interdependence may therefore have an impact on governments' demands for collaboration primarily through its impact on the domestic political economy equation, discussed in more detail in the next section. If greater openness inclines political and economic elites towards greater cooperation, is this new enthusiasm likely to be focused mainly on the regional or the global level? To raise this question is to focus on the issue of what measure of interdependence is relevant in predicting increased interest in regional collaboration. Is this the overall ratio of trade to GDP, or the share of economic interactions with neighbouring states in countries' total transactions? The conventional measure of economic openness – the aggregate ratio of trade to GDP – may disguise a powerful motive for increased collaboration at the regional level if the

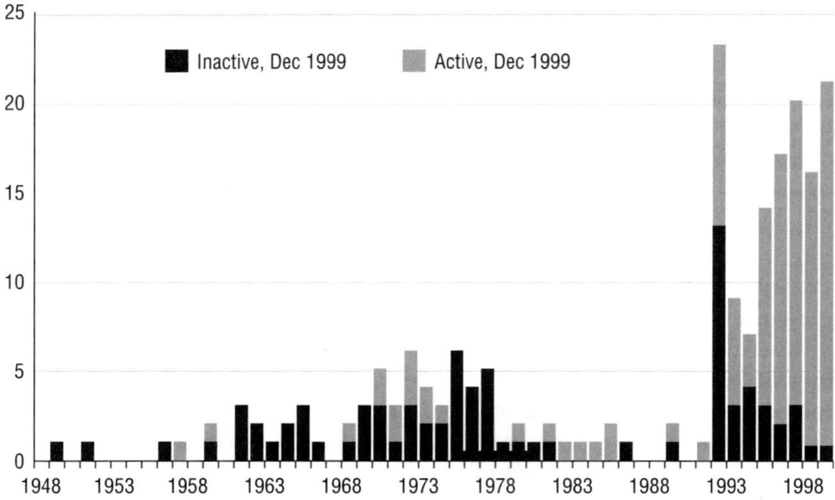

Figure 1.1 Regional trade agreements notified to the GATT/WTO
Source: WTO, 'Regionalism: Facts and Figures', http://www.wto.org/english/tratop_e/region_e/regfac_e.htm

share of intra-regional transactions in a country's total rises sharply without affecting overall openness. Such 'objective' indicators, however, may only provide an imperfect guide to governments' preferences on the preferred geographical scope for collaboration. If their aim is to press for trade or investment liberalization, governments may see that their most likely – and strongest – allies in such a venture will be found outside their specific geographical region, and that global forums may offer the best prospects for effective coalition-building in support of liberalization.[13]

Any optimism that increased interdependence will create a dominant domestic coalition in support of further economic collaboration has to be tempered – at least at the regional level – by the recognition that enthusiasm for regionalism has followed a cyclical pattern. Figure 1.1 presents data on the regional arrangements notified to the GATT/WTO. The lack of a strong relationship between the linear growth in interdependence and the cycles of regional collaboration suggests that, at the very least, other factors intervene. Moreover, no clear correlation exists between levels of interdependence between specific economies, measured by the relative importance of bilateral trade flows, and the emergence of economic regionalism. If such a straightforward relationship existed, one would have expected, for example, that Canada and the United States would have negotiated a regional trade agreement much earlier than the middle of the 1980s. The relative importance of trade with other members of a regional grouping may be a relevant variable in predicting which groupings are more likely to succeed. But a quick glance at the regional economic groupings that have appeared over the years suggests that no critical threshold of regional economic interdependence exists below which regionalism never occurs and beyond which such collaboration always takes place. At best, then, the evidence suggests that growing interdependence may generate increasing pressures for governments to collaborate, but such collaboration does not result automatically: agency in the form of leadership by individuals, governments or international secretariats is required to exploit the favourable change in international context.

Contagion

The data in Figure 1.1 point to another systemic or contextual factor that has a significant role in the incidence of regionalism: regionalism in one part of the world fosters emulation by governments elsewhere. The pattern of establishment of new regional arrangements is cyclical, with peaks in the 1960s and again in the 1990s. The driving influence behind the first wave of enthusiasm for regionalism was the establishment of the European Common Market in 1957. Behind the second lay the deepening of European integration with the move towards the Single Internal Market, finalized in 1992, and the new regionalism in North America: the 1988 entry into force of the Canada–US Free Trade Agreement and its subsequent conversion to the North American Free Trade Agreement.

Two impulses, which often operate together, are the principal drivers of contagion. One is the desire to use mechanisms for promoting national objectives in a regional context that appear to have worked successfully elsewhere. The second is a defensive motive: the perceived need to emulate others in order to defend domestic interests that appear to be under challenge by a strengthened external entity. The new interest of the Japanese government in the last years of the twentieth century in negotiating discriminatory free-trade arrangements (discussed in Chapter 5) can be traced to its belief that such agreements had contributed to the economic success of its principal competitors. Similarly, the perceived positive benefits of the European Economic Community (EEC) in the 1960s inspired imitators elsewhere. In some instances, as in West Africa, and in the Americas with the launch of the Latin American Free Trade Association and Central American Common Market in the early 1960s, collaborative ventures were begun in the hope of emulating the stimulus that regional integration gave to economic growth in Europe – albeit with very limited success. Defensive motives may also inspire emulation: a concern to increase bargaining power to counter the combined weight of the new grouping in international economic relations. An attempt to balance the new framework for European cooperation, which was seen as threatening access to markets, was a primary motive, for instance, in Japanese proposals in the mid-1960s for a Pacific Free Trade Area.

Knowledge

Like other elements of the international structure, the knowledge structure is both constraining and enabling. Conceived broadly, it embraces the store of scientific and technological information that conditions the manner in which states and other players in the international system interact. The state of technological knowledge affects other elements of systemic structure, such as interdependence. The advent of steamships and refrigeration transformed economic relations between the old and new worlds. Satellite telecommunications similarly have revolutionized international financial markets, and afforded new opportunities for firms to organize production networks on a regional or global basis. But much of the stockpile of technical knowledge in the international system is not a public good. Access to knowledge is highly asymmetrical – hence the emphasis that Strange (1988) placed on knowledge as one component of structural power.[14]

How do currently prevailing ideas affect policy? Ideas define what issues governments regard as important; they provide the basis for classifying events and for ranking perceived policy options. As Biersteker (1995: 175) notes, ideas have 'the power to determine what appears to be "natural," taken for granted, unquestioned, or not requiring any further explanation'.

Ideas, then, cannot simply be reduced to interests. Rather, they can have an independent effect on how governments conceptualize their interests, and how they see that their interests can best be pursued. Because ideas and interests interact, however, it is not easy to demonstrate the independent role that ideas play in policy-making, as recent review articles make clear (Jacobsen 1995; Woods 1995; Yee 1996; see also Haas 1990; Adler 1991). A crucial issue therefore is when and how the global knowledge structure, the generator of ideas, is likely to come into play in determining how states construct their interests.

Studies of foreign policy decision-making point to significant limitations on the learning capacity of states. New knowledge often threatens the privileges of currently favoured interest groups. Bureaucracies continue to operate according to standard operating procedures even in the face of changed circumstances. Leaders attempt to assimilate new information to existing beliefs: only when their belief structures are persistently challenged do they seek new knowledge as a guide to action (Stein 1989a: 264–5). Misleading analogies rather than a careful consideration of policy options often underlie the choice of action (Khong 1992). Yet learning, a process in which individuals embrace new beliefs, in response to observation and experience, about the nature of their interests and how they may best pursue them, does occur.[15] Evidence suggests that adoption of new ideas by political elites occurs most often in conditions of uncertainty, of repeated and/or severe policy failure, and when new elites come to office.

Uncertainty is pervasive in world politics, especially in economic relations (see, for instance, Putnam and Henning's [1989] study of the Bonn Economic Summit). It is particularly characteristic of those situations where new issues are emerging onto the public agenda. Even after a problem is well defined, however, there is often considerable uncertainty as to how international collaboration may best help resolve the issue. Uncertainty exists not only over the likely effects of economic policies on the international and domestic economies but also over the political process of coalition-building: what policies will be acceptable to potential partners? Uncertainty may reduce the incentives for collaboration or increase the transactions costs involved. On the other hand, it may also open the way for new ideas and provide opportunities for policy entrepreneurs to persuade governments of the wisdom of a particular course of action. Technical knowledge may be important in helping to change or clarify other actors' perceptions of their interests (Putnam and Henning 1989). Similarly, Winham (1986: Ch. 8) records the impact of international negotiations on how domestic actors conceived of their interests in the trade regime. Ideas are often prominent as a guide to action in the pre-negotiation stage of international collaboration when state elites and domestic interest groups may be particularly uncertain of the outcomes of alternative policy options (see Stein 1989; Bates and Krueger 1993: 454; Young 1998: 12).

Even where agreement exists on the desirability of collaboration and its goals, there is often uncertainty over the best way of pursuing these objectives. For many structures of strategic interaction, the Folk theorem holds that more than one equilibrium outcome is possible. Alternative Pareto-optimal solutions are available. Accordingly, outcomes cannot be predicted from knowledge of players' interests and the structure of interaction alone (Martin 1992; Goldstein and Keohane 1993a). In such circumstances, power – as realist theorists suggest – may play a decisive role in determining which equilibrium on the Pareto frontier is eventually chosen (Krasner 1991). But so too may ideas. In an environment of uncertainty over the best course of action, ideas may provide a focal point around which actors' expectations and behaviours converge (Goldstein and Keohane 1993b: 16–18). Garrett and Weingast (1993) give a persuasive illustration of the way in which ideas helped determine a focal point in negotiations for the European Union's Single Internal

Market. Ideas – as opposed to power – they suggest, are likely to be more significant the greater the uncertainty about policy outcomes, the smaller the differences in the distribution of benefits across various equilibrium outcomes, and the smaller the disparities in power among the negotiating states.

Uncertainty may increase at a time of perceived changes in the relative power of states. Such changes may open the way for new ideas if they appear to offer a cogent explanation for current developments or, indeed, a rationalization of them. One example is the influence of ideas derived from the strategic trade policy literature in the United States in the 1980s, a time of concern about apparent US relative decline vis-à-vis Japan. In contrast, this literature and its prescriptions generated far less enthusiasm by the mid-1990s – even before the East Asian financial crises of 1997–98 – when domestic confidence in the US economy and its competitiveness revived after a sustained period of strong domestic economic growth in contrast to relative economic weakness in Japan and other East Asian economies.

Repeated policy failure is another circumstance in which an opening for ideas may occur. Crises are frequently identified in the policy literature as occasions when governments are forced to search for new policy alternatives; they may be influenced by ideas they were previously unwilling to consider – ideas 'whose time has come'.[16] Crises change the configuration of domestic forces, weakening some interests that were previously ascendant, and strengthening others. Crises may introduce a new fluidity into domestic politics. Rodrik (1995: 1487), for instance, notes that crises can relegate distributional concerns to second place behind economy-wide concerns, thereby enabling governments to pursue previously impossible trade reforms alongside macroeconomic reforms. The structural adjustment programs embraced by some African governments in the wake of economic decline in the 1980s are an example of how crises can disrupt long-established domestic coalitions and patterns of public policy, and thereby provide opportunities for ruling elites to seize new ideas (Callaghy and Ravenhill 1993). But as many of the African experiences make clear, while crises may provide a permissive condition for the adoption of new ideas, they do not guarantee that governments will respond in a particular way. Such is the strength of vested interests – and, often, the limitations of state capacity – that many governments will choose, actively or by default, to muddle through with unchanged policies (see also Kahler 1993).

A second circumstance considered particularly propitious for an acceptance of new (or, more accurately, different) ideas is when a change of leadership takes place, particularly when this involves a generational change (Breslauer 1987; Levy 1994). Incoming elites have various incentives to question previous orthodoxies. Furthermore, new regimes may enjoy a honeymoon period with domestic constituencies in which it is easier for them than for long-established governments to adopt and apply new ideas about problem-solving. But again, the newness of a regime does not guarantee that it will be any more open to different ideas than its predecessors.

The likelihood that a new international orthodoxy will be adopted domestically will depend not just on the circumstances in which political elites find themselves. The possibility of learning will also be conditioned by the effectiveness of transmission mechanisms from the international to the domestic political system, by the institutional structure and current ideational structure of the domestic polity, and by the extent to which similar ideas have successfully been adopted elsewhere.

It is almost tautological, but accurate nonetheless, to suggest that the key to the acceptability of ideas is their promotion by political elites (Hall 1989). Ideas take on a life of their own if they provide signposts that help elites to redefine their interests in a way that promotes the building of coalitions, again emphasizing the crucial role that ideas play in fostering focal points. Ideas can provide legitimacy for political elites – a justification for the policies they pursue. Ideas are neither objective nor necessarily optimal solutions to the problem at hand. Rather, they are guides to policy that appear to suit the needs of decision-makers at a particular time. Their acceptability, therefore, may well depend on how well they 'fit' (or can be made to fit) with existing belief systems, and particularly with the approaches favoured by agencies within the state (Sikkink 1991). And once embedded in institutions, ideas themselves become gatekeepers, influencing which options are considered by political elites as feasible or legitimate (Hall 1989; Goldstein 1993).

Acceptance of ideas by political elites also depends on how effectively they are 'sold', an argument that points to the importance of another element of the international context: the provision of leadership.

Leadership

The creative role that an imaginative and energetic regional secretariat can play in stimulating cooperation by inducing governments to reorder their preferences is a central point in neo-functional theorizing (Haas and Schmitter 1966). Similarly, observers have noted a close correlation between the success of international organizations and the inventiveness of their secretariats (Cox 1969; Cox and Jacobson 1974), an argument taken up by recent writers using constructivist approaches (Klotz 1995a; Finnemore 1996a).[17] Leadership in regional cooperation may come not only from international secretariats and hegemonic powers but also from individual governments, including those of smaller states.

Oran Young (1991) provides the most comprehensive discussion of the role of leadership in the promotion of international cooperation. He acknowledges that the issue-specific capabilities possessed by states can indeed provide one source of leadership (in his terminology, 'structural leadership'). He argues, however, that power resources are not the only decisive factor in situations of uncertainty. Agreements that appear feasible are often difficult to realize in a context of lack of certainty over outcomes. Leadership can play a crucial role in bringing about agreement. The capacity to exercise such leadership rests not only on issue-specific capabilities but also on negotiating skills that promote integrative bargaining ('entrepreneurial leadership'), and on intellectual capital deployed to shape actors' conceptions of the problem at hand ('intellectual leadership').

This broader conception of leadership offers several possibilities not available when leadership is viewed solely in terms of power resources. First, rather than a single hegemonic actor occupying the position of leader, multiple leadership roles may be available depending on the issue, the capabilities and skills of various actors, and the commitment they have to engineering an agreement. Second, an emphasis on entrepreneurship and intellectual leadership affords the possibility that governments or individuals from states lacking in material capabilities can play leadership roles. Contrast this suggestion with Kindleberger's (1986) blunt statement that 'proposals of great technical appeal from individuals or small countries are not welcomed ... there needs to be positive leadership, backed by resources and a readiness to make some sacrifice in the international interest'. The rationale for much of Canada's activist postwar diplomacy, and more recently that of Australia, rests on the idea that 'middle powers' are able to exploit their capacity for entrepreneurial and intellectual leadership to help facilitate cooperative arrangements that otherwise might not be constructed.[18]

An acknowledgement of the potential importance of entrepreneurial and intellectual leadership moves the analysis beyond arguments derived from the collective goods literature that the public good of economic cooperation will be undersupplied unless states with the biggest share of potential gains provide leadership. What may be important in motivating a state to play a leadership role is less the *share* of the total potential gains that an individual state is likely to capture than how significant the *absolute* gains/avoidance of losses are for that state. For instance, asymmetries in market size make it likely that smaller countries will gain disproportionately from a regional trading arrangement. Although their share of the total benefits from collaboration may be relatively small, these potential gains loom large in their national income, and therefore may motivate political elites to invest resources in attempting to engineer an agreement. Similarly, the economic openness that is more characteristic of small economies makes many of them more vulnerable than larger, more closed economies should the global economy become more protectionist, for example by fragmenting into a world of trading blocs. This vulnerability motivates them to pursue active diplomacy to avoid such an outcome. Hence it was not surprising that the initiative for the Canada–US Free Trade Agreement should come from Ottawa, *and* that it occurred in response to a more aggressive policy by Washington towards Canadian trade barriers, a policy that appeared to pose a threat to future Canadian access to the US market.[19]

A pursuit of entrepreneurial and intellectual leadership by small and medium powers is, of course, no guarantee that they will succeed in their objectives – witness the inability of the Cairns Group to play a major role in the outcome of the agricultural negotiations in the Uruguay Round.[20] But small and medium powers may have more of an incentive to pursue such leadership than do their larger neighbours. Moreover, as the literature on middle powers emphasizes, initiatives taken under their leadership may be more acceptable to potential partners than if promoted by the largest states, which would enjoy the greatest absolute gains from cooperation (see e.g. Evans and Grant 1991). *Who* promotes an initiative can be a significant factor in whether or not it is successful. Leadership from smaller powers was important in the foundation and institutionalization of APEC, an argument developed in the next chapter.

Why would larger states countenance smaller states playing a leadership role, often in the promotion of initiatives from which the smaller states may seem to benefit disproportionately? One reason is that although the smaller economies may make relative gains, the larger states may still enjoy the lion's share of total absolute gains. Larger states may also have non-economic objectives, for example the promotion of a security agenda, that they can pursue by linking them to economic cooperation. Moreover, the executive of larger states may also be using an international agreement to strengthen its hand in its conflict with domestic groups. A more cynical interpretation is that larger states may use regional economic agreements, whose market access provisions appear, prima facie, to benefit small states disproportionately, to extract concessions on other issues of 'deeper integration' that they wish to promote, such as labour and environmental standards, treatment of foreign direct investment (FDI), or intellectual property rights. Furthermore, they may be able to deploy their bargaining leverage to limit the adjustment costs they face by excluding sensitive sectors from the agreement (Helleiner 1996). Perroni and Whalley (1994) suggest that smaller countries have paid premiums in the form of non-trade concessions to secure the insurance of a regional trade agreement with larger countries to avoid the possible negative consequences of a global trade war.

To confine the discussion of leadership to the state level would be to present an incomplete analysis. Leadership may be as much if not more a property of individuals than of bureaucracies or of governments considered collectively. In their comparative study of environmental regimes, Young and Osherenko (1993a: 232) go so far as to argue that the entrepreneurial role played by individual leaders 'may constitute a necessary condition for regime formation'. Policy entrepreneurship in promoting international collaboration may come from national politicians or from individuals based in the secretariats of intergovernmental organizations, or from prominent figures in non-government organizations (NGOs). A focus on individuals points to the significance for successful collaboration of the personal capabilities of individuals, such as their capacity and will to mobilize and invest resources in promoting cooperation. Variation in the activism of 'middle powers' in the international system, for instance, owes much to the personalities of the prime ministers and foreign ministers of the day and to the stature of these individuals within their governments, as well as to their party affiliations.[21]

Intellectual leadership may also come from transnational groupings of experts ('epistemic communities') that provide an effective means for the transmission to the domestic polity of new orthodoxies at the systemic level (see Haas 1992). Forward momentum on trade liberalization has occurred in part because of the influence in the governments of less developed economies of Western-trained technocrats who are part of a transnational community of economists (Biersteker 1992, 1995). Members of the community interact daily when officials consult with their counterparts in other governments and in international organizations. They also come together regularly in official and non-official forums. In regional economic cooperation in the Asia-Pacific, as Chapter 2 documents, the transnational community of academic economists played a significant role in keeping proposals for an intergovernmental regional organization on the agenda at a time when governments lacked enthusiasm for the idea. And transnational expert task forces in the Asia-Pacific region have frequently produced blueprints that identify new areas and mechanisms for collaboration.

The task for the analyst is to identify how these expert groupings have influenced the process of domestic decision-making, and why political elites at any given time are attracted to the ideas these communities advocate. Merely to document membership of such a transnational community does not demonstrate that ideas have been transmitted effectively to the domestic polity or that they have been assimilated by political elites.

The key question is how effectively their members have built alliances within the state and with the political elite.

The Domestic Context

Discussion of the role of ideas in causing a reordering of government preferences has already indicated several ways in which the systemic and domestic contexts interact. Take crises, for example. These may result from adverse developments in the international context which have a similar impact on economies that have – or are perceived by significant foreign actors to have – commonalities in structure. Or crises may be homegrown: the product of the consistent failure of a particular set of policies. Whatever their origins, crises often facilitate the adoption of a new set of policy preferences consistent with ideas currently popular in the international environment, such as those promoted by the Washington-based international financial institutions. Crises in turn may contribute to a change in domestic political leadership – witness the effects of the 1997 financial crises in Indonesia and Korea – which again may open the door for different ideas to inform the government's policy preferences.

A similar interaction between domestic and international contexts arises with the growth of interdependence. Increased interdependence inevitably has a differential impact on various sectors of the domestic society. In other words, it will generate important distributional consequences. The endogenous tariff literature suggests that the preferences of domestic actors towards economic liberalization will depend on the scarcity and specificity of the various factors of production. Relatively scarce factors and those specific to import-competing industries are likely to favour protection. But variance in factor specificity, and in the transactions costs of mobilization, makes it difficult, a priori, to predict the composition of pro- and anti-liberalization coalitions that will form (see Magee et al. 1989; Rogowski 1989; Frieden 1991; overviews in Alt et al. 1996; Frieden and Rogowski 1996). A more straightforward hypothesis that enjoys substantial empirical support is that companies with a stake in international trade can be expected to be more enthusiastic about economic openness and collaboration than their domestically oriented counterparts (Helleiner 1981; Milner 1988; for an application of these ideas to Japan see Yoshimatsu 1996).

The possibility exists, therefore, of a virtuous cycle emerging: greater interdependence (openness) gives more actors a stake in the international economy (and/or favours outward-oriented actors), which in turn generates more political support for government policies that promote collaboration in support of economic liberalization. But the preferences of actors have to be effectively aggregated and articulated if they are to influence government policy (Nelson 1988; Verdier 1994). Here the effects of transactions costs in political mobilization come into play. So too does the ability of strategically located actors, for example urban labour and the military, to construct coalitions that enable them to exert an influence on government policy that is disproportionate to their economic weight. In contrast, landowners and/or peasant farmers are often difficult to mobilize for political action and under-represented in dominant political coalitions in less developed countries (Lipton 1977; Bates 1981), but notably not so in industrialized economies. And in land-abundant economies with high per capita incomes, a relatively small percentage of the population derives its income directly from the land. This often causes land to be under-represented (in comparison with its economic weight) in politics in these countries.[22]

To the hypothesis that growing interdependence is likely to make governments have a greater interest in economic collaboration, an auxiliary argument should therefore be added: the greater the weight of export-oriented manufacturing industry in the domestic economy, the more likely is economic openness to produce a demand for transnational economic collaboration. Supporters of economic openness in the manufacturing sector are likely to be more easily mobilized and carry more political weight than their counterparts elsewhere in the economy. Moreover, the larger the share of the manufacturing sector in exports, the greater the likelihood that adjustment to economic openness will take the form of intra-industry trade. Such trade generally produces adjustment costs of a lower magnitude than when countries export and import the products of different industries (inter-industry trade) and is therefore likely to generate less political opposition to international collaboration in support of economic liberalization (Ruffin 1999).

A discussion of domestic economic structures points in turn to the importance of considering the various forces that transform these structures. The literature on interdependence and economic collaboration typically focuses mainly on trade as an indicator of interdependence. Flows of foreign direct investment are another significant dimension of interdependence. They too can have a direct influence on the way in which governments define their interests, as we will see in the discussion of APEC's formation in the next chapter – and not least because of the transformative effect they have on domestic economic structures.

The consequences of FDI for domestic political support for regional collaboration are not necessarily straightforward. FDI may cause conflict between host and home economy governments over the terms of transfer of technology or over the effects on bilateral trade imbalances (witness the tensions between some Southeast Asian economies, most notably Malaysia, and the Japanese government), and the bad feelings generated may make formal intergovernmental collaboration more difficult. Moreover, FDI creates another set of actors, corporate subsidiaries, with interests that may be for or against regional collaboration. Their preferences on regional collaboration will vary according to the purposes for which the plants were established. Where their primary goal is import substitution production for the host's domestic market, the subsidiaries may well be hostile to regional economic liberalization (for a West African case study, see Langdon and Mytelka 1979). If the main purpose of the plants is to export to third country markets, however, and/or if the parent company wishes to rationalize production on a regional basis, then FDI may create new support for regional collaboration. Another stimulus investment may give to regional collaboration is through its promotion of a convergence in business practices, the adoption of similar technical standards, and so on (for East Asia, see Doner 1993; Primo Braga and Bannister 1994).

Discussion of the complex relationship between changing levels of interdependence and governments' demands for collaboration suggests a further question that needs to be addressed: why does the private sector seek government intervention to assist in the promotion of economic collaboration? The answer would at first seem to be straightforward: the private sector will seek intergovernmental agreements because these can provide it with security and confidence in international transactions that it cannot engineer by itself. Yet behind this simple answer lie other questions. For instance, does the propensity of companies to seek and to support intergovernmental agreements vary by type of investment, by sector and by the domicile of the company? Companies whose investments constitute 'specific', that is, immobile (a mining operation, for example), assets in host economies may be keener to promote intergovernmental collaboration on the treatment of FDI than investors whose assets essentially are footloose (e.g. textile machinery).

Ethnic Chinese entrepreneurs have succeeded in building transnational empires in East Asia despite an absence of intergovernmental agreements to provide security for their investments.[23] A host of transborder, subregional economic entities, the 'growth triangles', have emerged in East Asia since the early 1980s, driven in many cases by ethnic Chinese capital (Lee 1991; Chia and Lee 1993; Toh and Low 1993; Pomfret 1996). In most cases, the role of government in promoting such transborder collaboration has been minimal. Indeed, private sector transborder activities have sometimes grown in the face of government hostility, for instance the long-standing prohibition on direct trade between Taiwan and the People's Republic of China. Does the capacity of some businesses to do well in East Asia without government support translate into variations in the pressure that private sectors in individual countries place on their respective governments to negotiate intergovernmental collaborative agreements? Transnationals from Asian countries, for example, seem less concerned about putting into place intergovernmental agreements on the treatment of FDI in other parts of Asia than do their North American counterparts – a factor that affected APEC's negotiation of investment principles, discussed in Chapter 4.

More generally, how does private sector pressure for intergovernmental collaboration affect governments' decisions on whether to undertake regional initiatives? This question is particularly pertinent in light of the conclusion that Evans (1993: 403) draws from case studies of domestic and international bargaining: 'International initiatives in direct response to constituency pressure were surprisingly rare'. Do private sector attitudes merely provide a supportive environment in which government initiatives can be launched? Or do these attitudes feed through into the political system to exert pressure on governments, but to an insufficient extent to prompt action until some other precipitant enters the equation? Existing studies provide few answers to these questions.

Another form of interaction between the international and domestic contexts is worthy of note. International agreements themselves may change the configuration of domestic political forces. By entering a cooperative arrangement, governments may be able to make a credible claim to domestic groups that their hands are tied on a particular policy issue. International commitments can help them to overcome domestic political economy problems (Putnam 1988; Evans et al. 1993; H. Milner 1997). Entry into international agreements may also change the balance of power between the various branches of the government, as Goldstein (1996) suggests has occurred in the United States through its participation in NAFTA. And in a federated state, the federal government may be able to exploit the obligations it has accepted by entering an international agreement to extend its competence into areas that are constitutionally defined as otherwise lying within the exclusive power of subnational territorial units.[24]

Why Regionalism?

The resurgence of regionalism in the global economy might be interpreted as another instance of the proverbial triumph of hope over experience. Even by the most basic measure of 'success' – longevity (or institutional survival) – few winners stand out among the large number of preferential trading schemes established in the postwar period. Repeated failures of geographically limited attempts at trade liberalization stand in marked contrast to the success of the multilateral trade regime, the GATT/WTO being widely regarded as one of the most successful of the universal organizations (Eichengreen and Kenen 1994).

Among economists, an almost universal tenet of faith is that cooperation on a multilateral (universal) basis maximizes welfare. Trade liberalization on a regional basis is a second-best option that may or may not enhance welfare, depending on the terms under which such cooperation proceeds.[25] Any study of the welfare effects of regionalism encounters the problem of accurate estimation of a counterfactual. Few analysts conclude, however, that even in the European Union, economic growth occurred at a substantially faster rate than the member economies would have experienced in the absence of the common market (Baldwin and Venables 1995; Winters 1996).[26] Moreover, simple measures of the 'success' of a regional arrangement, such as a growth in the share of intra-regional trade in member economies' total trade, may actually reflect the welfare-damaging effects of trade diversion.

Why, then, do states so often respond in an apparently perverse manner to the challenges posed by increased interdependence by seeking regional collaboration? It is now well accepted that no unique set of theories is necessary to explain regional collaboration. The theoretical challenges involved in explaining the construction of collaboration at the regional level are the same as for other forms of inter-state cooperation (Haas 1975; Moravcsik 1993). Nonetheless, the decision of states to collaborate within a geographically confined area rather than in a global forum still requires explanation.

The previous discussion of the economic impact of discriminatory trade liberalization points to one reason why governments prefer cooperation on a regional rather than a multilateral basis. Governments may pursue regional trade liberalization in the form of discriminatory preferential arrangements not *despite* but *because* it generates trade diversion. Non-competitive industries may succeed in lobbying governments to enter such arrangements rather than to engage in multilateral liberalization that would put their profitability at risk.[27]

Economic motives, however, may be secondary in governments' decisions to construct collaborative economic arrangements on a regional basis. Regional economic collaboration, like other economic regimes, is nested within broader frameworks of military and political power, at both the regional and the global level (Aggarwal 1985; Buzan 1991). Arguably, the ultimate goal of regional economic cooperation has always been to reap positive political and security externalities from the institutionalization of collaboration. Europe provides a classic example (Haas 1958). Similarly, the states of the Association of Southeast Asian Nations (ASEAN) pursued economic cooperation as a medium to build confidence within the region, to defuse inter-state tensions, and to forge a sense of community. The extent to which collaboration has to generate economic benefits in order to promote positive security effects may vary substantially across different regions. ASEAN, for instance, has generated significant benefits in the form of confidence-building activities even though the gains from economic collaboration have been minimal.

Security motives for regional cooperation are not confined to a desire to reduce the likelihood of conflict between states included within a regional organization. Regional collaboration has also been constructed to strengthen member states against outsiders perceived as posing a threat – whether it be the Soviet Union for the European Community in the Cold War era or, at various times, Vietnam, the Soviet Union, and China for ASEAN, or South Africa in the apartheid era for the Southern African Development Coordination Conference.[28]

A second political reason that often informs governments' demand for economic collaboration at the regional level is that it will enhance their bargaining leverage with non-members. Historically, this motive has been particularly important in the establishment of regional economic arrangements among less developed economies, as a way of attempting to encounter their perceived external dependencies. For instance, the founders of the Andean Pact hoped their collaboration would enable them to extract improved terms from foreign investors (Axline 1977; Mytelka 1979). Using a discriminatory regional economic grouping (or the threat to establish such a grouping) as a bargaining chip against outsiders is not confined to less developed economies, however. Pierre Uri, a significant figure in the early days of European integration, suggested that 'one reason for setting up the Common Market was to enhance the bargaining power in tariff negotiations of all member countries taken together' (quoted in Mattli 1999: 71). Several commentators have asserted that the creation of the EEC prompted the United States to seek to mitigate the possibility of trade diversion by seeking multilateral negotiations on tariff cuts (the Dillon and Kennedy Rounds) (Lawrence 1991; Sapir 1993). Others have argued that existing regional arrangements, the possibility of their extension, or the creation of new arrangements have had the effect of pressuring non-members of the grouping to make concessions in the GATT/WTO. Winham (1986) suggests that the first EEC enlargement was a significant factor in encouraging the United States to enter the Tokyo Round of GATT negotiations. And, as discussed in the next chapter, a significant factor in the timing of APEC's establishment was its members' frustrations with European recalcitrance in the Uruguay Round negotiations.

Finally, a familiar argument from the literature on collaboration is that regional arrangements may help governments to establish their liberalizing credentials by signalling and locking in their commitment to reform (Rodrik 1989). One component of this argument is a political economy dimension: by entering an agreement and being able to claim that their hands are tied, governments may strengthen their bargaining position against domestic protectionist forces. Another component is that governments that have entered a regional agreement will have greater concern about their reputations. Reputational considerations may overcome the problem of time inconsistency in welfare-enhancing policies; that is, they will reduce the temptations to defect from current policies when circumstances change.

Here, the salient question is why should regional commitments be more effective devices for locking in reforms than commitments made in the GATT/WTO, especially commitments that governments make through the binding of tariffs? One answer is that the smaller number of parties to regional arrangements makes it easier (and more important) for members to monitor behaviour. Furthermore, repeated interactions within regional arrangements may make governments more concerned with their reputations than they would be in more diffuse multilateral forums (for a detailed discussion, see Fernandez and Portes 1998). Yet how effective regionalism is as a signalling and locking-in strategy is questionable. Certainly, entry into NAFTA did not enhance the credibility of Mexico's monetary policies in 1993–94. On the other hand, Mexico's response to its debt crisis in 1994 was to continue to cut tariffs on its trade with its NAFTA partners while raising some tariffs on non-NAFTA imports, suggesting that it was more concerned with the credibility of its regional commitments than with those it had made within the WTO.

The literatures of economics and political science suggest five other factors that may encourage governments to pursue cooperation on a geographically limited basis:

- the existence of 'natural' economic regions
- the advantages of small numbers
- the importance of commonalities in culture and history among neighbouring countries
- symmetries in economic capabilities
- the relative ease of adjustment to liberalization on a regional basis.

Natural Regions?

For some economists, trade naturally takes a regionalized form because transportation and communication costs are lower between economies in the same geographical region (Krugman 1993). Furthermore, incomes and policies often converge between countries in a geographical region, thereby facilitating intergovernmental collaboration (Fishlow and Haggard 1992). These claims evidently contain an element of truth, but even a cursory glance at patterns of global trade suggests the limitations of the argument. Only among industrialized economies is it the case that the bulk of a country's trade takes place with neighbouring economies. For less developed economies, by far the most trade occurs with countries outside their geographical region. Among less developed economies, similarities in economic structure may be barriers to rather than facilitators of economic cooperation. Even in what is arguably the most institutionalized of all regional cooperative arrangements among less developed economies, ASEAN, three decades of regional economic cooperation has not increased the share of intra-regional trade in the total trade of member states beyond the 20 per cent level that prevailed when the grouping was established (Ravenhill 1995b) – and of this 20 per cent, most was trade between Singapore and other member economies. (In other regional economic groupings among less developed economies, intra-regional trade is often as low as 7 per cent of members' total trade.) Krugman may simply be wrong about the incidence of transportation and communication costs: for many less developed economies, these may be lower for trade with geographically distant industrialized economy partners than for cross-border exchanges with their regional neighbours, given poor regional transport infrastructure. Moreover, the share of transport costs in the retail price of many products has declined markedly in the last quarter of a century.

An alternative explanation for regionalized trade patterns rests on ideas of comparative advantage and the 'natural' complementarities of the member economies. Drysdale (1988) has developed this argument most fully in looking at the growth of trade and economic cooperation among countries of the Pacific Rim, a process that he argues builds on 'strengthening complementarities'. 'The densely populated, natural-resource-poor East Asian economies', he suggests, 'have been highly complementary to economies rich in natural resources such as Australia and North America and some of the Southeast Asian economies' (Drysdale 1988: 16). Again, this argument undoubtedly has some validity – witness the rapid growth of trade between resource-rich Australia and resource-poor Japan and Korea.

If natural complementarities explain Asia-Pacific economic integration then they should also predict low levels of integration and cooperation in Europe, given the similarities in economic structures. Furthermore, following the logic of Drysdale's argument, regional economic cooperation should take place primarily on a North–South axis rather than among industrialized economies. Yet exactly the opposite has been the case. The most successful integrative scheme, the European Union, rests on economic exchange that is characterized overwhelmingly by intra-industry rather than inter-industry trade. Until the establishment of NAFTA, Kahler (1995a) notes, no free-trade area existed that brought together Northern and Southern economies.[29]

The notion of natural complementarities was more characteristic of international trade before 1945 than that of the present day – and has limited relevance to the Asia-Pacific region. Indeed Drysdale (1988: 89) acknowledged that 'less than half' of the bilateral trade flows among

Pacific Rim economies 'reveal strong complementarity'. This proportion had changed little over the years 1964–66 to 1979–81; in the latter period the mean complementarity coefficient was lower than in the earlier years, as would be expected given the growth of manufactured exports from Southeast Asia (see Shinohara 1982). Fishlow and Haggard (1992: 12), in contrast to Drysdale, see regionalization resulting from intra-firm trade among geographically proximate economies.

The very lack of intra-industry trade has been at the heart of many of the trade disputes between countries of the Asia-Pacific region in the last two decades, most notably those between the United States and Japan. The latter's extremely low levels of intra-industry trade make it an outlier among industrialized economies, even when allowance is made for factors such as resource endowment and Japan's distance from other industrialized economies (Lawrence 1987; Lincoln 1990; Ravenhill 1993; for an opposite conclusion, see Saxonhouse 1986; Saxonhouse and Stern 1989). Trans-Pacific trade tensions began with the rapid growth of textile exports from Japan, culminating in the imposition of the Multi-Fiber Arrangement (Aggarwal 1985). Textiles was but the first of several industries – steel, colour televisions, automobiles, semiconductors – where East Asian countries' aggressive conquest of North American markets, while maintaining closed domestic markets, generated significant trade friction.

Ideas about 'natural regions' or natural economic 'complementarities' thus at best provide only a very limited contribution to an explanation of why states should choose to construct regional rather than global collaborative arrangements.

The Numbers Game

Economists and political scientists alike have long shared the view that 'the prospects for cooperation diminish as the number of players increases' (Oye 1985: 18). The difficulties that an increased number of players pose for economic cooperation are at the heart of Olson's (1965) work on collective action. They also figure prominently in discussions of international regimes, the essential argument being that larger numbers increase the transactions costs of dealing with potential free riders. In particular, the larger the number of members, the more difficult it is to monitor behaviour and to enforce sanctions in the event of non-compliance (Keohane 1984; Oye 1985; Putnam and Henning 1989: 18; Caporaso 1992: 609; Martin 1992: 773). Where a relatively small number of economies participate in a regional arrangement, they may well have not only a greater capacity to monitor the behaviour of their partners but a greater incentive to do so. Defection in a small numbers situation is likely to create a precedent that potentially will have a more adverse affect on other members than if such behaviour occurred in a global institution (Fernandez 1997).

Certainly, the existing membership of many regional organizations has behaved as if it accepted the logic of the case for limited numbers. Moratoriums on the admission of new members are common. In APEC, for example, as we will see in subsequent chapters, existing members on several occasions declared moratoriums on new admissions to their club on the grounds that an expansion would complicate the task of widening and deepening cooperation. Malaysia's support for enlarging APEC's membership – first in promoting Chile's application, then in leading the push at the Manila Leaders' Meeting against a further three-year moratorium on enlargement – was seen by some other members as a deliberate strategy aimed at weakening the grouping.

Various counter-arguments, however, are ranged against these a priori assertions about the deleterious effects of numbers on the prospects for cooperation. Increased membership may enhance the prospects for issue linkage and the construction of package deals. Larger numbers, in Keohane's (1984: 91) words, may produce a situation where more potential *quids* are available for the *quo*. The overall benefits from collaboration may increase (although here again a counterargument may be made: too large a forum with too many issues may complicate the reaching of agreements; no clear dividing line exists between 'big enough' and 'too big'). And in an environment where states are concerned about relative gains, the presence of a larger number of players may reduce these fears (Milner 1992: 473).

Undoubtedly, the larger the number of states, the more likely it is that they will have a greater diversity of interests. Axline (1994: 199), for example, highlights this issue in comparing the Andean Group with the Caribbean Community and Common Market (for further discussion, see Haggard 1997). Greater diversity can complicate negotiations. The larger the number of states, the greater the likelihood that some will not have an interest in reaching agreement on a particular issue, and/or be more reluctant to tie their hands through an international agreement (Triffin 1954: 533). On the other hand, numerous cases exist of large numbers of actors successfully concluding international agreements (Osherenko and Young 1993: 12). Much depends on institutional design, as Kahler (1992) cogently argues. Voting procedures and mechanisms for discussing issues can be adapted to counter the problems of numbers and diversity. Giving all states a veto power, however, will likely guarantee that a lowest common denominator approach prevails. Abundant evidence is available as to how inappropriate design can reduce the chances of reaching agreement. The negotiations under UNCTAD's auspices for a New International Economic Order were a classic example of how getting the institutional design wrong can vitiate attempts at collaboration (Rothstein 1979).

The bottom line is that the evidence from various forms of inter-state collaboration is inconclusive on the issue of the impact of numbers on the prospects for cooperation (Levy et al. 1995: 279). A priori, it is impossible to argue that successful collaboration will be more likely to result when pursued by a relatively small number of states in a regional forum rather than by the whole community of states in a global institution. Other variables inevitably enter the equation. Nor is it the case that regional negotiations or the issues they embrace will necessarily be 'less complicated' than those at the global level, contrary to Bergsten's (1996: 106) assertion. The complexity of the issues involved, the asymmetries in issue-specific power among the states, and the mechanisms for discussing and voting on the issues will all have an impact on the prospects for realizing a successful collaborative outcome.

Commonalities

Inter-state collaboration is easier to achieve within a geographical region than on a global scale, it is often argued, because neighbouring states are more likely to have cultural commonalities, similar legal systems and modes of business practice. Relations among states with similar political, legal and business systems may already have acquired a great deal of transparency. Triffin (1954: 533), for instance, writes of the 'intimate' integration of economic policies 'which is feasible among countries that are highly interdependent, keenly conscious of this interdependence, and easily amenable to close cooperation because of the similarity of national viewpoints and policies resulting from a common geographical and historical background and a relatively homogeneous stage of economic development'. Moreover, intensive interactions among neighbouring states may create mutual trust – the 'social capital' that helps to overcome collective action problems (Putnam et al. 1993). The greater the cultural commonalities, the argument goes, the better the prospects for regional collaboration – hence the frequent unfavourable comparison between the European experience and the prospects for collaboration in the more culturally heterogeneous Asia-Pacific region (e.g. Rostow 1986; Kahler 1988). The lack of cultural commonalities similarly is an explanation for the infrequency of regional collaboration on a North–South axis.

Again, however, the usefulness of such broad generalizations is questionable. Not all commonalities are necessarily propitious for cooperation. The characteristics that political systems have in common matter – hence the emphasis that neo-functionalist theorists placed on pluralism (Haas and Schmitter 1966). A region consisting of states governed by unstable autocracies manifests a political commonality that would be unlikely to favour sustained inter-state collaboration. Similarly, a region whose economies were all heavily dependent on the export of the same limited range of primary products would be an unlikely candidate for regional economic collaboration – another reason for the multiple problems encountered by many of the economic integration schemes in Africa.

State capacity is another dimension of commonality that is undoubtedly important for the prospects for successful regional collaboration. If states have doubts about the capacity of their regional partners to implement agreed arrangements, then the basis for cooperation is fragile indeed. Hamilton-Hart (1999) makes a persuasive case that differences in state capacity have been a significant factor inhibiting the emergence of effective regional institutions in East Asia to manage the effects of interdependence (see also Kahler 1995b).

The notion that commonalities facilitate collaboration may appear a self-evident truth, but clearly it requires further definition if it is to be useful. Even if a list of desirable commonalities could be agreed on, the question remains, as with levels of interdependence, as to what the critical thresholds are. How common must the commonalities be for them to have a favourable impact on the prospects for successful collaboration? Judgements on this issue can at best be qualitative. To these difficulties must be added two others. Some elements of heterogeneity are not fixed. Even seemingly unchanging characteristics such as geography or factor endowments can change in salience with the evolution of technology. And cultural identities are not objective phenomena; they are perceptions that political elites can manipulate (on the Asia-Pacific region, see Kahler 1995a). Their political significance may change according to the context and the elites currently in office. Moreover, the importance of commonalities in culture, political system and business practice will vary according to the form of regional collaboration proposed. To what extent will the scheme intrude on national decision-making? To what extent will political elites perceive it as threatening to a state's sovereignty?

Symmetries in Economic Capabilities

A similar inconclusiveness is evident in arguments about another dimension of commonality: symmetry in economic capabilities. Within a geographically confined region, greater similarities in relative capabilities may be found than within the global economy as a whole (though this clearly is not always the case). Such symmetry may provide a favourable condition for collaboration. It may be more likely to produce a relatively even distribution of benefits from cooperation, and thereby reduce conflicts over the distribution of gains – a problem that has bedevilled economic integration among less developed economies (Ravenhill 1979). Economies of similar size are more likely than asymmetrical partnerships to face similar trade-offs between benefits from integration and the loss of policy autonomy that inevitably accompanies regional collaboration. For example, a strong correlation exists between economic size and openness. Because of the greater importance of foreign trade to the small economy (Alesina and Wacziarg 1998), the political economy equation there – characterized by a substantial percentage of enterprises and jobs dependent on foreign trade – is likely to be more favourable to a government's entry into regional arrangements that constrain its autonomy (see Smith 2000). It is likely, therefore, that governments of similarly sized economies will be more willing to enter collaborative arrangements that provide for legal dispute settlement mechanisms (DSMs).

On the other hand, inequalities in economic size may, following the logic of arguments about the provision of collective goods, provide incentives for one economy, or a small coalition of larger economies, to make the disproportionate contribution necessary to underwrite collaboration. Moreover, a dominant regional economy may have both the capacity and the motivation to make side payments to induce collaborative behaviour by smaller states.

Neither of these arguments finds much support in the recent wave of integration. To an unprecedented extent, the new regionalism has involved countries at diverse stages of industrialization. A remarkable switch in the tactics of less developed economies has occurred since the first wave of regionalism in the 1960s and early 1970s. Many of the early collaborative efforts undertaken by less developed economies had the explicit objective of countering dependency and improving bargaining leverage against the industrialized world, that is, an attempt to balance against powerful states. The philosophy underlying more recent regional schemes in contrast is much closer to the idea of bandwagoning – linking up with the more powerful. Alliance with one or more industrialized economies has been driven in part by fears of a fragmentation of the global economy, in part by fears of increased protectionism by their main industrialized economy trading partners, and in part by a desire to make themselves more attractive as hosts to foreign investment. Regional economic agreements have become a form of insurance policy that relatively small or underdeveloped economies have entered into in an attempt to ensure relatively unimpeded access to the markets of dominant regional economies. Exemption from acts of contingent protectionism in turn is expected to increase their attractiveness to potential investors. Mexico's interest in NAFTA, and the desire of other South American economies to join an expanded free-trade area of the Americas, is a prime example (Fernandez 1997). Similarly, the desire of European Free Trade Association economies to become EU members, despite their already privileged access to the EU market and despite the significant net contributions they would have to make to the EU budget, can be attributed in large part to a quest for assured access (see Flam 1995).

And contrary to the collective goods-based arguments about the capacity of dominant economies to be the paymasters of regional arrangements, the more developed economies have not made disproportionate concessions in these new regional agreements. Indeed, exactly the opposite has been the case, particularly in the area of trade liberalization. The less developed economies are the ones that have made the major concessions (Lawrence 1996; Ethier 1998). They have essentially entered into a clientelist relationship, making a downpayment of trade liberalization in the hope that this will constrain industrialized economies from irresponsible behaviour – a process akin to the payment of protection money.[30]

The question again arises of why membership of a regional arrangement would provide better insurance than does the WTO against opportunistic behaviour by more developed economies. Two answers are plausible. The more developed economy may feel a greater obligation towards the less developed members of a regional grouping to which it is a party (possibly for non-economic reasons). Regionalism in these circumstances may lead to greater self-restraint on the part of the powerful. Alternatively, it may be easier for less developed economies to mount an effective protest against opportunistic behaviour within a regional arrangement either because it provides its own DSMs, or because their governments are better placed to attract the attention of publics, sympathetic interests (such as companies sourcing components or finished products from the less developed economy) or decision-makers in the dominant regional countries.

The new North-South regionalism has produced groupings with far greater disparities in economic size than have those founded in the 1960s. But it is yet to provide any definitive answer to the question of how important are commonalities of state capabilities to the success of regional institutions. A further quarter-century of case studies and theoretical arguments have not taken us much beyond the conclusion reached by Haas (1971: 11) that 'the relative size of the member states in a regional grouping is not a good overall predictor of the success of integration'.

Regionalism and Adjustment Costs

A final argument why regional collaboration may be attractive to governments is that economic liberalization on a regional rather than a global basis may impose fewer adjustment costs. Regionalism affords an opportunity for governments to expose domestic sectors to some international competition without necessarily forcing them to compete immediately with the world's most efficient producers. Because they generate fewer losses for domestic interests, such arrangements may be more politically feasible than an immediate move to the complete removal of protection. Regionalism may be a halfway house, or a stepping stone, that facilitates eventual global liberalization (Triffin 1954).

Arguments along these lines have been used to justify several regional economic arrangements in the Asia-Pacific, including ASEAN and the Closer Economic Relations Trade Agreement between Australia and New Zealand. Moreover, they underlie prescriptions from the international financial institutions that African countries should engage more effectively than in the past in regional economic collaboration as part of structural adjustment programs (World Bank 1990). And the WTO's sympathetic view of recent regionalism is premised on the belief that these arrangements can be a stepping stone to liberalization on a broader scale (WTO Secretariat 1995). Support for the notion that regional arrangements can be a foundation for broader liberalization also comes from arguments that the formation and extension of preferential trade arrangements provides a powerful incentive for outsiders to seek admission to the regional grouping (see Oye 1992; de Melo and Panagariya 1993: Introduction; Fernandez 1997).

Justification in economic theory for limited liberalization on a regional rather than a global basis might be found in arguments about the need to protect infant industry, or (courtesy of strategic trade theories) to enable domestic industries to capture the various advantages from a partially protected market. The case for regional liberalization, then, is both theoretically plausible and seems to have empirical support. The negative side of confining collaboration to a geographical region is that although the costs of adjustment may be lower, so too may the overall benefits from liberalization – while the costs in the form of trade diversion may be substantial. And the arguments for geographically limited liberalization may open the door for the cynical strategy, noted above, of deliberately pursuing trade diversion. Moreover, a danger exists that domestic protectionist interests may be strengthened by some forms of regional trade arrangements, especially free-trade areas, which do not require the negotiation of a common external tariff (Krueger 1997, 1999).

Conclusion

Regional institutions are the constructions of states. In attempting to explain why states established APEC in 1989, and why the grouping has evolved in the way it has, the central question the next chapter addresses is why state elites have redefined their interests or perceived that the best way of pursuing their interests has changed since proposals for Asia-Pacific regionalism were first mooted in the mid-1960s. States are reflective organisms rather than automatons that respond mechanically to some putative laws of the international system. Systemic influences are filtered and interpreted by domestic actors: an understanding of why states opt for regional collaboration therefore requires an analysis of changes in domestic as well as international structures. The assumption in this study, prominent in the neo-functionalist literature, is that the self-interest of actors 'is taken for granted' (Haas 1971: 23). To suggest that states are rational, self-interested actors is neither to argue that interests are unchanging nor that states have perfect knowledge of how best to pursue their interests.

Assumptions of state rationality have to be tempered by allowing for considerable uncertainty about where states' interests lie and how they might best be pursued, and for the possibility of unintended consequences arising from state actions. States rarely realize in advance how the process of collaboration will unfold. When APEC ministers met for the first time in Canberra in 1989, the idea that the organization would, within six years, adopt a timetable for the establishment of free trade among its member economies would have appeared preposterous. For the grouping's future, this was probably fortunate because such a proposition would have been decidedly unattractive to some member governments at the time of its establishment.

The literature reviewed in this chapter suggests, to paraphrase Haas (1971), that there may be more angst than joy in theorizing about regionalism. The literature presents a plethora of independent variables that may affect the construction of regional intergovernmental collaboration – a problem that has always afflicted the study of regionalism (see e.g. Lindberg and Scheingold 1971; Mansfield and Milner 1997). Yet, as neo-functionalist theorists such as Haas and Schmitter (1966) recognized, adopting an eclectic approach which acknowledges the complex interaction of factors that affect governments' decisions to pursue regional collaboration may have its own virtues. Only limited utility is gained by attempting to reduce a complex world to two or three variables.

Mutually contradictory hypotheses, frequently buffeted by inconclusive evidence, characterize much of the literature on cooperation. Moreover, generalizing about regional collaboration is complicated by the fact that only one integrative scheme, the European Union, can reasonably be judged to have enjoyed long-term success in the postwar period. Other examples of regionalism may have been long-lived – and, as in the ASEAN case, served significant non-economic purposes – but they have singularly failed in their stated objectives of widening and deepening economic collaboration.

But not all is angst. This chapter has identified a number of propositions about the factors that can change governments' interests in entering regional collaboration that are relevant to the APEC case. These include:

Changes in power relativities

While arguments about a simple relationship between hegemony and successful inter-state collaboration are deficient on both theoretical and evidential grounds, it is clear that changes in power relativities in the international system will add to uncertainty. Such changes can increase the unwillingness of previously dominant states to continue to assume the burden of underwriting collaboration. These states may become more concerned with issues relating to the distribution of gains from collaboration. Changes in power relativities can prompt a search for new mechanisms for sustaining collaboration, for keeping a declining hegemon engaged in a region, and for constraining it from taking unilateral action that may harm the short-term interest of other states. The uncertainties arising from changing power relativities may provide an opening for new ideas to take hold.

Increasing interdependence

This has an impact on the prospects for collaboration through several interrelated effects. It generates problems that can be addressed most effectively through collaborative action. It can change the balance of forces in domestic politics in favour of economic collaboration. It can change states' perceptions not only of their interests but also of their identities and generate a new sense of community. Economic collaboration, although not inevitable regardless of the level of interdependence, is more likely the greater the importance of intra-industry trade, and the greater the involvement of locally based companies in transnational production networks.

Ideas and norms

Ideas shape governments' conceptions of their interests and hence their willingness to enter into regional economic collaboration. New ideas are most likely to be embraced in conditions of uncertainty, of severe policy failure, when changes of government occur, and when they have been demonstrably successful elsewhere. The adoption of new ideas can also be affected by their transmission through transnational communities, and the socialization effects of international institutions. Ideas themselves may cause governments to redefine their interests.

Leadership

Creative leadership is often needed to exploit favourable developments in the international context. Contexts may constrain and facilitate. Creative agency is often able to overcome constraints; it is often required if favourable contextual developments are to result in new collaborative endeavours. Leadership may be based not just on control over material resources but on intellectual capital and entrepreneurial (coalition-building) skills. Smaller countries may have both the capacity and a disproportionate incentive to play an entrepreneurial role, and their playing this role may be more acceptable to other potential parties to a regional arrangement than would be attempted leadership by a large power.

Diversity of membership

Regional collaboration traditionally has enjoyed greater success when member states have substantial similarities in levels of economic development and political frameworks. The new regionalism, with its alignment on a 'North–South' axis, challenges the conventional wisdom about the relationship between successful regional collaboration and similarities in levels of economic development. But most regional schemes accept the logic of the desirability of similar political frameworks: the EU and the proposed Free Trade Area of the Americas limit their membership to democratically elected governments. APEC, like ASEAN, is unusual in accepting political diversity among its members – with predictable consequences, as we will see, for institutional design and effectiveness.

Chapter 2 examines how relevant these arguments are for an explanation of the evolution of regional intergovernmental economic collaboration in the Asia-Pacific, collaboration that, after a series of false starts, was institutionalized with the establishment of APEC in 1989.

CHAPTER 2

The Construction of APEC

At first sight, the effective regional organization of Asia seems to be more absurd than inevitable. (Rostow 1986: 18)

[T]he diversity and variety [of the countries of the Pacific littoral] means that the political will and trust for ... an overarching organization where their future economic collaboration could be planned ... is simply lacking, and shows no sign of developing sufficiently before the end of this century at least. (Wilson 1985)

[I]t will probably take many years before the unstructured enthusiasm of the present acquires a respectability and acceptance among the majority of the region's trading nations and results in concrete structural mechanisms designed to realize the common aspirations of Pacific rim countries. (Kohona 1986: 400)

[T]he puzzle with reference to the Pacific is not to explain the progress of regional initiatives, but their relative weakness. (Fishlow and Haggard 1992: 30)

When Australian Prime Minister Bob Hawke launched the initiative in Seoul in January 1989 that was to culminate in the establishment of the Asia-Pacific Economic Cooperation grouping later that year, he was building on more than two decades of diplomacy aimed at the creation of an intergovernmental institution to promote collaboration among the economies of the Pacific Rim.[1] Indeed, Hawke's proposals bore a remarkable resemblance to those made two decades previously for an Organization for Pacific Trade and Development (OPTAD). The academic economists Hugh Patrick and Peter Drysdale had refined this concept in a 1979 report commissioned by the US Congressional Research Service for the Subcommittee on East Asian and Pacific Affairs of the US Senate Committee on Foreign Relations (Patrick and Drysdale 1979). OPTAD, however, had first been placed on the regional agenda as early as 1968 by the Japanese economist Kiyoshi Kojima (1968) and by Drysdale (1968).

The case for an Asia-Pacific regional institution, which would operate in a manner different from that of the existing global forums, was clearly stated by two economists:

> They must seek ways to build mutual trust, find a surrogate for hegemonial power, design mechanisms to make countries aware of the limits to their macroeconomic goals, make countries aware of the implications of their macroeconomic policies on others, avoid excesses of export-led growth, face up to cyclical and structural problems, improve the functioning of the exchange rate market, promote international trade and contain protectionism, put limits on export promotion efforts and export controls, and design a system to reduce price fluctuations of commodities.
>
> If any of these goals are to be reached, a regular and continuous procedure for consultation among governments of the Pacific basin must be created. International co-operation will help to broaden and lengthen policy horizons of national governments. International consultations can help resolve economic problems in the Pacific basin if they encompass all of the interacting and overlapping aspects of economic issues and bring together both developed and developing countries. None of the international economic institutions, agencies and forums created in the twentieth century has been able to accomplish this task. Functionally narrow institutions such as the International Monetary Fund and the World Bank that perform well in their own field do not provide the basis needed for broader co-operation. The Organisation for Economic Co-operation and Development, though it has had some success in promoting co-operation, has a membership limited to advanced countries. Those institutions that have a universal mandate with respect to both countries and problems have not been successful. Their deliberations tend to degenerate into a morass of negative coalition politics in which it is easy to prevent progress and impossible to create it. The secretariats that governments have generously funded to search for the solutions that the countries could not find have soon become bloated bureaucracies, with ideological programmes often completely removed from the political reality of the member governments. (Krause and Sekiguchi 1981: 151–2)

Governments were slow, however, in coming to accept that a new regional grouping was needed. This chapter explains why it took so long for governments to see a need for such a grouping, and why they changed their minds at the end of the 1980s. In reviewing the origins of APEC, this chapter draws on the insights from the literature on international collaboration reviewed in Chapter 1. Before applying this literature to the emergence of regionalism in the Asia-Pacific, I briefly review the history of collaboration among the economies of the Pacific Rim.

The Historical Absence of a Regional Identity

The Asia-Pacific region, defined as the countries of the Pacific Rim,[2] has no history of institutionalized cooperation throughout the region. Indeed, the idea that the Asia-Pacific might constitute a 'region' is a recent construction. For centuries, the Pacific Ocean was viewed as a dividing rather than a unifying force (Segal 1990). In the very extensive academic literature on regionalism produced from the 1960s onwards, the absence of any reference to a 'Pacific' or 'Asia-Pacific' region is striking. Similarly, 'East Asia' does not figure in the discussion. Only Southeast Asia receives recognition as a 'region' – courtesy of the establishment of ASEAN in 1967.

One of the few widely accepted propositions in the literature on regionalism discussed in Chapter 1 is that certain commonalities are prerequisites for successful regional collaboration. In this context, the Asia-Pacific area appears an unlikely candidate. It includes an extremely diverse group of countries, whether viewed in terms of economic variables such as size of gross national product (GNP) or GNP per capita, or composition of exports, or in terms of economic and political systems and structures, or in terms of culture and history. And these divisions are not only between 'East Asia' on the one hand and the countries of predominantly European settlement of North America and Oceania on the other. Observers who look beyond the shallow rhetoric of 'Asian values' or a 'clash of civilizations' discover within East Asia itself a remarkable heterogeneity.[3] Although trading routes have long linked Southeast and Northeast Asia, the cultures and histories of the two subregions are quite distinct. And even within these subregions, substantial differences exist in ethnicity, culture and history. Inter-state relations within the subregions are often characterized by deep-rooted historical antagonisms – nowhere better illustrated than in the troubled relationship between Japan and Korea.

Table 2.1 provides basic data on APEC member economies at the time of its foundation.[4] The diversity of the founding member economies is readily apparent. Populations range from the 300 000 of Brunei to the 1.1 billion of China; GNP from the $3.1 billion of Papua New Guinea to the $5520 billion of the United States. In terms of purchasing power, real GDP per capita among the founding members at the end of the 1980s encompassed Indonesia at $1425 and the United States at $18 000. Land mass varied from the 600 square kilometres of Brunei and Singapore to the 1 million square kilometres of Canada. The diversity of the APEC founding members is arguably far greater than that found in other regional groupings – whether in Europe, Africa, or Central or South America – at the time of their formation.

Economic policies have been similarly diverse. Table 2.2 presents rankings by two conservative think-tanks, the Heritage Foundation and the Fraser Institute, of their estimates of the 'economic freedom' found in APEC member economies.[5] These rankings are subjective and inevitably contentious. Many regional specialists, for instance, would not share the Heritage Foundation's assessment that Indonesia's trade policies in the mid-1990s (ranked in the second highest category by the Foundation) were as open as those of Canada. Nor would many accept that Indonesia's trade policies were substantially more open than those of Malaysia,

Table 2.1 APEC member states: basic data, 1990

	GNP at market prices ($US bn current)	Total population (million)	Total labour force (million)	Real GDP per capita (1985 US$)	Manu-facturing as % GDP	Economic openness: (Trade as % GDP)	Stock of external debt ($US bn)	International reserves (US$bn)	Age depend-ency ratio	Area (sq km)	Adult illiteracy rate
Australia	282	17	8.5	14 445	14.6	34.9	.	19.3	0.5	7 713	< 5
Brunei	5.5	0.3	0.1		9.0	.	.	.	0.7	6	< 5
Canada	548	27.8	14.7	17 173	19.3	51.3	.	23.5	0.5	9 976	< 5
Chile	28.5	13.2	5.0	4 338		65.5	19.2	6.8	0.6	757	6.6
China	356	1 140	672	1 324	33.6	26.8	55.3	34.5	0.5	9 561	26.7
Hong Kong	74.8	5.7	2.9	14 849	17.6	260	.	.	0.4	1	< 5
Indonesia	109	178	78.3	1 974	20.7	49	69.9	8.7	0.7	1 904	23
Japan	2 990	124	64.1	14 331	28.2	20.6	.	87.8	0.4	377	< 5
Malaysia	40.9	17.9	7.0	5 124	18.4	150.6	16.4	10.7	0.7	333	21.6
Mexico	238	83.5	31.1	5 827	22.5	32.3	104	10.2	0.7	1 958	12.7
New Zealand	41.0	3.4	1.6	11 513	17.6	54.1	.	4.1	0.5	271	< 5
Papua New Guinea	3.1	3.8	1.9	1 425	9.0	89.6	2.6	0.4	0.8	463	48
Peru	31.8	21.5	7.4	2 188	27.0	23.6	20.1	1.9	0.7	1 285	14.9
Philippines	44.5	61.5	24.7	1 763	24.8	60.8	30.6	2.0	0.7	300	10.3
Russian Fed	578	148	77.2	3 905	38.0	36.1	59.8	.	0.5	17 075	.
Singapore	36.8	2.7	1.3	11 710	29.6	364.5	.	27.7	0.4	0.6	10.9
South Korea	252	42.9	19.6	6 673	29.2	60.1	.	14.9	0.4	99	3.7
Thailand	84.6	55.6	31.7	3 580	27.2	75.5	28.1	14.3	0.6	513	7
United States	5 520	250	126	18 054	18.8	21.4	.	173	0.5	9 363	< 5
Vietnam	20.4(a)	66.2	33.6	.	18.8	59.8	22.3	0.1	0.8	331	12.4

(a) data for 1995
Source: World Bank and Penn World Tables, accessed through the International Economic Data Bank, ANU

Table 2.2 Heritage Foundation and Fraser Institute indices of economic freedom: APEC country rankings

Overall rank	COUNTRY	Trade	Taxation	Government intervention	Monetary policy	Foreign investment	Banking	Wage/ prices	Property rights	Regulation	Black market	1995 overall score	Fraser Institute 1990
1	Hong Kong	1	1.5	1	2	1	1	2	1	1	1	1.25	9.3
2	Singapore	1	3	1	1	1	2	1	1	1	1	1.25	8.5
4	New Zealand	2	3.5	2	1	2	1	2	1	2	1	1.75	6.0
6	United States	2	4	2	1	2	2	2	1	2	1	1.90	7.4
8	Taiwan	2	2.5	2	1	3	3	2	1	2	1	1.95	5.9
11	Canada	2	4.5	2	1	3	2	2	1	2	1	2.00	6.9
14	Japan	2	4.5	1	1	3	3	2	1	2	1	1.95	6.9
18	Australia	2	4.5	3	1	2	1	2	1	3	2	2.20	6.0
22	Chile	2	3.5	1	3	2	3	2	1	2	3	2.50	5.7
24	Thailand	3	3	1	1	3	3	3	1	3	2	2.30	6.5
28	South Korea	3	4.5	2	2	3	2	2	1	3	2	2.15	5.2
39	Malaysia	5	3	2	1	3	3	3	2	2	2	2.15	7.1
54	Philippines	5	3	1	2	3	3	2	2	3	4	3.30	5.7
62	Indonesia	2	3.5	1	2	2	3	3	3	4	5	3.35	6.6
65	Peru	3	3	1	5	2	2	2	3	4	4	3.40	4.0
81	Papua New Guinea	5	3	3	1	3	4	3	3	3	3	3.10	n.a.
96	Mexico	3	3.5	3	5	2	4	3	3	4	3	3.05	5.3
117	Russia	5	3.5	4	5	3	2	3	3	4	4	3.50	n.a.
126	China	5	4	5	3	3	3	3	4	4	4	3.80	n.a.
146	Vietnam	5	5	5	5	4	4	4	5	5	5	4.70	n.a.

Source: Heritage Foundation and Fraser Institute web pages. Heritage Foundation data for 1995 except for New Zealand and Papua Guinea (both 1996), and last column. Heritage Foundation rankings on scale of 1 to 5, where 1 = best score. Last column is Fraser Institute composite index of economic freedom for 1990, on scale of 1 to 10 where 10 is best score.

Table 2.3 Freedom House, 'Comparative Measures of Freedom 1995–96'

Country	Political rights	Civil liberties
'Free'		
Australia	1	1
Canada	1	1
Chile	2	2
Japan	2	2
Korea	2	2
New Zealand	1	1
USA	1	1
'Partly Free'		
Malaysia	4	5
Mexico	4	4
Papua New Guinea	2	4
Peru	5	4
Philippines	2	4
Russia	3	4
Singapore	5	5
Taiwan	3	3
Thailand	3	4
'Not Free'		
Brunei	7	5
China	7	7
Indonesia	7	6
Vietnam	7	7

Source: Freedom House, 'Table of Independent Countries, Comparative Measures of Freedom 1995–96', (www.freedomhouse.org/Political/frtable1.htm), where a score of 1 is the most free, and 7 is the least free.

which (together with the Philippines, Papua New Guinea, and – less surprisingly – China, Russia and Vietnam) received the lowest ranking of 5. At best, such rankings provide a very rough evaluation of the content of economic policies. Nonetheless, treated with appropriate caution, they serve as approximations for some of the differences in policies among member states. Hong Kong and Singapore consistently score highly on rankings of economic freedom, indeed more highly than the Western industrialized economies of APEC. At the other end of the spectrum, the low rankings of China, Russia, and Vietnam reflect the continued prominent role of the state in their economies. Only four countries – Iraq, Cuba, Laos, and North Korea – received lower rankings on indices of economic freedom than that of Vietnam in the Heritage Foundation's sample of 150 countries.

A summary of the cultural and political diversity of APEC member states suggests other obstacles to the construction of regional collaboration. Political systems range from the absolute monarchy of Brunei to the polyarchies of most of the industrialized economy members. According to another conservative think-tank, Freedom House, only six of APEC's founding members – Australia, Canada, Japan, Korea, New Zealand and the United States – had 'free' political systems in the mid-1990s. Again, country specialists may well quibble with the assigned scores, for example Taiwan's categorization as 'partly free' compared with the placing of Korea in the 'free' category. The general picture painted by the rankings, however, is a reasonable approximation of the openness of the political systems of APEC states, and of the diversity found within the grouping.

After surveying the economic heterogeneity of the Asia-Pacific region, and its racial, religious, cultural and historical differences, Walt Rostow (1986: 19) concluded that 'a region with these characteristics is not, on the face of it, a logical prospect for organization on a reasonably harmonious, cooperative basis'. His view was shared not only by many academic commentators but also, for most of the postwar period, by key decision-makers in the countries of the region.

The discussion in the previous chapter of the literature on the relationship between hegemony and institutionalized inter-state collaboration showed that neither in theory nor in practice is there a straightforward link between these two variables. The absence of shared values among the countries of the Asia-Pacific region was a powerful factor inhibiting the emergence of a regional organization in the postwar years. Certainly, it would have complicated any effort to construct a regional economic or security organization. But why did the United States as the region's hegemonic power not even attempt to promote equivalent organizations in the Asia-Pacific to parallel the North Atlantic Treaty Organization (NATO) and the European Economic Community in response to the dual Soviet and Chinese threats?

Hegemons are able to choose between a variety of institutional forms to promote their interests (Weber 1992). Multilateralism is not necessarily the most obvious choice for a hegemon because a multilateral institution normally offers it less leverage than a series of bilateral hub-and-spokes arrangements. For some authors, the US choice of multilateralism in Europe and, in contrast, its preference for bilateralism in Asia was a simple reflection of differences in power relativities. Crone (1993: 503) argues, for instance, that '[w]hile the US was predominant in the Atlantic, power differentials were not that great and it was therefore never able to dictate. US relative power in the Pacific, however, was far greater than it ever was in the Atlantic'. The 'extreme' US hegemony in the Pacific, he continues, inhibited early attempts to organize the region 'by creating disincentives for the parties to institutionalize and multilateralize the relationships'. A multilateral alliance in the Pacific at best appeared to promise a meagre net addition to US capabilities while offering other states an opportunity to stake a claim to US resources (Kahler 1995a).

Like other single-factor explanations, a focus on power asymmetries in the Pacific provides only part of the explanation for the absence of US interest in promoting multilateralism in the Pacific. Many of the countries of the region (all of Southeast Asia with the exception of Thailand) were still under colonial rule at the end of the Second World War. Some (Indonesia and Vietnam) were about to embark on bloody nationalist struggles for independence. The continued presence of European colonial powers in the region would have immensely complicated the task of promoting a regional institution should the United States have desired to do so. US administrations were at best ambivalent towards European colonialism when not outwardly hostile, and the Dutch resistance to Indonesian independence attracted a great deal of criticism from Washington. European colonial powers, conversely, were not welcoming of American interference in their diminishing spheres of influence. Divisions between the United States and the European colonial powers were one of the reasons why the only major multilateral defence agreement established in the Pacific in the first decade after the Second World War, the South-East Asia Treaty Organization (SEATO), proved unsuccessful.[6] SEATO was indicative of another barrier to the construction of regionalism in the Pacific: Cold War divisions. The early regional organizations were directed primarily towards the defence of some countries in the region against other regional states. This orientation towards regional defence figured prominently in the motives for the establishment of ASEAN, even though the emphasis in collaboration was on the economic dimension.

A further factor that would have complicated the construction of regional collaboration in the Pacific was the bitter legacy of wartime hostilities between Japan and other states in the region. Whether popular resentment of Japanese colonization in other parts of the region was greater than equivalent European resentment of Germany's wartime activities is impossible to estimate. It is clear, however, that other Asia-Pacific states were unwilling to cooperate with Japan against a perceived common threat from China and the Soviet Union in the early postwar years. This contrasted with the official willingness, even if accompanied by substantial reservations, to welcome Germany back into the European fold in the context of the perceived Soviet threat. In the immediate postwar period, Japan was viewed as much as the problem than as part of the solution to Pacific insecurities. The 1951 ANZUS alliance, for instance, which linked Australia, New Zealand and the United States, was intended originally to provide assurance for the states of Oceania against any resurgence of Japanese militarism after the end of the US occupation. Official resentment in Asia of Japan's wartime aggression appears to have been longer lived than official resentment in other European states of Germany, a resentment that was exacerbated by the policy of denial maintained by some senior Japanese politicians.

The fear of Japan indicates the ongoing importance of power asymmetries in the region that go beyond the issue of US hegemony. For Japan had a much larger population than any other country in East Asia except China and Indonesia, and an industrial history unparalleled in the Western Pacific. Disparities between potential Japanese capabilities and those of other Pacific states were far greater than those between a divided Germany and other countries of Western Europe. Fear of Japan was thus not confined to the military sphere: other countries were concerned that a resurgent Japanese economy would have the capacity to recreate an East Asian Co-Prosperity Sphere even without military conquest. The Koreans, for instance, worried that US plans for postwar reconstruction of the East Asian economy would confine them to the roles of agricultural producers and providers of a market for Japanese industrial products (Woo 1991). The bitter legacy of Japanese colonialism endured for several decades. As we will see later in this chapter, it stymied any overt Japanese leadership role in the promotion of Asia-Pacific regionalism. Normalization of relations between Korea and Japan did not occur until 1965 (and, arguably, was not completed until President Kim Dae Jung's visit to Tokyo in 1998). Elsewhere in the region, the visit of Japanese Prime Minister Tanaka to Indonesia, Malaysia and Thailand prompted anti-Japanese riots as late as 1974.

The colonial legacy was to pose further complications for the organization of the Pacific: the emergence of a group of states that were jealous of their sovereignty, suspicious of the motives of Western powers, and dissatisfied with the structure of the existing international economic order. The Philippines and Indonesia gained their independence in the second half of the 1940s, joining a group of independent states in Asia whose views on economic cooperation differed markedly from those in Washington. These independent Asian states aspired to use the only multilateral regional institution – the UN's Economic Commission for Asia and the Far East (ECAFE), whose membership included the countries of Central and South Asia as well as Southeast and Northeast Asia – to extract development assistance from the United States and other Western powers. In particular, they pressed the United States to extend the Marshall Plan to Asia and to channel aid funds through ECAFE. In an early setback to regional collaboration, neither the US nor its European allies would oblige, and Australia and New Zealand backed their position.[7] ECAFE and its successor, ESCAP, were to remain divided along

North–South as well as Cold War lines, thereby inhibiting the role they could play in fostering regional collaboration.

Washington subsequently opposed Japanese plans for the establishment of an Asian Development Bank (ADB) until, in the mid-1960s, the Johnson administration made the promotion of Asian prosperity a central component in its strategies for resisting the expansion of Soviet and Chinese influence in the region. The change in US policy enabled in-principle agreement on the ADB to be reached in December 1965. The United States subsequently supported the establishment of ASEAN in 1967, again in the hope that economic development would bring new political stability to the region. But US enthusiasm for regional collaboration did not extend to the creation of a Pacific-wide economic organization: Washington repeatedly stated its preference for global over regional trading regimes. And the concern of ASEAN countries to maintain the integrity of their organization and its centrality in regional affairs was subsequently to prove a major stumbling block to the creation of a broader regional institution. Efforts to create institutionalized intergovernmental collaboration in the Asia-Pacific region faced not just indifference but active hostility from ASEAN.

Precursors to APEC

With the United States generally hostile to the establishment of region-wide collaboration in the Asia-Pacific, other sources of leadership were required. All the major initiatives for the institutionalization of Asia-Pacific cooperation from the mid-1960s onwards came mainly from Japanese academics, who acted in close association with the Japanese government, and in collaboration with counterparts in Australia. The origins of this cooperation lie in the Agreement on Commerce between the Commonwealth of Australia and Japan, signed in Hakone on 6 July 1957. The agreement owed much to two factors that have consistently driven the push for closer inter-state collaboration in the Pacific. One was defensive: a fear of the consequences of protectionism elsewhere in the world economy. The second was the desire to manage the challenges of, and take advantage of the opportunities provided by, increasing economic interdependence, in this instance driven by Japan's rapid economic growth and reindustrialization.

The Australian and Japanese economists who participated in the policy-making process perceived a considerable mutuality of interests across the two economies, a perception shared by the two governments.[8] Both feared that the establishment of the European Community would raise new barriers to their exports. Australia faced the loss of its preferred access to its traditional major market should the United Kingdom eventually join the European Community. And Japan, whose exports to Europe had already been adversely affected by European refusal to grant Japanese goods MFN status despite Japan's accession to GATT, faced additional barriers to its burgeoning exports of textiles.[9] Governments in both countries saw themselves as 'outsiders' to the 'region', and as having the capacity to play a bridging role between East and West. Collaboration in the promotion of regionalism would be a means of integrating the two countries with Asia – and not just on the economic dimension (see Korhonen 1994; Terada 1999a). Mutuality of interest extended to a new division of labour in the Pacific based on 'natural complementarities'. Australia would be the quarry to supply the raw materials to fuel Japan's industrialization drive.

Another reason behind Japanese promotion of regional collaboration was a concern that it should not bear the costs of Southeast Asian development alone – whether by providing financial aid or by absorbing the exports of ASEAN's nascent manufacturing industries. In 1962, Saburo Okita of the Japan Economic Research Center asserted that 'most of the products in the region should be bought by outside countries as the capacity of regional countries, including Japan, to absorb such products is quite limited; so-called open regionalism is thus necessary' (quoted in Terada 1999a: 175).

Concern about European protectionism and the Community's construction of a closed economic bloc with the former colonies of the European powers sparked the first major postwar initiative for Asia-Pacific regionalism: the proposal in 1965 by the Japanese economist Kiyoshi Kojima (1966) for a Pacific Free Trade Area (PAFTA). The organization was to embrace the five advanced economies of the Pacific: Australia, Canada, Japan, New Zealand, and the United States, with the developing economies of the region given associate membership – in Kojima's original terminology, the proposal was for a Pacific Advanced Countries Free Trade Area. In early 1967, Kojima undertook a 'study tour', financed by the Japanese Ministry of Foreign Affairs (MOFA), to promote the PAFTA idea in the other four industrialized countries. His arguments (Kojima 1971) that a Pacific Free Trade Area was desirable to counter the European Community, which had been strengthened by the completion of its program of removing internal tariffs, and that the complete freeing of trade on a regional basis was preferable to the partial liberalization of global trade likely to be achieved under GATT's Kennedy Round, fell on deaf ears in the other capitals.[10]

Although it did not bring about the desired intergovernmental collaboration, Kojima's tour laid the foundations for the first Pacific Trade and Development (PAFTAD) conference in January 1968, again financed by MOFA through the Japan Economic Research Center. PAFTAD brought together economists from academia, government, and regional and international organizations. The PAFTAD conferences, held on average every eighteen months over the three succeeding decades, have been the primary vehicle for the construction of an epistemic community of pro-liberalization economists in the Asia-Pacific region.[11] Meanwhile, as the result of another Japanese initiative, which grew out of the Australia–Japan Business Cooperation Conference, the Pacific Basin Economic Council (PBEC), a conference of business representatives, was established in Tokyo in April 1967. For the first three PBEC meetings, the business representatives invited came from the same five industrialized economies of the Pacific that Kojima had listed as candidates for membership in PAFTA (see Woods 1993: Ch. 5).

The lack of interest of other governments in Kojima's proposal for a Pacific Free Trade Area caused him to reformulate his ideas in the direction of a more modest organization to promote inter-state economic cooperation in the Pacific. At the first PAFTAD conference, he proposed that an Organization for Pacific Trade and Development (OPTAD) be established. He noted that '[p]ractical steps towards closer Pacific economic cooperation can be taken by strengthening *functional*, rather than *institutional* integration, and thus attempting to attain the favourable benefits of a free trade area whilst avoiding the unfavourable impact effects' (Kojima 1971: 168, emphasis in original). The model for OPTAD was to be the Organization for Economic Cooperation and Development (OECD). It would be an intergovernmental organization with the responsibility for coordinating policy in three areas: trade; investment; and aid and trade policies towards less developed economies. At the same conference, the Australian economist Peter Drysdale, a student of both Kojima and Sir John Crawford (of the Australian National University [ANU]), put forward a similar proposal. Neither variant generated any significant interest from governments in the region. The Australia–Japan Economic Relations Research project, headed by Okita and Crawford, kept the OPTAD project alive in the first half of the 1970s. Their joint report (Crawford and Okita 1976) recommended that their two governments should promote the OPTAD concept. But a decade passed with the proposal largely neglected outside Australia and Japan and PAFTAD circles until it was revived in a paper commissioned by the Congressional Research Service from Patrick and Drysdale (1979).

The revived arguments for OPTAD rested not so much on the defensive case that Kojima had put forward for countering regionalism elsewhere, as on the perceived need to construct new institutional structures to manage the growing interdependence of the Asia-Pacific region. A certain triumphalism is evident in the writings of the day. Patrick and Drysdale contrasted the rapid growth of the Asian economies, and of Asia-Pacific trade more generally, with the stagflation of Western Europe and the slow growth of the economies of the Western Hemisphere.[12] The growth of interdependence in the Asia-Pacific region, however, had produced uncoordinated national policies with consequent suboptimal outcomes.

Countries had resorted to protectionist actions in response to the increased costs of structural adjustment. Proponents of OPTAD singled out US unilateralism for particular criticism – from the 'Nixon shocks' of 1971 (the dollar devaluation and the soybean embargo against Japan) to US protectionism against East Asian exports of textiles, autos and steel.[13]

The interdependence of the region was now so complex that bilateral approaches to problem-solving were insufficient. As well as this, global institutions and mechanisms no longer provided an adequate framework for managing the interdependence of the region (Patrick and Drysdale 1979: 13). 'Established Atlantic and European interests', they asserted, dominated global institutions; these preferred a model of managed trade that would not provide 'positive encouragement to the accommodation of trade growth' from East Asia. Moreover, again reflecting a central concern in Japan's foreign policy, the search for 'comprehensive security' (Kiichi Saeki 1981), a regional institution was needed to ensure long-term security of supply of raw materials for the rapidly industrializing countries of the region. The institution would help to move trade in raw materials beyond the conflict between commodity producers and consumers that had become so prominent in the global economy following the initial success in 1973–74 of the Organization of Petroleum Exporting Countries (OPEC) (Drysdale 1978: 612). Membership in OPTAD, unlike that proposed for PAFTA, would not be confined to the industrialized economies of the region but would also embrace the less developed economies of Southeast Asia and possibly South America. The centrally planned economies of Northeast and Southeast Asia would be excluded, but Patrick and Drysdale suggested that one of the purposes of OPTAD would be to coordinate and improve relations with these economies.

Again, governments in the region were unwilling to commit themselves to the intergovernmental organization that the OPTAD proposal envisaged. The push for enhanced regional collaboration, however, did generate enough momentum to lead to the establishment in 1980 of a new organization, the Pacific Economic Cooperation Conference (PECC), in response to another joint Australian–Japanese initiative. PECC was designed as a tripartite organization that would bring together representatives of the academic world, business and governments of the region.[14]

As early as 1968, then, the model that was to be used by Australian Prime Minister Bob Hawke in his 1989 APEC initiative had already been formulated and proposed to the governments of the Asia-Pacific region. Certainly, with Patrick and Drysdale's 1978 reformulation of the OPTAD proposal, a detailed blueprint for APEC had been established. The model for Asia-Pacific regionalism was to be the OECD, but without the large-scale bureaucracy of that organization. National bureaucracies would provide support services for the regional organization instead – as per the model that ASEAN had adopted. Functional task forces would be the main agents of OPTAD's work. The institution was to operate informally, based on consensual decision-making (Drysdale and Patrick 1981: 81). This modus operandi was to become known as the 'Pacific Way' and the idea that regionalism in the Pacific should be non-discriminatory was already well established in the discussion of OPTAD in the late 1970s. The concept of 'open regionalism', a core theme in APEC, first appeared in a report of a study group appointed by Japanese Prime Minister Ohira in 1979:

> A regionalism that is open to the world, not one that is exclusive and closed, is the first characteristic of our concept. We are fully aware that a regional community without a perspective for a global community, a regionalism that excludes globalism, has no possibility of development and prosperity. Nonetheless, not a few problems that confront us today could be most suitably handled by first attempting regional co-operation and then developing this into global co-operation. (Pacific Basin Co-operation Study Group 1981: 184)

Why did it take more than two decades for governments to accept a variant of the OPTAD model as the basis for constructing a regional institution? To answer this question requires consideration of the reasons why governments initially expressed no enthusiasm for the proposal, the role of the organizations established in the late 1960s to promote Pacific collaboration, and how the context for cooperation, especially as reflected in changes in states' interests, evolved over the succeeding two decades.

The Lack of Official Enthusiasm for Pacific Regionalism

The report of the study group set up by Prime Minister Ohira advocated staging a series of international conferences for further exploration of the prospects for Pacific cooperation. Because the Japanese government, fearful of the possible reaction of other Asian states, did not wish to be seen to be taking a leadership role in sponsoring OPTAD, Ohira appointed a task force initially headed by Saburo Okita, former director of the Economic Planning Agency and subsequent head of the Japan Economic Research Center, to seek a formula for moving the process forward. Okita in turn contacted his co-organizer in the Australia–Japan Economic Relations Research project, Sir John Crawford, who persuaded the Australian Prime Minister, Malcolm Fraser, to co-sponsor a seminar on Pacific cooperation. This seminar, subsequently known as the first of the Pacific Economic Cooperation Committee conferences, was held under the auspices of the ANU in 1980. Although an 'academic seminar', the organizers consulted closely with officials from both the Australian and Japanese governments in their preparations for the meeting.

Following the seminar, Crawford wrote a report to the governments of all the countries represented at the meeting on how the cooperation program might be advanced.[15] Not a single response was received – even from the Japanese government. The reasons for governments' lukewarm reaction to the seminar tells us much about the scepticism at the time about the viability of regional intergovernmental collaboration, and the problems that had to be overcome before APEC was realized.

The reservations of individual countries (or groupings such as ASEAN) about the initial PECC meeting are elaborated below. Other concerns were common across most countries. The first related to the nature of the beast that was being proposed: what form would collaboration take? Although Patrick and Drysdale had elaborated the OPTAD proposal in detail, it was not the only proposition on the table. Besides the OECD model, others suggested that an intergovernmental regional organization should embrace security issues. Proposals for purely private sector arrangements along the lines of the Trilateral Commission or the inter-war Institute for Pacific Relations also received some support. Yet others argued that the organization should be private but with financial and organizational support from governments whose officials could participate in a private capacity (Morley 1987).[16] The open-ended nature of the discussions at the first PECC meeting caused substantial uncertainty about the benefits that regional collaboration would bring – and the responsibilities that governments would have in a process where they would not necessarily control the agenda. Some participants complained that the only substantive outcome of the seminar was a call for yet more academic conferences and discussion papers on the future of regional collaboration.[17] 'There is less here than meets the eye', declared one PECC participant (quoted in Weatherbee 1989: 13). The Australian Prime Minister, Malcolm Fraser, conceded that '[w]hile the idea of a Pacific Community has been around for some time, it has never been expressed in clear terms ... I could well understand some of the earlier diffidence with which ASEAN members approached the concept. How can you ask somebody to support something that cannot be and has not been defined ...?' (Fraser 1984: 3, 5).[18]

A second general problem that beset the PECC meeting was the absence of leadership. Neither of the governments of the two largest economies, Japan and the United States, was willing to take the initiative. Both Tokyo and Washington feared that their close identification with a proposal would alienate other countries within the region, especially some members of ASEAN – hence the Japanese desire to have Australia stage the first PECC meeting.[19] Factors peculiar to Japan and the United States were relevant also. In Japan, the Pacific Basin concept became entangled in leadership and bureaucratic politics. Ohira had launched the initiative as part of his campaign for the prime ministership, his initiative seen by some as related to factional politics (Gordon 1983). Zenko Suzuki, who succeeded to the premiership after Ohira's death in June 1980, was far less interested in the concept. Moreover, Ohira had reputedly announced his proposals without prior consultation of the relevant bureaucracies (Morley 1987: 28–9). The Ministry of Foreign Affairs and the Ministry of International Trade and Industry (MITI) subsequently engaged in infighting over which agency would have prime responsibility for managing relations with the region, a problem that was to beset Japanese action on Pacific regionalism throughout the 1980s. MOFA, moreover, was reluctant to promote any initiative that did not have the full support of ASEAN. Meanwhile, MITI reportedly feared that a new regional organization would merely act as another vehicle through which the less developed economies would make unwelcome demands for further economic aid – a concern shared by Washington.

Although Ronald Reagan had signalled an interest in pursuing a free trade agreement with Canada during the 1980 presidential campaign, the US government at the beginning of the 1980s was still hostile to regional approaches that might be seen to undermine its commitment to global trade liberalization (Patrick 1975; Borthwick 1987). In particular, the US government looked forward to the GATT Ministerial Meeting scheduled for November 1982 in the expectation that this would launch a new round of global trade negotiations. Moreover, pressure within Congress for a reduction in US contributions to regional and multilateral organizations posed a further obstacle to the launch of a major new intergovernmental organization (Morrison 1981). The failure of the GATT Ministerial Meeting did prompt a new interest in regional arrangements – seen in the announcement of a willingness to negotiate free-trade agreements with Israel and Canada. But the Reagan administration's change of heart on regionalism came far too late to save the 1980 Pacific Basin initiative. It was not until the advent of the second Reagan administration that Secretary of State George Shultz specifically endorsed a regional approach to Asia-Pacific cooperation and institutionalized US participation in PECC (Patrick 1996: 198).

Whereas the Japanese and US governments largely maintained an attitude of indifference in their public stances towards proposals for a new intergovernmental forum, representatives from the ASEAN countries were frequently outspoken in their opposition. One reason was the lack of clarity about the proposals and the benefits that a new forum would bring. Kernial Sandhu, head of the influential Institute of Southeast Asian Studies in Singapore, wrote of the 'meaningless rhetoric' of OPTAD proponents and their failure to demonstrate how the proposed organization would generate concrete benefits.[20] Another prominent academic with close government connections, Dr Noordin Sopiee from the Institute of Strategic and International Studies in Malaysia, complained that the process of 'muddling through' that OPTAD proponents were engaged in was inappropriate for negotiations among governments of the region (cited in Soesastro 1983a: 1259).

Underlying these objections were deeper concerns about the origins of the proposal, and the implications of a regional grouping for ASEAN itself and for its relations with other less developed economies including non-market states within the region. Some ASEAN governments saw the OECD model proposed for OPTAD as a means of institutionalizing a 'rich man's club'. A move to free trade in the region, it was feared, would freeze the current division of labour. They believed that the obligations that a new regional economic organization would impose would be asymmetrical: ASEAN governments would have to undertake liberalization of their economies whereas the organization would not address the increasing resort of industrialized economies to protectionist measures, especially in the form of non-tariff barriers (Tan Sri Ghazalie Shafie, Malaysian Minister of Home Affairs, cited in Gordon 1983: 247–8; see also Morley 1987: 26–7). The threat perceived was that ASEAN economies would be confined to the roles of suppliers of raw materials and providers of markets for the manufactured goods of the industrialized economies of the region. Concerns about North–South relations, often expressed in the rhetoric of demands for a New International Economic Order, extended also to the impact that OPTAD, an institution that would have bridged the North–South divide, would have for ASEAN's relations was other members of the grouping of less developed countries within the UN, the Group of 77.

Of even greater concern to some ASEAN governments were the implications of a new regional organization for ASEAN itself. Although ASEAN had been founded in 1967, the grouping was largely moribund in its first decade. Only in 1976 did it hold its first summit meeting. By the end of the 1970s, therefore, its leaders were still concerned that a new regional organization could put at risk ASEAN's fragile institutionalization. Its Secretariat was weak and lacked the capacity to provide effective input into discussions of a broader Pacific regional grouping. ASEAN had begun to forge an effective process of bilateral dialogues with industrialized economies: how would the proposed arrangements improve on the results of these meetings by providing substantive outcomes, ASEAN leaders asked? And what would the role of ASEAN, *qua* organization, be within the proposed OPTAD? (Akrasanee 1981: 172). The common fear in Southeast Asia was that the ASEAN identity would be lost within a broader regional arrangement.

ASEAN sensitivities had also been heightened by the way in which the Japanese government had put forward its ideas. In particular, some ASEAN governments took offence that Japan had decided to approach Australia rather than one of their own number to serve as host for the conference.[21] By choosing another OECD government as a partner for its regional initiative, Tokyo appeared to some ASEAN critics to be reviving Kojima's PAFTA proposal for a two-tier region. This offence was compounded when neither the Australian nor the Japanese governments consulted their ASEAN counterparts before the Canberra conference. Some ASEAN governments believed that ASEAN itself should be the core of a new regional organization, which would build on its bilateral dialogues with industrialized economies. (Building a new regional organization around ASEAN's post-ministerial conferences was an approach that Kojima [1983] himself subsequently proposed as a fallback position when the lack of enthusiasm for OPTAD had become clear.)

ASEAN was also alarmed that a regional arrangement that excluded the centrally planned economies of the region, as Patrick and Drysdale had proposed, would have strategic overtones. Sensitivities on this issue were particularly high given the unfortunate history of the two principal regional security organizations – SEATO and the Asian and Pacific Council. A strategic dimension to OPTAD would compromise the non-aligned status that some Southeast Asian governments professed, and the ASEAN commitment to the establishment of a Zone of Peace, Freedom and Neutrality in the region. Inevitably, Russia and Vietnam in particular would see a regional organization that excluded the centrally planned economies as directed against their interests. Indeed this was the official Soviet view of the proposal, which alleged that the primary focus of the Pacific Basin concept was strategic rather than economic in nature (see e.g. Kimura 1987; Primakov 1987).

What were the factors that changed in the course of the 1980s so that governments at the end of the decade accepted a proposal for a new intergovernmental institution that they had earlier rejected?

Why was the APEC Initiative Successful?

The remainder of this chapter reviews the reasons why the initiative for intergovernmental collaboration in the Asia-Pacific was successful in 1989. It addresses the principal factors that the literature reviewed in Chapter 1 identified as significant in causing governments to change their attitudes towards regionalism: hegemonic power shifts; the role of ideas, intellectual leadership and epistemic communities; the importance of crises for opening agendas to new ideas; and the growth of interdependence.

Hegemonic Decline and Asia-Pacific Regionalism

Theorists of hegemonic stability see the emergence of regionalism as both cause and consequence of hegemonic decline. A growth in regionalism is evidence that the hegemon's resources relative to those of its challengers have declined to the extent that it no longer has either the will or the capacity to enforce a multilateral liberal trading system (see e.g. Krasner 1976; Gilpin 1987). Hegemonic decline necessitates more pluralist arrangements for the governments of international economic regimes, arrangements that will be much more difficult to negotiate and to sustain. Challengers to the previous hegemon have an incentive to protect their position by excluding the hegemon's products and firms from their markets. The emergence of regionalism is thus seen in the literature on hegemonic stability as marking a move away from the collective good of an open trading system towards a more fragmented and mercantilist trading regime.

At first sight, the emergence of regionalism in the Asia-Pacific seems to provide support for these arguments (Crone 1992). The agreement of governments to form APEC occurred, in Crone's words, after the 'extreme' hegemonic position of the United States in the region had been eroded as other economies – first that of Japan and then those of the newly industrializing countries – grew at rates far in excess of that of the United States. Undoubtedly the relative decline of the US economy in the 1980s, coupled with the waning of the Cold War, did increase uncertainty in the Asia-Pacific and did open the way for new ideas and for the creative activities of policy entrepreneurs. Yet a simple structural explanation for governments' new interest in collaboration at the end of the 1980s immediately faces a number of problems.

First, the literature on the relationship between regionalism and hegemonic decline expects that the economies that are growing rapidly relative to the hegemon ('the challengers') will attempt to strengthen their own positions and weaken that of the hegemon by excluding the latter from a new regional arrangement. As we will see, however, proposals for a Western Pacific trading group that would exclude the United States generated little support at this time from the rapidly growing economies of Northeast Asia. Linked to the inclusive nature of the proposed region is a second characteristic counter to the arguments about regionalism and hegemonic decline: the proposals for Asia-Pacific regionalism were all directed towards promoting further economic openness rather than closure in the global trading regime. Clearly, even if the growth of government support for Asia-Pacific regionalism was connected with hegemonic decline, the directions taken by that regionalism were not those predicted by the structuralist approaches.

Moreover, the evidence pointing to any significant decline in US hegemony between the end of the 1960s when OPTAD was first mooted, and the formation of APEC in 1989, is not particularly persuasive. On many 'objective' measures of national power – even leaving aside the continuing US 'structural' power on which Susan Strange (1987) focuses, and the 'soft' power that is central to the analysis of Joseph Nye (1990) and writers in the Gramscian tradition – the relative position of the United States stabilized after 1970. In 1989, the US share of world trade (13.84 per cent) was almost exactly equal to that of 1970 (13.79 per cent). The importance of the US as a market for the rest of the world *rose* during this period: the US market share of world imports increased from 13.5 per cent to 15.8 per cent.[22] Of even greater relevance to Asia-Pacific cooperation was the share of the United States in the exports of the economies of the Western Pacific Rim. Rather than declining, this share *increased* substantially in the first half of the 1980s when the US dollar appreciated significantly against East Asian currencies. At the very least, the lack of any substantial decline in US capabilities suggests either a time lag between relative decline and the emergence of regionalism, and/or that factors other than objective economic indicators were important in determining state behaviours in the region at this time.

In particular, the perceptual element clearly had an important influence on Washington's trade policies in the 1980s. Hyperbole about 'Japan as Number One' compounded concerns that the United States had lost its technological edge. Persistent trade deficits with Japan and the East Asian newly industrializing countries (NICs) reinforced perceptions that these economies were 'unfair' traders, an argument made with great effect by a group of 'revisionist' writers (Johnson 1982; Prestowitz 1988; van Wolferen 1989). Meanwhile, the European Community continued to wage a trade war against the United States and other exporters by providing ever larger subsidies for its agricultural sector – again an apparent testimony to the inability of the United States to enforce open markets. One response from Washington was to impose non-tariff barriers (NTBs) against an increased proportion of its imports; by 1983, 43 per cent of US imports were subject to NTBs, compared with an average of 27 per cent for all industrialized economies (Nogues et al. 1986, cited in Webb and Krasner 1989, Table 8: 194).[23]

The United States, nonetheless, continued to perform one of the classic functions of a hegemon by providing the market not just of last resort but of first resort in the recession of the early 1980s. Increasingly, this role was incongruous not only with opinion-makers' perceptions of the declining relative capabilities of the US economy but also with the other policy priorities of the Reagan administration. The administration's solution to the resulting trade problem was an aggressive multidimensional foreign economic strategy. One policy thrust was to force a devaluation of the dollar against the currencies of major trading partners, achieved through the 1985 Plaza Agreement of the Group of 7 industrialized economies. The second element was a new activism in trade diplomacy. Bilateral pressure against trading partners was intensified – and here the administration was pressured by the passage by Congress of the 1988 Trade Act with its Super 301 amendment. Another dimension to the administration's trade diplomacy was the promotion of a new round of global trade negotiations under the auspices of GATT, with the intention of broadening and strengthening the disciplines imposed by the international trade regime. The third element was to signal a new willingness to enter regional trade agreements should progress in the multilateral talks be disappointing.

Were these developments testimony to a decline in the US hegemonic position? In one sense they obviously were. Washington was clearly no longer willing, or indeed able, to sustain the discrimination against its exports by the Europeans and East Asians that it had tolerated in the years of the reconstruction of their economies in the first quarter of a century after the end of the Second World War. It now behaved much more like a normal power in seeking a level playing field in international trade. Nonetheless, Washington continued to set the agenda. Other Asia-Pacific economies displayed a new interest in intergovernmental collaboration, not because they desired to mount a challenge to the hegemon by excluding the United States from a regional organization and thereby strengthening their own positions as rivals to the United States, but because they wanted to incorporate the United States in a new regional grouping in the expectation that this would provide them with increased leverage over US behaviour. In particular, they hoped to constrain Washington's resort to unilateralism and to reduce the likelihood that the US government would promote a regional bloc in the Americas that would discriminate against their interests. These concerns clearly weighed heavily on other governments in the Asia-Pacific as the 1980s progressed. In other words, while the behaviour of the United States was consistent with expectations of a declining hegemon, the policies of the other states in the Pacific did not correspond to the expectations that the theory of hegemonic stability raised about challengers to the dominant power.

Hegemony and Regionalism: The Strategic Dimension

On the economic dimension, the United States increasingly behaved as a declining hegemon, seeking to protect its domestic market as its exports lost competitiveness in the first half of the 1980s. On the strategic dimension, however, developments in the 1980s reinforced the dominant position of the United States. These strategic developments were to have important consequences for the prospects for intergovernmental collaboration in the Pacific.

As noted above, one reason underlying the unwillingness of some ASEAN governments to support a regional economic institution was the fear that the centrally planned economies would be excluded and that this (re)division of the Pacific would inevitably have strategic overtones. Until the mid-1980s, the Soviet Union maintained its hostility towards regional economic institutions in the Pacific, claiming that they were merely a front for an anti-Soviet strategic alliance (Bandura 1980). Soviet views on Asia-Pacific economic cooperation changed dramatically in the first half of the 1980s, however, culminating in Gorbachev's Vladivostok initiative of July 1986. In his speech, Gorbachev proclaimed that 'the Soviet Union is also an Asian and a Pacific country', and expressed an interest in Soviet participation in the previously vilified regional economic institutions.

PECC responded immediately by admitting a Soviet observer to its fifth conference, held in Vancouver in November of that year.[24] Gorbachev's Vladivostok speech in retrospect was an acknowledgement that the Cold War in the Pacific was for all practical purposes over – and that the United States had won. Strategic considerations would no longer pose a major barrier to the realization of institutionalized inter-state regional economic collaboration. But the movement of the Pacific towards a 'unipolar' moment had other important consequences for the relationship between the United States and other countries in the region. Other governments quickly appreciated the risk that a transition to a post-Cold War environment could cause Washington to lose interest in military involvement in the Pacific.[25] Such a possibility appeared all the more likely in the context of trade imbalances and the congressional perception that East Asian countries had not played an appropriate role in either economic or military burden-sharing.

Participants in the push for regional economic collaboration in the Asia-Pacific had always seen it as serving broader political and strategic purposes, a restatement of the functionalist optimism that collaboration on economic and technical issues would reduce the scope for inter-state conflict. The winding down of the Cold War added a new imperative and urgency to this quest. A trans-Pacific regional economic organization had the potential, its proponents believed, not only to help defuse trade conflicts between the United States and East Asia but also to sustain US strategic interests in the region.

Epistemic Communities, Ideas and Intellectual Leadership in the Asia-Pacific

The promotion of the idea of institutionalized intergovernmental collaboration on economic issues in the Pacific region came primarily from sources outside government. For the two decades after the first PAFTAD conference in 1968, an active group of policy-oriented economists promoted the OPTAD idea through PAFTAD, the PBEC, and subsequently through PECC. They succeeded in placing on the international agenda in the 1970s not only the idea of an institution governing regional economic interdependence but also a detailed blueprint for its realization. The significance for the eventual establishment of APEC of the promotional activities of these academics is indisputable. The length of time that elapsed between the original formulation of the proposals and their realization in APEC makes it clear, however, that these ideas in themselves were not sufficient to provide the desired outcome. Their acceptance by governments depended on a range of developments in the 1980s that made the ideas more attractive than they had been at the beginning of the decade.

The overlap and continuity of personnel across the various organizations established to promote Pacific regionalism is striking. As Hugh Patrick (1996: 191), one of the participants in the first PAFTAD conference and a leading proponent of Asia-Pacific regionalism, suggests, 'The road from PAFTAD to PECC, and then to APEC is direct … as one commentator recently put it, "the fingerprints of PAFTAD are all over PECC and APEC"'. 'Perhaps most important', he continues, 'two of the ongoing PAFTAD leaders from the very beginning – Sir John Crawford of Australia and Saburo Okita of Japan – were instrumental in 1980 in leading their countries to propose and carry out the establishment of … PECC, which in due course led to the formation of the government ministerial level APEC in 1989'.[26] Economists involved in PAFTAD came to play major roles in both the discussion of public policy and policy formulation – in their home countries and in regional organizations (Patrick 1996: 197, 190; see also Harris 1994). The PAFTAD group appears to meet the definition of an epistemic community that Peter Haas (1992: 3) offers: 'a network of professionals with recognized expertise and competence in a particular domain and an authoritative claim to policy-relevant knowledge within that domain or issue-area'.

Whether or not the PAFTAD conferees *initially* met the supplementary criteria for categorization as an epistemic community is more debatable. These criteria include a shared set of normative and principled beliefs, shared causal beliefs, shared notions of validity, and a common policy enterprise. Certainly, the economists from the five industrialized countries represented at the first PAFTAD conference shared a faith in the verities of the neo-classical approach, in the desirability of limiting state interference in markets, and in the benefits to be derived from constructing a regional intergovernmental forum to manage the problems arising from complex interdependence. Some of their counterparts from Southeast Asia, for example Hadi Soesastro of the Centre for Strategic and International Studies in Jakarta, shared these beliefs. Others, however, had less faith in the workings of an unfettered market system, viewing the global economy more through the lens of dependency analysis with its emphasis on the structural inequalities between industrialized and less developed economies.[27] At the very least, they were strong believers in the case for protecting infant industry. Moreover, they pushed for the establishment of preferential trading arrangements for the less developed economies of the region, equivalent to those established between the European Community and the ACP Group of countries under the Lomé Convention, including a mechanism similar to the Convention's STABEX scheme to stabilize the earnings of commodity-exporting countries. The Reagan administration's Caribbean Basin Initiative was also seen as a possible model for preferential trade arrangements in the Pacific (Harris 1994: 387).

One of the functions of PAFTAD, however, was to serve as an agency of socialization. Although economists from some of the less developed, and non-market, economies of the region may initially have been sceptical of the pro-liberalization message of PAFTAD, by the mid-1980s little dissent from the dominant line was evident in PAFTAD. Ideas informed by dependency analysis, and demands for preferential arrangements, largely disappeared from the discourse. The organization became an effective proselytizer of what became the pro-liberalization 'Washington Consensus' of the international financial institutions in the 1980s.[28] And with the establishment of PECC in 1980, even greater opportunities arose for the socialization of government officials.

Like other epistemic communities, the PAFTAD economists were largely a self-selected group. The PAFTAD International Steering Committee was responsible for issuing invitations to conferences in conjunction with a host organizing committee formed by the International Steering Committee members from the country staging the next conference (Woods 1993: 45). Neo-classical economists have controlled the International Steering Committee during its three decades of existence. Its Secretariat throughout this period has been located at the Australia–Japan Research Centre at the ANU under the direction of Peter Drysdale, one of the earliest proponents of Pacific regionalism. The Steering Committee seldom invited non-economists to participate in PAFTAD meetings. And challenges to the dominant consensus – on liberalization and on the desirability of establishing an intergovernmental organization for managing interdependence – have been unwelcome. For instance, at the eleventh PAFTAD Conference, a rare paper by political scientists David Yoffie and Robert Keohane (1981), which challenged the push for OPTAD, received a very cool reception (personal communication). (Yoffie and Keohane had suggested that an OPTAD could generate a more protectionist trans-Pacific trade regime. Whereas the newly industrializing countries of East Asia had previously been able to exploit the ambiguities of US trade legislation, the negotiation of a new trade organization, entailing greater specificity of rules, would be likely to entrench US protectionism.)

To demonstrate the existence of an epistemic community is relatively easy; to document its influence on policy is altogether more difficult (Milner 1992). Many of the participants at PAFTAD and PBEC meetings were involved in public policy in their home countries, and PECC brought government officials into the discussion process, albeit acting in a private capacity. But Stuart Harris, a former Secretary of the Australian Department of Foreign Affairs and Trade, a longtime participant in the Pacific economic organizations, points out that it is not clear how effective PECC has been as a transmission belt of ideas to governments. 'The message', Harris (1994: 391) suggests, may have been 'received, although not always passed on'.

In keeping the idea of a regional intergovernmental institution for managing interdependence in the Asia-Pacific on the agenda for more than two decades, the role of the PAFTAD-related economics community is indisputable. Undoubtedly the community exerted more influence in the 1980s than ever before as the case for liberalization became more widely accepted among the governments of the region, and more actively promoted by the international financial institutions. Was the role played by this epistemic community *necessary* for APEC to have been created? To pose this question is to seek a counterfactual that is difficult to define. In the absence of PAFTAD and the other organizations promoting Pacific regionalism, would governments have had the same interest in constructing a regional organization? The answer is almost certainly 'no' or, at least, 'probably not' – an acknowledgement that movement towards such an organization would most likely have taken longer without the blueprint provided by PECC. To recognize the role played by this epistemic community is not, however, to suggest that its promotion of regionalism was *sufficient* to guarantee a successful outcome. Clearly, this was not the case. That more than two decades passed between the original formulation of the OPTAD concept and the eventual agreement on APEC suggests that other factors had to intervene before the ideas of the PAFTAD economists were accepted by all governments in the region. Although the activities of the PAFTAD group influenced governments' views on the desirability of constructing an institution for managing regional interdependencies, the adoption of these ideas awaited a window of opportunity offered by changes in the economic and political contexts in the 1980s.

Crises, Ideas, and Liberalization

The majority of the ASEAN countries were not alone in being at best partial converts to the creed of economic liberalization in the early 1980s.

Table 2.4 Early 1980s economic shocks to commodity exporters

	1978	1979	1980	1981	1982	1983	1984	1985	1986
(a) Annual average rate of growth of per capita GNP (%)									
Australia	4.4	0.5	2.0	0.6	–4.3	4.8	3.2	2.2	0.7
Canada	6.2	2.2	6.5	6.5	–2.5	7.3	3.5	2.2	4.5
New Zealand	0.0	2.8	1.0	3.7	0.2	0.3	2.2	–0.5	2.5
Indonesia	6.2	2.2	6.5	6.5	–2.5	7.3	3.5	2.2	4.5
Malaysia	3.6	6.7	6.3	4.8	1.9	1.3	3.8	–3.9	–0.6
Philippines	3.1	4.0	2.2	0.7	0.3	–1.1	–10.9	–9.4	1.7
Thailand	7.0	1.6	3.2	2.2	3.2	5.1	3.3	2.5	2.2
(b) Current account balance as a percentage of GDP									
Australia	–3.7	–2.0	–2.8	–4.7	–4.9	–3.6	–4.7	–5.5	–5.6
Canada	–2.2	–2.0	–0.6	–2.0	0.4	–0.5	–0.3	–1.4	–2.9
New Zealand	–2.5	–4.0	–4.3	–4.3	–7.2	–4.1	–13.5	–11.7	–9.8
Indonesia	n.a.	n.a.	n.a.	–0.6	–5.6	–7.4	–2.1	–2.2	–4.9
Malaysia	0.8	4.4	–1.1	–9.9	–13.4	–11.6	–4.9	–1.9	–0.4
Philippines	–4.8	–5.5	–5.9	–5.9	–8.6	–8.3	–4.1	–0.1	3.2
Thailand	–4.8	–7.6	–6.4	–7.4	–2.7	–7.2	–5.0	–4.0	0.5

Source: World Bank data accessed through the International Economic Databank, ANU.

Economic nationalism was alive and well in the other economies identified as core participants in a Pacific regional economic grouping: Australia, Canada, Japan, Korea, and New Zealand. The economic crises that the economies heavily dependent on commodities for their export earnings experienced in the first half of the 1980s were to provide an opening for significant policy change that would facilitate subsequent regional collaboration.

Global economic recession followed OPEC's success in raising oil prices in 1979–80. The magnitude and timing of the effects on the commodity exporters of the Western Pacific Rim varied according to the stage of their domestic business cycle and the structure of their exports. All, however, suffered downturns in their rates of economic growth and experienced current account difficulties by 1982. For some economies, the problems were to recur in 1985–86 (Table 2.4). A principal source of difficulty was the decline in the prices of their major commodity exports.

The crises of the first half of the 1980s offered a window of opportunity for pro-liberalization intellectual entrepreneurs to forge new domestic and transnational coalitions. In some economies, such as Indonesia, the crisis led to 'technocrats' (public servants, usually economists, with pro-liberalization, pro-deregulation views) playing a greater role in the determination of economic policy (see e.g. Liddle 1987; Robison 1988;

Soesastro 1989; Barichello and Flatters 1991). In others, such as Australia and New Zealand, pro-liberalization departments, notably the Treasury, were able to seize the initiative on trade policies from the traditionally client-oriented departments of trade.[29] In these two countries and in Canada, reorganizations of the bureaucracy facilitated the marginalization in policy-making of departments traditionally hostile to liberalization. The common trend was a merger of the department of trade with the foreign affairs department in an unequal partnership in which trade was the subordinate party.[30] Some governments, notably Canada and to a lesser extent Australia, appointed autonomous commissions of inquiry into the future direction of economic policy.[31] In a context in which governments were seeking to promote non-traditional exports, and the previous import substitution emphasis of industrialization appeared to have paid few dividends, economic liberalization appeared an attractive option. This message, coming from economists within the domestic bureaucracy and from some industry associations, was reinforced by the international financial institutions and the US government itself, which were aggressively pushing this policy alternative. And one (selective) reading of the reasons for the success of the export-oriented economies of Northeast Asia enhanced the plausibility of liberalization as a strategy to revive sagging economies.[32]

The common response (albeit uneven and at times equivocal) to the economic difficulties of the first half of the 1980s, across all the economies that were potential partners to the United States in a Pacific regional economic organization, was domestic economic liberalization.[33] Once under way, the process became self-sustaining for several reasons. First, it did appear to bring success – the economies of Southeast Asia, in particular, quickly resumed and indeed accelerated their rates of economic growth in the last years of the 1980s. Second, the process of liberalization itself changed the parameters for domestic political coalitions, strengthening the position of pro-liberalization forces. In Southeast Asian economies, for instance, export-oriented industries exercised increasing 'voice' about the disadvantages they encountered from having to purchase high-cost inputs from heavily protected upstream industries (MacIntyre 1991; Doner and Ramsay 1993). The way was open for new coalitions between pro-liberalization technocrats and business groups. Third, liberalization became a core element of national competitive strategy. The fear that the domestic economy would lose out in the competition for FDI, if the conditions that it offered potential investors were not as liberal as those provided by competing hosts, became an important consideration in government policy.

Economic liberalization usually embraced four principal elements: a lowering of border barriers (tariffs and non-tariff barriers) to imports; a reduction in state intervention in the economy, especially of attempts to promote a particular pattern of industrial development through a process of 'picking winners'; a loosening of foreign exchange controls (often accompanied by a devaluation of the local currency); and a reduction in the constraints on foreign investment in the domestic economy. In Indonesia, the initial response to the collapse of oil revenue in 1983 was increased state intervention in the economy through the introduction of an extensive scheme of import licensing. This scheme was intended both to help alleviate balance-of-payments problems and to provide selective incentives for domestic industries. It soon gained notoriety, however, as a haven for rent-seekers (Barichello and Flatters 1991: 278–9). A deepening of the country's economic problems in the mid-1980s opened the way for trade liberalization and a reduction in state intervention. As Soesastro (1989: 859) comments, 'the drop in oil prices in 1983 and again in 1986 was responsible for precipitating and fueling a continued sense of economic crisis in the public's mind that allowed drastic measures to be taken'. From mid-1986 to the end of 1988, the government reduced the percentage of total imports subject to controls from 43 per cent to close to 20 per cent (Riedel 1991: 125).

Similar liberalization occurred in other Southeast Asian economies. In Malaysia, the government largely abandoned the ambitious program it had adopted in 1981 to promote heavy industries, privatized some state-owned industries, reduced tariff and non-tariff barriers, relaxed the conditions on foreign investment established by its New Economic Policy, and allowed the exchange rate to depreciate (Jomo 1993, 1995). In Thailand, the limits to import substitution industrialization were becoming increasingly obvious by the early 1980s. Elements of the business community proved to be allies for reform-minded technocrats located both in the Ministry of Finance and in the National Economic and Social Development Board (the government's economic planning agency, founded in the early 1960s) in their pursuit of a shift from import-substituting to export-oriented industrialization (Phongpaichit 1992). In the Philippines as in Indonesia, the initial response to economic problems in the early 1980s was further state intervention in support of the rent-seeking system of crony capitalism constructed by the Marcos regime (Haggard 1990b). The depth of the crisis by 1984, however, necessitated policy change to secure further assistance from the International Monetary Fund (IMF). Serious efforts at reform, however, proved impossible before the departure of Marcos. The successor government, led by Corazon Aquino, brought new vigour to a stalled process of trade liberalization, abolished domestic monopolies, promoted privatization, and drafted a new investment code.[34]

In Australia, the deterioration of the terms of trade and the current account led the Treasurer, Paul Keating, to warn in 1986 that without a process of significant adjustment and liberalization, Australia risked becoming a 'banana republic'. The economic crisis offered an opening for pro-liberalization forces within the government and the bureaucracy to set the economic agenda (Pusey 1991; Whitwell 1993). The emphasis was on a winding back of state intervention in the economy, in its two dimensions of support for specific industries and of offering social protection to workers (see Castles 1988). The New Zealand Labour government, faced by an even worse balance-of-payments crisis, embarked on a more radical course of economic restructuring. Along with Australia, New Zealand, of all the OECD economies, had traditionally maintained the highest trade barriers. These had been supplemented by a panoply of interventionist devices designed to insulate the domestic economy and society from world market forces. Within a few years, however, the New Zealand economy was transformed into one of the most open in the OECD (Boston et al. 1991; Douglas 1993). In Canada, although the multiple volumes of the Royal Commission on the Economic Union included studies from many different approaches, the overall thrust of the recommendations was in favour of liberalization and a dismantling of some measures of economic nationalism that had long irritated the United States. The new openness to liberalized trade with its giant southern neighbour paved the way for the negotiation of the Canada–US Free Trade Agreement, eventually implemented in January 1989.

Domestic economic deregulation and liberalization of trade policies went hand in hand. Indeed, for many governments, trade liberalization was an essential component of domestic deregulation. The increased competition from imports was a means of forcing inefficient industries to restructure, and a preferred alternative to additional governmental intervention through pro-active industrial policies. As Winham (1988: 44) comments in the context of Canada's pursuit of a bilateral trade agreement with the United States, 'although the [MacDonald Royal] Commission was ultimately proposing something similar to domestic deregulation, it chose a foreign policy, namely trade policy, as the main instrument by which to achieve its purpose'.

Throughout the region, governments evinced a capacity to change the direction of foreign economic policies largely unhindered by domestic economic groups. The pattern of decision-making varied considerably from country to country. At one end of the spectrum was Indonesia. The *Far Eastern Economic Review* concluded its survey of that country in 1995 by noting that '[a]ll key decisions are made by one man' (quoted in Root 1996: 100). Similarly, Mackie and MacIntyre (1994: 20) note that '[t]he locus of power and influence in the political system is confined to the upper echelons of the civilian and military bureaucracies, with little effective leverage being exerted by political parties or *Golkar* (the ruling party), or by other pressure groups, hence the appropriateness of the term "bureaucratic polity"'.[35] Although President Soeharto undoubtedly had to take some domestic interests into account, not least those of his avaricious family, he enjoyed a great deal of latitude in times of economic crisis to change some of the fundamentals of economic policy with the stroke of a pen.

The rapidity and ease with which other governments in the region effected fundamental policy change suggested, however, that all of the states enjoyed a great deal of autonomy in the area of foreign economic policy-making. In Malaysia, the government dramatically reversed course on its promotion of heavy industries only a few years after it originally introduced its policy. In Indonesia, Malaysia and Thailand, state autonomy from business interests derived in part from the dominance of the private sector by an ethnic Chinese minority vulnerable to state and civil society alike (on Thailand, see Laothamatas 1988). In Korea and Taiwan, the hallmark of the developmental state model was its relative autonomy from particular business interests (see e.g. Johnson 1987; Haggard 1988, 1990a; Amsden 1989; Wade 1990). Although democratization was changing the relationship between the state, politicians and business, foreign economic policy-making in the 1980s remained very much the preserve of the government of the day. In Japan, bureaucratic rivalries between MITI and MOFA complicated foreign economic policy-making towards the region. Nonetheless, it was the state that had the dominant role in decision-making on foreign economic policies; few private sector actors participated in the process (Hirata et al. 1996: 35).

In Australia, and even more in New Zealand, the liberalization of the 1980s not only embraced a reduction in barriers to imports but also a fundamental restructuring of the institutions of state–society relations. Many of these had prevailed since the countries attained self-government at the end of the last century. For most of the reforms undertaken, the governments concerned had neither published plans before election nor subsequently sought a popular mandate for them. Once elected, governments in these parliamentary systems (especially in New Zealand's unitary, unicameral form of government) were able to press ahead with reforms largely unhindered by countervailing pressures.

The capacity of governments to undertake pro-liberalization reforms was enhanced by changes in the attitudes of key 'stakeholders' – business groups and organized labour – towards the traditional insular protectionism of the two economies. Business and labour alike recognized the imperative of restructuring. Significant differences existed between and within the two communities over the preferred modes of reform, but these tended to enhance the capacity of the government to take independent initiatives. Pro-reform elements within these groups and the public more generally were reinforced by a press, especially the economics correspondents of the more serious newspapers, that was generally supportive of economic liberalization. And the economic problems of the first half of the 1980s undoubtedly brought home the urgency of economic reform. While ultimately having to balance the needs of multiple constituencies, governments enjoyed substantial room for manoeuvre.[36] If this statement was true of industry policy generally, it applied *a fortiori* to negotiations on economic issues within international forums. The absence of a coherent business input into, for instance, Australian government negotiating positions for the Uruguay Round of GATT negotiations is striking (Ann Capling, personal communication).

In sum, the liberalizing measures implemented in response to the economic crises of the first half of the 1980s removed some of the obstacles that had previously stood in the way of regional economic collaboration. These included a range of economic policies intended to protect and promote domestic economic groups. Attitudes about feasible policy alternatives also changed. The economic crisis finally destroyed the credibility of South–South collaboration as an alternative to economic liberalization. The UNCTAD V conference held in Manila in 1979 had exposed the divisions within the Group of 77, especially between oil-exporters and other less developed economies. The recession that followed the second round of oil price rises in 1979–80 was a powerful demonstration to the ASEAN group that their prosperity was intimately linked to that of their industrialized trading partners. Moreover, not only did the recession of the first half of the 1980s weaken a commitment to South–South alliances generally, but it also revealed the limitations of cooperation within ASEAN itself. In the first fifteen years of ASEAN, the percentage of their total trade that the member states conducted with one another actually declined. Neither the Preferential Trading Arrangements nor the various regional schemes to promote industry development had generated benefits of any significance to member states (for one Indonesian perspective on ASEAN's effectiveness, see Rezasyah 1996: 191).

A further factor that helped reduce the Southeast Asian states' resistance to a regionwide intergovernmental institution was their participation in the Cairns Group. The membership of this group of 'agricultural fair traders', established in an attempt to increase the leverage of relatively small agricultural exporting economies in the Uruguay Round, included Indonesia, Malaysia, the Philippines, and Thailand as well as Australia, Canada, and New Zealand (Higgott and Cooper 1990). Collaboration with some of the proposed industrialized economy members of a Pacific regional grouping was a further learning and socialization experience for the ASEAN countries. While it may not have produced a sense of community, it did help to dispel ideas that relations between North and South were necessarily antagonistic. And it also demonstrated the additional leverage that could be gained in international negotiations by collaboration with others.

Most ASEAN countries remained reluctant participants in a broader Asia-Pacific regionalism, but the developments in their own economies in the 1980s and the experience of greater interaction with other potential members of an Asia-Pacific grouping helped to break down the opposition that had derailed previous efforts at constructing an intergovernmental institution. The growth in interdependence within the Asia-Pacific region as a whole powerfully reinforced these more positive attitudes towards regionwide cooperation.

Growing Interdependence

The previous chapter noted how writers in the liberal institutionalist tradition often see the growth of interdependence as increasing the incentives for regional economic collaboration among governments. A rise in interdependence increases the number of problems requiring inter-state collaboration for efficient and successful resolution. Increased interdependence may also make governments more aware of the transactions costs that closer collaboration could help overcome. In the Asia-Pacific region in the 1980s, the growth of interdependence not only changed governments' attitudes towards regional collaboration but had a profound effect on their thinking about the shape that the region should take.

The share of trade that Asia-Pacific states conducted with other states in the region rose substantially in the 1980s (Table 2.5). By the end of the decade, intra-regional trade in the Asia-Pacific, defined as the APEC 15,[37] approached the levels prevailing in the European Community. This increase in trade interdependence occurred even though few preferential agreements existed to encourage trade between economies in the region, and none were in force throughout the region. Economists have studied the growth of Asia-Pacific intra-regional trade in detail. Employing gravity models, a form of regression analysis, they concluded that the recent growth in intra-regional trade occurred not because of an increase in intra-regional trade 'bias', but simply because East Asian economies were growing more rapidly in these years than the world economy as a whole (see e.g. Frankel 1991, 1993; Petri 1993). In other words, intra-regional trade was no greater than would have been predicted on the basis of factor endowments, geographical proximity, transport costs, etc.

For governments, the sophisticated economic models that showed, for example, a long-term decline in intra-regional trade bias were largely beside the point. The very fact that East Asian economies were growing more rapidly than those elsewhere encouraged a rethinking of foreign economic policy priorities. Governments in Canada and the United States, for instance, increasingly emphasized their economies' Pacific interests

Table 2.5 Interdependence among APEC economies: intra-APEC trade as a share of total trade (%)

Year	Share
1980	56.9
1981	58.9
1982	60.1
1983	63.0
1984	65.3
1985	66.4
1986	66.6
1987	67.5
1988	68.0
1989	68.5

Source: IMF Directions of Trade data accessed through the International Economic Data Bank, ANU.

and orientation. With a Californian in the White House, it was perhaps inevitable that the United States would give new emphasis to its Pacific interests, a trend that was reinforced in July 1982 when George Shultz was appointed Secretary of State. The US Under Secretary for Economic Affairs, W. Allen Wallis (1984: 50) noted, for instance, that since the late 1970s US trade with East Asia and the Pacific had exceeded that with Western Europe, and by 1983 was $26 billion larger than trade with Europe. 'Traditionally', he asserted, 'we have thought of Asia as the "Far East". We looked far, and we looked east, across Europe to Asia. Now we look west, across the Pacific, to Asia. East Asia and the Pacific region have become the "Near West".' The share of North American exports going to other Asia-Pacific economies rose from 47 per cent in 1978 to 59 per cent in 1988 (DFAT 1989c: 63). In Australia, an influential report by a former adviser to Prime Minister Hawke emphasized the importance of the East Asian economies for Australia's future prosperity (Garnaut 1989). The need to 'jump on board the Orient Express' became an overworked metaphor.

Two factors contributed significantly to the increase in intra-regional trade. The first was the growing importance of the US market for East Asian exports during the global recession of the first half of the 1980s, a development encouraged by the overvaluation of the US dollar. The second was the rapid growth of FDI, first from Japan and then from Hong Kong, South Korea and Taiwan, into Southeast Asia in the second half of the decade. These capital movements were driven by the desire of companies in Northeast Asia to relocate some of their manufacturing activities in response to the rapid appreciation of their domestic currencies following the Plaza Accord, by a substantial increase in the costs of labour

Table 2.6 Ratio of foreign direct investment to gross fixed capital formation

Country	1971–75	1976–80	1981–85	1986–90
Australia	4.5	4.6	5.1	10.2
Canada	3.6	1.7	–0.6	3.7
China	0	0.08	0.9	2.1
Hong Kong	5.9	4.2	6.5	13.6
Indonesia	4.6	2.4	1.0	2.0
Japan	0.1	0.05	0.1	0.0
Korea	1.9	0.4	0.5	1.3
Malaysia	15.2	11.9	10.8	10.6
Mexico	3.5	3.6	3.6	8.1
New Zealand	4.8	6.1	5.4	9.8
Papua New Guinea	–	8.7	16.4	21.5
Philippines	1.0	0.9	0.7	6.8
Singapore	15.0	16.6	18.1	33.9
Thailand	3.0	1.5	3.2	5.9
United States	0.9	2.0	3.4	7.1

Source: Chia Siow Yue (1994b: Table 6.3)

and land in the home country, and by pressures from the United States on Northeast Asian governments to reduce their balance of trade surpluses. These pressures included the removal of Korea and Taiwan's access to the US Generalized System of Preferences program in 1988 (for more detailed discussion, see Bernard and Ravenhill 1995).

Japan's new investment in manufacturing in other Asian countries in the years 1986–89 exceeded the *cumulative* total for the whole of the 1951–85 period. The growth in Taiwanese and Korean investment in ASEAN was even more spectacular. At the end of 1987 the total stock of Taiwanese investment in manufacturing in ASEAN stood at $78 million. In the following three years over $850 million was invested. As was true for Japanese investment, electronics was the single largest sector (with 39 per cent of the total).[38] A similar surge, though at lower levels, occurred in outflows from Korea: in 1985 the *cumulative* investment from Korea in ASEAN amounted to only $42 million; in 1989 alone, new investment from Korea amounted to $132 million. By the end of the decade, Taiwan had replaced the United States as the second most important investor in ASEAN and had overtaken Japan as the single largest investor in Malaysia. The share of the four East Asian NICs combined in foreign investment in all ASEAN countries except Thailand was comparable to or exceeded that of Japan.[39] Increasing flows of FDI between regional economies were one dimension in the growth of transnational production networks.

In aggregate, the share of FDI in gross fixed capital formation jumped substantially in many APEC economies in the 1980s (Table 2.6).

Table 2.7 Openness of APEC economies (foreign trade as a percentage of GDP)

	Australia	Canada	Chile	China	Hong Kong	Indonesia	Japan	Korea	Mexico	Malaysia	New Zealand	Philippines	PNG	Singapore	Thailand	USA
1970	29	43	29	5	181	28	20	37	15	80	48	43	72	225	34	11
1975	29	47	53	10	164	44	26	64	15	87	55	48	86	289	41	16
1980	34	55	50	13	181	53	28	74	24	113	62	52	97	423	54	21
1985	35	54	54	24	209	43	26	67	26	105	64	46	95	318	49	18
1989	35	51	66	25	255	46	20	63	32	140	53	59	93	368	72	21
1992	38	54	58	32	281	53	18	59	30	154	61	63	94	324	77	22
1995	40	71	54	40	297	53	17	67	48	194	62	80	106	n.a.	90	24

Source: World Bank data accessed through the International Economic Data Bank, ANU

Table 2.8 Share of manufactures in total exports (%)

	Indonesia	Malaysia	Philippines	Singapore	Thailand
1970	1.2	6.5	7.5	41.5	4.7
1975	1.2	17.3	11.7	.	14.7
1980	2.3	18.8	21.1	43.1	25.2
1985	11.0	27.2	26.6	51.0	38.1
1990	35.5	54.2	39.0	71.7	63.1

Source: World Bank data accessed through the International Economic Data Bank, ANU

From the perspective of their impact on governments' willingness to enter regional collaboration, the single most important contribution of these foreign capital flows was to effect a dramatic change in the export structure of many of the ASEAN economies (with the exception of Brunei, where petroleum continued to constitute the vast majority of exports). The previous chapter noted the hypothesis that an increase in economic openness will be associated with the formation of regional economic groupings. For the Southeast Asian economies, economic openness increased significantly for all economies apart from Indonesia over the course of the 1980s, especially in the last years of the decade (Table 2.7). Liberalization brought the desired move towards more export-oriented economies. Inevitably, the greater export orientation of the economies changed the domestic political economy of trade policy. More locally based interests, including many of the newly established subsidiaries of Japanese, Korean and Taiwanese companies, supported a liberal trade regime. Their motive, in some instances, was not only because trade liberalization would provide access to less expensive components and inputs, but because companies were concerned about the access of their products to foreign markets, a concern heightened by the increased US resort to bilateralism in its trade relations with East Asian economies.

Moreover, and probably even more important for the attitudes of ASEAN governments towards regional economic collaboration, was the dramatic shift in the composition of their exports. By the end of the decade, manufactures constituted more than half of the total export earnings of Malaysia, Singapore and Thailand, and more than a third of those of the Philippines and even those of oil-rich Indonesia (Table 2.8). The concerns that ASEAN governments expressed at the time of the first PECC meeting in 1980 that regional economic collaboration would condemn their economies to the perpetual position of commodity exporters were considerably allayed during the course of the decade. By the end of the 1980s, ASEAN governments were buoyed by a new confidence that their increasingly export-oriented economies were capable of competing with any in the rapidly globalizing world economy (see e.g. Lim 1995). Governments also perceived regional institutions as a potential tool in domestic politics: as economies became more outward-oriented, so governments became more interested in using commitments made in regional organizations as a way of increasing their leverage against protectionist domestic forces.[40]

Growing Interdependence and the Choice of 'Region'

Two factors profoundly affected the direction of East Asian exports in the 1980s. The first was the overvaluation of the US dollar in the first half of the decade. In conjunction with large budgetary deficits, the high dollar sucked a rapidly growing flow of East Asian exports into the United States. The second was the move of an increasing share of low-end manufacturing from Northeast Asia to Southeast Asian economies that were used as production platforms for exports to third-country markets, especially the United States. In addition, a number of major US electronics companies including Apple, Hewlett-Packard and Intel increased their investments in components and final products manufacturing in Southeast Asia. The net result was a significant increase in the dependence of the East Asian economies on the US market in the 1980s. Although the US share of Japanese and Korean exports by 1989 had fallen from its peak of a few years earlier, it remained substantially above the levels at the start of the decade. Meanwhile, the US share in ASEAN exports continued to increase throughout the decade (Table 2.9).

Despite East Asian economies growing more rapidly than the rest of the world, the intensity of trade between most East Asian economies (the exception is Taiwan) and other parts of East Asia actually declined in the 1980s (Primo Braga and Bannister 1994: 102 and Table 2).[41] The main reason was the increased share of their exports directed to the North American market. ASEAN governments believed, however, that the direction of trade was also a reflection of the difficulties of accessing the Japanese market, and that these also explained the ongoing deficits that

Table 2.9 Share of the US in the total exports of East Asian economies (%)

	1975	1980	1981	1982	1983	1984	1985	1986	1987	1988	1989
ASEAN	18.6	16.0	15.7	14.2	17.3	18.6	19.3	20.4	20.9	20.7	21.1
Japan	19.9	24.3	25.4	26.2	29.2	35.4	37.4	38.7	36.7	33.9	34.1
Korea	28.7	26.4	25.9	28.8	33.0	35.4	35.3	39.7	38.6	35.3	33.0

Source: IMF Directions of Trade data accessed through the International Economic Data Bank, ANU

Singapore and Thailand experienced in their trade with Japan. Governments in Southeast Asia region maintained a love–hate relationship with Tokyo. They admired and wished to emulate the Japanese economic model but complained bitterly that Tokyo had failed to support their industrialization efforts through market-opening measures for manufactures.[42] Moreover, the Japanese government was criticized for the alleged reluctance of Japanese corporations to transfer technology to Southeast Asian economies. An East Asian regional grouping that Japan would inevitably dominate accordingly held little attraction for other states in the region. It was hardly likely in these circumstances that the East Asian economies would choose to attempt to exclude the allegedly declining hegemon, the United States, from a new regional economic grouping.

Balancing the United States by aligning with the Europeans also had few attractions. Such a move would have been entirely contrary to the process of institutionalization of trans-Pacific relations that had occurred since the first PAFTAD conference. The PECC meetings brought government officials into the discussions, an institutionalized link that was lacking (at the multilateral level) in relations between East Asian economies and Europe. It may have been premature to talk of a Pacific 'community'. Nevertheless, far more of a sense of an evolving institutionalized multilateral approach to problem-solving existed across the Pacific than between the East Asians and the Europeans.

The European Community, moreover, was a far less important market than the United States for the East Asians throughout the 1980s. In 1989, the EEC consumed 14 per cent of ASEAN's total exports, 17 per cent of those of Japan, and less than 12 per cent of those of Korea. The Europeans had been far more ruthless than the United States in limiting the access of East Asian exports to their markets by employing non-tariff barriers and voluntary export restraints. One of the most prominent examples was EEC restrictions on imports of Japanese automobiles, the single most important item in America's trade deficit with Japan in the 1980s. And as Southeast Asian countries moved increasingly to being exporters of manufactures in the 1980s, the EEC market actually declined in significance for them (Langhammer 1998).

Moreover, East Asia's trade relationship with the EEC was far more asymmetrical than that with the United States. The EEC consumed more than 15 per cent of East Asia's exports in the late 1980s; in contrast, the EEC depended on East Asian markets for only 5 per cent of its exports. The trade dependency relationship with the United States was much more evenly balanced. East Asia as a whole provided a market for 26 per cent of its exports in the late 1980s, a figure not far removed from the US share (29 per cent) of East Asian exports – a balance that one might suppose would have provided a source of leverage if East Asia developed a capacity to act collectively.[43] Furthermore, the share of the EEC in investment stocks in East Asia was declining rapidly during the 1980s.[44] Any attempt to balance the United States by aligning with Europe would have placed East Asian economies in a particularly unequal relationship.

Context and Precipitants: Regionalism as a Defence against Closed Markets

Much of the attention of the Pacific regional organizations, especially PECC, in the 1980s was directed towards maintaining and enhancing liberal trade at the global level. Regionalism was valued as much for the perceived potential leverage it would give to states in their dealings with outsiders as for any immediate economic benefits it might bring in within-region relations. Member states did not conceive of regional economic collaboration as a substitute for but as a means of supporting global trade liberalization. The promise of a new round of GATT negotiations in the mid-1980s initially raised expectations. Frustration with the slow pace of the Uruguay Round, however, and alarm at the increasing resort by the Big Two – the United States and the European Community – to unilateral actions that both restricted access to their domestic markets and undercut the position of competitors in third-country markets propelled the economies of the Western Pacific Rim towards closer regional collaboration. As with previous proposals for new Asia-Pacific regional institutions, the primary motive was defensive.

In 1983, Australian Prime Minister Bob Hawke proposed at the third PECC conference that the trade ministers of Western Pacific economies should meet annually. The intention was to strengthen the participation by these economies in the anticipated new round of GATT negotiations. Hawke's proposal underlines two features of the emerging regionalism in the Asia-Pacific in the 1980s. One was a desire that it should reinforce multilateral trade liberalization. A second was a search for a way to establish an increasing government component to regionalism after the lukewarm response of governments to the launch of PECC in 1980. PECC sponsored the quest for a 'Pacific position' on the multilateral trade negotiations in subsequent meetings, most notably the First PECC Trade Policy Forum, held in San Francisco in March 1986, six months before the launch of the Uruguay Round (for details, see Woods 1993: 128–9).

The PECC process, however, provided an early indication of the limitations that Asian governments would place on interference by regional organizations in their sovereignty – an issue that subsequently has weighed heavily on decision-making within APEC. They rejected a resolution introduced by the US delegation at PECC IV in support of further trade liberalization and the initiation of a new GATT round. The main objection was not so much over the substance of the resolution as over procedure. The use of resolutions would have marked an unacceptable move away from a consensus approach in PECC towards legalism. It would thereby open the way in the future for voting, and the possibility that a majority might attempt to impose its will on a minority (Woods 1993: 116).

The quest for a new intergovernmental forum gathered pace in the mid-1980s, fuelled by growing concerns about the possible fracturing of the global economy into rival trading blocs. A number of factors combined to cause Western Pacific governments to worry not just about their future access to markets but also their capacity to maintain control over their domestic trade policies.

One significant development was the increasing resort of the United States to unilateralism in its trade relations. Congressional concern about trade imbalances with Northeast Asian economies, and a perception that Japan, Korea and Taiwan in particular were 'free riders' in a liberal global economy underwritten by the United States, pressured an increasingly receptive administration to retaliate against perceived unfair practices. The burgeoning literature on strategic trade policy gave such sentiments a new academic legitimacy. Retaliation appeared justified in situations where exclusion from foreign markets could lead in theory to a permanent disadvantageous shift in competitive advantage.[45] Moreover, breaking the multilateral rules could be justified as a temporary expedient if it led ultimately to others maintaining a greater respect for these rules (Hudec 1990).

By the late 1980s, Raymond Vernon commented, the US administration appeared to have 'an irrepressible propensity to place restrictions on its imports'. During 1988 alone, US government agencies were processing 133 cases under various provisions of US trade law, each of which had the potential to lead to further restrictions on imports (Vernon 1996: 624). Such actions would add to existing 'voluntary' export restraints that applied to East Asian exports of autos, steel, machine tools, textiles, clothing and footwear. US unilateralism was not confined to protecting its domestic market, however. After 1985, using section 301 of the Trade Act and the 'super 301' amendment introduced in 1988, the administration actively sought to prise open markets perceived as unfairly closed to US exports. In the second half of the 1980s, a marked geographical shift towards East Asia occurred in the cases brought under section 301. Japan replaced the European Community as the principal target of the cases – and unlike most actions against the Europeans, those against Japan targeted trade in manufactures. Moreover, Korea and Taiwan also appeared prominently on the list of alleged offenders (see data in Bayard and Elliott 1994, Table 3.2: 60–1).

Another facet of US trade policies alarmed other Western Pacific countries: the trade war that the United States was waging with the European

Community over subsidies for exports of agricultural goods. Inevitably, this conflict spilled over to affect third countries not only by depressing world agricultural prices but also by displacing their products from traditional export markets. The antipodean economies felt the impact of the subsidy war particularly strongly because their temperate agricultural products competed directly with those of the United States and Western Europe. Australian Foreign Minister Bill Hayden, paraphrasing the statement by the US administration that it would treat New Zealand as a friend but not an ally, after New Zealand's refusal to grant entry to its ports to US nuclear-armed or nuclear-powered ships, jibed that Washington was treating Australia as if it were an ally but not a friend.

A second factor of increasing concern to Western Pacific economies was the willingness of the United States to enter into regional trade agreements. Baldwin (1997) makes a persuasive argument that the United States did not undertake a dramatic U-turn in its attitude towards regional trade agreements in the 1980s. It had offered such an agreement to Canada on several occasions since 1945; the difference now was that Ottawa showed a new willingness to enter such an arrangement. In addition, Washington presented a credible argument that it looked to regional agreements as a way of pursuing its goal of global free trade, viewing them in part as a lever to induce concessions from an intransigent European Community. In a speech in June 1988, James Baker (1988), then Secretary of the Treasury, remarked: 'We need to enhance the resiliency of the trading system by promoting liberalization on a number of fronts. While we normally associate a liberal trading system with multilateralism – bilateral or minilateral regimes may also help move the world toward a more open system'. Nonetheless, this was another instance where perceptions were what counted. When coupled with the increasing unilateralism in US policy, the negotiations between Washington and Ottawa gave Western Pacific trading partners cause for concern that the United States was moving away from multilateralism, and that their exports would experience increasing difficulties in accessing the world's largest single market.

The slow rate of progress in the Uruguay Round of GATT negotiations compounded fears about a future fragmentation of the world economy. The first two years of negotiations brought minimal progress. Again, the significance of the lack of progress in the GATT round should be viewed in the context of the other concerns that Western Pacific economies held about trade policy developments. It was the cumulative effect of US unilateralism and a growth in regionalism (not only the Canada–US negotiations but also the European Community's plan to create a Single Internal Market), together with the disappointments in the multilateral talks, that created a sense of crisis for the Western Pacific economies. Proposals from the Bush administration for a bilateral extension of free-trade areas also spurred the efforts of the governments of Japan and Australia to create a regional institution as a viable alternative path to trade liberalization; Singapore and South Korea were both identified by Washington as possible participants in such bilateral arrangements.[46] These developments prompted defensive moves by Western Pacific governments to attempt to ensure future market access. The failure of the Montreal mid-term review of the Uruguay Round of GATT negotiations in December 1988, largely because of disagreement over agricultural subsidies, was the precipitant for Bob Hawke's APEC proposal in Seoul in the following month. In a speech to the Korean Business Association, he suggested a ministerial conference towards the end of the year to consider ways of 'creating a more formal intergovernmental vehicle of regional cooperation'.

Hawke's proposal followed several others made over the previous eighteen months. In May 1988, after a review of possible forms that new regional collaboration might take by a MITI Study Group, Japanese Prime Minister Nakasone proposed that a Pacific Forum be established to promote economic and cultural cooperation. Again, the reference was to creating a Pacific equivalent of the OECD. And by 1988, leading figures in the United States had also become backers of a Pacific intergovernmental regional organization. In July 1988, former Secretary of State George Shultz suggested the creation of a Pacific Basin Forum to conduct information exchange on general economic and sectoral issues. Senators Bill Bradley and Alan Cranston introduced variants on the theme in separate initiatives in December 1988 and January 1989. The US Under Secretary of State for Economic Affairs and Agriculture, W. Allen Wallis (1988: 25), spoke of the need to devise a way of bringing the market-oriented economies of the region together: 'it seems to me probable that before long an intergovernmental process may be appropriate ... it would resemble the OECD (in some respects)'.[47]

Governments in the region later squabbled over who should take credit for the APEC initiative – with MITI claiming that the idea originated in Japan (see Funabashi 1995).[48] The rash of proposals in 1988 suggested, however, that a growing body of official opinion in the region now shared the view not only that an intergovernmental organization was desirable but that its realization was merely a matter of time. PECC and its business counterpart, the Pacific Basin Economic Council, had lobbied governments in 1988 to establish a formal intergovernmental forum. That the final push for APEC should come from Australia is not surprising given Australia's association with Japan in earlier initiatives for Pacific regionalism and the perception that it was tactically preferable for the lead not to be taken by either Washington or Tokyo.[49] Moreover, the Australian economy had been the worst affected by the agricultural export subsidies war between the United States and the European Community. Not being a natural member of any of the triad of East Asia, North America, or West Europe, Australia also had much to lose from any fragmentation of the global economy (see Ravenhill 1998b). And its economic performance in the 1980s lagged far behind that of East Asia – another factor that encouraged Canberra to seek deeper integration with these rapidly growing economies.[50]

Also not surprising was the proposed form that the intergovernmental organization should take. Hawke's speech, following in the OPTAD tradition, made explicit reference to the OECD as a model for the new Pacific organization. And, in the tradition of Pacific regional economic cooperation of the previous two decades, the first objective that Hawke listed for the proposed organization was to assist in engineering a successful outcome to the Uruguay Round of multilateral trade negotiations. What was surprising, however, was the list of countries that Hawke subsequently proposed as members for the new grouping. Neither Canada nor the United States appeared on the list. Hawke and the Australian government later sought to explain this omission by suggesting that the intention was first to gain support from East Asian economies, especially the ASEAN group, and that tactically it was preferable for the East Asian governments to propose that the North American countries also be offered membership in the proposed organization (see e.g. Woods 1993: 121).

Such a convoluted explanation appears to be a *post hoc* rationalization. Hawke made his speech without prior consultation with the Department of Foreign Affairs and Trade. On his Seoul visit, he was not accompanied by either the Minister or the Secretary of the Department, neither of whom knew the contents of the speech in advance. The episode gives the impression of policy-making on the run, and of considerable ad hocery. And it is clear that within the Hawke ministry considerable pique was directed towards the United States, both because of the Export Enhancement Program and because Australia had been excluded from talks about a Pacific regional organization that Secretary of State James Baker had held in Asia in the previous year. The Australian Foreign Minister, Gareth Evans, spoke of the need to fire a 'warning shot' across Washington's bows.[51]

Whatever Canberra's intentions, only the Malaysian government subsequently gave support for a regional grouping that excluded the United States. The Japanese government, in particular, was insistent that any regional grouping must include the North American economies, as were the key ASEAN governments of Indonesia and Singapore. The reason is obvious. The continued (and indeed in the 1980s) increased dependence of East Asian exports on the US market would have made the exclusion of the United States from a regional institution a highly risky move, especially at a time when the United States was implementing its free-trade agreement with Canada. The preferred alternative to retaliating against US unilateralism by excluding the United States was to attempt to constrain Washington by bringing the United States within a regional arrangement.[52]

The Australian initiative required careful shepherding to avoid the diplomatic debacle of the 1980 Canberra meeting. As always, the key actor was ASEAN. Indeed, Tokyo and, more surprisingly, Washington indicated that their endorsement of the proposed ministerial meeting was dependent on its receiving a positive response from ASEAN.[53] Canberra sought to assuage ASEAN concerns by emphasizing that it supported the grouping and appreciated its achievements, that any new regional organization would not seek to supplant ASEAN, and that ASEAN would have a central role in the new institution. Moreover, the purpose of the Canberra meeting would be exploratory – a consideration of how best to proceed in promoting regional intergovernmental collaboration on economic issues. MITI also actively lobbied ASEAN governments – though its message was somewhat blunted by simultaneous lobbying against the proposal by MOFA. The approach seemed to work – for, despite an ongoing preference that ASEAN's own institutions should be at the heart of any new regional arrangement, ASEAN governments did agree, after initial reluctance, to participate in the Canberra meeting.[54] The Indonesian Foreign Minister, Ali Alatas (1994), in reflecting on the reasons why APEC came into existence, emphasized '*first*, its pragmatic focus on the substantive areas of clear common interest for such cooperation; *second*, its sensitive approach with regard to the possible operational modalities; *third*, the careful and extensive consultations undertaken by Australia in developing the idea and in preparing for its realization'. Learning had occurred: the Australian government presented the APEC initiative in a manner more acceptable to its proposed partners than was the case with the OPTAD proposal a decade before.

The initiative later went ahead surprisingly smoothly despite the rocky start, despite reservations on the part of some ASEAN members, especially Indonesia and Malaysia, and initial rejection by ASEAN's foreign ministers, despite infighting between Japan's MITI and MOFA, and despite Washington's resentment at the Australian government's failure either to include the United States in the initial proposal or to consult Washington before its launch.[55] The agreement on constructing a regional economic institution, however, did not go beyond a decision to stage an exploratory meeting, in other words to hold further discussions. The institutional shape of APEC and the roles that it was intended to play had still to be decided.

Conclusion

At the start of the 1980s, only the most optimistic of observers would have believed that a regional economic intergovernmental organization in the Asia-Pacific would be established before the end of the decade. Formidable obstacles appeared to stand in its way. These went beyond the obvious cultural, economic, and political diversity of the region. Some of the less developed economies saw other Southern economies as their natural partners, and were fearful of and hostile towards proposals for a Pacific regional organization that would bridge North and South. The determination of the Southeast Asian countries to strengthen their fledgling regional organization, ASEAN, made them reluctant to entertain proposals for new regional bodies that had the potential to diminish ASEAN's role. And the strategic situation further complicated proposals for regional economic collaboration by adding an East–West dimension. The Canberra conference that had led to the founding of PECC illustrated both the difficulties that proposals for institutionalized regional collaboration faced and the contemporary lack of enthusiasm of governments for proceeding down this path.

What does the successful establishment of APEC less than a decade after the disappointing outcome of the Canberra conference imply for the arguments about regional collaboration reviewed in the previous chapter?

At the most general level, the events leading to APEC's formation underline how important is the nesting of economic collaboration within a security context. The East/West divide posed two important barriers to the creation of a regional economic institution in the first half of the 1980s. The first was the reluctance of the Southeast Asian states to be involved in an institution they saw as inevitably having security overtones because its membership would be limited to market economies. The second was the unwillingness of Washington to encourage regional institutions in the Pacific for fear that they would enable the Soviet Union to gain access to a forum that might later be used for the discussion of regional security issues. The momentous changes that began in the Soviet Union in the mid-1980s helped to remove this obstacle. Gorbachev's Vladivostok speech signalled that the Soviet Union no longer saw regional economic institutions as merely a mask for an anti-Soviet strategic alliance. In promoting the APEC proposal, Australian representatives emphasized that membership should be determined on 'pragmatic economic criteria, rather than ideological grounds' (Woolcott 1989: 2). While the Australian government did not consider the Soviet Union a likely founding member, its omission was because of its current lack of strong economic links with the region; future membership was a possibility.

Gorbachev's Vladivostok initiative coupled with the winding back of the Cold War in the region somewhat assuaged Washington's concern about the Soviets' possible use of any regional institution to raise security issues. Nonetheless, the security question continued to constrain the Bush administration's attitude towards Pacific regionalism into the 1990s, and explains its general lack of enthusiasm for the APEC initiative (Baker 1998). Security concerns had another impact on APEC's founding. The fear of Western Pacific countries that the end of the Cold War would cause

Washington to lose enthusiasm for military involvement in the region, especially in the context of its growing impatience with both the trade policies of its regional partners and their perceived unwillingness to share the security burden, encouraged the promotion of closer regional economic ties in the hope that these would help sustain the US security commitment to the region. Changing power relativities in the region undoubtedly gave rise to uncertainty and to a quest by governments to establish new foundations for collaboration. Governments viewed cooperation on economic matters as a means of building confidence across the diverse states that constituted the Asia-Pacific region, thereby helping to ensure a more secure regional environment. Economic cooperation was undertaken in part in expectation of non-economic payoffs.

That the changing systemic distribution of power, and in this case in particular the declining hegemony of the United States, should affect governments' interest in regional economic collaboration should come as no surprise. As noted in the previous chapter, however, the literature contains a number of mutually contradictory hypotheses on the relationship between hegemony and regionalism. Hegemons have a menu of choices available to them in determining their preferences for organizing a global economy. In the Pacific, the intrusion of Cold War conflicts, the continuing presence of European colonial powers, and the subsequent North/South divide introduced by decolonization all weighed against the establishment of regional organizations.

Arguments about hegemonic stability correctly predicted that the United States, after a decline in its share of global exports, would be increasingly unwilling to play the role of market of last resort in the 1980s, even more so when it was asked to take an increasing share of the burgeoning manufactured exports of East Asia. Perceptual factors, however, particularly concerns about the strategic economic policies of Northeast Asian countries, were probably as important as changes in real economic relativities in these years in driving US behaviour, given the relatively small movement in the overall US economic position in the global economy. And the emergence of economic regionalism in response to the concerns of other Pacific economies did not take the shape that some theories of hegemonic stability would predict. The rapidly growing Pacific economies did not seek to form a coalition, possibly in combination with the Europeans, against the United States. Rather, both because of their commitment to multilateralism and because of their continuing dependence on the US market, they sought an inclusive regional organization through which they hoped to constrain US unilateralism.

The growth of interdependence across the Pacific conditioned how governments defined the geographical basis for regional collaboration. It also generated new problems whose efficient resolution was increasingly seen to require intergovernmental collaboration. Increasing resort to unilateral measures and to bilateral agreements threatened to hinder the growth of interdependence.

If the distribution of power and the growth of interdependence were important changes in the context for economic collaboration in the Pacific, so too were knowledge and ideas. Ideas derived from the new literature on strategic trade theory reinforced US perceptions that East Asian economies were 'unfair' traders, and that their policies were deliberately crafted to give them a strategic advantage over the United States. Through the pressure that Congress exerted over the Reagan and Bush administrations from the mid-1980s onwards, these ideas had a direct impact on US trade policies, and thus on the interests of other economies in the region in seeking an institution to defuse trans-Pacific trade conflicts. Ideas were also important in other ways in changing the attitudes of East Asian governments towards the desirability of a regional intergovernmental economic collaboration. The rapid growth of the four newly industrializing countries (Hong Kong, Korea, Singapore and Taiwan) appeared to attest to the virtues of an outward-oriented approach to development. Such a message, frequently advocated by the international financial institutions, was reinforced by the acceleration of economic growth in Southeast Asia from the mid-1980s when they switched from manufacturing based primarily on import substitution to an export-oriented approach. Some regimes may have implemented liberalization in a piecemeal manner and with less than total enthusiasm. Nonetheless, the overall direction was clear – and the reduction in domestic trade barriers not only helped pave the way for regional cooperation in trade liberalization but also significantly changed the domestic political economy calculus.[56]

Crises, as the literature predicts, offered a space for new ideas and for expert groups to exert an influence on decision-making that they previously lacked. Across the region in the first half of the 1980s, a move towards liberalization quickly followed economic crisis. The rapid switch in policies was facilitated by political systems that gave economic decision-makers significant autonomy from societal groups. Whether it was the patrimonial systems of Southeast Asia, the 'statist' systems of Korea and Japan, or the parliamentary systems of Australia, Canada and New Zealand, none of the political systems imposed checks and balances on the executive comparable to those in the United States. To be sure, changes in the domestic political economy facilitated liberalizing moves. But what was striking across the Western Pacific region was the relatively small input that business organizations had in the decision-making on foreign economic policies.

Whatever the favourable changes in context brought about by developments in security relations, interdependence and so on, APEC would not have come about without intellectual leadership and without the entrepreneurial role states played in brokering the agreement. The epistemic community that had at its core the leaders of the PAFTAD conferences kept the idea of an OECD-like organization for the Pacific on the agenda, and continued to press for greater government involvement in regional economic institutions. Despite the initial failure of the 1980 Canberra conference, the establishment of PECC eventually proved important in the emergence of intergovernmental collaboration. It reinforced the idea that economic collaboration should be based on a trans-Pacific definition of the region rather than on the Western Pacific alone. Moreover, once established, the institution played a role in confidence-building and in socializing elites. Identities were slowly being transformed. The idea of a Pacific Community might not yet have been realized, but some old assumptions and antagonisms were breaking down. As always, posing the counterfactual is hazardous. Would APEC have come about in the absence of this epistemic community? The answer is probably not, or at least not in the same form nor in the same time.

Intellectual leadership in itself was insufficient, however, to bring APEC into being. The momentum towards establishing an intergovernmental grouping only gathered pace when governments took up the idea and began to commit significant resources to working for its realization. The role of the Australian government as broker here was critical in exploiting the change in context that occurred in the middle of the 1980s.

The coincidence of a significant surge in US unilateralism, the agricultural trade war between Washington and Brussels, the conclusion of negotiations between the United States and Canada to establish a free-trade area, the move towards a single internal market in the European Community, and deadlock in the Uruguay Round of GATT talks generated increased anxiety among the economies of the Western Pacific about the future of the global trading system. By the late 1980s, all appeared open to suggestions that the time for an intergovernmental institution had arrived – as, indeed, did the US administration. The Australian economy, however, was perhaps uniquely disadvantaged by these trends.

It was a significant casualty of the agricultural subsidies war. Its agricultural exports had suffered from previous widening of the European Community. The Australian government believed that US unilateralism endangered the access of its exports to Northeast Asian markets.[57] And whereas the East Asian economies might, in the event of a failure of the Uruguay Round, form a regional trading bloc to oppose the North Americans and West Europeans, Australia was not assured of membership in any of these three blocs. In the words of a former Secretary of the Australian Department of Foreign Affairs and Trade, Australia faced the possibility that it would be 'totally friendless' in a fragmented global economy

(Harris 1989b: 19–20). The Australian government was also well placed to play a brokerage role. In association with the Japanese government, it had been at the forefront of previous efforts to institutionalize collaboration in the region. As a 'middle power', its role as broker was likely to be better received by other regional states than if the United States or Japan attempted to exercise leadership. And it had a sophisticated foreign affairs bureaucracy that had learnt over the years how to cope with the foreign policy sensitivities of ASEAN countries.

But what of the governments of other countries from which proposals for a regional organization had emanated? Could they not have played a similar leadership role? The Japanese government at the end of the 1980s appeared too divided even to provide 'leadership from behind' (see Calder 1988b; Rix 1993), with MITI and MOFA openly warring over proposals for a regional economic institution (although MITI's support for the Australian initiative may have been crucial in bringing some ASEAN governments on board; see Krauss 2000b). The US government took no formal initiative to follow up on the Shultz, Bradley and Cranston proposals, perhaps not surprisingly since they came at the time of transition from the Reagan to the Bush administration (see Baker 1998). Had Washington pursued such ideas, however, it is likely that its proposals for a regional economic institution would have differed from those of Australia – powerful actors in the United States were keen to see Mexico included as a founder member in any Pacific organization. Canada, often seen as the archetypical 'middle power' and good international citizen, was preoccupied with consolidating its relationship with its Southern neighbours, and unwilling to expend significant diplomatic effort in brokering an Asia-Pacific agreement.

ASEAN was too lukewarm about an Asia-Pacific intergovernmental grouping to take the lead itself in brokering an agreement. Once it appeared likely that such a grouping would eventuate from the flurry of diplomatic activity in 1988–89, it pressed to have its post-ministerial conferences be the core of any new regional institution – even though the primary focus of these meetings was on political rather than economic matters. It seems unlikely, therefore, that without the Australian brokership APEC would have materialized in the form that it did. 'APEC may arguably be termed a triumph of Australian foreign policy', wrote the Canadian academic and former diplomat Sylvia Ostry (1998: 343).

Agreement for a ministerial meeting in Canberra was, however, only a modest beginning for APEC. The shape that APEC would take had yet to be negotiated among its member states. Chapter 3 examines the influences that determined its evolution.

CHAPTER 3

The Evolution of APEC

The successful launch of APEC at the Canberra Ministerial Meeting in November 1989 owed much to the international context. Stalemate in the Uruguay Round of GATT negotiations and the emergence and/or deepening of regional trading groupings in North America and Europe caused particular concern to Asia-Pacific governments. This context provided a foundation for a new coincidence of interests among governments, which in turn was exploited by shrewd diplomacy. The centrality of the global context, especially the lack of progress in the Uruguay Round of GATT negotiations, to APEC's foundation is seen in the one-page Joint Statement issued by the Canberra Ministerial Meeting, fully a third of which is devoted to a discussion of multilateral trade negotiations (DFAT 1989b: 9). Besides voicing their support for a successful outcome of the Uruguay Round, the ministers agreed on little more than holding two further consultative meetings at ministerial level – in Singapore (not coincidentally the most enthusiastic ASEAN supporter of APEC) in the following year, and Korea in 1991.

The Canberra meeting, Rudner (1995: 410) notes, produced 'a studiously vague statement of intent'. The ministers recorded that it was premature to decide on any particular structure for the new body, or on a design for support mechanisms. In itself, this was a rebuff for ASEAN, whose members had argued that APEC meetings should be based on the ASEAN Post-Ministerial Conference and be serviced by the ASEAN Secretariat. The general principles of Asia-Pacific economic cooperation that the meeting approved, however, did recognize the concerns of ASEAN states that APEC should operate on the basis of consensus and with explicit recognition of the diversity of the member economies. The nine principles were:

- the objective of enhanced Asia Pacific Economic Cooperation is to sustain the growth and development of the region, and in this way, to contribute to the growth and development of the world economy;
- cooperation should recognise the diversity of the region, including differing social and economic systems and current levels of development;
- cooperation should involve a commitment to open dialogue and consensus, with equal respect for the views of all participants;
- cooperation should be based on non-formal consultative exchanges of views among Asia Pacific economies;
- cooperation should focus on those economic areas where there is scope to advance common interests and achieve mutual benefits;
- consistent with the interests of Asia Pacific economies, cooperation should be directed at strengthening the open multilateral trading system; it should not involve the formation of a trading bloc;
- cooperation should aim to strengthen the gains from interdependence, both for the region and the world economy, including by encouraging the flow of goods, services, capital and technology:
- cooperation should complement and draw upon, rather than detract from, existing organisations in the region, including formal intergovernmental bodies such as ASEAN and less formal consultative bodies like the Pacific Economic Cooperation Conference (PECC); and
- participation by Asia Pacific economies should be assessed in the light of the strength of economic linkages with the region, and may be extended in future on the basis of consensus on the part of all participants. (DFAT 1989b: 10–11)

Like its predecessor, the second Ministerial Meeting in Singapore focused primarily on the Uruguay Round of trade negotiations, and restated the principle that APEC was a 'non-formal forum for consultations'.[1] APEC's future membership, work program, and operating principles were still largely undecided. As APEC evolved, the question of whether or not the principles declared at the Canberra meeting were being respected became a matter of contention among participating governments.

In this chapter I examine the interests and ideas of the principal actors that have shaped APEC in the first decade of its evolution. In Chapter 4, using the literature on international regimes, I evaluate the effectiveness of APEC's rules and structures. This present chapter does not present a chronological approach to APEC's evolution. Readers not familiar with the development of APEC may wish to consult Appendix 1, which provides a brief chronology of the grouping.

Governments[2]

Governments are the appropriate starting point for a review of the principal forces driving APEC's evolution in its first decade. APEC is an intergovernmental organization. It had no Secretariat before 1992. Moreover, as we will see in this chapter and in Chapter 4, when the members decided to establish a Secretariat, they designed the institution in such a way as to minimize its autonomy. Members were determined that the Secretariat would not become a source of supranational authority or initiative. And, besides business groups, non-government actors have played a very limited role within APEC. The one important exception to this statement is the Eminent Persons Group (EPG), an advisory body created at the fourth Ministerial Meeting held in Bangkok in September 1992. I examine the role of the EPG later in this chapter.

One feature of policy-making towards APEC common to all of the governments was the significant autonomy they enjoyed. Such an argument applies not just to the authoritarian states of the region, where foreign policy has often been the personal preserve of the leader. In Japan, APEC was no exception to the tradition of foreign policy being determined primarily by the bureaucracy:

> The number of actors in the APEC-policy-making process in Japan is relatively limited as well as in other foreign-policy-making processes. APEC is less-known, less-understood or less-interesting to make a variety of actors participate in the policy-making processes. This is not only due to the lack of their understanding of APEC but also to somewhat broad and ambiguous nature of the institution and the lack of its concrete activities. Therefore the APEC-policy-making process is mostly confined to Government – especially, to the bureaucratic system. (Hirata et al. 1996: 35)

APEC is not a household word in most member states. A report from a consortium of APEC Study Centres recorded that 'questionnaires revealed a stunning lack of public awareness of APEC activities' (APIAN 2000: viii). Lack of knowledge about the grouping has been compounded by a lack of interest among those who have heard of it, a lack of interest born from a perception that the group was failing to achieve meaningful outcomes. As discussed in more detail below, business, in whose interests APEC ostensibly works, has seldom shown much enthusiasm for the body. Richard Baker (1998: 178), a former US diplomat, notes, for instance, that APEC's initial deliberations 'had little immediate significance for the American business audience'.[3]

Only when proposals for the acceleration of trade liberalization have threatened the protection enjoyed by business and agricultural interests in 'sensitive' sectors have governments faced significant pressure on

APEC issues from domestic lobby groups. Even in the region's democracies, few actors outside government have become sufficiently excited about APEC to attempt to influence government policy towards the grouping (except, occasionally, protesters at the venue of its annual leaders' meetings, most notably in Vancouver in 1997) (see Ericson and Doyle 1999).

The United States

American administrations were slow to warm to the APEC concept. Angered not only that Australian Prime Minister Bob Hawke had failed to consult Washington before announcing his initiative in Seoul in January 1989 but also by his omission of the United States and Canada from the list of countries proposed for membership, the Bush administration was lukewarm in its support of Australian and Japanese efforts that led to the initial Canberra meeting (*FEER* 11 May 1989: 20). Washington declared that its attitude towards the proposal would depend on whether or not it gained the support of ASEAN countries. Although Washington was keen to be a member once it was clear that APEC would get off the ground, and Secretary of State Baker produced the expected supportive hyperbole at the Canberra meeting,[4] the Bush administration throughout its tenure remained tepid to the new institution. Bush gave a polite but noncommittal response while visiting Australia in 1991 to a suggestion from the recently installed Prime Minister, Paul Keating, that a meeting of government leaders should accompany the APEC Ministerial Meeting scheduled for Seattle in 1993. Although it had moved to embrace regionalism elsewhere, the Bush administration maintained a reticence towards regional arrangements in the Pacific, arising in part from fears that Russia would exploit them to attempt to undermine US security interests in the region (Kerr et al. 1995). In the economic realm, the administration in its dealings with the Western Pacific Rim continued to prefer bilateralism to a regional approach. In his re-election campaign, for instance, Bush raised the possibility once again of developing bilateral free-trade arrangements on a hub-and-spokes basis with selected countries in Asia.

It was not until the advent of the Clinton administration that Washington took an active interest in and, indeed, seized the initiative on APEC. Clinton, reportedly against the advice of the State Department, accepted the arguments of pro-APEC activists in the administration to adopt Keating's proposal for a leaders' meeting and worked actively to bring it about (though such action consisted mainly of presenting other members with a *fait accompli*). The Clinton team saw APEC as a possible source of leverage against the European Union in its efforts to extract concessions from Brussels in the Uruguay Round negotiations. Saxonhouse (1996: 112) notes, for instance, that Washington realized that the negotiation of NAFTA would not itself provide any significant additional bargaining power against the Europeans. They were, however, expected to be more alarmed by the possibility that Washington might establish a Pan-Pacific preferential trading arrangement should the Uruguay Round negotiations fail. Whether the European Union really would have seen such a threat as credible, and whether the Seattle Leaders' Meeting was critical to bringing the Europeans back to the bargaining table is a matter of some contention. What is clear, however, is that key figures in the Clinton administration did see APEC as a potential source of leverage in the global trade talks. US Trade Representative Mickey Kantor said at the meeting, 'We trust our partners in Geneva will take careful note of [APEC's] solidarity and purpose' (quoted in *FEER* 2 December 1993: 13).[5]

The higher priority Washington gave to APEC did not rest exclusively, however, on the potential contribution the grouping might make to a successful outcome to the Uruguay Round negotiations. The new administration also saw APEC as a means of signalling its commitment to the Pacific region and as a vehicle through which it could pursue its activist trade policy, in particular its objective of opening up East Asian markets to American exports. The new administration's Assistant Secretary of State for East Asian and Pacific Affairs, Winston Lord, asserted at his confirmation hearing that the time was ripe for the United States to build a 'new Pacific community', a phrase that the President was later to take up (Clinton 1993). APEC was identified as a vital regional forum, one that the administration was determined to make 'more relevant and action-oriented' through the Seattle Leaders' Meeting (*FEER* 15 April 1993: 10–11). From the time that Washington assumed the chair of the grouping, the emphasis was that APEC should produce results rather than remain a consultative forum.[6]

A fundamental US interest in APEC was to build up this trans-Pacific organization so as to reduce the attractiveness of a grouping exclusively East Asian in composition, such as the East Asian Economic Group (EAEG) which Malaysian Prime Minister Mahathir had proposed at the end of 1990, and which the US government feared would reinforce Japan's economic dominance in the region. Washington's initial opposition to the Mahathir proposal had been unusually strident, with Baker reportedly exerting strong pressure on both the Korean and Japanese governments for them not to participate in the proposed arrangements. Baker is said to have told the Korean Foreign Minister, Lee Sang Ock, that 'Malaysia didn't spill blood for this country, but we did'. He also wrote to the Japanese Foreign Affairs Minister, Michio Watanabe, warning that Malaysia's EAEG would 'divide the Pacific region in half' (*FEER* 28 November 1991: 26–7). Michael Armacost, US Ambassador to Japan, warned that the EAEG could 'encourage economic rivalry' between Japan and the United States (quoted in Fishlow and Haggard 1992: 29).[7]

Besides this desire to discourage the emergence of a Japanese-oriented, yen-dominated East Asian trading bloc (Noland 1995), Washington had several other distinct interests in the trade field that set its views on APEC apart from those of most Asian governments. Chief among these was the desire to promote rapid trade liberalization through APEC. This objective lay at the heart of its emphasis on APEC as a results-oriented grouping, rather than placing a particularly high value (as many Asian governments did) on APEC as a process of consensus-building. East Asia continued to be the principal source of America's trade deficit as China's surplus with the United States rapidly approached and then surpassed that of Japan. East Asian economies continued to be viewed in Washington, by Congress as well as the administration, as free riders on the liberal trading system (Ryan 1995). The development of arguments from strategic trade theory gave a greater urgency to the perceived need to level the international trade playing field. Washington, therefore, was enthusiastic about the agenda of the APEC Eminent Persons Group, dominated as it was by the promotion of trade liberalization.

But Washington had particular concerns about how trade liberalization might best be promoted. As by far the largest economy in the grouping and the one least dependent on trade with other APEC economies, it had the most reason to be concerned lest actions within APEC reduce its leverage in trade negotiations with other parties, especially the European Union. In particular, it was unwilling to see unilateral trade liberalization adopted as the only approved modus operandi for APEC. With good reason, a requirement for reciprocity remained the preferred option for Washington.

The Clinton administration was also concerned about the comprehensiveness of APEC's efforts at trade liberalization. The elimination of border barriers was one objective. But the experience of trade with East Asia in the previous decade had shown, given the low levels of Japanese tariffs, that the elimination of border barriers was insufficient to ensure access to these markets (Lincoln 1990; Ravenhill 1993). American companies attempting to export to most East Asian economies faced a host of official and unofficial non-tariff barriers, the so-called 'structural impediments' to trade. Although APEC might make a useful contribution to trade liberalization through a focus on border barriers, in itself this would be only a partial solution to the problems faced by US exporters. Partly for this reason, Washington was unwilling to agree to the establishment of DSMs in APEC: it was concerned that such procedures might be used to attack the relatively transparent US barriers to trade while leaving untouched the more opaque obstacles to the penetration of East Asian markets. Moreover, Washington had little faith in a method of trade liberalization where member states decided for themselves what they would liberalize and when – the essence of APEC's 'concerted unilateralism'. The US Ambassador to APEC, Sandra Kristoff, argued that '[b]asically, the "C" and the "A" of CUA [concerted unilateral action] are not convincing, leaving only "U". The US doesn't see much value in the "U" alone' (cited in Funabashi 1995: 96). US representatives pushed repeatedly for members to be held to account for implementing commensurate liberalization measures.

The East Asian perspective on these matters, of course, was very different. With a Congress generally unsympathetic towards trade liberalization – and ultimately denying Clinton renewal of his fast-track negotiating authority – the US administration had little to offer on trade liberalization at APEC meetings. In its Individual Action Plans (presentations at annual APEC meetings of intended measures on trade liberalization), the United States failed to go beyond its Uruguay Round commitments. To other participants, therefore, Washington's enthusiasm for trade liberalization seemed lopsided. As Asian critics were quick to point out, American talk of trade liberalization in APEC appeared to mean liberalization by other governments so that the United States could gain access to their markets. The Japanese economist Ryutaro Komiya (1999: 297) noted:

> [T]he US government has not so far put in order the domestic preconditions for an extensive reduction of US tariff and non-tariff barriers, and seems to lack the willingness to do so, at least for the present. When the US representative talks about trade liberalization at APEC, therefore, it appears that what is meant does not include trade liberalization *by* the USA but seems to mean trade liberalization by other APEC members along the lines of US wishes. (Emphasis in original)

Moreover, Washington was not well placed to take initiatives in other areas of APEC's activities, to engage for instance in issue linkage to provide some carrots in the form of development assistance to offset the pain of trade liberalization. Policy was again constrained by the actions of Congress, in this case the cuts it had made to the budgets of the State Department and US AID. The administration simply had no funds available for APEC initiatives, as Baker (1998: 183) notes, and had to hope that its rhetoric alone would induce the desired policy response from its partners. In any event, Washington has not been enthusiastic about APEC's taking on the role of development agency. Ambassador Kristoff asserted that '[t]he APEC forum should not function in a "North-South manner" as a body to distribute official development assistance and other funds' (quoted in Mori 1997: 92).

American enthusiasm for APEC began to wane in 1994 when the weakness of the Non-Binding Investment Principles that the grouping adopted (see Chapter 4) provided a clear demonstration of the limitations of the grouping's lowest common denominator approach. APEC clearly was not going to be transformed into the results-oriented forum that the administration, facing a Congress sceptical of the grouping and of the good faith of East Asian trading partners, desired. Whatever the rhetoric of the early Clinton years, its subsequent approach to APEC was 'ad hoc, utilitarian or instrumental' (Snyder 1999: 77). Washington showed enthusiasm for APEC only when the grouping seemed to offer some potential to advance America's global trade goals as, for instance, in the promotion of the Information Technology Agreement in 1996. Overall, however, in the Clinton years, the administration did not see APEC as an institution that merited a significant or sustained commitment of material, bureaucratic or intellectual resources.

Asian Governments

To write of 'Asian' governments might appear to risk a gross over-generalization. Yet, with the partial exception of Singapore and Hong Kong, all the Asian members of APEC shared views about its goals and operating procedures that differed significantly from those of the United States. In particular, these governments valued APEC primarily for its contribution to the evolutionary process of confidence-building among the countries of the region. This view is expressed succinctly by the Indonesian economist Hadi Soesastro (1994b: 48), who wrote that APEC 'needs to be guided by the wisdom that processes are more important than structures' (cf. Mahbubani 1995: 110). Premature institutionalization was to be avoided. Moreover, Asian countries were insistent that the principles enunciated at the Canberra Ministerial Meeting be observed, especially the emphasis on acknowledging the diversity of the grouping's members, and on consensus and a respect for the views of all participants as the basis for decision-making within the grouping.

Asian economies tend to have much more diverse export markets than do most other countries. From the beginning of the institutionalization of the European Community, they have expressed concerns about the regionalization of the world economy and the possible detrimental impact of this trend on their interests. Accordingly, they have traditionally opposed discriminatory trading arrangements (though ASEAN has promoted its own, largely ineffective, regional trading agreement).[8] For most Asian countries, and here Singapore has consistently been the exception, trade liberalization should not be APEC's primary activity. Rather, Asian governments preferred to place emphasis on the centrality of economic and technical cooperation within the grouping. To the extent that APEC had potential value on trade matters, Asian governments saw this resting mainly on the possibility of using the organization to restrain US unilateralism.

Asian countries have also shown little enthusiasm for the construction of regional bureaucracies. ASEAN countries, in particular, have jealously guarded their fairly recently won sovereignty. But they are not isolated on this issue. China has also shown a marked reluctance to pool sovereignty in any regional forum. For related reasons, most Asian governments were suspicious of the APEC Eminent Persons Group, seeing it as a tool of the US government for forcing the pace of liberalization in the grouping, and as a threat to their own decision-making autonomy. Thailand's Deputy Prime Minister Supachai Panitchpakdi, for instance, was said to have emphasized the need to 'look at the hidden agenda' of the EPG, which he perceived as an instrument for the Western industrialized economies to move APEC in directions harmful to its less developed members (quoted in *FEER* 6 October 1994: 14).

Japan

As discussed in the previous chapter, the Japanese government had been the first to express an interest in the construction of a Pan-Pacific intergovernmental organization. It had worked, together with others, especially Australia, for more than three decades to realize this goal. Yet within a relatively short period after APEC's establishment, the Japanese government found that other members had hijacked the grouping's agenda, and that its vision for APEC was in danger of being subordinated to a 'Western' preference for a grouping whose primary goal was trade liberalization, and which operated as a negotiating rather than a discussion forum.

Commentators have frequently observed that bureaucratic divisions have prevented Japanese governments from pursuing a coherent, activist foreign policy (see e.g. Calder 1988b; Hellmann 1988; Rix 1993). Certainly, bureaucratic politics was much in evidence in Tokyo's policies towards the Pacific. In discussing the failure of the Japanese government to support the UN Economic Commission for Asia and the Far East's proposal in 1962 for an Organization for Asian Economic Cooperation, Singh (1966) recorded that even in these early years of postwar diplomacy 'various departments in the Japanese government were hopelessly divided on the issue'. These divisions were to re-emerge in APEC. As discussed in the previous chapter, in the months following Hawke's Seoul launch of the APEC initiative, Japan's Ministry of Foreign Affairs reportedly lobbied Asian governments to reject the proposal, which it associated with its rival, MITI. And, in the early years of APEC, other governments faced the extraordinary spectacle of MOFA and MITI demanding separate consultations and representation in APEC meetings. Officials from the two ministries served as co-chairs when Japan hosted APEC's senior officials meetings in preparation for the Osaka Leaders' Meeting in 1995 (see Funabashi 1995; Terada 1999a). The dispute was a classic fight over bureaucratic turf, with MOFA concerned that a new regional economic organization would give greater prominence to economics rather than foreign affairs ministers in regional relations, and that APEC would overshadow PECC, in which MOFA had played a prominent role. MOFA was also worried that a Japanese initiative would revive fears in ASEAN about Japanese economic domination of the region, and feared that a Western push to institutionalize APEC would alienate ASEAN and force the Japanese government into choices it wished to avoid.

Despite this ministerial disunity, and despite complaints that the Japanese government failed to play a leadership role when it hosted the grouping's annual meetings in 1995,[9] Tokyo's strategy towards APEC in reality has been a model of consistency. Tokyo may not have led APEC in a direction desired by its Western members; it certainly failed to give leadership to APEC's trade liberalization agenda.[10] But this approach was entirely consistent with Japanese views on what the grouping should do and the means it should use to achieve its objectives. Moreover, as discussed in Chapter 5, this consistency has paid off: APEC at the end of its first decade was much closer to the institution envisaged by Tokyo than that which Washington attempted to construct.

Japan's approach to APEC has involved a delicate balancing of three (not always compatible) sets of objectives: an attempt to reduce the scope for US unilateralism in trade policies; a desire to maintain access to the US market and to encourage US engagement with the region, in both economics and security; and a desire to maintain good relations with ASEAN and to encourage Japanese companies' activities in Southeast Asia.

If anything, the third set of objectives – the maintenance of good relations with ASEAN – has been paramount in Japan's APEC policies. Here, however, it is important to record that on many issues a substantial coincidence of interests exists between Japan and the ASEAN countries. The objective of being a good friend to ASEAN has coincided with the promotion of Japan's domestic economic interests. In particular, because of its desire to continue protection for inefficient sectors of its economy – mainly agriculture but also some service sectors such as finance – Tokyo has been entirely opposed to the US desire to turn APEC into a negotiating forum for accelerated trade liberalization. Having suffered a domestic political backlash to the Uruguay Round agreement for an in-principle opening of all agricultural markets, and the tariffication of non-tariff barriers, Japanese governments have been willing to countenance the United

States and other Western countries exploiting APEC to bring further pressure for liberalization.

Although Tokyo has recited the APEC mantra that the grouping's collaboration rests on three pillars – trade liberalization, trade facilitation, and economic and technical cooperation – it has never placed emphasis on the first of these pillars. 'The Americans are wrong to regard APEC as being primarily about trade' was the blunt comment of Isao Kubota, a senior official in Japan's Ministry of Finance (*Economist* 11 November 1995: 31). Similarly, Makoto Kuroda, a former vice-minister of MITI and former executive vice-president of Mitsubishi, told a meeting at the Brookings Institution that APEC was wasting its time in debating how comprehensive trade liberalization should be; instead it should focus on trade facilitation and economic and technical cooperation (quoted in Johnstone 1995: 10). Whatever the other divisions between MOFA and MITI, they shared the view that APEC's principal purpose should be to facilitate growth in the less developed economies of the region – primarily those in Southeast Asia, though China became of increasing interest with the dramatic surge of Japanese investment there in the early 1990s. Emphasis within APEC was therefore placed on the contribution the grouping might make to the strengthening of local institutions through economic and technical cooperation, consistent with Japan's interest in the export of its development model to other parts of Asia, and its sponsorship of the World Bank's study, the *East Asian Miracle* (World Bank 1993).

Japan's antipathy towards the use of APEC to promote trade liberalization has taken various forms. Elements of the Japanese government initially opposed the introduction of APEC leaders' meetings, fearing that this high-level forum would only generate more pressure on Tokyo for trade liberalization. The government has consistently attempted to exempt agriculture from APEC plans for trade liberalization. The Ministry of Agriculture, Forestry and Fisheries argued in meetings of APEC officials that agricultural products should be given the status of 'nontradeable goods' (Funabashi 1995: 216). In conjunction with MOFA and MITI, it lobbied the Indonesian government in 1994 to exclude agriculture from the trade agenda in the upcoming leaders' meeting that Jakarta was to host. Members of the agricultural 'policy tribes' in the Japanese *Diet* also visited Southeast Asia that year in an attempt to persuade local leaders to exempt agriculture from APEC's liberalization agenda (see Mori 1997: 87).

Having failed in this effort, the Japanese government again sought to exclude agriculture from the trade agenda at the Osaka Leaders' Meeting in the following year. Moreover, it gave every impression that it used its chairmanship of APEC that year to attempt to slow the momentum on trade liberalization. Indeed, in the first half of the year, the Japanese government appeared to be distancing itself not only from comprehensive trade liberalization but from the very concept of free trade in the region, thereby undermining the agreement reached at the previous year's Leaders' Meeting in Bogor. Only after sustained pressure from other APEC members, particularly Australia and the United States, did the Japanese government adopt an agenda that had some potential for moving the cause of trade liberalization forwards rather than backwards. Whereas in the previous year the Indonesian government had bypassed senior officials and worked directly with other leaders to establish for the Bogor meeting what became quite a radical agenda, for the Osaka meeting the Japanese government relied almost exclusively on meetings of senior officials to set a (much more modest) agenda – a process very much in accord with customary procedures of policy-making in Japan.[11] As discussed later in this chapter, senior officials have consistently been more conservative in their approach to APEC than have the heads of government.

Finally, when APEC attempted liberalization on a sectoral basis at the Vancouver Leaders' Meeting in 1997 (Early Voluntary Sectoral Liberalization [EVSL]; see Chapter 4), the Japanese government effectively torpedoed the process by refusing to agree to liberalization in forestry and fisheries.

The Japanese government's lack of interest in trade liberalization was evident in other behaviour. One of the reasons, commentators believed, for Tokyo's enthusiasm for Russian membership in APEC, agreed at the Vancouver Leaders' Meeting in 1997, was that the even greater diversity this would introduce to APEC membership would greatly complicate the grouping's trade liberalization agenda. (Russian membership had other attractions for Tokyo: it was seen as part of a package deal to tempt Moscow into agreeing to a resolution of the Kurile Islands [Northern Territories] dispute. Japan is also particularly interested in gaining access to the rich energy and mineral deposits of the Russian Far East.) Another illustration of Japan's views on freeing trade occurred when Japanese Prime Minister Ryutaro Hashimoto visited Australia, whose governments have consistently been among the most enthusiastic proponents of trade liberalization within APEC. Hashimoto warned the Australian Prime Minister against plans to introduce further cuts in tariff protection to the domestic automobile industry (in which Japanese firms – Mitsubishi and Toyota – have a significant stake). The irony of one APEC member government warning another against engaging in tariff-cutting was not picked up by local commentators.[12]

Japan's desire to avoid trade liberalization dominating the APEC agenda stems from a number of overlapping factors. Of paramount importance was the fear of a domestic political backlash should further pressure be brought to bear on sensitive sectors.[13] But a policy of resisting trade liberalization served other purposes. It enabled Japan to side with the vast majority of other Asian members of the grouping that were also resentful of US efforts to use APEC to promote more rapid liberalization. And, by placing emphasis not on trade liberalization but on trade facilitation and on economic and technical cooperation, both domestic and foreign policy interests were promoted. These were the issues of most interest to the less developed economies of the region, and Japan was able consistently to claim to be their champion in APEC forums.

At the Osaka meeting, Japan was successful in gaining acceptance from other APEC leaders of its proposed 'Partners for Progress' scheme. This was to provide 10 billion yen (approximately $100 million) to APEC's central budget to promote economic and technical cooperation initiatives. The scheme agreed on, however, was considerably watered down from that originally proposed by the Japanese Foreign Minister, Yohei Kono, at a Ministerial Meeting in Jakarta. The Ministry of Foreign Affairs had wanted to establish a separate 'Partners for Progress Centre' within the APEC Secretariat. The proposal was opposed by the US government for several reasons: it did not wish to see attention diverted from the 'main game' of trade liberalization, it feared that Japan would inevitably have a significant competitive advantage should APEC become involved in development cooperation, and it did not wish to see an enlargement of the Secretariat. The scheme was also opposed from within the Japanese government – by MITI and by the Ministry of Finance. Even though the proposal was watered down, Japan did gain kudos from the less developed economies in the grouping for the initiative. Moreover, the program provides an ongoing publicity bonus for Tokyo when APEC meetings are financed by 'Partners for Progress' funds.[14]

The Japanese government shared the view of the less developed countries in APEC that economic and technical cooperation were essential to help these economies make the necessary adjustments so that trade liberalization could proceed. APEC's economic and technical cooperation activities also served another purpose: they were often beneficial to Japanese companies (including their subsidiaries in Southeast Asia). Upgrading the skills of companies in Southeast Asia facilitated the development of Japanese production networks in the region (see Bernard and Ravenhill 1995; Doner 1997).

If trade liberalization was to occur within APEC, the Japanese government was determined that it should take place through a voluntary process of unilateral measures that would be applied to members and non-members alike in a non-discriminatory manner.[15] Tokyo generally did not share Washington's concerns about European free-riding on APEC trade liberalization. More troubling was the possibility that discriminatory liberalization in the Asia-Pacific would encourage a fragmentation of the global economy into rival trading blocs. APEC should therefore proceed through a process of 'open regionalism'. Washington's pressure for legally binding measures within APEC risked undermining Tokyo's delicate diplomacy of courting other Asian governments: a leading Japanese newspaper warned that the Western approach to APEC 'is a challenge to Japan's very policy toward Asia and the Pacific' (cited in Deng 1997a: fn. 13).

Under pressure from other member economies to retreat from its refusal to participate in two of the sectors the grouping had identified for liberalization in its EVSL programme, the Japanese government again emphasized the voluntary nature of APEC commitments. Japanese Foreign Minister Masahiko Komura stated bluntly in a press conference at the Kuala Lumpur APEC meetings in 1998, when the EVSL approach broke down: 'Although I am not very familiar with the English language, I understand that the V in EVSL stands for voluntary, which means this is not a process for negotiation' (*AFR* 2 November 1998). Japanese officials were reported to have warned other APEC governments at the Kuala Lumpur meetings that Tokyo would withdraw its offer of a substantial aid package in the wake of the Asian financial crises should it be forced to cut tariffs in the fish and forestry sectors (Skelton 1998)

Japan's other principal concern was to ensure that APEC continued to operate according to the principles laid down at the Canberra meeting. The Japanese government was alarmed at President Clinton's use of the phrase 'Pacific Community' at the Seattle meetings, with its possible implication that APEC would evolve towards a more institutionalized grouping akin to the European Community. The Japanese government has consistently stressed the importance of markets rather than the construction of supranational institutions for the region's development. 'Organic economic integration guided by market mechanisms' was Japan's belief on the appropriate mode for economic cooperation in the region.[16] In response to Clinton's proposal for a 'Pacific Community', Tsutomu Hata, Japanese Foreign Minister and soon to be Prime Minister, proposed at Seattle that all members should respect five basic principles of APEC cooperation: due attention to the different stages of development of members and the diversity within the grouping; gradualism based on consensus and consultation rather than negotiation; consistency with GATT; open regionalism and unconditional extension of APEC liberalization on an MFN basis; and intensive consultation and dialogue with non-members (cited in Yamamoto and Kikuchi 1998: 203). His summary characterization of APEC's operations was 'creeping incremental gradualism by consensus' (cited in Pyle 1995: 37). The consistent Japanese emphasis within APEC on unilateralism and consensus was very much in accord with the views of other Asian governments on how APEC should proceed.

ASEAN

Gaining ASEAN's confidence was an essential component of the diplomacy that led to APEC's creation. ASEAN's resistance, as discussed in Chapter 2, had stymied earlier efforts to create a trans-Pacific regional intergovernmental grouping. Foremost among ASEAN concerns was the fear that a new organization would overshadow ASEAN itself; moreover, new coalitions in APEC might divide ASEAN members against one another. Exacerbating these anxieties were other issues central to the identity and interests of some Southeast Asian states: a preoccupation with North–South topics in the global political economy, and with fashioning coexistence with the states of the region where communist parties continued to govern (see Crone 1996). Chapter 2 noted how contextual factors changed in the 1980s in a manner that reduced the intensity of some of these concerns. The most important developments were the evolution of the structure of ASEAN economies away from their previous dependence on primary product exports, and the winding down of the Cold War. Nonetheless, ASEAN states remained particularly exercised about the possibility that APEC would become more than a discussion forum and be used by Western members to apply pressure for more rapid economic liberalization. Although most of the ASEAN economies had implemented significant liberalization measures in the late 1980s, their concern was that APEC should do no more than provide a supportive environment for policies that they themselves had decided to implement.

Other APEC member governments had attempted to mollify ASEAN at the Canberra meeting by agreeing to a special status for the ASEAN Secretariat at APEC meetings, and to ASEAN states' hosting alternate APEC ministerial meetings. ASEAN governments nonetheless still harboured considerable concerns about APEC, seen in their decision to force postponement of the first senior officials meeting after the initial Ministerial Meeting in Canberra, a signal of their displeasure at the perceived excessive speed of institutionalization of the APEC process, and at its domination by the wealthier member economies. ASEAN leaders also were not content with the statement of principles for Asia-Pacific economic cooperation adopted at the Canberra meeting. At an ASEAN joint Ministerial Meeting in Malaysia in February 1990, governments adopted a further list of principles for ASEAN participation in the APEC process, a list known as the Kuching Consensus. The principles were:

- ASEAN's identity and cohesion should be preserved, and its cooperative relations with dialogue partners and third countries should not be diluted in any enhanced APEC.
- An enhanced APEC should be based on the principles of equality, equity and mutual benefit, taking fully into account the differences in stages of economic development and socio-political systems among the countries in the region.
- APEC should not be directed towards the formation of an inward-looking economic or trading bloc but instead it should strengthen the open, multilateral economic and trading systems in the world.

- APEC should provide a consultative forum on economic issues and should not lead to the adoption of mandatory directives for any participant to undertake or implement.
- APEC should be aimed at strengthening the individual and collective capacity of participants for economic analysis and at facilitating more effective mutual consultations to enable participants to identify more clearly and to promote their common interests and to project more vigorously those interests in the large multilateral forums.
- APEC should proceed gradually and pragmatically, especially in its institutionalization, without inhibiting further elaboration and future expansion.

Besides a great deal of redundancy in characterizing the APEC process as being voluntary in character, the other major theme of the Kuching principles is that APEC should not develop as a discriminatory trading arrangement. ASEAN economies generally are highly outward-oriented; intra-ASEAN trade constitutes but a small fraction of their overall commerce (see Ravenhill 1995b). Low levels of dependence on trade with other members largely explain the governments' historical lack of enthusiasm for ASEAN's own preferential trading arrangements, and their support for non-discriminatory liberalization.

At first the ASEAN caucus at the senior officials meetings provided an effective united front and gave ASEAN a central decision-making role in APEC (see Bodde 1994: 55). ASEAN issued a joint statement at the second APEC Ministerial Meeting in Singapore, critical not only of the European Union but also of US and Canadian textile quotas. The group initially managed to paper over divisions over the desirability for APEC to play a role in trade liberalization, and over the pace of its institutionalization. But the decision of the Clinton administration to promote APEC as an action-oriented vehicle for trade liberalization exposed the fragile basis of ASEAN unity on many APEC issues. In several ways, APEC's subsequent development realized the worst fears of some ASEAN governments about APEC's potential not only to overshadow their own grouping but also to split it. Although many ASEAN as well as other Asian governments were annoyed at what they saw as Clinton's attempt to impose a new agenda on them (cf. Ariff 1994b: 48), they were divided on the substance of this agenda. From 1993 onwards, ASEAN has been unable to speak with one voice on the most important issues APEC has confronted, especially on trade liberalization.[17]

Singapore and Malaysia have been at the two extremes on the spectrum of ASEAN opinion on APEC. Singapore has consistently supported a push for trade liberalization under APEC's auspices, and for further institutionalization of the grouping. The most open of the ASEAN economies with zero tariffs on most products, it has shown little interest in or faith in

ASEAN's own efforts at economic integration. Its interest – from the days of the Bush presidency – in a bilateral free-trade agreement with the United States has been a further indication of its reservations about ASEAN's effectiveness. Singapore successfully bid to host the APEC Secretariat by offering to meet the body's local costs for its first two years. In contrast, the Malaysian government, as discussed below, at least in its public pronouncements, has been the most resolute opponent of efforts to promote an action-oriented trade agenda for APEC. Other ASEAN governments have held views between these two poles, with enthusiasm for APEC varying from one administration to the next, as has been the case for the Philippines and Thailand. The most remarkable turnaround in an ASEAN government's views on APEC, however, was that of Indonesia under President Soeharto.

Indonesia

The Indonesian government initially shared Malaysia's lack of enthusiasm for APEC. It had several concerns about the new grouping. As the long-standing leader of the non-aligned movement, the Soeharto government perhaps inevitably initially viewed APEC through a North–South prism, fearing that the grouping might jeopardize its relations with other less developed economies. Indonesia had been among the foremost supporters of ASEAN's Zone of Peace, Friendship and Neutrality initiative, an effort to keep great powers out of the conflicts in the region. Moreover, Indonesia had particular problems with proposals that APEC membership should be extended to China: it still had not resumed diplomatic relations with the People's Republic, broken after the bloody suppression of an allegedly communist-led coup attempt in 1965. Indonesia also had the lowest per capita income in ASEAN even though its economy had grown at high rates in the 1980s. Despite successive rounds of liberalization, key domestic sectors continued to enjoy very high levels of protection. And the principal beneficiaries of the rents generated by tariff and non-tariff barriers were often political allies or relatives of the President.

The Indonesian Foreign Minister, Ali Alatas, had been ASEAN's most prominent spokesman in arguing in the lead-up to the Canberra meeting that ASEAN's post-ministerial conferences and the (Jakarta-based) ASEAN Secretariat should be the core around which Asia-Pacific economic cooperation might be constructed. And after ASEAN had been rebuffed, Indonesia had echoed Malaysia's reservations about institutionalizing APEC. The position of the Indonesian government underwent a sea change, however, beginning with the Leaders' Meeting in Seattle. The decision to invite Soeharto to host a follow-up meeting was particularly astute. It appeared to pay tribute to Soeharto's role as the elder statesman of ASEAN, and to Indonesia's long-standing claim to be the most important of the ASEAN countries. Moreover, a leaders' meeting in Jakarta would pose a vexatious dilemma for Malaysian Prime Minister Mahathir, who had boycotted the Seattle meeting. To fail to participate in a meeting hosted by a fellow ASEAN member would be regarded in the region as a grave insult.

Having successfully appealed to Soeharto's vanity, the Americans and Australians then strove to convert him into a missionary for trade liberalization within APEC. To a significant extent they succeeded. We will probably never know for sure the real reasons for Soeharto's conversion. They almost certainly included continuing appeals to his vanity – especially to his desire to be seen as a leading international statesman who left a mark on the fledgling organization.[18] Sustained diplomatic pressure supported these appeals, probably accompanied, in the American case, by promises of substantial foreign aid. Various domestic pressures also played a part. Indonesia had experienced a significant downturn in inward FDI flows in the early 1990s (the figure for FDI approvals in 1993 was down 22 per cent on the previous year). Like other ASEAN economies, Indonesia was concerned at increasing competition from China for investment funds, a factor in the formation of the ASEAN Free Trade Area (AFTA). AFTA, alone, appeared insufficient to stem the diversion of foreign investment: a renewed commitment to domestic liberalization was called for, and APEC could help in this objective. Drysdale (1996) suggests that Soeharto took the initiative to promote trade liberalization at the Bogor APEC meeting because of his desire to lock in domestic reforms.

Whatever the causes, the consequences of Soeharto's conversion to the cause of trade liberalization through APEC were dramatic – not just for APEC but also for ASEAN solidarity within the Asia-Pacific grouping. For one US official, the change of policy of the Indonesian government was 'a historic moment' (quoted in *FEER* 10 November 1994: 30). Having decided to promote the trade liberalization agenda in APEC, the Indonesian President pushed ahead regardless of the objections of some of his ASEAN colleagues. With the support of the Singaporean government, Soeharto rejected a proposal from the Philippine and Thai governments to hold an informal ASEAN summit before the APEC Bogor meeting (*FEER* 10 November 1994: 30). Contrary to the 'ASEAN Way' of proceeding according to consensus, Ali Alatas asserted that Malaysia would simply be left out of the arrangements should Dr Mahathir refuse to agree (cited in Pillai 1994). Moreover, once the Leaders' Meeting began, Soeharto refused to take significant amendments to the draft agreement he presented. 'Consensus', he declared, 'does not require unanimity' (quoted in Srinivasan 1995: 12). Malaysia and Thailand consequently issued declarations with their own interpretations of the accord that the leaders had reached.

The Bogor meeting decisively showed that ASEAN governments were no longer able to reach agreement about the desirable pace of trade liberalization or the role that APEC should play in promoting it. The latter issue spilled over beyond the setting of distant targets for trade liberalization, however. It was a matter of whether APEC should go beyond the narrow conception of its role as a discussion forum that had been presented at the Canberra meeting. To set a timetable for trade liberalization, as the leaders did at the Bogor meeting, would inevitably require some form of *negotiation* of what was to be done by whom and when.

Malaysia

President Soeharto's conversion to the trade liberalization cause is an illustration of the decisive role that individual leaders play in the foreign policies of Southeast Asian countries. This point is nowhere better illustrated, however, than in Malaysia's policies on APEC.

Malaysian foreign economic policies would be an inexplicable paradox without reference to the dominant influence of the enigmatic Prime Minister, Datuk Seri Mahathir bin Mohamad. Malaysia is one of the most open economies of the region, with an extremely high ratio of trade to GDP. After abandoning a brief flirtation with state-led development in the 1970s and early 1980s, governments set out to create an environment as hospitable towards foreign investment as that of neighbouring Singapore (regularly judged by international surveys as among the most welcoming in the world). They were largely successful. FDI in Malaysia contributes a higher percentage of gross fixed domestic capital formation than in any other Asian state except Singapore. Subsidiaries of foreign corporations are responsible for close to 90 per cent of the manufactured exports of Malaysia.

Despite the economy's ongoing dependence on foreign investors and despite generous government incentives to attract yet more foreign capital to the Malaysian economy, Prime Minister Mahathir has been a consistent and outspoken critic of the global economic order. Whereas Soeharto had been the champion of independence in the strategic dimension of less developed countries' foreign policies, Mahathir has seen himself as the South's standard-bearer on economic issues. Mahathir is one of the last representatives in office of the independence generation of leaders, a prime minister whose outlook has been coloured by the real and perceived injustices of the colonial period. He has been an outspoken proponent of ASEAN, seeing in its collective action a means through which the economies of Southeast Asia could enhance their bargaining power.

APEC symbolized a double threat for Mahathir. It raised significant questions about identity – whether the relevant 'region' was trans-Pacific in nature or one based on the Asian countries of the Western Pacific Rim. APEC, moreover, had the potential to undermine ASEAN's efforts to establish itself as the dominant regional institution in the Asia-Pacific. Although ASEAN's membership inescapably would be confined to Southeast Asian states, its influence could be extended beyond Southeast Asia through its post-ministerial conferences (and later through its consultative group on security issues, the ASEAN Regional Forum). To supplement ASEAN's influence and counter the threat posed by APEC, Mahathir proposed at the end of 1990 that the countries of East Asia should join together in an East Asian Economic Group, in which ASEAN countries would be in the majority.[19] Membership in the EAEG, later watered down to be a caucus within APEC, would be open only to those countries with populations of Asian origin – a 'Caucus without Caucasians' as one wit dubbed it. In a speech to the United Nations, Mahathir defended this racial demarcation:

> In East Asia we are told we may not call ourselves East Asians as Europeans call themselves Europeans and Americans call themselves Americans. We are told we must call ourselves Pacific people and align ourselves with people who are only partly Pacific but more American, Atlantic, and European. (Quoted in *FEER* 3 October 1991: 13)[20]

Besides the question of identity, the other threat that APEC would pose to ASEAN in particular would be through the opportunity it would give to industrialized economies to pressure the weaker economies to move in unwelcome directions. 'It would be unrealistic and grossly unfair', Mahathir asserted, 'to coerce particularly the less advanced member economies to undertake liberalization measures at a pace and manner beyond their capacity' (quoted in Australia 2000: 27–8). Mahathir continued to deploy the rhetoric of the New International Economic Order debate: APEC, he asserted, might become 'a vehicle to perpetuate existing asymmetries and policies that place [its smaller, less developed members] at a disadvantage' (quoted in Bates 1996: 323, n. 172). ASEAN would always be a relatively small player in APEC, even if it provided close to half of the grouping's membership. Mahathir (1994: 95) wrote of these fears:

> When the Asia Pacific Economic Cooperation (APEC) forum was proposed by Australia, all the ASEAN countries, with the exception of Malaysia, welcomed it. Malaysia's fear was that the inclusion of economic giants like the United States, Canada, and Japan would result in the domination of the grouping by

> these countries ... Fear prevails that ASEAN will disappear as a group within the very much enlarged and more powerful APEC grouping. There may be conflicts between the ASEAN interest and the broader Pacific interest. APEC is likely to dominate ASEAN and hinder its progress toward greater intra-ASEAN cooperation.[21]

From Mahathir's perspective, therefore, it was imperative that the grouping operate according to the principles agreed at the Canberra meeting: it should not evolve beyond a consultative forum. Writing of Malaysia's concerns, he noted that Malaysia at the time of APEC's formation 'was reassured that APEC would remain an informal consultative group dedicated to helping the less developed members upgrade their overall performance' (Mahathir 1994: 96).

Mahathir and his feisty Minister for International Trade and Industry, Datuk Seri Rafidah Aziz, have been thorns in the flesh of those pushing for APEC to move beyond a role as a confidence-building forum. Dr Mahathir and his government have adopted a number of strategies designed to prevent APEC from gaining momentum as a body promoting trade liberalization. Malaysia downgraded its representation at the Seoul Ministerial Meeting in response to James Baker's attack on Mahathir's proposal for an East Asian Economic Group. Lingering resentment on this issue caused Mahathir to boycott the first APEC Leaders' Meeting in Seattle. And Malaysia refused to send representatives to a ministerial meeting on telecommunications in Taipei in 1996 on the grounds that its economy was not yet ready for liberalization, and that it had nothing to gain from the meeting (*Asian Business* 11 November 1986: 20). Few commentators, moreover, believed that Mahathir was unhappy at the results of the Kuala Lumpur Leaders' Meeting where the grouping failed to reach agreement on its program of sectoral liberalization, a meeting variously described by media commentators as a 'fiasco' and a 'public relations disaster' for APEC (see e.g. Millett 1998).

Malaysia has consistently supported the addition of new members to the grouping, a none too subtle attempt to ensure that efforts at deepening cooperation within APEC would be a casualty of widening the membership of the group (*Asian Wall Street Journal Weekly* 28 November 1994, quoted in Johnstone 1995: 6). And Malaysia has never tired of reminding other governments that agreements within APEC are voluntary – even to the extent of issuing a unilateral declaration at the Bogor meeting when Soeharto refused to include its reservations in an annex to the official statement. Malaysia's statement declared:

- Malaysia will only commit to undertaking further liberalization on a unilateral basis at a pace and capacity commensurate with our level of development.

- The liberalization process to achieve [the Bogor goal] will not create an exclusive free trade area in the Asia Pacific.
- The liberalization process will be GATT/WTO-consistent and on an unconditional most-favored [nation] (MFN) basis.
- The target dates of 2020 and 2010 are indicative dates and nonbinding on member economies.
- The liberalization process will only cover a substantial portion of Asia Pacific trade and should not go beyond the provisions of the GATT/WTO.
- It is Malaysia's understanding that decisions in APEC should be on the basis of consensus.
- The EPG has fulfilled its mandate, its duration should not be extended. (Quoted in Funabashi 1995: 92)

After the Subic Bay Leaders' Meeting, which supported the negotiation of an Information Technology Agreement at the upcoming Singapore Ministerial Meeting of the WTO, Mahathir again emphasized that compliance with any agreement must be voluntary. And, not surprisingly, he emphasized the *voluntary* in the EVSL negotiations.

> The most important thing is that this is voluntary. Early voluntary. Those two words are very important. It means that you must make the decision yourself, if you are ready. If you are not ready, you can wait until the time comes for you to make the decision. But to say that because there is early voluntary liberalisation, therefore you must agree now, that is wrong. You can do it at your own pace depending upon your own country's situation. ('PM to Keep Raising Real Concerns', *The Star Online* 15 November 1998)

After a decade of Malaysian obstructionism in APEC, Mahathir's tactics apparently brought the results he desired. The broadening of membership to twenty-one states was accompanied by increasing concern that APEC had become too unwieldy a grouping to deliver on its ambitious agenda. Trade liberalization has been immensely complicated by the addition of countries, most notably, Russia, for whom other APEC members are insignificant trading partners. Moreover, the expansion of APEC membership and its impact on the grouping's effectiveness has made Mahathir's proposal for the establishment of an East Asian Economic Group more attractive to other East Asian governments.[22] Besides establishing an East Asian Economic Caucus within APEC, Mahathir was successful through the Asia–Europe Meeting (ASEM), the first of which was held in 1996, in finding a forum in which his proposed group was realized.[23] Institutionalization of the group in everything but name has occurred more recently through the 'ASEAN Plus Three' dialogue which brings together China, Japan and Korea and the ASEAN members after the ASEAN summits (discussed further in Chapter 5).

Mahathir has also succeeded, in conjunction with the wishes of most other Asian economies, in deflecting the push by APEC's 'Western' members to give priority to trade liberalization. By the end of its first decade, APEC's agenda was becoming reoriented back to the trade facilitation and economic and technical cooperation to which Malaysia and other Asian economies wished to give priority. The revised agenda would impinge much less on the members' sovereignty than one centred around negotiated trade liberalization.

China

Like the Soviet Union, China historically had been hostile to regional groupings in the Asia-Pacific, viewing them as a vehicle for US and Japanese imperialism. Attitudes changed only slowly after the initiation of the economic reform process in 1978: it was not until the mid-1980s that Beijing began to see some value in participating in a regional economic organization.[24] As with other members of APEC, a principal motive was defensive: a fear that a world of regional trading blocs would exclude China. For China the concern was not just about North American and European regionalism but that it might even be excluded from an Asia-Pacific grouping. Beijing also came to see a regional economic grouping as a potential shield against US unilateralism. Moreover, its participation was seen as having positive consequences for how potential investors perceived China – and Beijing was particularly concerned at competition from Southeast Asia for incoming investment. And whereas China either was excluded from some global forums, most significantly the World Trade Organization, and was a relatively late entrant to others, it had an opportunity in APEC to join early (albeit not as a founding member) and thereby potentially to play a significant role in shaping the new institution.

Participation in a regional organization also served other foreign policy purposes. China approached APEC very much from a *realpolitik* orientation. APEC could become a vehicle through which the influence of its principal adversaries – Japan and the United States – could be balanced. China was particularly anxious to be a member of any pan-Asian grouping to reduce the possibility of an institutionalization of Japanese hegemony in the region. Such concerns caused Beijing to want the United States in APEC to reduce the risk that the grouping might fall under Japanese domination. On the other hand, Beijing actively supported efforts to offset the influence of Western, and more generally industrialized, economies in APEC. Thus China was one of the few governments to give active encouragement to Mahathir's promotion of the East Asian Economic Caucus. And Beijing supported the application of the Russian government for APEC membership, to help offset Western domination of the grouping.

Beijing also saw APEC as a vehicle to help China build relations with other countries in the region, especially the ASEAN group, a relationship that had historically been adversarial. China was able to portray itself as the champion of less developed economies in APEC, part of its broader claim to be the natural leader of the 'Third World'. Although China was forced to accept Taiwan's membership as a condition for its own entry to APEC, once Beijing was in the grouping it was able to prevent Taiwan from being represented by its political leadership. Taiwan's membership was also conditional on its acceptance of the status of an economic entity, with the designation of 'Chinese Taipei'. China, however, has been willing to send officials to Taipei for APEC-sponsored discussions and to permit Taiwanese officials to participate in similar meetings on the mainland (see Klintworth 1995: 505). China's membership in the organization gave Beijing the capacity to keep other rivals out, a particularly pertinent consideration in the case of India's application.

Membership in a regional economic organization also offered China an opportunity to build support for its application for admission to the WTO, and for its associated argument that trade agreements should be applied in a non-discriminatory manner. With the introduction of leaders' meetings, APEC also provided a forum for high-level bilateral discussions in otherwise uneasy relationships – not least that with the United States for most of the 1990s.

Within APEC itself, China has pushed to ensure that the organization not become a negotiation forum for trade liberalization, contrary to Washington's wishes. Moore and Yang note that 'Beijing's policy toward APEC has been anything but *passive*. Indeed, China has been uncharacteristically *pro-active* recently in its diplomatic efforts to slow the process of trade and financial liberalization and, more generally, obstruct U.S.-led efforts to transform the forum into a more formal rules-making organization' (1999: 363, emphasis in original).

Like most other East Asian countries, China has shown little interest in APEC's trade liberalization agenda except, somewhat cynically, to see benefits in a proposal which does not require it to liberalize until 2020 yet which is supposed to deliver unimpeded access to the markets of APEC's industrialized economies a decade earlier. China initially opposed the idea that a deadline be set for trade liberalization but eventually accepted the consensus agreed at Bogor. Although China announced some concessions at APEC that were best viewed as part of its efforts to gain admission to the WTO, its proposals for its own trade liberalization have generally been very modest. China offered 'only relatively weak commitments' on non-tariff barriers, and 'offered no tariff bindings at all' (Anderson 1997: 766). Beijing was suspicious of the Eminent Persons Group, seeing it as an instrument for promoting Washington's trade agenda. It has consistently placed emphasis on economic and technical cooperation within APEC, arguing that this is essential if the less developed economies are to move towards liberalized trade and investment policies.[25] For Beijing, APEC's promotion of trade liberalization inevitably will mainly be of benefit to the grouping's developed economies.

Beijing has also been outspoken in demanding that the Canberra principles on APEC's modus operandi should be respected. Gradualism and consensus are the name of the game. In his statement to the APEC Leaders' Meeting in Seattle, President Jiang Zemin emphasized that regional economic cooperation must be based on principles of equality and of mutual respect, benefit, and trust, and should proceed 'step by step based on the practical situation and the characteristics of the region'. APEC must remain an 'open, flexible and practical forum for consultations on economic cooperation'. APEC should not stray beyond its mandate to promote economic cooperation: 'so-called democracy and human rights and other ideas were not in the least related to economic cooperation'. At the Bogor meeting, President Jiang reiterated these principles and added that APEC should embrace comprehensive cooperation, common prosperity and a reduction in the development gap. And Beijing has been particularly scathing about suggestions, such as those by US Defense Secretary Perry at the Osaka Leaders' Meeting and by Australian Prime Minister Keating, that security issues should be added to APEC's agenda.

Australia

No governments had been more enthusiastic boosters of APEC than those of the Australian Labor Party headed first by Bob Hawke and then by Paul Keating in the years from the grouping's foundation to Keating's departure from office in 1996. Hawke had been responsible for the original proposal for APEC; active Australian diplomacy in the region had been critical to bringing the proposal to fruition in the Canberra Ministerial Meeting in 1989. Keating in turn had originated the proposal to stage a leaders' meeting, and had actively lobbied other APEC leaders in 1992–93 to forge an agreement on the matter. He had also suggested that the 'C' in the APEC acronym should stand for 'Community'. Keating's persistent lobbying of Indonesian President Soeharto played a positive role in the latter's decision to press ahead with proposals that the grouping adopt a timetable for freeing trade.

As discussed in Chapter 2, the Australian government had powerful incentives to promote an economic grouping that extended beyond the economies of East Asia. The country's trade orientation had changed more dramatically than that of any other industrialized economy, following the United Kingdom's application for and eventual membership in the European Union, and the growth of Australian minerals and agricultural exports first to Japan and then to other Northeast Asian economies. Australia was not a natural member of any regional trading bloc, beyond the preferential trade agreements it already had with New Zealand and the islands of the South Pacific.[26] Promotion of APEC was seen as a means of demonstrating Australia's claim to be part of the Asian region (or 'East Asian Hemisphere', the phrase adopted by Gareth Evans, the Minister for Foreign Affairs under both Hawke and Keating). And APEC had an important role in two-level games for the Australian government (Higgott 1991). Promotion of trade liberalization in the region was essential if the domestic public was to accept the radical program of economic liberalization that the Labor government was pursuing within Australia. As Prime Minister Keating (2000: 15) noted, 'Australia's economic success at home was heavily dependent upon what we did, and how we related externally'.

Australia was home to several of the most active members of the PAFTAD and PECC communities. The APEC proposal was consistent with ideas that had emerged from a group of influential economists, many of whom had combined academic and public service careers. The group included Stuart Harris, former secretary of the Department of Foreign Affairs and Trade (DFAT), and head of the Northeast Asia Program at the Australian National University; Andrew Elek, who was a member of Hawke's entourage in Seoul, and was the head of the Economic and Trade Division within DFAT and sometime fellow in the Department of Economics in the Research School of Pacific Studies at the ANU; Ross Garnaut, a professor in the Department of Economics in that Research School at the ANU, former ambassador to China and chief economic adviser to Hawke; and Peter Drysdale, head of the Australia–Japan Research Centre at the ANU and longtime collaborator with Japanese academics close to the Japanese government. Their views were influential in the trade policy bureaucracy and shaped Australian attitudes on the form that APEC should take and the role it should play.

As a Western industrialized economy located on the fringes of East Asia and with a government dominated by 'economic rationalists', however, Australia had somewhat of a split personality as far as APEC was concerned. On the one hand, Australia was impatient with what it saw as Washington's lack of understanding of Asia, siding with Tokyo in its trade dispute with the United States and arguing for a more complete relationship between Washington and Jakarta that went beyond a concern with human rights and labour standards to appreciate the importance of Indonesia for stability in the region. In attempting to draw closer to 'Asia', Canberra was making every effort not to offend ASEAN sensitivities and to respect the grouping's desire to proceed on the basis of consensus. On the other hand, the dominant economic orthodoxy in

Canberra suggested that trade liberalization would bring its own rewards and certainly did not require 'compensation' in the form of economic aid. And a respect for Asian concerns with consensus sometimes sat uneasily with a desire that APEC should bring concrete results within a short time, not least to placate domestic constituencies upset by Australia's unilateral trade liberalization.

In trade disputes between East Asian countries and the United States, Canberra's sympathies lay entirely with East Asia. Ross Garnaut (1996: 40) wrote of the dangers of an aggressive American unilateralism associated 'with misperceptions of the reality of official trade restrictions in East Asia'. Anti-American sentiment was rife among trade officials given the difficulties that Australian primary producers had experienced in gaining access to the US market and, more recently, the damage that the Export Enhancement Program had done to Australian agricultural exports. Since Australia was in the unusual situation of running large trade surpluses with Japan and most other East Asian economies, yet a large trade deficit (on a per capita basis, larger than that of the United States with Japan) with the United States, few officials had sympathy with US complaints about access to East Asian markets – even though some Australian exporters of manufactures complained of similar access problems. And some evidence existed that previous bilateral pressures on Japan had increased the market share of American products at the expense of Australian exports (George 1983). Even though US officials insisted that US demands were for market opening in Asia on an MFN basis, the context – disputes over US trade deficits – within which such negotiations took place caused great scepticism among Australian officials regarding whether a 'fair market' would be the outcome of US bilateral pressures. Prime Minister Keating was outspoken in his criticism of US efforts to introduce quantitative targets for Japanese purchases of US goods.

On the other hand, Canberra was perhaps even more dogmatic than Washington in its advocacy of trade liberalization. The 'Canberra consensus', to paraphrase John Williamson's shorthand description of the views of the Washington-based international financial institutions and the US government, rested on a faith in the neo-classical argument that unilateral trade liberalization mainly benefits the country that is removing its trade barriers. Accordingly, and consistent with the recommendations of the report from Garnaut (1989) on Australia's domestic adjustment to the rapid growth of Northeast Asian economies, Australian proposals for APEC made no reference to adjustment assistance. Similarly, the government gave no consideration in the initial APEC proposals to offering special treatment for the less developed participants. The dominant economic orthodoxy portrayed GATT Part IV (which allows for non-reciprocal trade concessions to less developed economies) as a significant mistake that had delayed necessary reform and adjustment in those economies. Tariff rates in many East Asian countries were still (too) high. The obvious gains in the mid-1980s from unilateral liberalization, especially in Indonesia, Malaysia and Thailand, were seen as demonstrating the benefits to the local economies of further trade liberalization. Moreover, in a context in which foreign aid was being drastically pared back as part of governments' preoccupation with budget deficits, Australia was not just unwilling but also unable to offer any substantial assistance to the less developed economies of the region. Canberra was simply opposed to engaging in a strategy of tactically linking aid to trade as part of its efforts to sell its APEC initiative to its proposed partners.

The Australian government's ideas of issue linkage were confined to the three areas of trade liberalization identified in the Hawke proposal: unilateral liberalization would be linked to a diffuse reciprocity through a successful conclusion of the Uruguay Round; greater transparency on intra-regional trade would again link domestic freeing of trade with that undertaken elsewhere; and, a significant incentive for several East Asian countries, there was the hope that a regional grouping pursuing liberalization would construct trade dispute resolution mechanisms that would inhibit the US resort to bilateralism. To be sure, Canberra like other member states saw a host of other possible links arising from APEC: a means of encouraging a continuing US security commitment to the region at a time when isolationist forces were on the rise in Congress, a bargaining chip in negotiations with the European Community, and so on. But Canberra's ideas on specific *substantive* links within the provisions of APEC itself were minimal; it was left to the Japanese to develop an explicit technical cooperation dimension to the body.

Australia's desires to be accepted as part of a broader East Asian community, reflected in efforts to accept consensus as the foundation for regional cooperation, sat uneasily with its desire to move APEC forward rapidly and, in particular, for the grouping to realize concrete achievements. Canberra appreciated not only that domestic communities in Australia, including business, would lose interest in the grouping if results were not immediately forthcoming, but also that Washington's attention span would be extremely limited in these circumstances. The tension between a willingness to operate on consensus and the impatience for results is clearly illustrated in Keating's remarks about Mahathir's reservations on the Bogor Declaration:

> Malaysia [according to Mahathir] would accept the 2010–2020 dates, but only if they were on a 'best endeavours' basis and were conditional and non-binding. In addition, APEC decisions should be based on consensus – in other words, unanimity – rather than majority agreement. He concluded that apart from these concerns, he was quite happy to go along with the document.
>
> Well, yes. But it was a fairly big proviso. (Keating 2000: 111)

The principle that APEC decisions should be based on consensus was enshrined, however, in the declaration at the Canberra Ministerial Meeting that Australia had supported. Moreover, it had been repeated in the Seoul Declaration (Principle 4b), which committed member economies 'to open dialogue and consensus-building, with equal respect for the views of all participants'.

Australian enthusiasm for APEC waned considerably with the election of a conservative coalition government in 1996. In its White Paper on Foreign Affairs and Trade, the government announced that it would place greater emphasis than its predecessor on bilateralism as a practical means of promoting national interests. The implicit criticism was that its predecessor had devoted too many resources to being a 'good international citizen' through its launching of regional and multilateral initiatives. Part of the new pragmatism in support of the national interest related to trade liberalization: the government was far less committed to the canon of free trade. John Howard, Leader of the conservative Coalition, declared in the lead-up to the 1996 election that he was not 'Captain Zero' as far as tariffs were concerned. In the new government's first year in office, it announced a tariff freeze on the two most heavily protected sectors of Australian manufacturing: cars, and textiles, clothing and footwear. The domestic component of the two-level trade liberalization game was thereby eroded.[27] This change in attitude towards domestic tariff reduction not only affected Australia's credibility as a driving force for trade liberalization within the region but also the country's stance on unilateralism: in its Individual Action Plan for the Manila meeting, the government gave a new prominence to requirements for reciprocity. It made its commitment to review Australia's general tariff level conditional on an assessment of the progress made by other APEC economies in liberalizing their trade (*AFR* 20 November 1996).

The diminution of Australian support for trade liberalization in general, and for the regional dimension in particular, re-emphasizes the limitations of explanations of state action that focus only on structural factors, such as economic size, or those that concentrate on ideas. The influence of such factors is inevitably dependent on how they are filtered through the mindsets of the individuals holding the key decision-making positions in foreign affairs. Moreover, the personality of and the stature of relevant ministers within the government affected both the desire and the capacity to provide leadership to regional activities.[28]

Explaining Governments' Policy Preferences

What explains the differences in governments' attitudes towards what agenda APEC should pursue and especially to the push for trade liberalization that dominated most of APEC's first decade? Undoubtedly, a

Table 3.1 Major economic characteristics of APEC members

Developed economies (per capita income over US$10 000 p.a.):
Australia, Canada, Hong Kong, Japan, Korea, New Zealand, Singapore, Taiwan, United States.
Small economies (populations under 10 million):
Brunei, Hong Kong, New Zealand, Papua New Guinea, Singapore
Open economies (trade as a percentage of Purchasing Power Parity GDP over 50%):
Brunei, Canada, Hong Kong, Malaysia, Singapore, Taiwan
Heavily protected economies (unweighted average tariff over 10% in 1993)
Chile, China, Indonesia, Mexico, Philippines, Thailand

Source: World Bank (n.d.), save for tariff rates (from PECC 1996)

combination of factors was at work here. The relevant literatures suggest close to a dozen propositions that might explain this policy divergence.

Level of Development

Historically, free trade has been the policy of the strong. Less developed economies have feared that free trade with more developed partners will inevitably produce asymmetrical results, that is, it will perpetuate a structure in which they are condemned to the export of lower-value-added products. As noted above, despite the greater acceptance of the 'Washington Consensus' by Southeast Asian economies in the 1980s, they still expressed concerns about the impact of free trade on their 'infant economies'. And the entry of China into APEC brought a powerful new actor not afraid to voice these concerns. The correlation between level of development and support for the trade liberalization agenda within APEC was very strong: the one Southeast Asian economy consistent in its promotion of the agenda was Singapore, the country with by far the highest per capita income in that region (see Table 3.1 for a summary classification of APEC members by economic characteristics). On the other hand, the correlation was not perfect: the outlier was Japan, a high per capita income economy but one that expressed serious reservations about trade liberalization under APEC's auspices.

Japan was also an outlier among the higher-income economies in its support for APEC's economic and technical cooperation agenda. Not surprisingly, the less developed member economies were the strongest advocates of this agenda.

Existing Levels of Tariffs

Countries with the lowest levels of tariffs had most to gain from regional trade liberalization. Their required domestic adjustment to such liberalization would be relatively small, while their exporters might expect significant gains from improved access to the markets of regional partners. Not surprisingly, the most enthusiastic Asian advocates of the trade liberalization agenda were Hong Kong and Singapore, two countries with minimal tariff protection for domestic producers. The correlation between existing tariff levels and support for trade liberalization is very strong, with Japan once more the outlier.[29]

Economic Size

Small economies are generally more dependent on trade than their larger counterparts (Alesina and Wacziarg 1998). The domestic political economy equation therefore might be expected to be more favourable for trade liberalization in smaller economies since a larger percentage of the workforce and of businesses is dependent on the export sector. Moreover, as Katzenstein (1985) demonstrated, small economies often have little choice but to adjust to the world market if they are to maintain their standards of living. They are price-takers. Small economies are typically strong advocates and beneficiaries of a rules-based trading system, whether at the regional or multilateral level. Large economies, on the other hand, may have the opportunity to dictate prices through the setting of optimal tariffs; they may have recourse to considerable leverage in bilateral economic relations and they depend to a much lesser extent on access to others' markets for their overall welfare.

In the APEC experience, the relationship between economic size and support for trade liberalization is not strong. Two of the smallest economies, Singapore and Hong Kong, were indeed strong supporters of the trade liberalization agenda. But for many of the other economies, the effects of size were swamped by other factors, most significantly the level of development.

Transparent Economic Decision-making

Those countries with a system of economic governance characterized by transparency and by administrative or legal procedures, to which groups may have recourse if they believe they have been unfairly treated, might be expected to be more enthusiastic about the promotion of trade liberalization in the region. Regional trade agreements could be expected to put their exporters on more of a level footing – to provide them with some mechanisms for appeal if they believed that they had been unfairly treated in countries where the administration of trade policy is less transparent. Accordingly, stronger support for trade liberalization would be expected from the 'Western' governments in the grouping, where competition policies are well developed and where specialist institutions, such as Australia's Productivity Commission, provide 'independent' monitoring of the effects of government trade policies (see Lloyd 1998). Against this argument, however, is ranged an alternative.

Prevalence of Non-tariff Barriers

Countries where various official and unofficial non-tariff barriers (NTBs) successfully protect domestic economic interests may be more willing to enter into regional trade liberalization – if the focus of these arrangements is solely on the removal of border barriers. Removal of such barriers may do little to expose their domestic producers to foreign competition. Many Asian economies are characterized by a host of official and unofficial NTBs ranging from government regulations on foreign investment, especially in the distribution system, to government actions against purchasers of foreign goods (Korean government targeting of purchasers of luxury foreign automobiles for tax audits is one of the most notorious examples), to control by domestic producers of exclusive distribution systems, to campaigns (sometimes finding substantial resonance in the nationalism of local political cultures) to buy domestic products.[30] In contrast, the prevalence of such barriers in potential regional partners may make countries with more transparent systems unwilling to enter liberalization arrangements. In the terminology of game theory, they fear they will end up with the bunny's payoff because NTBs enable their partners to defect from the trade liberalization project. These reservations also focus on both the will and the capacity of other governments to comply with any agreements. International commitments may lack credibility if domestic institutions are not conducive to their enforcement (see Cowhey 1993a).

Overall, the evidence does not support the argument that economies more reliant on non-transparent NTBs will be most positive in their attitudes towards a regional trade liberalization agenda. Governments were apparently concerned that a significant liberalization push would soon be broadened to NTBs, as had occurred in other regional and global forums. Such economies, however, were supportive, as the above line of reasoning would predict, of the introduction of dispute settlement mechanisms whose focus would have been on the formal barriers to trade.

State–Society Relations

Support for trade liberalization might be expected to be weaker in countries where governments have entered into social bargains that provide significant social protection through redistribution. Northeast Asian economies are often portrayed as characterized by such relations: governments protect inward-oriented domestic sectors, particularly but not exclusively agriculture, as a way of ensuring that they share in the prosperity achieved through rapid economic growth. The politics of domestic compensation features prominently in many Asian countries (see Calder 1988a on Japan).

In contrast, in some Western countries business communities have lobbied successfully over the years against the costs that social protection and compensation impose on aggregate economic efficiency. But the structure of domestic political institutions affects the balance between pro- and anti-liberalization forces. The congressional system in the United States, with its porosity to interest groups, ensures that US governments continue to supply extensive protection to agricultural producers, and to some sensitive sectors such as textiles. In contrast, governments in parliamentary systems have been able to act with fewer constraints in promoting trade liberalization that imposes costs on domestic constituencies – Australia and New Zealand are excellent examples.[31] Reference to the Australian and New Zealand examples, though, is a reminder of how fluid state–society relations may be on the issue of social protection. Both made a rapid transition away from policies of domestic insulation towards open economies, driven not only by changing economic circumstances but by a changing configuration of hegemonic ideas (Castles 1988; Pusey 1991; Kelly 1992; Castles et al. 1996; Ravenhill 2000).

In general, the experience in APEC supports arguments that enthusiasm for trade liberalization will be weaker in countries that are pursuing policies of societal protection.

State–Business Relations

The greater the dependence of the business community on the state for opening foreign markets, the more enthusiastic a government might be expected to be, other things being equal, in its support for a trade liberalization agenda. Government–business relations vary dramatically not only between Asia and North America but also within Asia itself (see MacIntyre 1994). It is a reasonable generalization, however, to suggest that most businesses from Asia that undertake international operations have not depended to a significant extent on their governments for market opening. Governments may have played a significant role in providing opportunities in foreign markets, as the Japanese government has done, for example, through its aid program (Arase 1995). But companies based in Asian economies have generally been comfortable with the informal networks that are so important throughout the Asian region, and have seen little need to mobilize the heavy hand of government to intervene on their behalf on trade matters.[32] Networks can be not only an alternative to hierarchy as an organizing principle for firms but also an alternative to international regimes in overcoming transactions costs (Borrus et al. 2000).

The contrast with businesses in many Western countries is marked. Some Western companies have been perfectly capable of promoting their own interests without recourse to home government intervention (on the experience of US firms in Japan see Encarnation and Mason 1990). Others have found Asian markets extremely difficult to penetrate, and subject to the NTBs noted above. They have looked to their home governments to promote market-opening policies, reflected in the initial enthusiasm of Western business for APEC's agenda. Business desire for government assistance in penetrating Asian markets is therefore one explanation for the greater support Western governments have given to APEC's trade liberalization agenda.

Sovereignty Sensitivities

Trade liberalization under the auspices of a regional organization usually impinges on the policy autonomy of national governments. They sacrifice some degree of sovereignty in that they agree to tie their hands on some measures that might otherwise have been available to support domestic constituencies. Their expectation is that greater aggregate gain will be achieved for the domestic economy in the long run when their partners' hands are similarly tied.

It is commonplace to observe that former colonies often have particular preoccupations with safeguarding their sovereignty. They would be expected, therefore, to eschew regional trade arrangements altogether, to enter arrangements with little intention of compliance, or to choose an institutional design that emphasizes unilateralism and voluntarism rather than legally binding arrangements.

How well does this factor explain divergence in countries' policies towards trade liberalization in APEC? Certainly, it is true that some of the most outspoken opposition to APEC's trade liberalization agenda and to any move away from decision-making based strictly on consensus has come from some Southeast Asian countries that were former colonies. On the other hand, Singapore, which came to independence in the same era as Malaysia, has held quite the opposite view to its erstwhile partner in the Malaysian Federation. And China and Japan, with little reason to feel insecure in their sovereignties, have been among the least enthusiastic APEC members on the trade liberalization question. Other factors thus seem to counteract the date at which countries gained their sovereignty as a determinant of attitudes to trade liberalization.

Cultural Factors

Scholars generated an enormous literature in the 1990s on the topic of Asian values. Whether a single set of 'Asian values' actually exists remains a matter of considerable debate. And the link between values and state behaviour also remains contentious. As easily as with other cultural characteristics, governments can manipulate Asian values and/or use them as a justification for policies that they wish to pursue for reasons quite divorced from any culural factor. These qualifications notwithstanding, scholars have suggested that Asian governments interact with one another in regional and global forums in a manner distinct from the interactions of other governments. The 'ASEAN Way', with alleged roots in traditional Indonesian (Javanese) culture, is characterized as emphasizing consensus and non-interference with the sovereignty of other governments. Elsewhere in the region, Asian governments are said to place considerable emphasis on the importance of 'face' in their interactions: they avoid words or deeds that would embarrass their partners.

Asian governments' approaches to international negotiations, therefore, would be expected to be wary of any form of regional interaction that impinged on the sovereignty of their fellows. They would value consensus more highly than achieving agreements if these were forced through against their partners' reservations on the issues. They would prefer to leave areas for cooperation loosely defined, subject to further consultation, rather than establish rules subject to juridical interpretation. Asian governments often seem willing to engage in 'regionalism by declaration', to 'agree first and talk after' as some have interpreted the acronym for the ASEAN Free Trade Area, AFTA. In contrast, Western governments have a preference for 'regionalism by treaty' (see Ravenhill 1995a). This is the basis for the distinction often made between the 'Asian Way' and the 'Cartesian' approach of the West, the latter symbolized by its emphasis on legally binding and enforceable agreements.

To what extent have these considerations influenced governments' behaviour in APEC? Generally, it has been the case that Asian governments have emphasized the importance of proceeding according to consensus, as agreed at the Canberra Ministerial Meeting, and wished to see APEC enshrine the principle of voluntary compliance with 'guidelines'. APEC's Western members, on the other hand, have led the push for more rapid results regardless of whether consensus has existed; for the possibility of APEC's proceeding on an $n - x$ formula whereby the organization would go beyond a lowest common denominator approach; for establishing more clearly articulated and binding rules; and for negotiated rather than unilateral approaches to trade and investment liberalization.

Yet once again, the fit is not perfect, and Asian governments' attitudes on the appropriate modes of cooperation have evolved over time. Singapore, largely an ethnic Chinese Southeast Asian state, and one whose former leader, Lee Kuan Yew, was a principal advocate of Asian values, has been active in pushing APEC forward at a rate faster than that desired by most other Asian governments. And, in other forums, China, which in

APEC has generally conformed very closely to the 'Asian' model, has had no reservations in engaging in tactics that more closely resemble Machiavelli's advice to the Prince than any emphasis on consensus in 'Asian values'. Within Southeast Asia in particular, attitudes to non-intervention have shifted as the failures of some states in the region to confront domestic problems – environmental and financial – have generated negative externalities for the region as a whole (see Dupont 2001).

Locking In and Signalling

As discussed in Chapter 1, entry into regional trade arrangements has sometimes been used by governments as a way of tying their hands with domestic constituencies that are resisting trade liberalization and/or signalling to potential foreign investors their commitment to a reform agenda. Governments pursuing a program of domestic liberalization might therefore be expected to be more willing to embrace trade liberalization at the regional level.

One problem is immediately obvious in applying this proposition to the APEC economies: the lack of variance within the grouping. Almost without exception, APEC economies all continued to pursue policies of domestic liberalization throughout the 1980s and 1990s: this factor is not a good source of variance among countries. Although some correspondence can be found between a commitment to domestic liberalization and enthusiasm for APEC – as seen, for instance, in the fall in enthusiasm in Australia following the election of a more populist, conservative government in 1996 – this factor generally has little explanatory value.

To what extent can Occam's razor be applied to cut through this proliferation of variables that purport to explain governments' attitudes to regional trade liberalization? In the discussion above, some variables were found to have little explanatory value. One variable – level of economic development – is generally very successful in predicting governments' approaches to trade liberalization in APEC. As always in the social sciences, the anomalies are of particular interest. A couple stand out.

One is Japan's policies. With the highest level of per capita income in East Asia, measured in current dollars, Japan might have been expected to be at the forefront of the push for trade liberalization. To explain its failure to play this role, one has to look to other factors, in particular the continued emphasis given in Japan to societal consensus and 'compensation' to sectors that would otherwise not share in the wealth generated by the success of its export-oriented manufacturing. An electoral system that traditionally has significantly overrepresented rural areas has reinforced this preoccupation with domestic constituencies, as has the 'money politics' that provides openings for disproportionate political influence for the inefficient construction sector. Japan's behaviour also has to be understood in the context of continuing unease about its relations with 'Asia', the legacy of conflict and conquest in the first half of the twentieth century. Its desire to be accepted as a true partner by other states has accentuated the desire of a consensus-oriented society to emphasize 'Asian values' in its interactions with other Asian governments.

A true anomaly in the context of the propositions discussed above would be for a large low-income, high-tariff Asian economy that is not highly dependent on trade to push for trade liberalization in APEC. This set of characteristics precisely defines Indonesia. What explains that country's leadership role in promoting a deadline for the realization of free trade in APEC when it held the chair of the grouping? As noted above, one explanation given relates to the desire of the government to 'lock in' a program of domestic economic liberalization. Also of importance was the desire of President Soeharto to leave a mark on the organization commensurate with his aspiration to be seen as a distinguished regional leader. Personalities matter in the provision of leadership to institutions. A more cynical interpretation, however, would suggest that APEC's provisions were so weak, ambiguous and distant that governments – Indonesian or others – could safely make commitments in the knowledge that they would not be held to account for them.

Other Actors

The APEC Eminent Persons Group

As noted in the previous chapter, NGOs provided much of the intellectual rationale and organizational design for APEC. APEC governments in turn looked to an independent body for a blueprint for raising the grouping's profile. At their meeting in Bangkok in 1992, APEC ministers accepted an Australian proposal for the establishment of an advisory committee of independent experts, the Eminent Persons Group. The idea was sold to a somewhat sceptical ASEAN by referring to the role that a similar group had played in the proposals for an ASEAN Free Trade Area – emulation, as always, being the best form of flattery. The Australians more likely had in mind, however, the role that similar groupings had played in the Commonwealth, particularly in the development of policies on South Africa in the apartheid era. The EPG was composed of academics (all except one of them being economists), a government official, and businessmen (none of its members were women).[33] Many had long-standing links with efforts to promote Asia-Pacific regional cooperation through their participation in PAFTAD and/or PECC.

The appointment of the EPG was recognition that the first three years of APEC had produced little substantive achievement. The joint statements from the first two ministerial meetings had given as much attention to the global economic situation, especially the Uruguay Round of GATT talks, as they had to developments within the region and within APEC itself. The third Ministerial Meeting at Seoul had defined APEC's objectives, its scope of activity and its mode of operation; nonetheless, the Seoul Declaration was largely aspirational and provided little guidance as to where APEC might be able to carve out a unique niche for itself. The risk of the grouping suffering an early demise was underlined by the failure of the US administration (during a presidential election campaign) to send any ministerial-level officers to APEC's fourth 'ministerial' meeting in Bangkok in 1992.

The EPG, created at that meeting, worked quickly under the energetic, if sometimes abrasive, leadership of Fred Bergsten to formulate a comprehensive vision for APEC in time for the first of the leaders' meetings in Seattle in 1993. Timing and location were fortunate. It is questionable whether the first EPG report would have received as warm a welcome had the chair of APEC not been held by the United States at the time, and had its first report not coincided with the first Leaders' Meeting. Indeed, the first executive director of the APEC Secretariat, William Bodde, noted that the APEC Ministerial Meeting's response to the report was 'somewhat restrained'. Nonetheless, the ministers renewed the EPG's mandate for a further year (Bodde 1994: 45).[34]

The singular achievement of the EPG was to make trade liberalization the dominant issue on APEC's agenda for the remainder of its first decade. Although its first report emphasized that multilateralism was the preferred option for trade liberalization, it argued that regional trade liberalization on a GATT-consistent basis could help to 'ratchet up' (one of Bergsten's favourite phrases) the process of global liberalization (APEC 1993: 31). The EPG proposed that leaders should agree at their first meeting to reach accord by 1996 on a target date and timetable for the achievement of free trade in the region (the 1993 Leaders' Meeting did not endorse this proposal but a target date was announced at the following meeting, in Bogor). The report recommended that leaders should meet at least once every three years, that finance ministers should begin to meet regularly, and that APEC should adopt an investment code and DSMs. Table 3.2 lists the principal recommendations from the three EPG reports and the actions that APEC has taken on them.

The agenda of the EPG was very much that of the Western industrialized members of the grouping. Indeed, cynics might view it as a clever device that provided legitimacy for policies that promoted the interests of the more powerful members of the grouping. Economic and Techni-

Table 3.2 Action on EPG recommendations

EPG I	
Change name to Asia-Pacific Economic Community	Rejected
Adopt commitment and timetable for regional trade liberalization by 1996	Adopted 1994
Commencement of Trade and Investment Facilitation Programs	Implemented
Adoption of Asia Pacific Investment Code	Adopted 1995
Adoption of dispute settlement mechanism	Rejected
Introduce regular meetings of finance ministers	Adopted 1994
Mutual recognition of product standards and testing	Under negotiation.
Staff Secretariat with permanent officials	Not implemented
EPG II	
Recognition that trade liberalization may be conditional (negotiated) or unconditional (unilateral)	Not disputed
Aim to complete liberalization by 2020	Agreed 1994
Adopt a safeguard mechanism more rigorous and more comprehensive than WTO's.	Rejected
EPG III	
Implement Uruguay Round commitments within half of agreed WTO period	Rejected
Address anti-dumping policies	Rejected
Introduce Asia Pacific Technology Fund	Rejected
Strengthening and application of Non-Binding Investment Principles	Not implemented

EPG Reports[35]: APEC 1993, 1994a, 1995a.

cal Cooperation (ECOTECH), the principal interest of many of the Asian members of the grouping, was a largely neglected appendage in the reports. Only four and a half pages of the total seventy-eight pages of the first report and one and a half pages of the thirty-eight-page second report were devoted to ECOTECH. On that subject, the reports had a striking absence of specifics, particularly in contrast to the detailed attention given to trade liberalization. In its final report, the EPG did pay more attention to this pillar of APEC's activities and recommended that the grouping should create an Asia Pacific Technology Fund. Governments have failed to endorse this proposal.

Although the EPG was unified in wanting to make trade liberalization the centrepiece of the APEC agenda, it was split on how APEC should proceed. The reports asserted that liberalization should be consistent with GATT. Two ways exist, however, for regional groupings to comply with GATT. One is to adopt a policy of 'open regionalism' through which any trade 'concessions' made to other members in the grouping would be extended on an MFN basis to all GATT/WTO members. The other method is by seeking exemption from the MFN requirement through the use of Article XXIV, which permits the establishment of preferential regional trade groupings as long as they meet specified criteria. The first report was clear that APEC's preferred method was 'open regionalism'. It explicitly rejected the alternative of constructing a discriminatory free-trade arrangement by extending NAFTA membership to other APEC members. In the second report, however, the EPG asserted that APEC's trade liberalization benefits should be offered to non-members on a reciprocal basis – raising the possibility that, in the absence of reciprocity, APEC might liberalize on a discriminatory basis – a proposal that Bergsten (1994) referred to as 'temporary conditional MFN'. This requirement that third parties should offer reciprocity was a reflection of growing US concern that APEC's process of unilateral liberalization would deprive it of the leverage it enjoyed in negotiations with third parties. Bergsten (1994, 1996) asserted that non-discriminatory free trade was both impractical and undesirable. It opened the way for free-riding by outsiders, and this uncertainty about realizing reciprocity would cost APEC domestic support. Moreover, it would prevent APEC countries from using their considerable bargaining strength to induce others to negotiate in global forums.

The discomfort of many Asian countries with the EPG became increasingly obvious after the Seattle Leaders' Meeting. They perceived the EPG as driving APEC's agenda too far too fast. After the presentation of its second report, ASEAN economic ministers, meeting in Chiang Mai in September 1994, called for the dissolution of the group. They judged its proposals as too specific. Suggestions that APEC should adopt investment principles and a dispute mediation service threatened to lead to excessive institutionalization of the grouping. Indonesia Trade Minister S. B. Joedono summed up the ASEAN sentiment in his assertion that the EPG was 'insufficiently pragmatic'.[36] Perhaps realizing that its days were numbered, the EPG in its third and final report was more outspoken and even less 'pragmatic' in its criticisms of APEC's efforts to date, especially the ineffective investment principles the grouping had adopted in 1994 (discussed in Chapter 4). Moreover, in a recommendation certain to antagonize most Asian governments, the third report advocated that APEC economies should speed up the implementation of their Uruguay Round commitments. The EPG did not have its mandate renewed by the ministers and leaders at their meetings in Osaka in 1995.

The EPG in APEC is further powerful testimony to the independent role that intellectual leadership can play in the promotion of international agreements. The EPG had no 'power' resources at its disposal other than its creativity and its capacity to embarrass governments by persistently exposing their lack of action. It was largely because of the EPG that APEC's agenda was changed dramatically away from that of an

OECD-like body for trade facilitation and economic and technical cooperation, which Australian Prime Minister Hawke had proposed, to one where trade liberalization was centre stage. To be sure, the agenda advocated by the EPG coincided with the interests of APEC's dominant economy, the United States. But because the EPG rather than a national government was the source of the trade liberalization push, the chances of its being incorporated into the APEC agenda were probably higher. Indeed, a former senior US official, Richard Baker (1998: 170), notes that the EPG proposal that a deadline for freeing trade in the region be announced was more ambitious than the Clinton administration would have formulated, given the known sensitivities of its Asian partners.

Why, then, did APEC's Western governments acquiesce in the EPG's demise? One reason was Washington's loss of interest in APEC following the disappointment at the effectiveness of APEC's Non-Binding Investment Principles. As discussed above, Washington's attention to APEC was spasmodic; it was not until it saw that APEC could play a positive role in the conclusion of the Information Technology Agreement in 1996 that Washington regained some enthusiasm for the grouping. A second factor was the leader of the EPG himself. Bergsten's abrasive personality had alienated senior officials in the Clinton administration, and his actions and statements were not always consistent with short-term US interests. Some other Western governments meanwhile, notably Australia, which might otherwise have been expected to have supported the EPG's determination to push the trade liberalization agenda, were alarmed at the movement discernible in the second EPG report away from an emphasis on open regionalism and unilateralism in APEC towards negotiated reciprocity. A requirement for reciprocity raised the unwelcome spectre of APEC's evolution into a preferential trading group. These Western governments also had some concern (reflecting the ambiguity noted above about a desire for immediate results versus a wish to respect Asian concerns for decision-making consensus) that the EPG was alienating Asian governments.

The Eminent Persons Group would qualify as a small epistemic community. But its experience shows that like other such communities, if effective links are not established with national bureaucracies, its capacity to move beyond a temporary agenda-setting role to effect a change in governments' attitudes and policies will inevitably be limited.

The APEC Secretariat

When the OECD was suggested as a model for APEC by the Australian government in 1989, the emphasis was on replicating OECD-like activities without creating a centralized bureaucracy akin to that of the Paris-based organization. APEC would be supported by PECC and by national governments, which would assume responsibility for being 'lead shepherd' of particular working groups (the model followed by PECC). Objections to the establishment of a significant bureaucracy ranged across concerns that this would make APEC inflexible, would diminish the influence of smaller members,[37] and would impinge on the sovereignty of member governments. The last was of particular concern to the ASEAN countries, which had been most reluctant to give any autonomy to their own grouping's Secretariat.

When the Bangkok Ministerial Meeting agreed in 1992 to create an APEC Secretariat, the decision was accordingly greeted with some misgivings in several member states. Subsequently, however, the member economies have ensured that the Secretariat enjoys negligible autonomy and lacks a capacity to play an independent leadership role in promoting Asia-Pacific cooperation. When it was established, APEC ministers declared that '[t]he APEC Secretariat should be small in size, simple in structure, and flexible enough to meet APEC's evolving needs' (quoted in Bodde 1997: 218). And, in November 1996, ministers approved the recommendation of the Task Force on Management Issues that the Secretariat should *not* develop a comprehensive research and analysis capability. Rather, the Secretariat was authorized to 'coordinate, oversee and undertake, where necessary, a limited amount of research and analysis work' but in collaboration with PECC and the APEC Study Centres (APEC 1998).[38]

The Secretariat (at the end of 2000) had only twenty-one professional staff, all of whom were on secondment from member governments rather than being permanent employees. In addition to these professionals, the Secretariat is headed by an executive director and a deputy executive director, both of whom enjoy ambassadorial status. These positions, however, rotate each year: the executive director comes from the country hosting the leaders' meeting in that year, the deputy from the country hosting the meeting in the following year. With a maximum of two years in a senior position in the organization, the executive director is not well placed to take any significant initiatives, which was exactly the intention of the member economies. As the first executive director of the Secretariat noted, the annual turnover of executive directors and their deputies 'makes management of the organisation very difficult' (Bodde 1994: 57). Member economies have ignored the recommendation of the EPG that the Secretariat be given permanent staff. The Secretariat's initial budget was paltry – a mere US$2 million – a marked contrast to the OECD's budget in 1988 of US$128.2 million (*FEER* 16 November 1989: 13).[39]

The individual professional members of staff are each responsible for four or five areas of the group's activities and can scarcely monitor them adequately, let alone provide any leadership. The Secretariat, in Soesastro's words, 'continues to function mainly as a clearing house'

(1999: 148). It is certainly not an organization that provides any impetus for initiatives that APEC might undertake. The weakness of the Secretariat has been central to APEC's lack of forward movement since the demise of the EPG, given the unwieldy character of its principal official forum, the senior officials' meetings. The first executive director, William Bodde (1997: 219), comments that the numbers in attendance at senior officials' meetings had 'grown out of hand', and that the unwillingness to limit the number of countries represented on the various committees and working groups had produced bodies 'that are often too large and cumbersome for timely decision-making'.

The Secretariat itself controls no funds for the group's activities: this factor, coupled with its inadequate staffing, currently prevents it from playing any part in resolving the lack of coordination in the group's economic and technical cooperation projects. APEC's Working Groups and Economic and Technical Cooperation program are often criticized for their lack of focus. Bodde (1994: 31) records that the Secretariat was unable to undertake substantive analysis of the proposals from the program.[40] The consequence was a proliferation of uncoordinated projects. The output from the Working Groups has been decidedly uneven. Bodde (1997: 221) makes a strong argument that some of the groups should be abolished, some consolidated, and new ones created. Member economies, however, have given the Secretariat neither the resources nor the authority to provide active guidance and coordination to APEC's work program.

Conclusion

APEC is an intergovernmental organization whose members have ensured that other actors are confined to minor supporting roles. Tolerance for initiatives from other bodies has been very limited. The Eminent Persons Group was an exception, but one that was short-lived. Its attempts to force the pace of trade liberalization were simply unacceptable to most Asian governments. Furthermore, members so restricted the Secretariat's resources and autonomy that it was incapable even of playing the limited support role intended for it, let alone serving as a coordinator or innovator. In APEC, one of the questions that has preoccupied students of European integration – whether the main source of the impetus for the deepening of regional collaboration has been national governments or the supranational European Commission – simply does not arise. The consequence of having an ineffective Secretariat was that, after the demise of the Eminent Persons Group, no source of leadership existed in APEC outside member governments themselves. APEC's future rested on the continued interest of governments and their senior office-holders in driving the grouping forward. As discussed in

Chapter 5, this interest waned considerably, to APEC's detriment, in the second half of the 1990s.

APEC's diverse economies held radically different views on what the central goals of the institution should be and on what methods were appropriate for their realization. Chapter 4 examines how this diversity affected the rules of the APEC regime.

CHAPTER 4

Does APEC make a Difference? Trade, Regimes, and Compliance

When economists call for free trade, this is not a blind prejudice. Rather, it is based on a theoretical framework that is compelling in its logic ... To say that our government must depart from free trade because other governments are not free traders is like saying that because other countries have rocky coasts, we must block up our own harbors. (Krugman 1986: 10–11)

A naïve observer, trained only to appreciate the overall welfare benefits of trade, might assume that trade relations would be harmonious. (Keohane 1984: 54)

Politics is the study of ways of transcending the Prisoner's Dilemma. (Elster 1976: 249)

Why is a Trade Regime Necessary?

For students of trade policy, the lack of congruence between the prescriptions of economic theory and the practice of governments poses an immediate puzzle. If free trade is as beneficial as economic theory suggests, why have governments practised it so rarely? Does the option of free trade not provide a rare instance of international harmony – a situation in which self-interested governments will pursue policies that maximize not only their individual welfare but also the common good? Most economies have so small a share of global trade or of total trade in a particular product that by their own actions they are not able to improve their terms of trade. Unilateral liberalization is the preferred policy prescription of economic theory. Yet it is one that governments have rarely embraced.

Four sets of reasons might explain governments' failure to practise free trade. One is that governments are simply lacking in knowledge, unaware of the purported benefits of trade liberalization. Such an explanation is scarcely credible in an era of easy global communication, at a time of almost universal participation by states in the World Bank and the

International Monetary Fund, and when the international donor community is keen to 'sell' the message of liberalization to aid recipients.

A second set of explanations revolves around a failure by governments to accept the logic of the neo-classical case for free trade and thus around their conscious rejection of the accompanying policy prescriptions. Such objections to trade liberalization may be based on economic theory or alternatively on governments' giving higher priority to non-economic objectives than to the purported gains to be made from trade liberalization.

A starting point here is the exceptions to the case for free trade that neo-classical theorists allow. One of the most distinguished of modern trade theorists, Max Corden (1974: 415–16), concluded a major survey of trade theory with the statement that '[i]t is undoubtedly true that much of the discussion implies that governments could frequently benefit their peoples by removing trade restrictions, perhaps gradually, especially if they replace them with other, more suitable, forms of intervention. But this can hardly be a firm, dogmatic conclusion since there are too many qualifications'. Neo-classical theory allows several such qualifications, leaving aside for the moment the case for optimal tariffs because this argument applies only to large players in the world economy. Perhaps the best known is the argument for infant industry protection. Often associated with the mercantilist ideas of Alexander Hamilton and Friedrich List, the argument nonetheless received the endorsement of one of the most enthusiastic of the nineteenth-century proponents of free trade, John Stuart Mill. In the postwar years, the case for infant industry protection became one of the cornerstones of development economics.

The costly failures of import-substituting industrialization in many less developed economies, especially in Africa, South America and South Asia, have done much to discredit the case for protecting infant industries – albeit often as much for reasons of political economy than for those derived from economic theory itself. In an era of global (or regional) production networks when production is frequently for the world rather than the domestic market, the economic case for infant industry protection is also less compelling. Moreover, the advent of post-Fordist production techniques, often based on the application of numerically controlled machine tools, renders the economies of scale that infant industry protection is often designed to achieve far less important in many sectors of manufacturing industry than they were in the first three postwar decades. The move towards lower tariffs and the emphasis on export-oriented production that has been so prominent in many less developed economies since the mid-1980s are testimony not only to the power of the ideas promoted by the international financial institutions but also to the loss of faith in many parts of the world in infant industry protection as a method of fostering rapid economic growth. Nevertheless, the infant industry argument continues to hold some attraction for governments, particularly those involved in the promotion of domestically oriented industries – witness the protection given the automobile industry in parts of Southeast Asia.

Neo-classical economic theory allows several other exceptions to the prescription of free trade. These include the imposition of duties where foreign producers hold a monopoly or engage in short-term dumping, and the use of tariffs to raise revenue when other means are less cost-effective. In addition, a failure in various domestic factor markets justifies the use of tariffs as a second best instrument to correct distortions in the domestic economy. More influential than these arguments in recent years, however, have been two new strands of economic literature: strategic trade theory and the 'new' growth theories.

Strategic trade approaches build on the infant industry argument by marrying it with insights from the industrial organization literature. These approaches begin by discarding the neo-classical assumption of perfectly competitive markets. Instead, they portray the contemporary industrialized world as characterized by oligopolistic competition and by intra-industry trade in products often differentiated primarily by brand name. With imperfectly competitive markets, the possibility exists that firms will be able to earn rents even in the long term.[1] In a market in which few players compete, where entry costs are high, where firms face steep learning curves and can gain 'first mover' advantages, strategic moves become an important determinant of who will prosper. Credible commitments may deter rivals from entering the market, enabling the domestic firm to gain first-mover advantages and capture the lion's share of rents. In a competitive structure where credible commitments are important, governments can improve the prospects of their domestic firms through a variety of measures. These include the exclusion of competitors from the domestic market, and the provision of subsidies for infrastructure and for exports, research and development, and so on (see especially Krugman 1986, 1990; Venables and Smith 1986; Lipsey and Dobson 1987). In certain circumstances, international economic relations take on adversarial attributes. Trade becomes a zero-sum rather than a positive sum game.

In its emphasis on path dependencies, and on promoting industries that generate positive externalities and ensuring these are captured within the domestic economy, strategic trade theory overlaps with the new growth theories. These suggest that small initial differences in economies' trajectories can translate into large long-run differences in growth rates (see e.g. Romer 1986, 1987; Dosi et al. 1990; Grossman and Helpman 1990). In such circumstances, the case for free trade is no longer unqualified.

For many economists, the case for strategic trade policies is far stronger in theory than in practice. They see the probability (and negative consequences) of government failure in the pursuit of interventionist policies as far outweighing those of market failure. In particular, rational policy-making is likely to succumb to particularist influences, the victim of political economy problems (Krugman 1992). The new growth theories are less vulnerable to such criticisms from a political economy perspective.

These objections of most professional economists notwithstanding, the new trade and growth theories provide a significant set of theoretically informed reservations to the case for free trade that supplement the exceptions that the neo-classical approach allows. Certainly there is enough material here to make governments have reservations about an unqualified economic case for free trade. And the economic policies of Northeast Asian governments in the postwar period suggest that they practised a strategic approach to trade – through the protection of local markets and the provision of assistance to domestic firms to penetrate export markets – even before economists devised models to show why in theory these policies might be successful (Yamamura 1986; Matthews and Ravenhill 1994).

Governments may accept the case for free trade on economic grounds but reject the policy prescription nonetheless because they place a higher value on political and social concerns. Again, classical economic theory suggests a number of grounds why governments may legitimately decide against free trade. The best known of these is the case for protection on grounds of national security or of protecting public welfare or morality. Most governments are also inclined to limit trade if they believe it threatens social consensus. Japanese, Korean and French governments have protected their farmers, not just because they constitute powerful political lobbies but because these governments have made a commitment to the countryside, which they view as an essential part of the social fabric. The 'embedded liberalism' compromise that underpinned postwar economic regimes was an attempt to reconcile the conflicting imperatives that governments face. Governments were not to be forced to sacrifice social goals on the altar of free trade (Ruggie 1982).[2] Good politics cannot be reduced to good economics.

A more cynical interpretation of government behaviour is that political incumbents often face short-term non-economic incentives that can override the perceived gains from economic liberalization. Politicians are concerned with their re-election and wish to avoid alienating domestic groups that may suffer short-term damage from trade liberalization.[3] Although free trade may enhance overall societal welfare in the long term, politicians can seldom afford to adopt that time-frame. Moreover, politicians and bureaucrats alike may have an interest in creating rents, and then extracting a share from their societal beneficiaries.

A third set of reasons why governments may not implement economic liberalization rests not on their disagreement with the policy prescriptions of neo-classical theory but rather, using the language of the literature on compliance, on 'involuntary defection'. That is, governments may accept the logic of the theoretical case and wish to implement trade liberalization but find that powerful interest groups are able to block their aspirations. In practice, it is often difficult to distinguish between involuntary defection and a decision by governments not to push for trade liberalization for fear of adverse political consequences. The likelihood that involuntary defection will occur often depends on differences between various branches of government and on the constitutional separation of powers. Involuntary defection is more probable in a political system where making and implementing trade policy rests not just in the hands of the executive but is shared with a powerful legislature in which party discipline is weak.

An emphasis on domestic opposition indicates why governments may reject a unilateral approach to trade liberalization. To liberalize without reciprocity from trading partners will stimulate domestic political opposition to a government without generating any offsetting support for government policies from domestic groups that might expect to benefit from improved access to foreign markets. In contrast, concerted liberalization will have a more positive effect on the domestic political economy equation if export-oriented interests are confident of gaining improved access to foreign markets and mobilize in support of trade negotiations. The political requirement for reciprocity is in the forefront of most politicians' thinking. For instance, former Australian Prime Minister Malcolm Fraser (1984: 9) asserted that 'it is almost impossible for any one middle ranking power to move too far alone unless they can get better access to other people's markets'.[4]

A final reason why governments may not follow the unilateral trade liberalization prescription of economic theory is that they see their capacity to reduce tariffs or non-tariff barriers as a bargaining chip in international negotiations. Governments may believe that they can achieve even greater gains, possibly not just for domestic welfare but for the world economy as a whole, by making improved access to their own markets conditional on reciprocal action by others. Such an approach has been the dominant one in international trade liberalization in the postwar years. Although GATT contained no reference to reciprocity as a principle for trade negotiations, the negotiating parties proceeded on the basis that 'diffuse' reciprocity should guide their approach to trade liberalization (Keohane 1986; Zacher with Sutton 1996). And GATT's use of the term 'concessions' to refer to tariff offers made in negotiations further emphasized notions of reciprocity.

To couch tariff reductions in terms of concessions has irritated most economists, who maintain that the principal gains from such 'concessions' will accrue to the economies that make them rather than to their trading partners. Nevertheless, governments have consistently held out for reciprocity, not just because they see it as essential to placate domestic constituencies but because they believe that the overall gains from liberalization can be enhanced when it occurs on a concerted basis rather than unilaterally. Some economists concur with their approach (see e.g. Snape 1996: 49–50; Anderson 1997: 752).[5] Reciprocity should produce improved terms of trade for exports as well as improved access to foreign markets. Moreover, the case for reciprocity extends beyond the gains for welfare in the aggregate to considerations of efficiencies at the firm level. The economist Neil Vousden (1990: 244–6), for instance, notes that in the contemporary global economy in which many firms face increasing returns to scale, access to foreign markets enabling the realization of scale economies is an important consideration in the negotiation of regional agreements. Moreover, it provides an economic rationale for the preference for reciprocity over unilateral tariff reductions.

Governments may fail to follow the free-trade prescription of liberal economic orthodoxy for any or all of the four sets of reasons listed above. Economic gain, political gain, the possibility of private gain for politicians or bureaucrats, a desire to maintain social consensus or to use tariffs as a bargaining chip: all of these concerns may cause a 'rational' government to maintain barriers to trade. The relatively small gains that economic theory suggests arise from trade liberalization reinforce these temptations to practise protection.[6] Even when governments are aware that opportunistic behaviour may attract retaliation from their trading partners, they may still persist in such behaviour because they are uncertain whether in fact retaliation will occur and, if it does, of its costs. And governments are notorious for their short time-horizons.

How should other governments respond to such a 'defection' from a policy of trade liberalization? Neo-classical economists typically argue that the government that fails to practise free trade does more damage to itself than to its trading partners. Domestic industries will not face the stimulus to efficiency that competition in the world market provides. In the long run, they will be placed at a disadvantage compared with their competitors who are forced to respond to market disciplines. Trading partners are unlikely to view the situation in that way for several reasons.

First, they are likely to believe that the protectionist economy in some circumstances can gain from free-riding on the liberalization of others. The logic of infant industry arguments and of strategic trade and new growth theories is that domestic firms may benefit from predatory trading policies. These benefits take on even greater significance where path dependence is a critical factor in firms' performances.

Second, even if protection of inefficient domestic sectors mainly causes damage to the economy that is imposing the restrictions, trading partners are still likely to want to reverse these policies because they cost sales opportunities for their own export industries. A prime example is the efforts by the United States and other agricultural exporters to open agricultural markets in Northeast Asia, attempting to reverse policies that impose huge costs on consumers in these economies and thus on these countries' national welfare – but which also impose income losses on agricultural exporters.

Third, trading partners are likely to be concerned about the reaction of their publics to trade protection elsewhere. The absence of market opportunities for domestic exporters will greatly complicate the political economy problem associated with domestic trade liberalization. Reciprocity is a necessity in the international trade sphere less for economic reasons than because it is a political imperative. Moreover, governments face a potential domestic image problem: they do not wish their constituents to perceive them as 'soft' or ineffective negotiators.

The temptations – whether economic or political – that governments have to 'cheat' their trading partners by protecting domestic interests lead most observers to characterize international trade as a mixed motive structure that often parallels that of a Prisoner's Dilemma game (see e.g. Stein 1982: 308; Axelrod 1984: 7; Abbott 1985; Krasner 1987).[7] Unless a trade regime provides mechanisms that reassure governments about the likely behaviour of their partners, specifically by reducing their incentives to cheat, it is very difficult to realize a cooperative strategy of trade liberalization.

Asia-Pacific Trade: Prisoner's Delight or Prisoner's Dilemma?

APEC's approach to trade liberalization rejects the conventional wisdom among political scientists (and many economists), outlined in the first section of this chapter, about the problems of realizing cooperation in international trade. This section of the chapter looks at how APEC's modus operandi is grounded in an alternative logic of trade liberalization.

APEC has adopted a unique approach to regional economic cooperation. The two guiding principles are 'open regionalism' and 'concerted unilateralism'. The term 'open regionalism', first coined by a Japanese study group in 1981, has become a catchword for APEC. It is shorthand for a process of 'regional economic integration without discrimination against outsiders' (Garnaut 1996: 1). The phrase has generated considerable contention. Some commentators (e.g. Srinivasan 1995) see it as an oxymoron: for them, regionalism is inevitably discriminatory. The extension of the benefits of cooperation to non-members of a regional grouping would rob it of its 'regional' nature. Others disagree on the essential characteristics of the non-discriminatory approach implied by the phrase 'open regionalism'.[8] APEC itself has never spelled out what it understands by this phrase. For the community of economists, business representatives, and officials active in PAFTAD and PECC, however, the meaning of 'open regionalism' is unambiguous. It is a continuation of the process of unilateral liberalization that has characterized the economic policies of countries in the region for several decades, a market-driven process rather than one directed by government efforts to construct formal free-trade areas.

Increasing interdependence within the region generated a need for intergovernmental collaboration to reduce the transactions costs exposed by the higher levels of economic interaction. But governments had no interest in these efforts taking the form of a free-trade area. Garnaut (1996: 9–10) identifies three main reasons. First, given the diversity of the region, it would be impossible for members to meet (even the ambiguous) requirements to qualify for the GATT/WTO consistency under Article XXIV. Second, the trading interests of Asia-Pacific economies extend beyond the region, causing governments to avoid any moves that might trigger the disintegration of the global economy into rival trading blocs. Third, open regionalism avoids the potential costs of trade diversion generated by a free-trade agreement.[9]

APEC's second key principle has been 'concerted unilateralism', a term that Funabashi (1995: 96) attributes to Tony Miller, the Trade Secretary of Hong Kong. Concerted unilateralism is an instance of what some have termed the 'constructive ambiguity' widespread in APEC's principles. 'Concerted unilateralism' was APEC's answer to the tension between those members who favoured a non-discriminatory unilateral approach to trade liberalization and those who favoured a process grounded in reciprocity.

The emphasis on unilateralism flows from the experience of Asian economies in the 1980s when rapid economic growth accompanied trade liberalization, Asian governments' frequently stated preference that regional arrangements must be grounded in consensus, and the arguments of economic theory that the principal gains from liberalization accrue to the states implementing this policy. The concern of Asian governments to maintain decision-making autonomy ruled out any pooling of sovereignty on economic policies. The Japanese Minister of Foreign Affairs, Yohei Kono (1995: 1–2), asserted that 'we have adopted the approach of concerting members' voluntary efforts on the basis of mutual trust ... APEC liberalization and facilitation should be implemented not by an excessively negotiation-like framework'. The APEC unilateral approach would therefore diverge dramatically from the negotiated, rules-based environment of the GATT/WTO, and from the vast majority of arrangements for regional intergovernmental collaboration on trade. The concerted component of 'concerted unilateralism', on the other hand, was intended to address concerns over lack of reciprocity, and to increase the magnitude of gains arising from the liberalization process. This would be the value added by APEC to an ongoing process of unilateral liberalization. 'What we are talking about', according to Gareth Evans, 'is *neither* strict, hard edged GATT-style multilateral offer and acceptance negotiations *nor* very loose voluntarism, in which every member economy is absolutely free to choose the pace at which it unilaterally liberalizes' (Evans 1995: 3, emphasis in original).

For APEC's proponents, a combination of a positive demonstration effect and a fear of missing out on the benefits of liberalization would provide countries with a powerful inducement to follow those that pioneered liberalization (see e.g. Elek 1992; Drysdale and Garnaut 1993). The result would be what might be termed a 'spill-in' process, through which liberalization would be successively adopted by all members of the grouping. For Drysdale and Garnaut, the unique circumstances of trade in the Asia-Pacific region have converted the traditional Prisoner's Dilemma structure of trade cooperation into one of 'Prisoner's Delight':

> Observation of the highly beneficial effect of one country's liberalization on its own trade expansion has led each Western Pacific economy to calculate that, whatever policies others follow, it will benefit more from keeping its own borders open to trade than from protection. Each country's liberalization in its own interest has increased the benefits that trading partners receive from their own liberalization. This prisoner's delight game consists of a series of movements toward sets of trade policies that are more favorable for all countries. (1993: 187–8)

The argument is essentially a restatement of the case for trade liberalization made in neo-classical economic theory. From this perspective, participants in international trade face a structure of interaction that is characterized not by dilemmas of collaboration but by harmony: 'each country's unilateral decision to maximize its own welfare, with or without co-operation, leads inexorably towards the best possible outcome for each country and the world as a whole' (Garnaut 1996: 31).

The record of some Asia-Pacific governments – especially those in Southeast Asia and Australasia – in undertaking unilateral trade liberalization in the 1980s and 1990s appears to provide support for Drysdale and Garnaut's thesis. Logical flaws are obvious, however, in an argument that views international trade as a situation of harmony yet simultaneously makes the case for an international regime – in this instance, APEC (Fane 1995). If governments acting rationally in their self-interest pursue a policy of unilateral trade liberalization then no international regime or institution is necessary for achieving the desired outcome. To salvage a case for an international institution, the authors could fall back on the argument that 'unilateralism is good, but concerted unilateralism is better'. However, following the logic of their argument, an institution is not even required to assist in the coordination of liberalization because governments' desire to liberalize will be driven in part by the demonstration effects of the success of others.

Ultimately, the most serious objection to the 'Prisoner's Delight' conceptualization is that even if the authors are correct in asserting that the observed benefits from liberalization cause governments to abandon the idea that such measures are 'concessions' to be hoarded for use in international negotiations,[10] their argument does not address the various other reasons discussed above why governments may be tempted to resist a cooperative approach.[11] The political rationality of economically irrational behaviour is ignored by exponents of the Prisoner's Delight approach. Yet, as we will see, such calculations have impeded APEC's efforts at trade liberalization.

The political economy of trade among the economies of the Asia-Pacific is no different from that in any other part of the global economy. Governments approach trade issues with a mixture of motives. True believers in the desirability of the abolition of all impediments to trade that protect domestic economic and social interests are very rare worldwide – although the Asia-Pacific region contains two governments, Hong Kong and Singapore, which have come as close to any to meriting that status. Other governments in the region often either see economic or political value in opportunistic behaviour – in the protection of domestic interests and in attempting to export the costs of structural adjustment – or find their hands tied in the domestic component of the two-level game that trade negotiations constitute. To be sure, significant unilateral trade liberalization did occur in many Western Pacific economies in the second half of the 1980s and early 1990s. Nonetheless, substantial protectionist barriers remain. These tend to be concentrated in sectors regarded as politically sensitive, for example agriculture in Northeast Asia, textiles in the more developed economies, or those sectors, such as automobiles, seen as strategically important to the local economy.

Considerable variation occurs across countries and across time in governments' proclivities to protect domestic interests. (For a consideration of the principal factors involved see, for instance, Gourevitch 1977; Goldstein 1988; Milner 1988; Magee et al. 1989.) Trading partners, however, face an ever-present *possibility* that a government will 'defect' from a cooperative approach. The structure of interaction in trade therefore often resembles a Prisoner's Dilemma game in which both parties would maximize their welfare through cooperation but where temptations to 'cheat' may be overwhelming. Trade agreements can help reduce the concern that parties have that their partners will engage in opportunistic behaviour.

Moreover, by requiring reciprocal 'concessions', they not only can provide potential sanctions to be employed in the event of non-compliance but also help overcome the resistance of domestic interest groups to trade liberalization. (On the importance of reciprocity to international cooperation, see Keohane 1986 and, from a game-theoretic perspective, Axelrod 1984.)

The next section of this chapter reviews the various ways in which international regimes can contribute to overcoming the obstacles to international collaboration in trade. I then evaluate the extent to which APEC makes a similar contribution.

Regimes and International Collaboration

International regimes – 'principles, norms, rules, and decision-making procedures around which actors' expectations converge' (Krasner 1982: 185) – can contribute to overcoming barriers to international collaboration in several ways. (For comprehensive surveys of the literature on international regimes, see Rittberger with Mayer 1993; Levy et al. 1995; Hasenclever et al. 1996, 1997.) These effects of regimes may conveniently be grouped under three headings: changing the incentives for states to collaborate; changing actors' conceptions of their interests and identities; and changing the balance of bargaining power in domestic politics:

- Changing the incentives for collaboration: Monitoring; reciprocity; sanctions; DSMs; reduction of transactions costs; issue linkage; iteration.
- Changing actors' interests and identities: Knowledge creation and diffusion; facilitating new transnational alliances; provision of new organizations; broadening the scope of policy options; raising domestic awareness; building domestic institutional capacity; reshaping domestic institutions.
- Changing the domestic political economy equation: Strengthening pro-reform forces; enabling governments to claim their hands are tied; locking in domestic reforms.

Changing the incentives for collaboration

Regimes can help rational actors to achieve their existing goals and overcome problems associated with collaboration in an anarchical international system mainly by helping to reduce uncertainty. Regimes may help to reduce fears that potential partners will behave opportunistically, and thereby move the structure of interaction away from that associated with a single-play Prisoner's Dilemma game. Collaborating parties look to regimes to constrain the behaviour of other members (Aggarwal 1995).

Uncertainty can be reduced by several features of a regime.

Monitoring

The principal way by which regimes can help to reduce uncertainty is increasing the transparency of behaviour of their members. The exchange of information in response to reporting requirements is an essential step in facilitating monitoring of partners' behaviour. Moreover, regimes often feature either the establishment of a central monitoring body and/or provide for monitoring activities carried out by interested third parties such as NGOs (on the important role of NGOs in monitoring, see Haas et al. 1993; Chayes and Chayes 1995). For many observers, a capacity to monitor partners is crucial in determining how conditional cooperators will behave in structures that resemble a collaboration game (see e.g. Ostrom 1990; Caporaso 1992: 609).

Reciprocity

Uncertainty about the behaviour of other parties, and particularly fears that concessions will be unrequited, can be reduced where the rules of the regime require reciprocal behaviour from all parties. Such prospects are enhanced when the obligation of reciprocity leads to coordination of behaviour. The possibility of withdrawing reciprocal concessions also offers contracting parties a potential sanction in the event of others behaving opportunistically.

Sanctions

Besides legitimising the withdrawal of reciprocal concessions should others behave opportunistically, the regime may include provisions for individual or collective sanctions against parties that transgress its rules and norms.

Dispute settlement mechanisms

Regimes may establish formal mechanisms or even an independent organization to help in resolving disputes. Again, such mechanisms may increase confidence among contracting parties about the likely respect for the rules of the regime, enhance parties' concerns about their reputations, and increase the range of sanctions available in cases of non-compliance.

Besides helping to reduce uncertainty, regimes can encourage a collaborative approach to goal attainment by facilitating the negotiation of international agreements. In particular:

Transactions costs

Regimes may facilitate negotiation on a multilateral basis. Multilateral negotiations have the potential to reduce the transactions costs associated with negotiation compared with those incurred when conducting a plethora of bilateral discussions with potential partners.

Issue linkage

Multilateral negotiations for constructing or maintaining regimes may provide opportunities for issue linkage in which it is possible to compensate parties that perceive losses from collaborative activities in some areas of a regime by providing them with obvious gains on other dimensions. The range of collaborative policy options may thereby be increased. The possibilities for issue linkage may be enhanced in the presence of institutions such as secretariats that have as one of their tasks a search for ways of linking various components of a regime.

Iteration

The extensive literature on game theory argues that iterated interaction has a profound effect on outcomes in a context where the parties have mixed interests. Indeed, a pattern of repeated contacts among participants undermines some of the core assumptions of the Prisoner's Dilemma. These include the inability of players to influence others' strategies through interaction, and the inability of players to adopt contingent strategies dependent on their partners' behaviours (the best-known strategy being 'tit for tat'). Moreover, repeated negotiations with partners in the context of an international regime can enhance the 'shadow of the future'. Parties contemplating opportunistic behaviour will give greater attention to the damage that such behaviour might do to their credibility and thus to their future opportunities to collaborate with other parties in an increasingly interdependent global system. Questions of reputation take on increasing import (see especially Chayes and Chayes 1995).

Changing actors' interests and identities

The rationalist approach to regimes usually (but not always) takes actors' interests as given and exogenous to the process of interaction with other parties to the regime. A broad range of arguments from constructivist and cognitivist approaches suggests, however, that regimes can also change actors' conceptions of their interests and even their identity. Again, regimes can have an impact on interests and identities in multiple ways:

Knowledge creation and diffusion

Regimes can assist in the diffusion and even the creation of knowledge relevant to problem-solving in the issue areas they govern. To the extent that interaction within the institutions of the regime generates consensus about the optimal approach to problems, parties may change their minds not only about the best means for pursuing their original goals but also about the definition of the goals themselves. If parties redefine their goals in the context of new consensual knowledge, they will, in Nye's terminology, have engaged in complex learning (1987: 380).[12] New knowledge may help change conceptions of what behaviour is legitimate.

New transnational alliances

Frequent interaction with officials from other governments and with representatives of non-government parties to the regime can lead to the formation of new transnational alliances. Such links can serve as transmission belts to national governments for new knowledge generated within the regime. Moreover, transnational alliances may help strengthen pro-cooperation elements within national bureaucracies (Keohane and Nye 1972).

The formation of the regime may also provide new opportunities for transnational interaction among societal interests and a new focal point for their lobbying. The establishment of new transnational lobbying groups may in turn help to transform domestic identities.[13]

New organizations

New organizations may be established as part of a regime that are able to play a leadership role through policy entrepreneurship. They may succeed in placing new ideas on the agenda, in formulating and promoting new policy options, in transmitting knowledge to national bureaucracies, and thus in promoting a transformation of parties' conceptions of their interests. The secretariats of international organizations collectively, and their chief executives individually, have frequently been identified as effective policy entrepreneurs (see e.g. Cox and Jacobson 1974; Haas 1990; Finnemore 1996a). Organizations may unexpectedly acquire autonomy and competence in policy-making, implementation or adjudication, developments that underline the importance of *unintended consequences* in the formation and institutionalization of regimes. A prime example is the European Court of Justice (Garrett and Weingast 1993; Stone Sweet and Sandholtz 1997; Stone Sweet and Brunell 1998).

New policy options

Patterns of cooperation within regimes may generate policy options that were not previously available. In turn, the availability of new options may cause parties to rethink their ordering of preferences.

Raising awareness

In their study of international environmental regimes, Haas and colleagues (1993) found that transnational collaboration was often hindered by some parties not sharing the concern of the most activist participants. Regimes often helped to boost the level of domestic awareness of the issues under consideration, with the possibility that the public as well as state agencies may place pressure on recalcitrant governments for action. This proposition can be generalized beyond these authors' case studies of environmental regimes. Collaborative reviews of scientific evidence generated concern among governments that previously had shown little interest in issues such as ozone depletion. Parties to the regime, especially non-government actors, also helped to create domestic interest in and awareness of the issues through their criticism of government policies. NGOs also often run effective educational campaigns that can raise public awareness. Increasing levels of concern in government circles can in turn translate into a redefinition of interests and attitudes towards collaboration.

Increasing domestic capacity

For international agreements to be implemented they have to be translated into domestic policy. States, particularly those outside the industrialized world, often lack the administrative capacity to elaborate and execute effective policy instruments to implement agreements reached in the international arena. At the 1996 WTO Ministerial Meeting in Singapore, for instance, the government of Indonesia noted that technical assistance to developing countries would be needed to ensure full implementation of the Uruguay Round agreements (WTO 1996). Moreover, weak states often lack the capacity to collect the information necessary for monitoring not only the effects of their own policies and those of their partners but also domestic trends in the issue areas that the regime incorporates. As part of collaboration within a regime, weak states may receive finance or technical assistance that helps them build relevant administrative capacity. Policy conditionality may accompany such assistance. Perhaps as effective as conditionality in changing domestic attitudes, and thereby potentially policies as well, are the socialization effects arising from the training of local officials. Whether it be the IMF or environmental institutions, ample evidence exists of the power of socialization in creating pro-regime sentiments among administrators in domestic ministries (Keohane 1990; Haas et al. 1993; Chayes and Chayes 1995: 198).

Reshaping domestic institutions and procedures

Much of the behaviour of bureaucratic agencies is habit-driven, organized around particular roles, rules and norms (March and Olsen 1989; Haas 1990: 180; Crawford and Ostrom 1995). Organizations adopt standard operating procedures to 'maintain habitual compliance with the internalized norms' (Koh 1997: 2654). Human interaction reshapes such practices – albeit constrained by the way things have been done in the past. The interaction of domestic bureaucracies with other actors in the context of an international regime can induce domestic agencies to absorb new norms, which in turn are reflected in changes to their standard operating procedures.[14] Domestic law itself may change in response to the new norms that domestic agencies internalize. Not just interests but identities may also be reshaped in the process.

Changing the Domestic Political Economy Equation

The negotiation of international collaboration is a two-level game. Governments not only have to deal with their potential international partners but must also put together a domestic coalition in support of policy change. Failure of efforts at international collaboration is more often the result of 'involuntary defection' by governments – a reflection of their inability to construct a domestic pro-reform coalition – than a consequence of governments' deliberate efforts to evade their responsibilities (Putnam 1988; Putnam and Henning 1989; H. Milner 1997). Participation in international regimes may change the domestic political equation that governments face by several means:

Strengthening pro-reform forces

In international trade negotiations it would be rare for there to be no domestic losers. Economic theory suggests that the sum of individual losses will be more than offset by aggregate gains to the domestic economy, and that some of these gains can provide compensation for the losers. In the short term, however, losses are often concentrated in particular sectors and/or geographical areas whereas gains are more likely to be spread across the whole economy. In such circumstances, theories of collective action predict that losers will be easier to mobilize for political action than will the beneficiaries of trade liberalization. And studies of two-level games suggest that when the costs are concentrated and the benefits diffuse, international agreements 'are usually, though not invariably, doomed' (Evans 1993: 400).

In constructing pro-liberalization coalitions, governments need to mobilize support from groups that will benefit from free trade. Usually, these beneficiaries are the economy's major exporters. Where trade regimes contain provisions for reciprocity, they strengthen the hand of these groups and thus that of pro-liberalization forces in the economy more generally. In contrast, a process of unilateral liberalization generates no certainty for domestic groups about their future access to export markets. Reciprocity may also appease other domestic forces that are opposed in principle to their government unilaterally making 'concessions' to foreign interests. Reciprocity provisions within a regime therefore not only increase the incentives for pro-reform elements to mobilize in support of the government, but may also reduce the likelihood that others will mobilize against trade liberalization.

Enabling governments to claim their hands are tied

When governments accept specific international obligations in negotiating a regime, they are able to strengthen their bargaining position with domestic constituents by claiming that their international obligations dictate the domestic course of action they prefer – a process Putnam (1988: 447) refers to as *synergistic* linkage. A recent example was the use by the Spanish and Italian governments of their obligations under the European Monetary Union to claim, in a phrase made popular by Margaret Thatcher, that 'there is no alternative' to the policy reforms they favoured. The use of synergistic linkages in the trade sphere is common.[15] Such a strategy of linkage may be even more effective if domestic groups are afforded at least some token representation in government delegations to international talks: they 'own', or may be alleged to own, any agreements reached at the international level.

Locking in domestic reforms

The logic here is an extension of the 'hand-tying' strategy. In this instance, however, rather than governments being able to assert that international commitments have constrained the range of policy options available for the future, the claim is that previously implemented policies are not reversible. A classic example of this phenomenon is the 'binding' of tariffs within the GATT/WTO, a practice whereby governments make a commitment not to raise tariffs beyond a specific level.[16]

The impact of international regimes does not occur independently in each of these three areas. A reduction in transactions costs, increasing the interests of parties in cooperating with one another, may in turn spill over into the parties' redefining their interests. Similarly, a change in the domestic political economy equation in one party will affect others' estimates of the likelihood that this party will behave opportunistically. The likely interaction among the various effects of regimes opens the possibility of a virtuous circle developing in which developments favouring collaboration reinforce one another. Equally, it opens the possibility that a vicious circle of unravelling will occur if parties lose confidence in one another's capacity or commitment to implement their obligations.

The Effectiveness of International Regimes: Why Do States Comply?

A first step in addressing the effectiveness of any international regime is to pose the question of why states comply with their international commitments. One approach is to view compliance as largely a managerial problem. This school, of which Oran Young and Abram Chayes and Antonia Handler Chayes are leading representatives (Young 1979, 1989; Chayes and Chayes 1993, 1995), views non-compliance as a problem to be resolved through negotiation rather than a violation that warrants the application of sanctions. Non-compliance arises for the most part not from wilful opportunism; rather, states fail to meet the obligations they have assumed because of ambiguities in the obligations themselves, limitations in states' domestic capacities, and/or because of the time-lag between treaty negotiation and the execution of the domestic social or economic changes necessary for its implementation, or for treaty provisions to be adapted to changing circumstances (Chayes and Chayes 1993: 187–97).

From this perspective, in an interdependent world in which states are frequently interacting in seeking joint solutions to problems, the problem of non-compliance is best resolved through communication among the parties. Measures such as improving dispute resolution procedures and providing assistance to improve state capacities can enhance prospects for compliance. Because states in a situation of complex interdependence will be concerned with their reputations, measures to improve the monitoring of behaviours can also improve the prospects for compliance. Sanctions, on the other hand, will seldom be successful in changing states' behaviour in the desired direction. Besides the host of reasons the literature provides for doubting the efficacy of economic sanctions (Hufbauer et al. 1985; Miyagawa 1992; Cortright and Lopez 1995), sanctions are simply inappropriate where non-compliance has not been a deliberate choice by decision-makers. Moreover, sanctions may poison the relationship between parties to such an extent that they jeopardize cooperation in other areas concurrently and in the future.

Other commentators have criticized the managerial approach for its failure to acknowledge that enforcement is required to complement other measures aimed at increasing the capacity and propensity of states to meet their international obligations. Critics assert that the managerial model, in making an analogy with municipal law, fails to take into account the shadow of sanctions that hangs over discourse among parties to domestic contracts (Koh 1997: 2639). Downs and colleagues

(1996) provide the most complete discussion of the implications for international regimes. They suggest that the generally good record of states' compliance with their international obligations owes much to utilitarian considerations. International treaties rarely require states to engage in behaviours that are contrary to their perceived short-term interests. Consequently, violations of treaty provisions are rare. On the other hand, states avoid agreements that require 'deep' cooperation, that is, compliance with provisions that would adversely affect their perceived short-term interests.

For deeper cooperation to occur, regimes have to be endowed with enforcement mechanisms. They acknowledge, however, that enforcement will not always be practicable. Sanctions are seldom acceptable or effective. Contracting parties often build ambiguity into regime provisions to allow for deliberate defection by states, an acknowledgement that the costs of enforcement would outweigh the potential benefits (see also Downs and Rocke 1995). Their conclusion, therefore, is a pessimistic one: enforcement and sanctions may be essential if deeper integration is to occur and the reluctance of states to act against their perceived short-term economic or political interests is to be overcome. But such measures are seldom practicable in international regimes.[17]

To what extent does the experience of cooperation in the global trade regime lend support to these competing interpretations of compliance? On the one hand, substantial progress has occurred in lowering tariff barriers to trade in manufactured products. Among industrialized economies, GATT's monitoring of the policies of contracting parties made a significant contribution to increased transparency, and helped to reduce fears that trading partners were cheating on their obligations. Among less developed economies, pro-liberalization ideas and the influence of socialization effects have been important in changing states' conceptions of the relative efficacy of alternative policies, in particular in convincing them of the limited utility of strategies of import substitution and, instead, of the desirability of export-oriented development.

On the other hand, the various escape clauses of the trade regime reflected the 'embedded liberalism' compromise on which collaboration rested. Moreover, as tariffs were lowered, states came to depend on ever more ingenious concoctions of non-tariff measures to maintain protection of 'sensitive' sectors. These measures ensured that cooperation in international trade was often 'shallow' in the terminology of Downs and colleagues. Moreover, dispute settlement mechanisms, seen by Chayes and Chayes as an important element in inducing compliance, largely fell into disuse in GATT after the mid-1970s because contracting parties used their veto power to preclude judgements that may have been contrary to their interests. Nor was there any indication that the parties had progressed towards a more comprehensive interpretation of the norms of the regime. If anything, by the mid-1980s the agreed understanding of the nature of the embedded liberalism compromise had increasingly unravelled. The primary cause was the disputes between the European Community and especially the United States on the one hand, and Northeast Asian economies on the other, over whether domestic economic structures might legitimately be scrutinized within the GATT/WTO as potential barriers to international trade. The nature of the embedded liberalism compromise was also increasingly contested in relation to agriculture, where European and Northeast Asian states asserted that agriculture's 'multifunctional' character should continue to exempt production in that sector from the rules that apply to trade in other goods. By the middle of the 1980s, the trade regime appeared to be in considerable disarray, weakened by parties' creative efforts to circumvent its principles and by the ineffectiveness of its DSMs. Pronouncements of GATT's imminent death became commonplace.

The revival of the global trade regime through its rebirth as the WTO rested on measures to increase transparency through changes to reporting and monitoring procedures, and on significant improvements in the regime's DSMs. Strengthening the enforcement procedures associated with the DSMs also enhanced the prospects for compliance.[18] Deeper integration, in the sense of cooperation among countries in areas where short-term domestic economic and political interests may have been jeopardized, for instance in reducing agricultural protection or subsidies to specific industrial sectors, depended to a considerable extent not only on enhanced DSMs but also on the probability that opportunistic behaviour would attract centrally legitimized sanctions. The strengthening of the DSMs undoubtedly led to an anticipatory adjustment of behaviours on the part of governments. Meanwhile the existence of improved mechanisms in turn affected the domestic political economy equation.

The recent history of the global trade regime therefore appears to support the argument of Downs and colleagues that deeper integration requires enhanced monitoring and enforcement capabilities. In trade regimes it is difficult to escape the premise that cooperation is a mixed-motive game in which parties often have powerful domestic reasons for defection. Monitoring of behaviour and the possibility that violations of the rules may be punished by sanctions cannot guarantee that conflicting interests will always be successfully reconciled. In some instances, however, they can induce governments to comply with measures they regard as contrary to their short-term (political or economic) interests.

APEC from the Perspective of Regime Theories

An obvious danger in the evaluation of any real-world institution is to compare it with what would essentially be a caricature – an ideal-typical international regime. All real-world international agreements contain various ambiguities. Some of these result from (often intentional) lack of specificity in a treaty's terminology. Others arise because circumstances may change in a direction that the original drafters of the agreement failed to anticipate. As Chayes and Chayes (1995: 123) note, international law is largely an 'interpretive practice' concerned with 'discursive elaboration'. The provisions of GATT (Article XXIV) relating to the conditions under which exemptions from the MFN requirement are granted to regional agreements provide an excellent example of ambiguous terminology in a trade treaty. Article XXIV allows an exemption from the non-discrimination requirement of Article I provided that the regional agreement applies to 'substantially all' trade between the parties and that 'on average' the agreement does not raise barriers to third country trade. The ambiguity of these criteria allowed political considerations to dominate in contracting parties' determinations of whether the provisions of regional agreements actually complied with the Article.

Indeed, if the GATT/WTO is an appropriate real-world yardstick against which other trade regimes should be compared, the thresholds for both specificity and compliance with treaty provisions are far lower than if the comparison is with an ideal-typical regime. Not only does considerable ambiguity exist in the GATT/WTO provisions, in many cases an ambiguity deliberately built into the treaty to accommodate the divergent preferences of contracting parties, but the record of compliance with treaty provisions is far from perfect. Moreover, contracting parties frequently preferred to ignore instances of non-compliance rather than risk alienating their partners by trying to enforce compliance. From the mid-1970s, they seldom allowed the regime's DSMs, the most significant centralized element for interpretation and enforcement of obligations, to play any significant role. Regional trade regimes, including that of the European Union, have for many years manifested a similar mixture of ambiguous provisions and far from perfect compliance.

A second danger in evaluating a regime is premature dismissal – writing off a regime because it fails to deliver significant outcomes in its initial years of operation. In their survey of international environmental regimes, for instance, Haas and colleagues (1993: 413) note that most environmental institutions were initially considered deep disappointments. However, they continue, 'our studies show that there is cause for optimism even following inauspicious starts, and that effective institutions seize opportunities to expand the consequences of their activity'. At the time of writing, APEC is only just over a decade old. The risk of premature dismissal is an obvious one – but one that has to be balanced against the negative assessments of observers and participants alike that originate in the frustration of (what were often exaggerated) expectations.[19]

Supporters of APEC can reasonably claim that it has on several dimensions made significant progress from the initial Canberra meeting, which was little more than an agreement to talk further on how best to advance regional economic collaboration in the future. To recapitulate briefly, these include an expansion of membership, institutionalization (with the addition of a secretariat, annual leaders' meetings, and meetings of finance ministers) and goal definition.

Despite these developments in APEC, and the cautions about the criteria by which APEC should be judged, considerable weaknesses are evident in APEC that limit its capacity to overcome collective action problems.

Ambiguities

Ambiguities are present in all international agreements and treaties. But APEC compounds ambiguities over how its goals might best be realized with further ambiguities over what the goals themselves should be.

Cooperation in APEC rests on three 'pillars': the liberalization of trade and investment, the facilitation of trade, and economic and technical cooperation. Among the member economies, tension has always existed over which of the three pillars should receive priority. The original formulation of APEC's objectives, as discussed in Chapter 2, was based on long-standing proposals for an Organization for Pacific Trade and Development, to be modelled on the OECD. In this model, the emphasis was on trade facilitation and on economic and technical cooperation. This model held through the initial ministerial meetings – Nobutoshi Akao (1995: 170) commented that the 1991 Seoul Declaration envisioned APEC as an 'Asia-Pacific version of the OECD'. As discussed in Chapter 3, however, the appointment of the Eminent Persons Group provided impetus for the push from Washington and Canberra for trade liberalization to become the principal focus of the group's activities from the 1994 Bogor Leaders' Meeting to the 1998 Kuala Lumpur meeting.

For some governments, of which the most vocal has been Malaysia (but others undoubtedly have been hiding behind its outspokenness), the priority given to trade liberalization has been a betrayal of APEC's original purposes. Moreover, the change in APEC's agenda also corrupted the institution's previously agreed modus operandi. For other members, this change in emphasis and process was welcome. The chair of the EPG, Fred Bergsten (1994: 21), noted enthusiastically that 'leaders in Seattle began the process of converting APEC from a purely consultative body into a substantive international institution'. But it was precisely this transformation that was worrying to many East Asian governments. Rafidah Aziz, the Malaysian Minister for Trade and Industry, commented in March 1994 that 'APEC is slowly turning out to be what it wasn't supposed to be, meaning that APEC was constituted as a loose consultative forum'.[20] Rather than a body that would assist in the concertation of unilaterally determined trade policies, APEC was increasingly being turned into a forum for trade *negotiations*.[21] The Japanese ambassador to the international organizations in Vienna, Nobutoshi Akao, evidently with the behaviour of the United States in mind, warned that 'we must beware lest a coercive bilateralism becomes a coercive regionalism' (Akao 1995: 173). To the extent that some members saw the new emphasis on trade liberalization as an external imposition, APEC's 'procedural legitimacy' (in Franck's terms) was undermined.

That tensions should exist among member states over the purposes and operating procedures of a new institution is not surprising, and they are no less common in even the most advanced of regional organizations, the European Union, more than forty years after its foundation. Indeed, such tensions might offer opportunities for creative initiatives by policy entrepreneurs. And rather than being a drawback, that APEC should have several dimensions to its cooperative activities might provide scope for issue linkages and trade-offs of concessions among the various parties. Yet little evidence exists that APEC member economies have moved forward in reaching a common understanding on the purposes of the organization, or in achieving linkages among its various objectives. And policy entrepreneurship has been notably lacking since the demise of the EPG.

To address the issue of linkage first: most Asian members have accorded highest priority to APEC's activities in the area of economic and technical cooperation. The less developed economies view such cooperation in terms of 'compensation' for the 'concessions' they have agreed to make in trade liberalization. As noted in the previous chapter, the Western members of APEC have refused to acknowledge the legitimacy of a link between trade and aid grounded in notions of 'compensation'. To the extent that 'Western' governments have been willing to provide economic and technical assistance in APEC, it has been directed overwhelmingly at improving the capacity of the governments of the less developed member economies to implement liberalization and facilitation measures, and to monitor developments in the various sectors that are covered by APEC's working groups. Such assistance may be more limited in scope and quantity than the less developed economies hoped for. It is nonetheless very much in accord with one of the contributions discussed above that international regimes can make to the resolution of collective action problems – capacity-building.

More serious for APEC's contribution to resolving collective action problems are the continuing ambiguities on the question of the commitments that member economies have made, particularly on trade liberalization, the subject to which APEC gave greatest attention in the mid-1990s. But it is one on which it has been possible to preserve the unity of the institution only by deliberately maintaining sufficient ambiguity so that individual governments have been able unilaterally to interpret their obligations.

The commitment made by economic leaders at the Bogor meeting in 1994 appears relatively straightforward:

> We further agree to announce our commitment to complete the achievement of our goal of free and open trade and investment in the Asia-Pacific no later than the year 2020. The pace of implementation will take into account differing levels of economic development among APEC economies, with the industrialized economies achieving the goal of free and open trade and investment no later than the year 2010 and developing economies no later than the year 2020. (APEC 1994b, paragraph 6)[22]

It was evident within a few months, however, that member economies disagreed in their interpretation of their obligations under the Bogor Declaration, especially on the question of how much flexibility was afforded by the clause stating that the pace of implementation would vary according to level of economic development. In a context in which some East Asian economies were seeking to exempt some sectors, especially agriculture, from the liberalization process, the next leaders' meeting attempted to provide greater specificity to the commitment (in the Osaka Action Agenda). Part One of the agenda established a set of 'General Principles' for the 'entire APEC liberalization and facilitation process':

> 1. COMPREHENSIVENESS: The APEC liberalization and facilitation process will be comprehensive, addressing all impediments to achieving the long-term goal of free and open trade and investment.
> 2. WTO-CONSISTENCY: The liberalization and facilitation measures undertaken in the context of the APEC Action Agenda will be WTO-consistent.
> 3. COMPARABILITY: APEC economies will endeavor to ensure the overall comparability of their trade and investment liberalization and facilitation, taking into account the general level of liberalization and facilitation already achieved by each APEC economy.
> 4. NON-DISCRIMINATION: APEC economies will apply or endeavor to apply the principle of non-discrimination between and among them in the process of liberalization and facilitation of trade and investment. The outcome of trade and investment liberalization in the Asia-Pacific region will be the actual reduction of barriers not only among APEC economies but also between APEC economies and non-APEC economies.
> 5. TRANSPARENCY: Each APEC economy will ensure transparency of its respective laws, regulations and administrative procedures which affect the flow of goods, services and capital among APEC economies in order to create and maintain an open and predictable trade and investment environment in the Asia-Pacific region.
> 6. STANDSTILL: Each APEC economy will endeavor to refrain from using measures which would have the effect of increasing levels of protection, thereby ensuring a steady and progressive trade and investment liberalization and facilitation process.

> 7. SIMULTANEOUS START, CONTINUOUS PROCESS AND DIFFERENTIATED TIMETABLES: APEC economies will begin simultaneously and without delay the process of liberalization, facilitation and cooperation with each member economy contributing continuously and significantly to achieve the long-term goal of free and open trade and investment.
>
> 8. FLEXIBILITY: Considering the different levels of economic development among the APEC economies and the diverse circumstances in each economy, flexibility will be available in dealing with issues arising from such circumstances in the liberalization and facilitation process.
>
> 9. COOPERATION: Economic and technical cooperation contributing to liberalization and facilitation will be actively pursued. (APEC 1995b, Part One)

The lack of specificity in the language (e.g. 'apply or endeavor to apply', 'endeavor to refrain') of some of these provisions is by no means unusual in international agreements. More damaging to the prospect that member economies could be held accountable for specific commitments within APEC is the extent to which these various principles potentially contradict one another, and the lack of criteria by which compliance might be judged. Consider, for instance, Principle 2, 'WTO Consistency'. The Action Agenda provides no indication which of the two routes available – liberalization on a non-discriminatory basis, or an exception from MFN requirements under Article XXIV – APEC would use to qualify for WTO consistency. This ambiguity sidesteps the dispute between Washington and most other APEC economies as to whether APEC should develop as a discriminatory regional arrangement. Rather than providing a focal point around which actors' expectations and behaviours converged, APEC has failed to bring members to an agreed definition on a preferred method of trade liberalization.

Of even greater political consequence is the apparent contradiction between Principle 1, 'Comprehensiveness', and Principle 8, 'Flexibility'. The inclusion of the principle of comprehensiveness represented a victory for the 'Western' group, which opposed East Asian attempts to exclude specific sectors, most notably agriculture, from the liberalization process. Yet the provision that implementation would be 'flexible' immediately undermined the commitment to a comprehensive agreement. The Action Agenda provides no indication as to what criteria would be employed (or by what body) to determine whether flexibility was justified in any particular circumstance. If left to individual governments to determine, the obvious risk was that the 'diverse circumstances' of a national economy could be used to invoke a flexible interpretation of the liberalization imperative whenever this posed problems for economic or political reasons.

The provision for flexibility, however, is consistent with the preference of most APEC members that liberalization will occur unilaterally. APEC's contribution to the process is to promote 'concerted' unilateralism – underlined by Principle 7, with its emphasis on 'simultaneous start' and 'continuous process', and by Principle 3, 'Comparability'. To the extent that regimes assist in coordinating the actions of contracting parties, they can help overcome fears that others will 'cheat', an outcome that would leave compliers with the 'bunny's' payoff. Again, however, escape clauses immediately undermined the injunctions of the Osaka Action Agenda's principles. The simultaneous start and continuous process of Principle 7 were compromised by reference to 'differentiated timetable'. The requirement for comparability, already expressed in the weak terminology of 'endeavour to assure' was further qualified by the requirement to take into account the existing level of liberalization and facilitation achieved by the individual economy.

Moreover, no consensus exists among the member economies on the exact meaning of even the fundamental objective of the Bogor Declaration, the commitment to free and open trade and investment in the region by 2020. Some governments have taken this literally as a removal of all tariff and non-tariff barriers, and of obstacles to FDI. Others have preferred the definition originally adopted by ASEAN for its Free Trade Area, namely that intra-regional free trade will be achieved when tariffs do not exceed 5 per cent.[23]

Not only is there no consensus on the definition of the target, but none exists on the nature of the commitment that member economies have made to it. Here the ambiguities introduced by the concept of flexibility are paramount. Prime Minister Mahathir was typically outspoken following the 1995 Osaka Leaders' Meeting in asserting that Malaysia was not bound to abolish tariffs by the target date. He reinforced the argument of his government's trade minister, Rafidah Aziz, that the Osaka commitments were merely 'indicative' (*Age* 21 November 1995; *Economist* 25 November 1995: 79). Statements from other senior Asian officials in the following days indicated, however, that other countries shared Malaysia's views. 'The key word is flexibility', asserted South Korea's Deputy Foreign Minister, Ban Ki Moon. 'It allows members to voluntarily decide on the speed, extent, timing and method of implementing liberalization' (*Los Angeles Times* 17 November 1995). According to Japan's Foreign Minister, 'flexibility will be available not only with regard to the pace but also the ways, modalities and so forth of liberalization and facilitation' (Kono 1995).[24] Similar ambiguities were evident in the member economies' interpretations of their obligations under the EVSL program, discussed below.

From the perspective of the literature on international regimes, the great disadvantage of a process of trade liberalization based on a unilateralism that is qualified with multiple escape clauses is that it provides no certainty of outcome for other parties to the agreement. Even if other parties make their best endeavours to comply – and this is a very big 'if' in APEC – they may have quite a different definition of the target of free trade. This uncertainty is particularly important in undermining the effects that a trade regime might otherwise have on the domestic political economy equation.

The voluntary nature of APEC commitments to trade liberalization may seem an attractive approach if the main barrier to trade liberalization is a principled (and unified) opposition from political elites and bureaucracies. APEC's voluntary approach rests on a belief in the power of socialization: that the exposure of member governments to iterated peer pressure will lead them to conform to the norms of trade liberalization. The growing acceptance of trade liberalization by East Asian governments over the decades is testimony in part to the power of socialization of political elites in PECC and then APEC itself.

If, on the other hand, the main obstacle to liberalization lies not in a lack of belief by political elites but in the opposition of key domestic groups, a voluntary approach is disadvantageous in that it fails to provide any leverage for pro-liberalization forces against these opposition groups. In their interaction with domestic groups opposed to liberalization, governments undertaking liberalization within a 'voluntary' framework cannot claim that the agreements they have negotiated have tied their hands. Moreover, in the absence of certainty about reciprocity and thus about future access to the markets of trading partners, mobilization of the country's principal exporters, the most likely supporters of trade liberalization initiatives, will be more difficult. The ineffectiveness of APEC in addressing the domestic political economy equation has been acknowledged by even the institution's most fervent supporters, who admit that APEC is unlikely to bring trade liberalization in 'sensitive' sectors. They see this as a task to be left to the WTO (see Drysdale 1997).[25]

Moreover, the ambiguities in the commitments of APEC governments greatly complicate the task of *monitoring*, an important element in providing assurance against opportunistic behaviour by partners. Measuring progress in a liberalization process not scheduled to be completed for twenty-five years, and one, moreover, where states are not obliged to achieve interim targets by a specific date, poses obvious problems in determining compliance. Furthermore, in outlining their individual action plans (IAPs) through which the commitment to liberalization is to be implemented, member governments for the most part deliberately avoided a clear statement of the obligations they had assumed. In its assessment of the Manila Action Plan, the Pacific Economic Cooperation Council notes of the IAPs: 'It is clear that only very few economies clearly specify their intentions and include a timetable' (PECC 1996: 17). Similarly, the American economist Peter Petri (1997: 1) comments that the IAPs 'are vague on overall goals and short on specifics'. Interpreting the action plans is all the more difficult because they do not list ongoing barriers to trade, merely those that governments intend to reduce. APEC's Business Advisory Council complained in its 1999 report to APEC economic leaders that the IAPs lacked transparency, accessibility and comprehensiveness. This complaint was echoed by PECC in its 1999 evaluation of the IAPs. 'The IAPs', PECC chair Roberto Romulo asserted, 'are not very accessible and user-friendly ... The IAPs must improve transparency and provide a clear record of commitments but they don't do either very well at this stage' (PECC 1999). Similarly, for non-tariff barriers, identified by PECC as a 'critical challenge' for APEC, Soesastro (1999: 161) records that 'commitments are still expressed in relatively vague terms'.

In APEC, unilateral interpretation of the nature of commitments that governments believe they have entered into voluntarily, and the absence of a precise timetable for their realization, precludes parties from reaching a judgement on whether non-compliance has occurred. Axiomatically, the application of sanctions is simply not an option, and of course no reference to sanctions appears in any APEC document.[26]

Ambiguity has other detrimental effects on international agreements. It is likely to affect whether contracting parties view the rules of the regime as legitimate, which, as noted above, can be a significant factor in influencing their propensity for compliance. Thomas Franck (1990) sees clarity and determinateness as the first factor influencing parties' views on whether rules are legitimate. APEC's rules meet neither of these criteria. Moreover, ambiguity in the rules of a regime will diminish the possibility that reputational concerns will have a significant impact on state behaviours. Chayes and Chayes (1995: 118ff.), the champions of the view that reputational concerns are a primary factor in determining parties' compliance with the norms and rules of a regime, acknowledge that such concerns will apply only if a mutually agreed interpretation of these norms and rules has come into existence. If, as in APEC, no agreement exists on the interpretation of the rules, parties cannot be held accountable for a particular course of action. Their reputations will not suffer if they do not behave according to the prescriptions another party derives from its interpretations of the rules.

Weakly specified rules and unilateralism also preclude APEC's playing a role in governments' use of membership as a signalling device to convince potential partners of their commitment to a particular agenda. APEC does not add to the credibility of commitments or provide governments with an advantage over potential competitors for foreign investment; the most that can be said is that by participating in the institution, governments keep themselves on a par with other members.

One of the important roles that regimes often play is to enable states to arrive at mutually agreed interpretations. The weak institutions that APEC has established, however, have manifestly failed in this task to date. It is not just a matter of the presence of ambiguities in the original agreements that underlies APEC's ineffectiveness. It is also the failure of the contracting parties subsequently to reach an interpretation of the rules and norms that gives their obligations a more precise definition. Moreover, they have been unwilling to agree to institutions that could play a role in defining members' obligations. A key instance is the inability of the member economies to agree on DSMs within APEC.

The development of DSMs has been an important element in many regimes in rule interpretation and enforcement. Gourevitch (1996) identifies credible commitments to institutions that manage policy disputes as the second major source of international cooperation, supplementing cooperation that derives from a convergence of policy objectives. Within the WTO, the new DSMs adopted as part of the Uruguay Round negotiations were arguably the most significant change in the global trade regime since 1947, and a major step forward in the institutionalization of the regime. As discussed in the previous chapter, member economies failed to adopt the recommendation from the Eminent Persons Group that they should immediately develop an APEC Dispute Mediation Service. In its initial report, issued before members of the WTO had agreed to the proposed changes in DSMs, the EPG advocated that APEC should adopt the new DSM proposed in the draft final act of the Uruguay Round should the WTO fail to do so. Such an act 'would represent an extremely positive example of the "ratcheting up" effect' that APEC, as a regional institution, could have on global liberalization (APEC 1993: 39).

In its second report, however, which was issued after the WTO had adopted the reforms to its DSM, the EPG argued that an APEC dispute mechanism should still be established but 'should be crafted carefully to supplement, rather than compete with, the GATT/WTO machinery at the global level' (APEC 1994a: 16). APEC's initiative should be targeted at issues not covered by the WTO mechanisms. The EPG recognised difficulties that any dispute mediation service in APEC would face:

> First, binding arbitration requires the existence of agreed rules against which to judge compliance. Second, external review of an economy's implementation of its domestic laws requires a significant degree of comparability of those laws among the participating countries. Neither of these conditions applies as yet to any extensive degree in APEC. (APEC 1994a: 15)

Accordingly, any dispute mediation service in APEC, the EPG asserted, would have to be entirely voluntary, with disputants having to agree on the terms of reference and on the make-up of a review panel.

Despite the modest nature of these proposals, APEC members have failed to adopt them. The essential reason has been that while member economies would like to install such mechanisms to constrain the behaviour of their partners, they have been unwilling to accept similar constraints on their own behaviour. East Asian governments aspire to use such mechanisms to constrain the US resort to bilateralism.[27] Washington, on the other hand, wants any DSMs to be grounded in more clearly defined obligations of its partners under APEC. Given the ambiguities in APEC's rules, the US government has been concerned that any DSMs within APEC will have an asymmetrical effect in the constraints they impose on the behaviour of member economies. Those states with the most transparent barriers would be most vulnerable to complaints. Moreover, effective DSMs would potentially deprive Washington of recourse to bilateral actions, generally judged to have been effective in opening up East Asian economies in the last two decades (Bayard and Elliott 1994). Washington continues to prefer to rely on the DSMs of the WTO because the obligations of its trading partners are more clearly elaborated in this multilateral regime than within APEC.[28]

The absence of DSMs denies APEC an authoritative voice in *rule interpretation.* Moreover, it robs APEC of a significant role in locking in domestic reforms. As discussed in Chapter 1, the availability of DSMs in regional trade arrangements has been central to encouraging governments to abide by their agreements lest they be taken to arbitration by other member economies (or by private parties in the case of NAFTA, where such mechanisms are available to them also).

APEC's reliance on flexibility and coordinated unilateralism contrasts not only with the contractual obligations of the WTO but also with those of most other regional trade agreements. Essentially, APEC's members are left to decide for themselves what their obligations are and when they will aspire to meet them. APEC can at best rely on socialization and peer pressure to attempt to move its liberalization agenda forward. In concluding that the Osaka Action Agenda committed 'nobody to anything', the *Economist* (25 November 1995: 80) perhaps went too far in arguing that 'shame seldom bothers politicians'. The regime literature does demonstrate that in a world in which states frequently interact and depend on collaboration to achieve many of their goals, concerns about their reputation can influence their propensity to comply with regime prescriptions and proscriptions. Nonetheless, in a grouping as diverse as APEC, reputational concerns are unlikely to carry much weight in governments' minds. Accordingly, the efficacy of socialization and peer pressure will be limited.

A brief comparison of APEC with the WTO illustrates the various weaknesses of the APEC approach to trade liberalization.

APEC versus the WTO

For some of APEC's supporters, the 'constructive ambiguity' of its provisions has several advantages (e.g. Soesastro 1997a).[29] It reinforces the principles of voluntarism and unilateralism within the grouping, and

Table 4.1 Comparison of WTO and APEC regimes

WTO	APEC
Clearly specified obligations: Facilitates monitoring	*Ambiguous obligations*
Legally binding commitments: Permits retaliation and sanctions Helps resolve domestic political economy problems	*Voluntary and unilateral commitments*
Reciprocity: Reduces fear of free-riding Generates domestic political support for liberalization Mobilizes export-oriented industries Facilitates global welfare-maximizing coordinated liberalization	*Reciprocity not assured* – either within APEC or by non-members
Dispute settlement mechanisms: Inspires confidence among members that rules will be obeyed	*No mechanisms for resolving disputes*
Effective monitoring procedures: Enhances transparency	*Limited monitoring mainly through non-APEC institutions*
Non-discrimination and universal application:	*Ambiguity on open regionalism*
Reduces role of power in international economic relations Avoids inefficiencies arising from trade diversion	Disagreement whether APEC agreements should be applied on a MFN basis to all WTO members

contributes, in a region with little history of intergovernmental collaboration, to a process of building confidence in the benefits that cooperation can generate. Member economies undoubtedly have purposely built ambiguity into APEC rules because they valued the latitude such ambiguity afforded them. But ambiguity has its costs. These are evident when APEC is compared not only with other regional institutions but also with the WTO.

Table 4.1 provides a summary of the principal differences between the WTO and APEC. For many observers, the global trade regime has been the most successful of the postwar economic regimes, a performance particularly impressive when contrasted with the breakdown of international commerce in the inter-war years.

The GATT/WTO has helped to produce a virtuous circle in which a coherent economic and political doctrine has supported a changing balance of domestic economic interests in favour of liberalization. The strength of the GATT/WTO lies in its combination of flexibility and rigidity (Eichengreen and Kenen 1994). The GATT/WTO has been sufficiently flexible, especially in its escape clauses such as its safeguard provisions, to allow governments in the postwar period to undertake trade liberalization without jeopardizing domestic political and economic stability – the 'embedded liberalism' compromise noted above. Yet the rules of the trade regime were also rigid enough to provide some assurance for trading partners that governments would comply with the liberalization project save in exceptional circumstances. It is the capacity of trade agreements to reduce uncertainty that is their principal contribution to fostering international collaboration (Zacher with Sutton 1996: 219, citing Winham 1992: 21).

The WTO's success in large part stems from the following:

- Clearly specified obligations for member economies (facilitating the task of monitoring).
- Legally binding commitments (facilitating retaliation against non-compliance, and raising the possibility of the application of sanctions).
- Reciprocity, that is, the provision of an equivalent value in trade concessions (which reassures domestic constituencies and facilitates the construction of pro-liberalization coalitions).
- Effective monitoring through the trade policy review mechanism, which enhances transparency and builds confidence that others will comply with their obligations under the regime's rules.
- Non-discrimination and universal application among a majority of states in the global economy.

In contrast to the WTO, APEC is all flexibility and no rigidity. The APEC process of trade liberalization is characterized by:

- Lack of clarity of obligations, with key concepts undefined.
- Voluntary commitment to goals.
- No assurance of reciprocity among member economies (at least, that is, until 2020, assuming that by that date governments will meet their obligations and that 'free trade' is eventually defined as free trade, commonly understood). The lack of assurance regarding either simultaneous or phased reciprocity imposes significant political costs. For instance, the US administration faces the near political impossibility of selling to Congress the idea that it should remove all barriers to trade with China by 2010 while US exporters would have to wait for a further ten years before China may (or may not) reciprocate. Moreover, APEC's 'open regionalism' raises the possibility that non-members will free-ride on APEC liberalization, failing to provide reciprocity.[30]
- Ambiguity over whether the principles of 'open regionalism' will cause APEC to extend its trade liberalization to non-members on a MFN basis.

Institutions in APEC

'Intellectual leadership', 'policy entrepreneurship': these are various phrases for the creative role that institutions created in international regimes can play – both in providing a new dynamism for the regime itself and/or in transforming the interests and identities of the various parties to the regime. Cognitive and constructivist analyses of regimes have often noted how leadership provided by individuals or secretariats can play a crucial role in moving a regime well beyond the purposes for which governments originally established it. To what extent are APEC's institutions capable of playing this leadership role?

Advisory groups

As noted in the previous chapter, the APEC Eminent Persons Group, established by the fourth Ministerial Meeting in Bangkok in 1992, did play a leadership role in the first half of the 1990s, much to the discomfort of some of the member governments. Although the EPG was divided over the merits of open regionalism as opposed to the creation of a discriminatory regional grouping, significant consensus existed on the desirability of APEC member economies making explicit commitments to trade liberalization. Charged by the Bangkok Ministerial Meeting with the responsibility to 'enunciate a vision for trade in the Asia Pacific Region', the EPG did precisely that. In doing so, it transformed the APEC agenda away from the OECD model with its emphasis on harmonization of rules and procedures, and on trade facilitation, to one where trade liberalization occupied the central role. Moreover, by producing annual reports, the EPG pursued a policy of attempting to embarrass the governments of the member economies into action. The adoption of the Bogor Declaration in 1994 owed much to the EPG's efforts at moving APEC's agenda forward.

It was soon evident, however, that the annual reports of the EPG, and the high profile enjoyed by its chair, Fred Bergsten, irritated many of the member governments. Taking advantage of the Japanese government's lead role in the year of the Osaka Leaders' Meeting, East Asian governments led a successful push for the abolition of the EPG, a move that met with little resistance. With its disappearance, APEC lost the only effective leadership source independent of national governments that it enjoyed in its first decade.

In the year that the economic leaders decided to abolish the EPG, they created an alternative advisory group, the APEC Business Advisory Council (ABAC). Some have looked to ABAC to fill the leadership void left by the EPG. To date, it has not proved capable of filling this role. Several reasons account for its limited influence. The Council lacks the autonomy that the EPG enjoyed. Its members are appointed (three per economy) by the governments of the member economies – and the fate of the EPG was a warning to individuals of the risks of stepping beyond the boundaries of proposals acceptable to the member economies. With a membership of sixty-three, and a chair that rotates from year to year, ABAC is too unwieldy and diverse a body to provide effective leadership.[31]

Secretariat

Rather than advisory groups, a more common source of leadership in international regimes is their secretariats. The policy entrepreneurship of the secretariats (especially their executive directors) of international regimes figures prominently in constructivist accounts of the role that regimes can play in transforming states' identities and perceptions of their national interests. Two schools of thought exist, however, on the question of whether a centralized secretariat is necessary for a regime to be effective. Haas and colleagues (1993: 409) conclude from their study of environmental regimes that centralized secretariats are not only unnecessary but may be counter-productive in that they distract leaders from the political task of changing governments' own conceptions of their national interests. Instead, they argue that a more effective route to promoting cooperation lies through the construction of transnational networks among domestic bureaucracies. Moreover, to their argument may be added a further case for national bureaucracies to play a central role in servicing a regional organization. To the extent that national governments undertake the secretariat role for a regional organization, they may be more likely to see the programs of the organization as their own rather than as an externally imposed agenda.

In contrast to this emphasis on the potential role for national bureaucracies in servicing regimes is a second view on the importance of regime secretariats to their success. Chayes and Chayes (1995: 271) note that 'it is no coincidence that the regimes with the most impressive compliance strategies – ILO, IMF, OECD, GATT – are operated by substantial, well-staffed, and well-functioning international organizations'.

The previous chapter detailed the origins of the APEC Secretariat and the sources of its institutional weaknesses. The capacity of a secretariat to control a grouping's agenda is often regarded as a core component of its influence (see Chayes and Chayes 1995: 275ff). For APEC, the Secretariat is completely lacking in this capacity. Bergsten (1997a: 16) asserts that the APEC Secretariat 'can barely manage the logistics of the meetings; it makes no pretence of offering substantive inputs'. In APEC, the agenda is not controlled by the Secretariat but by senior officials' meetings, that is, by meetings of officials from the member economies; these meetings also determine the Secretariat's budget and the financing of other APEC initiatives.[32] With such a small staff and limited mandate, the Secretariat plays a minimal role in monitoring the behaviour of member economies.

If the Secretariat itself cannot provide leadership and effective monitoring, what of the role of PECC, to which much of the responsibility for research and analysis in APEC has been delegated? PECC has proved to be an effective cheerleader for APEC. It suffers, however, from the same handicap as the Business Advisory Council: it is not autonomous from the member governments. Indeed, PECC is in the anomalous situation of having government officials as part of its membership, albeit serving in a non-official capacity. Moreover, governments often determine the non-government membership of their national PECC committees. For instance, membership of AUSPECC, the Australian Pacific Economic Cooperation Committee, is by invitation of the Minister of Foreign Affairs and Trade. Camroux (1994) notes that Malaysian participants in regional organizations are essentially representatives of 'Malaysia Incorporated' (see also Jayasuriya 1994, on Singapore). Stuart Harris has written, 'the relatively clear line that separates government, the private sector and, indeed, the academic world in the West in not evident in the region' (1989b: 18). As far as PECC is concerned, however, the distinctions between the three groups, especially between academics and government, may not be conspicuous even in its Western members. PECC is too close to governments to play a significant independent leadership role in APEC. The problems that the lack of autonomy of PECC poses for its monitoring capacity are discussed below.

Summitry

With advisory bodies and the Secretariat confined to such limited roles, much of the responsibility for leadership in APEC has fallen on the shoulders of governments themselves. In this context, the introduction of APEC 'summits' – the economic leaders' meetings – in 1993 proved to be an important development. For one leading constructivist writer, Alexander Wendt (1994: 391), summits can play an important role in changing ideas about identity and collective action. They may thus be of greater significance for their symbolic purposes than for any substantive outcomes.

In fact APEC leaders' meetings have had both symbolic and substantive outcomes. The meetings were the first to bring together the heads of state of the countries of East Asia, Oceania, and North America. Symbolically, the annual meetings have focused attention on the Asia-Pacific *as a region*, arguably of particular import in Washington given the range of foreign policy issues competing for attention there. The leaders' meetings push APEC higher up the political agenda than would otherwise be the case. Although APEC may still not be a household word, the meetings have also increased public awareness both of the organization and of the emphasis it gives to trade liberalization. And they have had substantive outcomes. Summits have proved important at APEC in breaking logjams; leaders have had the authority to make decisions that their officials had shunned (a capacity particularly important in, but by no means exclusive to, the hierarchical and patrimonial regimes of many of the East Asian members). Australia's former Prime Minister, Paul Keating (2000: 102), suggested that without the leaders' meetings (which he had originally proposed in 1992), APEC would go nowhere: 'Left to its own devices the official machinery of APEC – the APEC Senior Officials' Meeting – would not move beyond agreements based on the lowest common denominator'.

The importance of summits in APEC was reinforced by its borrowing the practice of PECC of rotating meetings among its member economies (with alternate summits, by agreement at the initial Canberra Ministerial Meeting, being held in an ASEAN member state). Here the logic is that each summit will give the institution new impetus because the host government will feel obliged to take initiatives to ensure that the summit is a success or else risk a loss of face. Certainly this logic seemed to work with the second of the leaders' meetings when President Soeharto of Indonesia unexpectedly seized the initiative in pushing for a commitment to the freeing of trade and investment in the region. But subsequent summits failed to generate a similar 'bounce'. The Japanese, Philippine and Canadian governments proved either unwilling or incapable of generating a new leap forward for the organization. This is scarcely surprising. Other organizations, like the Group of 7, also rotate their summits among member states with no expectation that the responsibility of the host is to do much more than to get the logistics right. Once the rotation of summits becomes routinized, the practice in itself is unlikely to provide any significant momentum for an intergovernmental grouping.

Hadi Soesastro has suggested that 'in accordance with the nature of the APEC process in general, each year it will need heroes' (1998a: 16). In its formative years, there were the makings of APEC's own pantheon: President Soeharto for steering the group towards adoption of the EPG's recommendations on setting a deadline for free trade, Bill Clinton for taking up Paul Keating's suggestion of staging a leaders' meeting, and so on. In its second five-year period, however, no charismatic individuals have stepped forward to play a heroic role. None of APEC's institutions or advisory groups is well placed to provide leadership. APEC has become routinized, a process that poses risks for the organization given the lack of immediate results generated by a liberalization process that has a time-frame of twenty-five years.

Information exchange and monitoring

For many observers, the main contribution that international regimes make to overcoming collaboration problems is through the greater assurance they give participants by increasing the transparency of partners' behaviour. As APEC numbers have grown, and the diversity of the economies of its member (including currently and formerly centrally planned) economies, so the monitoring task might have been expected to take on even more importance.[33] The objective of increasing transparency is an important component of one of APEC's three pillars: trade facilitation.

One of APEC's most important contributions to regional economic collaboration has been to increase the exchange of information among member states through the activities of its various working groups. One Australian business representative has testified to the significance of this information exchange:

> For a number of countries, just being required to participate in APEC and produce the chapters for those guidebooks has been useful because for business it has made that information, if nothing else, available and transparent. A lot of countries have held that intellectual capital within their governments, within their bureaucracies, but business has either never been able to get at it or been given various interpretations of what it is from time to time. (Davis 1997: 31)

In the important area of trade liberalization, however, APEC's efforts at increasing transparency and monitoring have had mixed results. One of the principal initiatives of the APEC Secretariat was the establishment of an on-line tariff database for all APEC economies (http://www.apectariff.org/). The effort has been applauded but the results have received less enthusiastic endorsement. Two main problems currently afflict the tariff database. First, it is not comprehensive. Two founding members, Malaysia and Thailand, initially failed to provide data to the Secretariat (and two recent members, Russia and Vietnam, had yet to provide the requested data by the end of 2000). Second, comparable data in machine-downloadable format is available for only a small subset of economies (Australia, Canada, Indonesia, Mexico, Taiwan and the United States). Comparison across countries remains a labour-intensive and time-consuming affair. With the current gaps and imperfections, the utility of the database to governments or business is limited. As noted above, the IAPs that countries have filed also lack transparency and comprehensiveness; moreover they were not in compatible formats.

The task of monitoring compliance with the APEC goal of free trade is complicated by the ambiguities of the commitments and by the lengthy timetable for achievement of the stated goals. APEC leaders have entrusted PECC with the main responsibility for research and for much of the evaluative activities it has commissioned. Here a significant constraining factor is PECC's ambivalent relationship with governments. Essentially, PECC's capacity to monitor APEC's performance is limited by what governments authorize it to do. Consider, for instance, the major study of non-tariff barriers that PECC undertook at APEC's request in 1995. This exercise illustrated not only the multitude of data problems that characterize this area but also the extreme reluctance of governments to provide information on trade restrictions and to allow its publication. Because of government sensitivities, the report's terms of reference stated explicitly that it was not to 'focus on specific economies' (PECC 1995, Appendix A: 123). Members placed a similar prohibition on publishing data on individual economies when APEC commissioned PECC to conduct a study of the IAPs.

PECC's capacity to embarrass governments through its monitoring of behaviour is constrained both by the participation of government officials in national delegations and by the limitations that APEC imposes on the scope of the studies it commissions from PECC. Moreover, the overlap of participants between PECC and APEC itself leaves PECC in an ambiguous situation, and its participants torn between playing the role of cheerleader and that of impartial monitor.

Despite APEC's goal of increasing transparency on trade issues, the institution itself is far from being a model of transparency. The first executive director of APEC (Ambassador William Bodde [1997: 222]) notes that the obsession with secrecy within APEC is such that most of its documents are not made public. Even information about the grouping's budget has been treated as confidential. The grouping has failed to make public the assessments by senior officials of the progress individual members have made in the implementation of the trade liberalization agenda.

Engagement with NGOs

Commentators have noted the important role that NGOs have played in the implementation of regimes, particularly in the environmental area. Chayes and Chayes, for instance, argue that 'Nongovernmental organizations perform parallel and supplementary functions at almost every step of the strategy for regime management we have begun to identify ... In a real sense, they supply the personnel and resources for managing compliance that states have become increasingly reluctant to provide to international organizations' (1995: 251).

Haas (1998: 25) records that Greenpeace International attempts to monitor national compliance with many environmental treaties, while the Natural Resources Defense Council collects data on compliance with the UN Framework Convention on Climate Change. The World Conservation Union and Greenpeace also monitor compliance with various species conservation treaties.

APEC has not benefited to any significant extent from monitoring activities undertaken by NGOs. To date, APEC has not sought to engage systematically with these organizations, save those representing business. APEC's list of official observers is confined to the ASEAN Secretariat, the South Pacific Forum, and PECC.[34] Of these, only PECC is not an intergovernmental organization.

Individuals who are not government officials have participated in APEC working groups and have been members of government delegations. For the most part, however, the relationship between APEC and NGOs has been adversarial. Rather than being constructive critics included within APEC deliberations, most NGOs have been opposed in principle to the APEC agenda. They have viewed free trade as antithetical to their own agendas of promoting human rights and environmental objectives. The frequent statements of governments that 'APEC is all about business' have done little to assuage NGOs' fears.

Neither has business sponsorship of APEC leaders' meetings assuaged these fears. Given their exclusion from the official meetings, some NGOs have attempted to stage 'alternative' summits on several occasions, with 135 representatives from twenty-two countries present in Kyoto in 1995.[35] Protests at APEC leaders' meetings, most notably those surrounding the meeting in Vancouver 1997, were dress rehearsals for the demonstrations that disrupted the Seattle Ministerial Meeting of the WTO in December 1999 and reinforced APEC's image as an institution failing to engage with civil society.[36] The lack of tolerance of many East Asian governments for criticisms, even of a constructive nature, from societal actors is likely to ensure that NGOs remain excluded from playing a role in APEC for the foreseeable future. Moreover, governments' sensitivities on many issues of concern to NGOs, such as labour standards, have prevented such issues from being included on the APEC agenda (see e.g. Bowles 1997).[37]

APEC's lack of interaction with NGOs is symptomatic of a broader failure to engage the public. The US economist Lawrence Krause (1997: 243), a longtime member of the PAFTAD community, has commented that 'APEC has done a disastrous job of making itself understood'. It has failed to promote a wider sense of community in the region: 'societal exchanges at different levels have not been promoted, and even informal APEC-wide parliamentary gatherings have yet to be suggested'.

APEC's principal efforts at engaging with NGOs have been directed towards the business community. The most comprehensive statement of the centrality of business in APEC's agenda was made by US Under-Secretary of State Joan Spero (1995):

> APEC also has a customer. APEC is not for governments. It is for business. Through APEC, we aim to get governments out of the way, opening the way for business to do business. It is our goal to make APEC the most user friendly forum in the world. That is why business participates in APEC's working groups. That is why APEC established a business advisory group – the Pacific Business Forum – to advise APEC leaders on business priorities and provide a vision for APEC's future. And that is why increasing the role for the private sector in APEC is a key objective for this year's meetings in Japan.

APEC, however, has even failed to attract much interest from its core constituency. In Australia, for instance, government officials and Australian members of the APEC Business Advisory Council informed a parliamentary committee of inquiry that business had responded apathetically to invitations to forums intended to explain the relevance of APEC to the business community. A senior official of the Australian Customs Service told the committee that only twenty out of 350 companies invited actually participated in a government-sponsored meeting on APEC. He continued: 'A group of our clients has a very good knowledge of what is going on [in APEC] ... There is probably a much larger element of companies exporting into the region that do not choose to have that understanding'.[38] My discussions with business representatives and officials in other APEC member economies indicate that the Australian experience on this issue is by no means unusual.

Despite the message from governments that 'APEC is all about business', business perceives APEC as being 'all about governments'. With few exceptions, businesspeople have yet to be convinced that APEC adds value – and warrants an investment of their time or resources. So negative were business perceptions of the lack of concrete outcomes from the grouping's extensive deliberations that the chairman of PBEC was quoted in 1999 as calling for APEC's abolition.

APEC remains the domain of bureaucrats. Such exclusiveness has obvious negative implications for the impact that APEC has had on members' conceptions of their identity.

APEC, Identities and Interests

The concept of 'Asia-Pacific' was not in the international relations lexicon two decades ago. APEC has played an important role in popularizing this new identity, one previously largely confined to participants in the PAFTAD and PECC processes. By fostering a trans-Pacific community,

APEC played a significant role both symbolically and practically in providing an alternative basis for organization to one built on a narrower East Asian definition.

The material interests of East Asian economies, as discussed in Chapter 2, clearly disinclined them in the 1980s against the construction of a closed East Asian trading bloc. Antagonism towards US trade policies, however, coupled with irritation at the development of regional groupings elsewhere, had provided a potentially fertile terrain for the construction of an 'Asian' (or Western Pacific) rather than an 'Asian-Pacific' identity. Such possibilities were foreshadowed both in Australian Prime Minister Hawke's exclusion of the North American economies from his original proposal for APEC, and in Malaysian Prime Minister Mahathir's December 1990 proposal for the establishment of an East Asian Economic Group. At the time, Mahathir did not specify the economies eligible for inclusion in the proposed grouping but it was clear that his proposed grouping would be confined to 'Asians', that is, he intended to exclude not only the Americas but also Oceania.

The institutionalization of APEC, coupled with pressure from the US government, succeeded in frustrating Mahathir's proposal in the early 1990s. Moreover, the idea of an open trans-Pacific region infused with a global outlook such as APEC represented was a counterpoint to the increasingly strident assertion of Asian values, which at least until the financial crises of 1997 were argued by some proponents to produce not merely social but also economic outcomes superior to those associated with Western culture (see Mahbubani 1992, 1993; Muzaffar 1993; Freeman 1996; Rodan 1996; Mauzy 1997).

If APEC won the initial battle in constructing regional identities, the war is far from over – and by the end of APEC's first decade appeared to be turning against APEC. Indeed, in at least one way, the evolution of APEC has arguably had the unintended consequence of weakening trans-Pacific loyalties. The efforts of the United States and other 'Western' member economies to enshrine trade liberalization as APEC's principal objective, in a manner that apparently gave little regard to Asian concerns about consensual approaches, may have encouraged support for an exclusively Asian institution. Such an organization has gradually come into existence, albeit currently in a loosely institutionalized format. The establishment of the Asia–Europe Meeting in 1996 brought into being the East Asian Economic Group in another guise – the Asian component of the meeting. In APEC itself, the East Asian Economic Caucus has become more prominent at the leaders' meetings. The extension of APEC's membership to twenty-one economies, and especially the accession of Russia, increased APEC's heterogeneity, a development that in itself made an East Asian grouping more attractive to its potential members (discussed further in Chapter 5). The 1997–98 financial crises, and the involvement of the IMF and Western governments in promoting what was often unwelcome economic liberalization and the dismantling of the previous framework for relations between the state and business, encouraged greater collaboration among Asian governments on economic matters. This collaboration has been institutionalized in the 'ASEAN Plus Three' meetings, discussions between the ten ASEAN member states plus China, Japan and Korea, that follow ASEAN summits. In 1999, for the first time this meeting occurred at head of state level.

APEC has undoubtedly increased public consciousness of the Asia-Pacific as a region and contributed to raising and sustaining trade liberalization to the top of many political agendas. Yet APEC's role again is somewhat of a two-edged sword. The debate on trade liberalization in some economies at certain times was couched in terms of the necessity of opening markets to compete more effectively, especially in an era of very mobile foreign capital. But such debates are easily transformed into a preoccupation with identifying the inadequacies of the policies of trading partners, and a focus on their failures to pursue comparable liberalization to that being implemented domestically. The outcome can be an increasingly mercantilist outlook that rebounds to APEC's disadvantage, particularly if it leads to increasing doubts about the grouping's efficacy in addressing market access problems.

Two Instances of Weakness: APEC's Investment Principles and EVSL

Two episodes in APEC's first decade provide decisive evidence of the weakness of its modus operandi. The first is the negotiation and adoption of Non-Binding Investment Principles (NBIP) in 1994. The second is the program of Early Voluntary Sectoral Liberalization, negotiated between 1996 and 1998.

Non-Binding Investment Principles

APEC's 1994 adoption of principles to govern investment had particular symbolic importance. As Graham (1994: 24) noted, the negotiation of the principles was to be the first tangible action of APEC economies, an initial attempt to translate into concrete reality the grandiose principles of Asia-Pacific cooperation enunciated in previous ministerial meetings and at the first leaders' meeting in the previous year. APEC stumbled badly at this first practical hurdle. Its inability to move beyond a common denominator approach, which generated a set of investment principles variously described as 'ineffective' and 'worthless', played a significant role in Washington's loss of interest in the grouping. Moreover, the ineffectiveness of

APEC action on this issue contributed to the early disillusionment of business organizations in Western economies about APEC's prospects.

Foreign direct investment had been at the heart of the economic transformation process in many East Asian economies. As discussed in Chapter 2, the substantial increase in FDI flows into Southeast Asia and China in the 1980s had been largely responsible for their success in moving to export-oriented manufacturing. Although many of the economies in the region had liberalized their inward FDI regimes, and most had entered into bilateral investment agreements with major partners, in many East Asian countries foreign investors still faced an uncertain legal framework. In some countries, notably Singapore, foreign investors received more generous treatment than that afforded local investors. Elsewhere, however, treatment of foreign investors was sometimes arbitrary and often lacking in transparency.[39] In the event of disputes, few countries in the region allowed foreign investors recourse to mechanisms beyond local courts. The absence of common investment principles across the region also potentially disadvantaged host countries: with competition for FDI intensifying in the early 1990s, foreign investors had the opportunity to play governments off against one another in shopping around for the best package of incentives.

An APEC Investment Code appeared to offer an opportunity to resolve some of these problems while avoiding the transactions costs involved in negotiating bilateral agreements (well over a hundred of these would have been required between the then membership of APEC). Proposals for an APEC investment code originated in PECC in a paper prepared by the American economist Stephen Guisinger (1991; see also Guisinger 1993; Lloyd 1995; Soesastro 1995b). PECC did not endorse the proposed investment code but the EPG picked up the idea and promoted it in its first report. The issue thus found its way onto APEC's agenda, becoming one of the first responsibilities of the newly established Committee on Trade and Investment. Officials developed the proposal throughout 1994, the debate coming to a head at that year's Ministerial Meeting in Jakarta.

The Eminent Persons Group (APEC 1993: 38) had recommended that APEC adopt an investment code that embraced four fundamental principles: transparency, non-discrimination, right of establishment, and national treatment. The code, the EPG suggested, should also provide assurances about the free transfer of funds for investors, about compensation in the event of nationalization, and about access to commercial arbitration to resolve disputes. Governments should refrain from imposing new performance requirements or investment incentives, and seek to roll back those currently in effect. The code, the EPG suggested, 'should probably begin' as a voluntary agreement but member economies should subsequently consider movement to a binding agreement.

While officials were able to reach agreement on the general areas that an investment code would cover – national treatment, transparency, and right of establishment – they disagreed on the extent of obligations that the code would impose on member economies. That the code at least initially would have to be non-binding was not a matter of great contention. What was controversial was the demand by many Asian governments, not content with having ensured that the adoption of all provisions of the code was not obligatory, that its provisions be further watered down through the use of terminology that lacked specificity. Rather than an injunction against certain prescriptions, such as mandatory performance requirements, the principles stated merely that these should be 'minimized' (see Appendix 3: APEC Non-Binding Investment Principles). Moreover, government observation of the principles would be subject to 'exceptions as provided for in domestic laws, regulations and policies'. The principles offered multiple loopholes for any government intent on circumventing their provisions.

The principles were substantially weaker than the recommendations of the EPG. Indeed, in its final report, the EPG issued a stinging criticism of the principles. In a detailed assessment, it found that half of them not only fell short of best international standards but also of what was required 'to provide an adequate investment environment'. The provisions deemed inadequate were those pertaining to the transfer of funds, capital movements, national treatment (including right of establishment), performance requirements, and investment incentives.

For the transfer of funds, the APEC principle provided only that member economies would 'further liberalize' towards the goal of free and prompt transfer of funds, a wording the EPG perceived as falling short of standards established in other international agreements, such as in the OECD Code on the Liberalization of Capital Movements, and in NAFTA. On capital movements, the relevant principle used the word 'minimize' but failed to specify the criteria against which to evaluate governments' performances. The EPG judged that the 'current language would allow almost any such barrier to be unchallenged'. Similar language was incorporated in the principle on performance requirements, with the consequence that no criteria were established to evaluate government behaviour. The language, the EPG asserted, was 'inconsistent with the new WTO obligations on local content and trade balancing requirements' that were banned under the Uruguay Round's Trade-Related Investment Measures (TRIMs) agreement. The NBIP wording on national treatment permitted 'exceptions provided for in domestic laws, regulations, and policies' without setting a deadline for the adoption of such exceptions. In other words, any policy a government adopted in the future would be consistent with the principle, which, consequently, the

EPG judged as falling 'well short of comparable international standards'. Finally, on investment incentives, the relevant principle provides merely that member economies will not relax existing health, safety and environmental standards – rather than obliging governments to commit themselves to tightening these standards. The EPG recommended that member economies 'make a major effort' to strengthen the NBIP (see APEC 1995a, Annex 3: 66–70, 27–8).

An acrimonious debate over the investment principles at the Ministerial Meeting in Jakarta almost prompted a US walkout. Washington had reluctantly agreed to the code being non-binding but on the understanding, as per the EPG's recommendations, that it would be an interim step towards a mandatory code, its preferred model being Chapter XI of the NAFTA. US officials argued that the principles should be no less favourable to investors than those in existing bilateral agreements, the draft Multilateral Agreement on Investment that was being negotiated by the OECD, and the TRIMs agreement within the WTO.

Asian governments on the other hand saw the principles as a direct threat to their sovereignty. They feared – reasonably – that if they agreed to inflexible principles in a non-binding agreement, Western governments would soon exert pressure to make the arrangements mandatory. Although competition for inward investment had intensified between China and ASEAN economies in the early 1990s, this in itself was insufficient to cause governments to change their attitude towards the proposed code. Foreign investment continued to flow into developing APEC economies at record levels, particularly to China, apparently unhindered by the absence of binding principles on treatment of investors (Table 4.2) (see also the data in Chia 1994).

Meanwhile, little evidence existed of any demand at this time by Asian investors for an investment code. Japanese investors had significantly expanded their investments in other Asian economies since the mid-

Table 4.2 Foreign direct investment into Asian APEC ($US m)

	1986	1987	1988	1989	1990	1991	1992
China	1 875	2 314	3 194	3 393	3 487	4 366	11 156
Indonesia	258	385	576	682	1 093	1 482	1 774
Korea	435	601	871	758	715	1 116	550
Malaysia	489	423	719	1 668	2 332	4 073	4 118
Singapore	1 710	2 386	3 655	2 773	5 263	4 395	5 635
Thailand	263	352	1 105	1 775	2 444	2 014	2 116

Source: Lloyd (1995, Table 1) citing IMF *Balance of Payments Statistics* data.

1980s, as had Chinese investors from Hong Kong and Taiwan. They were comfortable with the informal arrangements that existed in their production networks in East Asia. The demand for intergovernmental agreements came exclusively from Western firms. The views of a Korean businessman (Park 1995: 642–4) are typical of the attitude of the private sector in most Asian economies towards investment agreements:

> Attempts to achieve open investment in the region through multilateral negotiation seems [*sic*] somewhat futile ... Overseas investment decision-making is strictly the role of the private sector ... I find it extremely difficult to understand what the governments can negotiate on behalf of the private sector in promoting better international investment conditions in the region. East Asian prosperity will continue and proliferate because of the market-oriented international mechanics of industrial migration and intra-industry division of labor, not because of APEC.

A last-minute agreement following the interventions of US Secretary of State Christopher and US Trade Representative Kantor enabled leaders to endorse the Code. A face-saving compromise allowed the United States to accept the principles in return for a ministerial statement that work on improving the principles would continue (no progress has been made to date). The damage had been done, however, to APEC's credibility.

The Indonesian economist Mari Pangestu (1994) has argued that the Non-Binding Investment Principles serve a useful purpose in that they will force governments to consider issues pertaining to investment, not just from a narrow national perspective but from the perspective of their international implications. This process, she suggests, is important as a confidence-building measure among APEC economies. In contrast, I would argue that the ineffectiveness of the proposals had a confidence-*destroying* effect, confidence in APEC's capacity to adopt consequential measures, that is. Whatever the grand principles for trade liberalization endorsed by the leaders at Bogor, the negotiation of the investment principles in the same year demonstrated that APEC's consensus-oriented, lowest common denominator approach was not going to deliver the concrete outcomes that Washington wanted. The NBIP episode caused a loss of credibility for APEC, not just with the US government but also with the private sector in many of the Western members. Messing (1995: 59) is representative of private sector views: 'As a nonbinding ministerial statement of mere aspirations to mere principles, unsigned, unratified, unenforceable, unincorporated into national law, and lacking meaningful clauses on national treatment, financial transfers, and dispute settlement, it does not protect investors against the risk of unfair, arbitrary or unpredictable treatment'. See also Murofushi (1996).

Early Voluntary Sectoral Liberalization (EVSL)

By the middle of the 1990s, the euphoria generated by the leaders' meetings in Seattle and Bogor had largely evaporated. Although the Osaka meeting had produced an 'action agenda', the obvious contradiction between its simultaneous emphases on comprehensiveness and on flexibility did not bode well for APEC's trade liberalization agenda. The unambitious 'individual action plans' that governments drew up as part of the Osaka agenda reinforced the scepticism of many observers that APEC could not deliver on trade liberalization.

The Osaka Action Agenda had committed governments to identify industries where they supported early liberalization; APEC's Western members now used this commitment to promote sectoral approaches to move the trade liberalization agenda forward. Sectoral approaches had figured prominently in US tactics from the early 1990s. The Uruguay Round had left several sectoral negotiations unfinished; those in the information technology sector and in financial services resumed not long after the signature of the Round's Final Act.

In the information technology sector, the Quadrilateral Group (Canada, the European Union, Japan and the United States) agreed in principle at a meeting in Japan in April 1996 to liberalize trade across a wide range of products. The APEC Leaders' Meeting at Subic Bay in November 1996 gave support to the Information Technology Agreement the Quad Group had proposed. Taking this agreement in the most rapidly growing segment of world trade as a model, APEC then commissioned a study to identify sectors where 'early voluntary liberalization' would have a 'positive impact on trade, investment and economic growth in the individual APEC economies as well as in the region' (APEC 1996).

Following the May 1997 trade ministers' meeting in Montreal, governments were asked to nominate sectors for possible inclusion in the EVSL program. Over sixty proposals covering more than thirty sectors were received (including nominations from Mexico and Chile, both of which later declined to participate in the program). Senior officials then faced the task of consolidating the proposals and determining priorities, a process that inevitably involved negotiation to ensure that all members stood to gain something from the final package deal. Member economies were polled to determine the sectors for which liberalization proposals enjoyed most support, a process that culled the list of sectors to fifteen, nine of which were designated priority sectors for immediate liberalization.

At the May Ministerial Meeting, agreement had been reached that the EVSL program would contain not just timetables for liberalization but also a package of economic and technical cooperation elements and trade facilitation elements: all three pillars of APEC thus were to be represented in the program, a gesture towards the concerns of the less developed economies. The EVSL program did not propose uniform treatment across all sectors: in some, the emphasis was on mutual recognition of standards rather than on tariff elimination (see Table 4.3).

APEC leaders endorsed the EVSL program at their meeting in Vancouver in November 1997. It soon became apparent, however, that the in-principle endorsement provided by the leaders left many questions unanswered. Familiar problems from APEC's earlier debates on trade liberalization reappeared. Indeed, the meaning of each of the four words in 'early voluntary sectoral liberalization' remained contested:

- the date by which EVSL would be finalized had not been agreed; it was unclear whether less developed economies would receive special dispensation through a longer time-frame, as per the Bogor Declaration;
- what was meant by 'voluntary' was understood differently by various governments;
- the exact product coverage had still to be specified (the agreement on sectors had yet to be translated into tariff codes);[40] and, most importantly,
- the tariff levels to be reached at the end of the EVSL program were not specified (again, there was disagreement on whether these should be zero or some level between zero and 5 per cent).

For some governments, mainly the Western participants, 'voluntary' was taken to refer to the willingness of members to take a decision to move forward rapidly on the specified sectors: in other words, governments had already chosen, and had exercised their choice voluntarily. The program had to be implemented as a complete package otherwise the balance that had been laboriously negotiated would be undone. Others did not share this view. Some saw the voluntary component as enabling them to choose when they would commence their obligations under the program. Some believed that the voluntary nature of the exercise would allow them to liberalize trade in some of the specified sectors but not others. Some asserted that the voluntary nature of the exercise would allow them to participate in some elements in some sectors of the program, such as the economic and technical cooperation dimension, but not require them to partake of other elements, notably the trade liberalization components.

Disagreements came to a head at the trade ministers' meeting in Kuching, Malaysia, in June 1998. The Japanese government refused to accept that the package should be treated in a unitary manner, arguing that voluntarism and flexibility were more important than comprehensiveness.[41] Because of pressure from domestic interests, represented in

Table 4.3 Sectors proposed for EVSL program

Sector	Nominating countries	Proposed measures
First Tier		
Chemicals, rubbers and plastics	Australia, China, Hong Kong, Singapore, US	Harmonize and then eliminate tariffs; facilitate and liberalize customs and regulatory procedures; harmonize chemical standards and testing.
Forest products	Canada, Indonesia, New Zealand, US	Remove all tariffs on forest products over period 2000–2004; conduct study of NTBs; introduce standards and conformance measures; phytosanitary measures; and economic and technical assistance.
Energy	Australia, Thailand, US	Accelerated removal of tariffs; work programs to identify and address NTBs; application of transparency principles in government procurement of energy-related equipment and services; work program on facilitation and standards.
Fish and fish products	Brunei, Canada, Indonesia, New Zealand, Thailand	Eliminate tariffs by 2005, NTBs by 2007. Conduct study on subsidies. Harmonization of sanitary and phytosanitary measures by 2003; economic and technical cooperation initiatives to improve effectiveness of fisheries management.
Environmental goods and services	Canada, Japan, Taiwan, US	Eliminate tariffs on environmental goods. Study to identify NTBs.
Medical equipment and instruments	Singapore, US	Eliminate tariffs; identify and address NTBs; technical assistance in cooperation with private sector.
Telecommunications Mutual Recognition Agreement	US	Implement agreement for mutual recognition of test results and certifications for telecommunications equipment.
Toys	China, Hong Kong, Singapore, US	Eliminate tariffs preferably by 2000 and no later than 2005; identify and eliminate NTBs in same period.
Gems and jewellery	[illegible]ailand, Taiwan	Reduction/elimination of tariffs and NTBs.

Second Tier		
Food	Australia, Canada, New Zealand, Thailand	Eliminate, reduce or harmonize tariffs on selected processed and unprocessed food products before 2010/2020. Compilation of comprehensive data base on trade flows, tariffs and NTBs.
Oilseeds and oilseed products	Canada, Malaysia, US	Eliminate tariffs, NTBs, export subsidies and other trade-distorting measures.
Natural and synthetic rubber	Japan, Thailand	Establish timetable for elimination of tariffs and NTBs; transfer of production and manufacturing technology to promote development of domestic industries in rubber-producing economies.
Fertilisers	Canada, Japan	Elimination of tariffs; implementation of transportation regulations contained in the International Maritime Dangerous Goods Code. Economic and Technical Cooperation projects to assist liberalization of trade.
Automotive	US	Facilitation measures; identification and liberalization of trade and investment barriers; economic and technical cooperation.
Civil aircraft	Canada	Elimination of tariffs and binding at zero by 2000.

Source: Compiled from data in Dee et al. (1998).

the government through the Ministry of Agriculture, Forestry, and Fisheries, Japan refused to agree to participate in two sectors in the program: fish and fish products, and forestry products. Other countries with similar interests in maintaining domestic protection in these sectors, most notably Korea, were happy to hide behind Japan's veto. The *Korea Herald* (24 November 1997), for instance, quotes an official from the Ministry of Trade, Industry and Energy as stating at the Vancouver meeting that '[w]e made it clear that the Korean government opposes slashing tariffs on fish and wood products in the early trade liberalization sectors'. Because the agreement reached was voluntary, Korean officials continued, governments were not bound by it. China and Taiwan also were known to have reservations about accelerated liberalization in these sectors. Chile and Mexico, meanwhile, had announced that they would not participate in the program at all, preferring to take across-the-board measures to promote liberalization rather than a sectoral approach. Chile did not wish to modify its tariff structure, which provides for a flat *ad valorem* rate (scheduled to reach 6 per cent by 2003) except on certain agricultural products and on used goods. Mexico asserted its preference for multilateral liberalization through the WTO over APEC's sectoral approach.

Contrary to the principle of consensus, however, the program was not dropped at the Kuching meeting but instead referred to the upcoming Leaders' Meeting in Kuala Lumpur. Other member governments (the Western Four plus Hong Kong and Singapore) subjected Tokyo to considerable pressure in the intervening months to attempt to change its mind. Japan meanwhile sent ministerial missions to other APEC economies to seek support for its position. It may not have been a coincidence that Japan at this time launched its New Miyazawa initiative, under which it pledged $30 billion to assist recovery in the Asian economies subject to economic crisis in 1997–98. Certainly, by the time of the Leaders' Meeting in Kuala Lumpur, Japanese efforts appeared to have been successful: other Asian governments were also expressing reservations about the program: China, Indonesia, Thailand, and Malaysia all refused to support it. With the host of the meeting, the Malaysian government, being the APEC member most insistent on the principle that the grouping should operate through consensual decision-making, the meeting seemed doomed to fail. Leaders were unable to agree on the package; in an attempt to save face, they decided to send it to the WTO – a move described by the chairman of PBEC as a 'fig-leaf to save embarrassment all around' (Sohmen 1998). Attempts by the New Zealand government to revive interest in the package in the run-up to the Auckland Leaders' Meeting went nowhere, though working parties continued to implement trade facilitation measures in some of the sectors.[42]

Conclusion

The abortive negotiations over the EVSL program demonstrated clearly that the obstacles to trade collaboration in APEC were no different from those in other parts of the global economy. Governments 'defected' from the program not because they were wilfully ignorant of its possible benefits but because they were unable to overcome the opposition of domestic groups, including their own ministries, that opposed further liberalization in politically sensitive sectors.[43] Trade continues to be a mixed motive game, one that contains powerful incentives to defect.

APEC's modus operandi was ill-equipped to deal with these problems – and, indeed, may have contributed to them. For the process of voluntary, unilateral trade liberalization that had been prevalent among some Western Pacific economies over the previous two decades had left the most politically sensitive and hence heavily protected sectors largely untouched. APEC's institutional weaknesses stemmed not from an oversight but from conscious design. The unwillingness of APEC members to pool sovereignty made for a particularly weak set of rules, a Secretariat that was confined to secretarial activities, ineffective procedures for monitoring, and no mechanisms for resolving disputes among members. A lack of engagement with civil society compounded these failings. An institution with these flaws could generate few of the contributions that international regimes can make to the realization of inter-state collaboration. The next chapter discusses why, a decade after its foundation, APEC could claim few concrete achievements.

CHAPTER 5

APEC Adrift

APEC to some appears as a loose and woolly forum replete with task groups and committees superimposed on the insubstantial and more narrowly regional fluff of ASEAN. Discussing the shadow battles among these acronyms, a business editor in Singapore cites an old Chinese adage: 'Hollow drums make the most noise'. (Clad 1992: 80)

APEC has been more about political posturing than real policy achievement. (*AFR* 15 November 1995)

APEC has never been more than a travelling photo op. (*FEER* 31 October 1996: 5)

When APEC had its tenth birthday in Auckland in September 1999, few participants were in a mood for celebrations. Not only did the violence in the Indonesian province of East Timor overshadow the meetings, but the overall mood was one of disappointment at the lack of tangible progress members of the grouping had made during the first decade of collaboration. Illustrative of the frustration with APEC's achievements was the report of APEC's Business Advisory Council to the host of the 1999 Leaders' Meeting, New Zealand Prime Minister Jenny Shipley. The report suggested that APEC's approach to trade and investment liberalization was not delivering results, and lacked transparency and specificity (*AFR* 25 August 1999). The chairman of PBEC, Helmut Sohmen (1998), had a similar assessment of APEC's first decade:

> Despite the hype and the positive political spin that surrounds the APEC process, little of real substance has been achieved in the ten years of summiteering, except for the setting of targets in the fairly distant future. One wonders which specific results can really be attributed to APEC, as a conferencing procedure of governments, that individual member countries could not have pursued at their own pace and time-frame ... Even on those issues where

agreement had been reached in principle, specific follow-up measures and actual implementation are frequently not proceeding as planned.

Discussions leading up to the Auckland meeting centred on what had gone wrong in recent years, and on a search for new directions to make the grouping more relevant to the twenty-first century. Despite an appreciation of the need to demonstrate APEC's continuing relevance for Asia-Pacific collaboration, the meeting made negligible progress on APEC's economic agenda.[1]

At one level, APEC did appear to have made substantial progress in its first ten years. From its foundation as a ministerial-level meeting of twelve economies in 1989, it had developed into a grouping of twenty-one countries. Its membership had expanded more rapidly than that of any other regional economic organization. The grouping set itself an imaginative target: free trade in the region by the year 2010 for developed and 2020 for less developed economies. The annual leaders' meetings provide the only institutionalized forum that brings together heads of government from all Pacific Rim countries. The grouping had established a Secretariat; its ministerial working groups held more than thirty meetings each year. And close to 300 projects designed to promote economic and technical cooperation were operating under APEC's auspices.

APEC's very existence and its survival over a decade were, for some observers, a triumph in itself. Yet mere survival is a weak criterion by which to judge the success of an international regime. Moribund institutions that survive – often little more than in name only – litter the international landscape. Establishing criteria for regime effectiveness that go beyond the question of survival remains a matter of some contention, however. A recent comprehensive survey of the literature suggests two criteria: the extent to which members abide by its rules, and the extent to which the regime achieves the objectives or purposes for which it was established (Hasenclever et al. 1997: 178). But neither of these is straightforward. Members may dispute the purposes for which the regime was established, which has been a fundamental problem for APEC. Moreover, objectives may change as the context and the interests of actors evolve. And if the rules of the regime are unclear or weak, member compliance with them may not lay a strong foundation for successful collaboration.

Haggard and Simmons (1987: 508) provide a more useful starting point for evaluating a regime: to ask whether it brings about a change in actors' behaviours because of the benefits provided 'uniquely, or at least most efficiently, through the regime, or by reputational concerns connected to the existence of rules'. While this is a useful starting point for assessing APEC's effectiveness, a focus on actor behaviours, as analysts of regimes acknowledge, runs the risk of incorrectly attributing changes to regimes when they may be due entirely to extra-regime influences. Testing a counterfactual is never easy in the social sciences and APEC is no exception to this. The Haggard-Simmons criterion also fails to address the constructivist suggestion that regimes may shape the identity of actors and thereby effect a change in their interests (see Levy et al. 1995: 306). Criteria for evaluating the success of regimes should include an assessment of their impact on actor identities.

In the following section, I attempt to assess the extent to which APEC has made a difference to the behaviours and identities of its members and to explain the limited results it has produced. Given the centrality of trade liberalization to APEC's agenda in its first decade, it is appropriate to begin with that area.

APEC's Impact

Trade Liberalization

Most commentators, including many of APEC's most enthusiastic supporters, acknowledge that APEC in its first decade accomplished little in the field of trade liberalization. Neither of the two methods APEC adopted – across-the-board liberalization through individual and collective action plans, and a sectoral approach through the EVSL program – was successful. The previous chapter identified some of the chief problems with the action plans. Although they were intended to go beyond the commitments countries had made in the Uruguay Round, few of the submissions did so. Particularly notable here were the failures of APEC's two largest economies – the United States and Japan – to improve on their Uruguay Round commitments in their action plans. And while countries had pledged to improve the plans each year, 'their additions turned out to be minimal' (Yamazawa and Urata 1999: 2). APEC's cheerleaders could claim that a linear projection of the rate of tariff cuts undertaken in the first half of the 1990s would enable economies to meet their free-trade commitments by the 2010 and 2020 deadlines (PECC 1996). To make such a linear projection was to make a heroic assumption, however: that the political economy difficulties encountered in attempting to promote trade liberalization for the remaining sectors, the most heavily protected and politically sensitive parts of member economies, would be no more severe than those encountered to date.

The results of the action plans may have been disappointing but these paled in comparison with APEC's second attempt to accelerate trade liberalization, the EVSL program, which turned into a public relations disaster for the grouping. It was the EVSL, as discussed in the previous chapter, that fully exposed APEC's lack of capacity to promote trade liberalization in areas where domestic political economy considerations were to the fore. Even APEC's strongest supporters now admit that its approach will be unable to deliver the desired results in sensitive sectors: 'As Bogor target dates loom closer and the sectors which remain to be tackled are increasingly sensitive, it is becoming more evident that voluntary co-operation alone will not achieve free and open trade and investment by 2010/2020' (Elek and Soesastro 1999: 23).

Perhaps the most telling commentary on APEC's ineffectiveness in promoting trade liberalization has been the increasing tendency of governments to move away from the grouping's modus operandi. Some governments have retreated from liberalization commitments they had made in previous years. Some appeared to have abandoned APEC's commitment to unilateralism and were increasingly insisting on reciprocity – both from members and non-members of the grouping. Even more striking, however, was a repudiation of 'open regionalism' as an increasing number of members sought to negotiate bilateral or regional free-trade agreements, seeing these as a more promising alternative than APEC's concerted unilateralism for accelerating trade liberalization within the region. Such discriminatory trading arrangements were exactly what APEC's founders hoped the institution would help to prevent. Of particular note was the reversal of the long-standing opposition of the Japanese government to entry into discriminatory regional agreements.

Tokyo's stance had previously been grounded in fears that as an economy with an unusually diverse range of export markets, it would be particularly vulnerable to discriminatory regional trade arrangements (and officials in Tokyo would recall that other countries continued to discriminate against its exports even after Japan was admitted to GATT). The 1999 MITI White Paper on International Trade signalled a dramatic alteration in Japanese government policy, explicitly calling for the development of a free-trade agreement in Northeast Asia. The White Paper noted that Japan's abstention from preferential arrangements increasingly placed it in an anomalous position in the world trading system: close to eighty regional trade agreements had been reported to the WTO in the 1990s. The MITI report identified three benefits from regional arrangements. First, they had contributed to the expansion of trade and investment flows among participants. The White Paper pointed to NAFTA and to the EU as successful schemes in this regard. Second, regional arrangements had forced participating economies to become more competitive; the reduction of government and commercial barriers to trade was beneficial to countries competing in a globalized economy. Finally, regional groupings had played an important role in advancing trade negotiations within the multilateral framework of GATT.

Japan's first move towards negotiating a free-trade agreement was with South Korea, initiated by the annual meeting of the countries' leading business groupings – Keidanren and the Federation of Korean Industries

– but then given a high profile by the invitation for negotiations on such an arrangement from South Korean President Kim Dae Jung in a March 1999 visit to Tokyo. Again, it is noteworthy that South Korea was another member of the small group of countries that had hitherto eschewed discriminatory regional trade agreements. Japan subsequently also entered into discussions with Singapore and Mexico for bilateral deals.[2] Other APEC governments involved in discussions of new free-trade arrangements include Australia, Canada, Chile, Mexico, New Zealand, Singapore, Thailand and the United States. They clearly have discounted the warnings from some economists (see e.g. Garnaut 1996) about the potential costs of trade diversion.

To be sure, governments could make these agreements compatible with APEC. The third report of the EPG (APEC 1995a: 29–37), for instance, devotes a section to the possibilities of 'open sub-regionalism'. It acknowledges, however, that such a proposal would inevitably require countries to negotiate reciprocity: 'we know of very few cases where the benefits of negotiated trade liberalization, multilateral or regional, have been extended to nonparticipants on a nonreciprocal basis'. Moreover, it would be far-fetched to deny that the new government interest in these arrangements reflects their lack of faith in APEC's capacity to deliver on its trade liberalization agenda.

The surge in proposals for bilateral trading agreements indicates that governments appeared to have lost patience with APEC on trade liberalization matters.[3] This sentiment applies *a fortiori* to the business community. As noted in the previous chapter, APEC has consistently stressed that business is its core customer and has afforded business groupings a privileged role in its meetings. Business organizations throughout the region continue to voice their support for an acceleration of trade liberalization. But increasingly they expressed the view that APEC had failed to deliver on this issue. Typical of business disillusionment with the grouping's performance were the comments of Bob Lees, executive director of the Pacific Basin Economic Council: 'I would not be able to put together a list of bite-size digestible deliverables that APEC has delivered to business' (quoted in *Australian* 11 November 1998). Similarly, the *Far Eastern Economic Review* (31 October 1996: 5) editorialized: 'We don't know of a single business deal that has gone through because of APEC'. In countries where business groups have an important input into foreign economic policy-making, APEC's loss of credibility with its core constituency had particularly damaging consequences for the priority that governments gave to the forum. Business has also become disillusioned by what it regards as APEC's top-down mode of operation, which leaves little room for business input into government decisions, and by the limited representation of the business community that ABAC affords.

For APEC's supporters, its voluntary, unilateral approach to trade liberalization poses particular problems in isolating APEC's contribution to trade liberalization, and in demonstrating how APEC itself has 'added value' to the process. Because the individual action plans published by member economies lack transparency and specificity, comparison across countries and demonstration of the part that APEC itself played in governments' plans is almost impossible. Furthermore, the effects of peer pressure on governments' decision-making are difficult to document. APEC can be credited with *all* the liberalizing actions that member economies have undertaken since its formation – or none at all.

Most observers have adopted the latter view. A comprehensive World Bank survey of regionalism at the turn of the century (World Bank 2000) concluded that 'there has not yet been any APEC liberalization'. Similarly, Fred Bergsten (1997a: 10) conceded that there was 'no hard evidence to date that any APEC country has taken additional liberalization steps solely due to APEC'. The most that might be claimed for the grouping's record in this field is that peer pressure at APEC meetings has produced a modest acceleration of liberalization processes to which governments had already committed themselves.

APEC's record in its other activities is no more substantial.

Trade Facilitation

APEC's efforts at trade facilitation encompass a wide range of activities including, for instance, harmonization of customs codes, mutual acceptance of testing standards, and compilation of databases on tariff and non-tariff barriers. Much of this work – the compilation of databases, holding of seminars, and so on – is ongoing, low-key, valued by some sections of the business community (though no studies have been conducted, for instance, of the use that business makes of the various databases APEC has compiled), and not of great political sensitivity to member governments. High-profile projects in this sector, however, have aroused political sensitivities and showed again the underlying weaknesses of an approach that relies on consensus. APEC has not been able to forge agreements where these would involve governments accepting significant constraints on the autonomy of their action.

The two most important examples are the negotiation of principles for investment and for competition. Discussion of the Non-Binding Investment Principles in Chapter 4 illustrated how APEC's consensual decision-making process generated a set of rules that were not only non-binding but were inferior to those adopted by other regional and global institutions. Similar problems beset the negotiation of competition principles, adopted at the Auckland Leaders' Meeting in 1999. Most economists agree that harmonization of competition policies is essential if a regional grouping is to progress towards deeper integration. In 1999, PECC recommended that APEC adopt four competition principles: comprehensiveness, transparency, accountability and non-discrimination.[4] The Leaders' Meeting adopted these principles but once again placed emphasis on 'flexibility' of implementation, and on the non-binding character of the principles.

As Australian economist Peter Lloyd (1999a: 17) notes: 'Unfortunately, the history of non-binding multilateral principles/rules is that they are usually agreed when there are obstacles to agreement on binding principles/rules and they have little influence on policies'. The non-binding nature of the competition and investment principles gives business no recourse should governments decide not to respect them. Lloyd's scepticism about rules that are of a non-binding character appears to have been borne out by the failure of APEC members to honour their commitment to improve on the NBIPs.

Unfortunately for APEC, its high-profile failures in establishing enforceable principles for competition and investment have overshadowed the more positive results from a multitude of seminars, study groups, and so on.

Economic and Technical Cooperation

The previous chapters noted how APEC neglected the economic and technical cooperation agenda relative to trade liberalization for most of the 1990s. Some governments, mainly those of Western members, were reluctant to see APEC become involved in foreign aid. As Yamazawa (1997: 138) records, leaders could not even agree on a name for APEC's program, rejecting President Soeharto's suggestion that it be termed 'development cooperation' in the Bogor Declaration. Gradually, however, governments came to appreciate the link between the role that APEC could play in the enhancement of domestic capabilities and the prospects for moving the trade facilitation and liberalization agendas forward.

In the Osaka Action Agenda, member economies gave 'economic and technical cooperation', as officials eventually named the program, equal status with trade liberalization on APEC's agenda. The following year's Manila Action Plan identified six areas in which APEC would develop ECOTECH activities: developing human capital; fostering safe and efficient capital markets; strengthening economic infrastructure; harnessing technologies of the future; promoting environmentally sustainable growth; and encouraging small and medium-sized enterprises.

The American political scientist Charles Morrison (1997) suggests that APEC's ECOTECH program was intended to differ from conventional programs of development assistance in two ways. The first was that APEC itself would not coordinate nor have any hand in the provision of the funds. The second was that assistance from government would be secondary in size and importance to that generated from private sector activity.

By the end of its first decade, APEC had 220 ECOTECH projects running under its auspices. Categorized according to the themes outlined at the Manila meeting, the distribution was as follows: developing human capital (70 projects); developing stable, safe and efficient capital markets (7); strengthening economic infrastructure (21); harnessing technologies for the future (49); promoting environmentally sound growth (51); and strengthening the dynamism of small and medium enterprises (22). Approximately a quarter of the projects were in the human resources development area, with energy, science and technology, and agricultural technology the other most active areas (each contributing about 12 per cent of the total projects).[5] At first sight this may seem to be an impressive program. In reality, the record is marred by several weaknesses.

A triumph of process over substance has again characterized APEC's program in this field. So has a general lack of coordination and setting of priorities, itself partly a reflection of the weaknesses of the APEC Secretariat noted in Chapter 3. ECOTECH has yet to be integrated with the trade liberalization and facilitation agenda. The grouping has launched projects when a member has sufficient enthusiasm to put up some money for them.[6] They reflect the particular interests of bureaucracies in the individual members. Projects range from the promotion of the understanding of culture in schools to an improved seafood inspection regime, from research on best gender practices in the workplace to risk assessment in customs procedures. As early as 1993, the EPG had criticized the proliferation of projects and called for their rationalization. Similarly, in the environmental field, to which APEC has given priority, the Australian government's Department of the Environment (1998) asserted that APEC's ECOTECH activity is 'ad hoc' and 'lacks cohesion'.[7]

A report by senior officials to ministers on ECOTECH concluded that many projects were not goal-oriented with explicit objectives, milestones and performance criteria; they were oriented more to process than to easily measurable results (cited in Curtis and Ciuriak 1999: 10). Surveys, research and seminars constituted two-thirds of the outputs of the projects.[8] APEC's ECOTECH subcommittee (ESC) worried at the lack of substantive outputs of the projects:

> [I]t remains concerned that not sufficient attention is being paid, when projects are being formulated, to the outcomes of projects, how they actually relate to specific ECOTECH objectives and initiatives, and how the results can be used for outreach purposes. Furthermore, the ESC considers that more can be done by APEC fora to ensure that projects have the active participation of a large number of economies. (APEC 2000b: 37)

The ESC also found deficiencies in the processes for project development and evaluation:

> [T]he current project funding guidelines do not comply with technical cooperation methodologies – such as the Logical Framework – used widely by international cooperation agencies and organizations. This has limited the ability of some APEC developing economies to successfully develop project proposals. (APEC 2000b: 37)

Moreover, neither the ESC nor the Secretariat had the expertise or resources to conduct an evaluation of individual projects. Evaluation of the contributions of a project to APEC's objectives depended on self-assessment by the relevant working group: the ESC found that for thirty-seven of forty-four projects subject to self-assessment, working groups had failed to submit the appropriate documentation or supporting information (APEC 2000b: 38).

Inadequate finance has also hampered ECOTECH activities. The total annual expenditure on projects has not exceeded $2 million. Most of the projects have been of a very small scale, with funding of less than $50 000. The failure of APEC to adopt Japan's 'Partners for Progress' proposal denied it any significant funds for the pursuit of ECOTECH activities. And, contrary to the expectation that the private sector would supply the bulk of funding for ECOTECH activities, business has taken little part in them. Only a third of ECOTECH projects have had any business input or participation, let alone financial support. In a survey conducted by the Australian branch of PECC, none of the business respondents 'saw any potential in economic and technical cooperation activities' (quoted in Australia 2000: 174).

The lack of substantive outputs from APEC's ECOTECH program renders it vulnerable to criticisms that it is 'activity masquerading as progress' (Flamm and Lincoln 1997: 6). Ippei Yamazawa (1998: 172), an enthusiastic supporter of APEC, acknowledged that during APEC's first decade the ECOTECH program had produced 'no visible achievement'. APEC's less developed economies were able to use the lack of progress on ECOTECH as an excuse for slow implementation of the trade liberalization agenda.

Financial Cooperation

APEC began as a meeting of ministers drawn predominantly from departments of trade and foreign affairs. The first Leaders' Meeting, at the urging of the Eminent Persons Group, added gatherings of finance ministers to APEC's program. As the European experience has demonstrated, financial sector cooperation is critical to the promotion of deeper regional integration. APEC members, however, have never committed themselves to specific proposals in the finance area: liberalization in the financial field simply has not figured on the forum's agenda. Before the Auckland meetings in 1999, gatherings of finance ministers were not even coordinated with the annual leaders' meetings or with those of trade ministers: finance has never been carefully integrated into the APEC framework.

In part, the explanation lies in bureaucratic politics. Trade and foreign affairs ministries of the member economies rather than their treasuries continue to dominate APEC gatherings and tend to guard jealously what they perceive as their turf. But the lack of progress on financial cooperation reflects other factors also. One is the unwillingness of many Asian governments to cede to a regional institution any role on even basic matters in the financial area, such as establishing principles for improving financial sector transparency. Another is the overwhelming importance of global forums in the financial regime – not only the IMF but the Bank for International Settlements.

To blame APEC for failing to resolve the Asian financial crises would be entirely unreasonable – clearly, the crises were primarily a matter for the global institutions, especially the IMF. It is, however, a telling commentary on APEC's perceived lack of effectiveness that the regional financial groupings established in the wake of the crisis – the Manila Framework and the Group of 22, whose memberships substantially overlapped that of APEC – were not placed under APEC's auspices. Moreover, APEC's failure, at its Vancouver Leaders' Meeting, to support Japan's proposals for an Asian Monetary Fund ensured that Japanese finance for Asian economic recovery would be supplied through bilateral mechanisms rather than channelled through the regional forum. APEC's endorsement of the centrality of the IMF to the resolution of the crises showed little empathy with the sensitivities of Asia's crisis economies.

The Sources of APEC's Ineffectiveness

This brief review of the various areas of APEC's activities suggests that the grouping's officials at their Auckland meeting had every reason to be concerned about the lack of achievements from the first decade of cooperation. APEC's weak implementation capacity, coupled with an ever-widening agenda and the quest for 'announceables' for each leaders' meeting, produced an enormous credibility gap. The failure to realize the ambitious agenda that leaders proclaimed stemmed not from countries' inadvertent or involuntary 'defection' from the rules of the APEC regimes but rather from 'defection' from the agreed objectives at an earlier stage, in the formulation of the rules that the grouping chose to adopt.

APEC's rules, discussed in the previous chapter, are characterized by flexibility and ambiguity. The existence of these rules and their simultaneous weakness is a consequence of the different incentives and pressures governments face in the two-level game of trade negotiations. In international meetings, governments are under considerable pressure to reach an agreement of some form with their counterparts – to deliver an 'announceable'. Failure to negotiate an agreement can cause loss of face not only for the government identified as the source of breakdown of negotiations but also for the host of the meeting. Reaching an agreement is one matter, however; implementing the agreement brings another, different set of pressures to bear (see e.g. Haas 2000).

Faced by the prospect that implementing an agreement will bring a costly domestic political backlash, governments have several alternatives available to them. One is to enter the agreement with no intention of complying with the rules they have negotiated. Another is to ensure that the rules are so vague that members can interpret them in a way that minimizes constraints on government action. In APEC, a broad gap is evident between the ambitious statements of intention made at the leaders' meetings and the modesty of the rules members have adopted supposedly to realize the stated aims. It is difficult not to conclude that states have lacked sincerity in their articulation of APEC's aspirations, and that they had no intention of implementing the measures that would have been necessary if the stated goals were to be achieved. Equally important, however, has been the strategy of deliberately constructing rules that fail to prescribe or proscribe with any specificity. APEC has its own lexicon of deliberately ambiguous phrases.[9]

In their negotiation of trade liberalization measures, governments for the most part did not confront a situation where significant uncertainty existed over policy outcomes. The cause of their reticence to agree to specific rules lay rather in the opposite – they knew all too well the likely domestic political consequences of liberalization that would have exposed sensitive sectors to greater international competition. Marked differences are observable within APEC in the willingness of governments to impose costly adjustment on domestic sectors. This variance reflected not just the strength or weakness of the governments of the day (though the succession of weak governments in Japan in the 1990s was certainly not propitious for the making of hard choices). It was also a function of differences in the compacts between government and civil society across the APEC region. In most of Northeast Asia, the market remains more firmly embedded in a framework of consensual social relations than it does in Western economies. East Asian governments have been unwilling to risk this social compact by subordinating it to the forces of the global market. These concerns, rather than any preoccupation with relative gains, hindered progress on the trade liberalization agenda. The variance in social compacts was more significant than competing forms of capitalism (variance in the relationship between the state and the private sector) in determining the differences between the enthusiasm of most East Asian governments and that of their Western counterparts for trade liberalization. But even in APEC's Western members, the good intentions expressed at Bogor frequently foundered when confronted with the lobbying of comparatively inefficient, highly protected industries such as textiles.

Domestic political constraints have prevented governments from concluding agreements even when overwhelming evidence was available to them that the aggregate economic benefits from collaboration would be positive. In APEC, the classic example was the failure to reach agreement on fishery and forest products in the EVSL program. Despite its flaws in selective liberalization in some sectors, the program promised to deliver substantial benefits in others. APEC simply failed to change the incentive structure for governments sufficiently for them to be willing to allow rules adopted at the regional level to tie their hands.

Moreover, APEC has not produced a greater agreement on principles. Despite the existence of the 'Washington Consensus' and the experience of two decades of (largely unilateral) liberalization, the governments of the less developed economies of the region, championed by China, have continued to regard free trade as the policy of the strong. They fear, consequently, that any binding rules for trade liberalization will not produce the desired balance in the distribution of benefits and still voice the case for 'infant economy' protection. Their attitude towards trade liberalization is akin to that of St Augustine towards abstinence as expressed in the *Confessions*: Give me free trade, but not yet.

The decision to adopt a voluntary, unilateral, and flexible approach to integration has provided governments with an excellent excuse for inaction, for maintaining face but complying neither in letter nor in spirit with APEC's lofty aspirations. Emphasis on consensus ensures that APEC seldom goes beyond a lowest common denominator approach. These characteristics of the 'APEC Way' weaken the regime in other ways. In general, where the rules of a regime are ambiguous, subsequent interpretation by members or regional institutions becomes particularly important if the regime is to succeed (as argued, for instance, by Cowhey 1993b: 157). APEC lacks institutions for interpreting rules. As noted in the previous chapter, the emphasis on unilateral action and voluntary compliance eliminates the possibility of APEC's adopting binding dispute settlement mechanisms that would arbitrate on the appropriateness of members' behaviour. It is not that APEC has eliminated friction between its members and thereby negated the demand for DSMs. More than a third of the cases taken to the WTO's Dispute Settlement Panels have involved conflicts between two or more APEC members.[10] Rather, it is that APEC itself provides no guidelines on what is legitimate for members to do. Agreement to disagree allows APEC's institutional survival but prevents 'progress' in the sense of a deepening of cooperation based on a process of cognitive evolution (see Adler and Crawford 1991).

Furthermore, while APEC is not entirely a 'reputation-free zone', the capacity of members to interpret rules to match their preferred behaviours ensures that reputational factors seldom come into play.

A puzzle remains. All APEC members were either already in the WTO at the start of the new century or desperately scrambling to gain entry to it. Why are these governments willing to agree to legally binding and enforceable rules in the WTO but not within APEC? It is difficult to sustain a cultural explanation for the behaviour and preferences of Asian members within APEC when these same governments have accepted quite different rules of the game in the WTO.

One explanation of this apparent anomaly would point to the timing of entry. Few East Asian governments were founder members of GATT, where the major Western economies drew up the rules. When East Asian countries joined, therefore, they had to accept GATT's *acquis communitaire.* In contrast, East Asian governments were in a majority in APEC from its initiation: they could dictate the rules of the game and have done so in a manner that has kept the rules weak.

A second explanation points to the relationship between these two trade institutions. Given the domestic political difficulties that the requirements for liberalization within the GATT/WTO were causing them, the last thing that most East Asian governments wanted from APEC was an institution that would 'ratchet up' the WTO commitments. Yet this was precisely the role that the EPG prescribed for APEC.

A related argument points to the overlap of membership between the two institutions. With the exception of the European Union, Switzerland, Brazil and India, all of the top twenty-five world traders are in APEC (and when one reaches number twenty-five, India, the country's contribution to total world trade is less than three-quarters of 1 per cent). Members would be unlikely to wish to duplicate the WTO on a regional level – if APEC was to have a *raison d'être,* it would have to carve out a separate niche for itself.

A further explanation revolving around membership takes us back to the argument as to whether governments will tend to view trade liberalization as constituting concessions that should be hoarded for ultimate exchange in global negotiations where more parties are involved. In global negotiations, governments may be able to demonstrate to their domestic constituencies that their concessions have brought broader gains than would be achieved at a regional level, which appears to be one reason why the Japanese and Korean governments are unwilling to discuss further liberalization of agricultural, fisheries or forestry trade within APEC.

Membership issues point to another possible consideration: some East Asian governments were uncomfortable with APEC's definition of the 'region'. They did not wish to see the institutionalization of a trans-

Pacific region that might detract from the possibilities of constructing more formalized cooperation within East Asia.[11]

In sum, APEC's ineffectiveness in its first decade reinforced governments' scepticism over whether collaboration in this particular forum would deliver the results that many of them desired. Neither the benefits that the grouping provided, nor concern that their reputations would be damaged by failure to comply with APEC's lofty objectives, had any significant impact on government behaviour. So weak are APEC's rules, so minimal is the shared commitment of member governments to a set of principles, and so ineffective has APEC been in changing governments' behaviours and their conceptions of their interests that it is probably a misnomer to refer to APEC as a 'regime'. Kratochwil and Ruggie (1986: 764) suggest that we know regimes by their principled and shared understandings of desirable and acceptable forms of social behaviour: the statements by ministers and leaders within APEC suggest the absence of such shared understandings. Similarly, APEC is found wanting in meeting Keohane's (1989: 3) definition of regimes as 'persistent and connected sets of rules (formal and informal) that prescribe behavioural roles, constrain activity, and shape expectations'. APEC does little to constrain government behaviours and consequently fails to shape expectations of how other parties will behave.

The Implications of APEC for Arguments about Regional Cooperation

APEC is *sui generis.* Its 'open regionalism' approach is unique among intergovernmental schemes promoting economic integration. Generalization from an *N* of one is hazardous. Nonetheless, the APEC experience does provide some further insight on various propositions about factors that assist or obstruct regional collaboration.

Hegemony

The United States is by far the largest of APEC's economies, close to twice the size of the second biggest. Although most Asian APEC economies grew at a faster rate than the United States throughout most of APEC's first decade – with the notable exception of the crisis period of 1997–98 – the main 'challenger' to US pre-eminence in APEC, Japan, grew much more slowly. By the middle of the 1990s, the 'Japan threat' that had been so prominent in US discourse at the beginning of the decade was giving way to a new self-confidence in the domestic economy, based on the extraordinary growth in productivity from the application of information technology. Moreover, the United States was basking in the unipolar moment of unrivalled military supremacy. By no objective or subjective measure could US hegemony within the APEC region be said to have declined during the grouping's first decade. Yet Washington appeared not to be able to impose its will on APEC, leading some analysts (e.g. Nesadurai 1996) to argue that the grouping had been more effective in restraining the United States than as a tool for US domination of the region. What explains this apparent paradox?

Or was there a paradox? US leadership in fact drove all the major initiatives in APEC's first decade. The establishment of leaders' meetings, the Subic Bay statement in support of the Information Technology Agreement, and the EVSL program (where the United States nominated more than twice as many sectors than any other economy) were all US-led projects. The ideas for these initiatives may have originated elsewhere but it was the US government that carried them to fruition. And it was arguably US pressure, acting in conjunction with Australia, that nourished President Soeharto's commitment to establishing a deadline for trade liberalization in the region at the Bogor meeting. When Washington spoke, others listened. When Washington lost interest, the grouping floundered – for instance when President Clinton decided against participating in the Osaka leaders' meeting. *Business Week* (4 December 1995) noted that the pressure on Asia to make trade concessions had been 'visibly reduced' with Clinton's absence from Osaka.

Yet if Washington played a major role in pushing through the principal initiatives of APEC's first decade, it by no means always secured the outcomes it desired. Despite the best efforts of the American chair of the Eminent Persons Group, the United States failed in its efforts to move APEC away from the concept of open regionalism, defined as non-discriminatory economic integration. On this issue, US interests diverged from those of its APEC partners. As the world's largest economy, the United States has enormous leverage in bilateral economic relations. Unilateral trade liberalization within APEC, without the requirement of reciprocity from non-members (and with no assurance of reciprocity even from members) would largely rob Washington of this leverage. Other APEC countries (the other Western members, particularly Australia and New Zealand) which shared Washington's enthusiasm for trade liberalization, and which would normally have been its allies in promoting this agenda, had different interests, dictated both by the size and structure of their economies and by their geographical locations. And the US resort to unilateralism against East Asian trading partners had alienated them. Washington therefore lacked supporters in its efforts to promote what Bergsten (1994: 24) termed 'temporary conditional MFN'.

The outcome of the debate on APEC's method for trade liberalization was similar to that noted by Putnam and Bayne (1987: 272–3) in their study of the Group of 7 summits: when the United States acted alone, without strong support from some other country, its initiatives failed.

Their other conclusions on US leadership also appear to be borne out by the APEC experience: when the United States asserted strong leadership in alliance with at least one other major power, significant advances in cooperation often resulted. And in APEC, as in the G7, 'the summits were generally inconsequential' when the United States was not prepared to take the lead, often because of preoccupation with domestic elections (APEC leaders' meetings were unfortunately timed to coincide with the election season in the United States).

Having failed to turn APEC into the institution that it desired, Washington largely lost interest in the grouping – except, as noted in Chapter 3, when it occasionally saw APEC as potentially serving US interests in global trade, as in the Subic Bay meeting's support for the proposed WTO Information Technology Agreement. Not surprisingly, given the leverage it could exert through unilateral pressure, Washington was unwilling to allow other economies to use APEC as a device to constrain its actions, opposing, for instance, the introduction of dispute resolution procedures. This was an instance where asymmetries in size had an impact on members' propensities to agree to dispute settlement mechanisms.[12] But it was not just that the United States had a low overall dependence on international trade. Until Russia joined APEC, the United States also had the lowest share of intra-APEC to total exports of any member economy – despite the presence within the grouping of its single most important export market, Canada, and its other partner in NAFTA, Mexico.

Could the United States not have used its considerable bilateral leverage to induce a change in the policies of its APEC partners? A partial answer is provided by Nesadurai (1996), who points to the constraints that growing interdependence in the region – strategic as well as economic – placed on the capacity of the United States to exercise bilateral leverage. Other factors were also important, however. The United States was essentially a *demandeur* in APEC. Its economy was already the most open in the region, with the exception of those of the small city-states of Hong Kong and Singapore. Even critics of US economic policies conceded that it had already made large reductions in protection 'of great value to East Asia and Australia' as part of its Uruguay Round commitments, and that no additional liberalization by Washington would be required until APEC's second decade for its policies to remain consistent with the Bogor target (Garnaut 1995: 40). Even if Washington had wanted to pursue more rapid liberalization, it found its hands tied: the denial by Congress of renewal of the Clinton administration's fast-track negotiating authority further reduced the likelihood of the United States undertaking additional liberalization.

Washington's position in APEC, therefore, was one of making demands on others to accelerate their trade liberalization but without the capacity to offer 'concessions' of its own. As the country most desirous of change on the trade liberalization issue, whereas many others were content with the status quo, the United States immediately faced an uphill battle in an institution where consensus was required. The US task was further complicated because it lacked other instruments to induce policy change in its partners. Not only was it philosophically opposed to linking development assistance to trade liberalization, and hostile to the possibility that APEC would build up a substantial bureaucracy to administer its own development cooperation program, but Congress was also simply unwilling to provide additional funding for its development assistance program. The United States thus came to APEC largely empty-handed. Conscious both of its own lack of leverage and of the low probability that APEC would deliver the outcomes it desired, Washington soon lost enthusiasm for the grouping, reflected in an unwillingness to invest significant bureaucratic resources in it.

Prisoner's Delights, Prisoner's Dilemmas, Compliance and Enforcement

Earlier in this chapter, I noted the difference between the willingness of governments to engage in tactical compliance in the APEC forum so as not to block (or be seen to be blocking) agreements, and their unwillingness to comply with the spirit and letter of agreements in their domestic implementation. Peer pressure was sufficient to produce token cooperation – indeed, it can be credited with pushing some East Asian states further than they wanted to go, for example in setting a *target* for trade liberalization.[13] It was not enough, however, to deliver the results that advocates of trade liberalization desired.

Proponents of APEC's unilateral approach to trade liberalization underestimated the enforcement problems arising from domestic resistance to the reduction of protection, and thus the incentives for governments to free-ride on the liberalization of others (Fane 1995; Flamm and Lincoln 1997). American and European concerns over the terms of China's admission to the WTO illustrate that the fear of cheating is very real. Statements from some East Asian governments gave their APEC partners every reason to doubt the sincerity of their nominal commitments to the trade liberalization agenda. China's chief trade negotiator, Long Yongtu, for instance, stated that China would not honour the 'meaningless' commitments it had given in its talks on accession to the WTO (quoted in *Australian* 24 November 1999: 30). The Korean government, meanwhile, had stated that it would not take any decision on liberalization on rice and other sensitive agricultural products until 2004 when the Uruguay Round grace period expires (*Korea Herald* 27 November 1999).

Governments are acutely aware of the domestic sources of resistance to trade liberalization in their partners. Concerns about such resistance are often amplified by doubts about the lack of transparency in making and implementing trade policy in their partners, and about the capacity of institutions in some APEC countries to enforce policy decisions taken at the centre. APEC's concerted unilateral approach and reliance on peer pressure gave them little reassurance on these issues. Concerted unilateralism, Peter Lloyd (1999b: 19) notes, is 'a weak substitute for reciprocity'. It provides no way of addressing the problem of governments' recalcitrance in meeting their trade liberalization commitments. Peer pressure may have played a modest role in inducing the hosts of APEC meetings to accelerate their liberalization commitments, as was said to have occurred in the Philippines in 1996, but was largely ineffective in a context where governments faced substantial domestic resistance to trade liberalization. Overall, the APEC experience confirms the conclusion that Putnam and Bayne (1987: 257) reached from their study of the Group of 7 summits: 'moral suasion is important only at the margins'.

APEC governments that failed to comply with the commitment to move towards trade liberalization would suffer no penalties, other than the damage that continued protection might inflict on their domestic economies. Even assuming that their behaviour was not grounded in the possibility of economic gain (based, for instance, on infant industry arguments), compliance simply became a victim of the clash between economic and political logics. The APEC record provides strong support for the argument of Downs and colleagues (1996): without enforcement mechanisms, economic integration will be shallow.

Leadership and Secretariats

APEC's experience attests to the creative role that individual leaders can play as intellectual entrepreneurs and policy-brokers. President Clinton, Australian Prime Minister Keating and Indonesia's President Soeharto all made significant contributions to the evolution of the institution through their championing of ideas.

APEC also underlines the creative role that smaller countries can play in international institutions. Leadership was not solely the preserve of the big powers. Smaller APEC members had a significant role in setting agendas. They were able to move the institution forward in the direction they wanted – provided they gained at least the acquiescence of the major powers. Sometimes, as with Keating's idea for leaders' meetings, this entrepreneurship involved selling the idea to a major power on whose support implementation would depend.

Nonetheless, power mattered within APEC. The governments of the United States and Japan essentially enjoyed a veto power within APEC. It was unfortunate for APEC that neither of these governments, for different reasons, was willing to make commitments to trade liberalization in

APEC that went beyond their Uruguay Round pledges, and were therefore either not well placed or unwilling to provide leadership on what became APEC's most high-profile project.

Small economies could be, and were on occasion, ignored in APEC deliberations. Despite the emphasis the grouping placed on consensus, it was sometimes possible, given the appropriate leadership, for major initiatives to be taken despite the opposition of one or more of the smaller members – witness Soeharto's ability to ignore Malaysian objections to the Bogor Declaration.

Mention of Malaysia is a reminder that individual leaders can play the role of wreckers as readily as that of institution-builders. Mahathir in APEC played a similar role to that of De Gaulle and later that of Margaret Thatcher in the European Union. Dr Mahathir's opposition to the institution was manifested in various forms – frequent public criticism of its activities, efforts to weaken it through enlarging its membership, and so on. Such tactics undoubtedly contributed to APEC's credibility problems and hampered efforts to promote deeper collaboration within the grouping.

The first executive director of the APEC Secretariat makes a persuasive case for the grouping's need for an independent source of leadership:

> The corporate culture of APEC is conservative, cautious, and incremental, and APEC's tradition of decision making by consensus reinforces these qualities. The senior officials who determine and monitor the work of APEC also reflect this culture. In addition, they have a tremendous workload. So it is unrealistic to expect them to also put forth bold and innovative ideas every year. They are too busy minding the day-to-day work and determining how the organization should accomplish its goals to have time for reflection on the big picture. (Bodde 1997: 217)

Not surprisingly, the former chair of the EPG, Fred Bergsten (1996: 115) shares these views: 'it is essential to move outside official circles to produce bold ideas for major initiatives'.

APEC's Eminent Persons Group – an epistemic community rampant – demonstrated the creative role that an independent expert body can play in shaping the agenda of an international institution. Indeed, the EPG, in conjunction with the Western members of the grouping, essentially hijacked APEC's agenda in the middle of the 1990s. The EPG supplied the ideas that were to become APEC's principal initiatives after the first leaders' meeting. Some of these, for example the proposal that leaders should declare a timetable for the freeing of trade in the region, were more radical than the initiatives that national governments were otherwise willing to sponsor. No doubt some of the EPG's success was because its ideas were those favoured by APEC's most powerful country, the United States, and by the other countries most willing to launch initiatives in APEC – the other Western members. Nonetheless, its achievement in reshaping APEC's agenda was impressive.

On the other hand, the APEC experience is also instructive in demonstrating the limits of an epistemic community. The APEC record provides no evidence that the EPG had any success in changing the policies of governments that were not already sympathetic to its agenda. Although its members enjoyed high status and often a high public profile in their home countries, they were not necessarily closely integrated into the policy-making process. As with other elements of the epistemic community, such as the PAFTAD conferences, the EPG at times gave the impression of a group of missionaries talking mainly with others who had been converted to the faith, but largely removed from the day-to-day issues of inter-state relations in the region. In the end, the EPG's supply of integrative ideas simply exceeded governments' demands for them.

The role of the EPG compensated in the 1993–95 period for the inability of the APEC Secretariat to provide the grouping with any intellectual or entrepreneurial leadership. APEC members deliberately structured the Secretariat so that it would play no independent role in the grouping. The short tenure of the executive directors and their deputies ensured that they had little scope themselves to try to strengthen the Secretariat. Clearly, it is possible for international institutions to survive and maybe even prosper without a strong secretariat. The APEC experience, however, demonstrates the risks in attempting to do so – especially after the abolition of the EPG deprived the grouping of its principal source of intellectual leadership.

Reliance on national governments to play the role of 'sherpa' or 'shepherd' is problematic in a region where the capabilities of national bureaucracies, and the commitment of national governments to the institution, are so diverse. Some national bureaucracies were obviously ill-equipped to play any significant role in the grouping. This diversity in national bureaucratic capacity had the unfortunate consequences of raising the question of 'who owns APEC', and of reinforcing the image that its more developed economies, especially its 'Western' members, were the dominant forces in the grouping. Of the 201 economic and technical cooperation projects reviewed by Yamazawa (1997, Table 2: 142), Australia (38 projects) and the United States (36) were lead shepherds in by far the largest number. Japan was responsible for twenty-four projects. In contrast, Brunei, Papua New Guinea, Mexico and Chile were leaders of none.[14] Malaysia was responsible for only one. Earlier in this chapter, I noted the problems that stemmed from the inability of the Secretariat to play a coordinating role in the diverse ECOTECH program, and in rationalizing the working groups.

Effective leadership in APEC did not necessarily entail the provision of material resources; rather, it was a matter of individuals and governments being willing to commit the energy, bureaucratic resources and their credibility in efforts to mobilize support for particular initiatives. Smaller countries could play the role of entrepreneur and broker but initiatives were more likely to succeed when they attracted the support of one of APEC's major powers. The EVSL debacle therefore was a double blow to APEC. It reinforced perceptions in Washington that the institution was ineffective – and consequently doubts about the wisdom of investing scarce resources in it. Simultaneously, it alienated the government of Japan, which subsequently directed its energies to building regional collaboration into other channels.

Summitry

The introduction of leaders' meetings provided APEC governments with a new forum for the pursuit of foreign policy objectives. The leaders' meetings in 1993 and 1994 provided the impetus for transforming APEC from a low-key meeting of officials with a very narrow agenda, to an institution that, at least temporarily, caught the world's imagination. The involvement of heads of government was particularly important for an institution the majority of whose members were from Asia, where political power in many countries is concentrated in the hands of the political leader (with some notable exceptions, of course – most importantly, Japan). In these political systems, bureaucracies are often very conservative, a characteristic, noted in the quote by Bodde above, reflected also in APEC's meetings of officials. The intervention of political leaders was required to break through deadlocks among officials in APEC that prevented action. As Paul Keating (2000: 102) noted, '[l]eft to its own devices the official machinery of APEC – the APEC Senior Officials' Meeting – would not move beyond agreements based on the lowest common denominator'. Summits were the venue for intellectual entrepreneurship. Leaders, drawing on ideas from national governments and from the EPG, were responsible for all the major initiatives added to APEC's agenda.

Summits, however, were only as good as the quality of leadership supplied. The 'bounce' effect that they initially gave to APEC soon disappeared, a reflection in some instances of the absence of key leaders (most notably President Clinton from the Osaka and Kuala Lumpur meetings), of changes in government and consequent change in leadership (the replacement of Keating by John Howard in Australia), or of disappointment with the results that APEC had delivered. Arguably, the summits themselves contributed to disillusionment with APEC by raising expectations unrealistically. Each of the early summits, driven not just by the leaders but by the desire of the host government to leave its mark on the institution, strove to define its own 'announceable': a new target, 'action plan', or 'agenda'. And with each announceable, the credibility gap between the stated aspirations of the grouping and its actual achievements widened.

Numbers

Some see the rapid growth in APEC membership as an indicator of the institution's success. On the other hand, it greatly complicated the tasks faced by an institution that, from its establishment, was extremely diverse.

APEC members have given priority to a widening rather than a deepening of the scope of its cooperation. The poorly defined rules of the institution made it easy for new members to be added. They did not face a substantial *acquis communitaire* with which they had to comply – merely a commitment to move, voluntarily, towards an (undefined) target of freeing trade two decades hence.

Unlike the EU or the proposed Free Trade Agreement of the Americas, APEC has not specified that applicants would have to be democratically elected governments – for obvious reasons given its existing membership. Moreover, APEC even went beyond its own weak rules on criteria for admission when it approved Russia's application. Both the Canberra ministerial statement and the Seoul Declaration had emphasized that 'open regionalism' did not imply that membership would be available to all economies, only those in the Asia-Pacific that 'have strong economic linkages in the Asia-Pacific region' (APEC 1991). It is difficult to sustain a case that Russia meets this criterion. Russia conducts only 20 per cent of its total trade with other APEC members, most of which is with China. This figure contrasts with an average for intra-grouping trade of more than 70 per cent; even the United States, the APEC member least integrated with other APEC economies, sells more than 60 per cent of its total exports in other APEC markets. And although Russia had been a member of PECC for a decade, it had not been an active participant in this organization (Soesastro 1999: 148).

The decision to admit Russia to the institution was a triumph of political expediency over economic logic. Governments of APEC's three biggest economies – China, Japan and the United States – all wanted Russia admitted for their own reasons: China because of its desire to improve relations with Moscow and to counter Western domination of APEC; Japan because of its efforts to normalize relations with Russia and resolve the Kuriles dispute, plus its longer-term interests in securing access to the mineral riches of the Russian Far East; the United States because it saw the offer of membership in this Pacific grouping as compensation to Moscow for the eastwards expansion of NATO.[15]

Greater numbers meant greater diversity. This further compounded problems in an institution that the *Economist* (21 November 1998: 27) had already characterized as 'too disparate a group to work together effectively on detailed trade and investment issues'.[16] APEC appeared to be embroiled in a non-virtuous circle. Its ineffectiveness encouraged existing members to admit others without much concern for their impact on the institution. In the meantime, the continuing growth in numbers further diminished the prospects for its engaging in meaningful action.

APEC's supporters and opponents alike recognized the likely consequences for the grouping of greater diversity. Prime Minister Keating (2000: 93–4) was typically outspoken in his memoirs in discussing the membership issue that had arisen in the run-up to the Bogor Leaders' Meeting:

> The regular ministerial meeting held before the leaders arrived took a couple of decisions that disappointed me, especially in extending APEC membership to Mexico, Chile and Papua New Guinea. In fact, this decision didn't just disappoint me, it infuriated me. My opposition to expanded membership had nothing to do with any antipathy to these countries, but to the belief that if APEC got too big, or its membership became more diffuse – for example, by drawing in Latin America – we could not achieve what we wanted to do strategically …
>
> The differences in opinion about membership lay in conceptual confusion about whether APEC was a Pacific-Rim body, or an Asia-Pacific one … Malaysia was enthusiastically encouraging new members, presumably because it made its own East Asian Economic Caucus seem a more workable alternative. Its lobbying for the entry of these countries should have been seen for what it was: an attempt to make APEC ineffective before it had really begun.

A grouping whose geographical scope stretched from the European borders of Russia to the southern tip of Latin America, and containing countries some of whose economies were still governed by communist parties, is not an obvious institutional design for effective action. APEC's diversity was particularly unfortunate for an institution that relied on voluntarism and peer pressure. The diversity of the grouping reinforced the problem of member governments being subject to contending pressures, to some of which they would inevitably give higher priority than APEC. Diversity, coupled with the lack of familiarity of elites with one another, ensured that peer pressure would have little impact. Moreover, the variety of regimes represented in APEC provided little foundation for members to have any confidence in how other governments would behave.

Context

Context, Oran Young (1998: 174) has emphasized, is frequently critical in the formation and evolution of international regimes. Context played a significant role in APEC's foundation, as argued in Chapter 2. Subsequently, the context turned far less favourable to APEC.

To the extent that APEC was seen as an insurance policy in the event of the failure of the Uruguay Round of GATT/WTO talks, the success of these negotiations robbed it of one component of its *raison d'être*. Although the Uruguay Round ended with central issues unresolved in several areas of negotiation, such as trade in services, the final agreement produced some surprisingly strong outcomes, particularly the improved dispute settlement mechanisms. Indeed, the very strength of some Uruguay Round agreements underlined the ineffectiveness of APEC's own efforts. No one disputed that the WTO was the 'main game' in trade liberalization and APEC but a minor sideshow.

APEC's establishment had occurred in a context of growing concerns around the Western Pacific Rim at the increasing resort by Washington to bullying tactics in bilateral trade relations. The unexpected success of the WTO's new DSMs helped reduce fears in the region about the worst excesses of US unilateralism, and weakened the demand for an effective regional mechanism which countries hoped would constrain the United States. Even governments that were usually loyal 'followers' of the United States on trade policy issues, those of Australia and New Zealand, made use of the WTO mechanisms to restrain US unilateralism – in this case over American restrictions on lamb imports. For East Asian governments, the failure of the Kodak/Fuji film case, lodged by the United States against the Japanese government, provided assurance that the WTO was unlikely to become involved in support of an American crusade against East Asian 'structural impediments'. Meanwhile, the strength of the US economy in the 1990s, at least for the time being, had reduced US preoccupation with bilateral trade imbalances with Asian governments. The advent of a Republican administration in Washington in the new millennium also reduced Asian fears about the propensity of the US government to resort to unilateralism.

By the end of APEC's first decade, another round of global trade talks loomed. For some commentators (e.g. Petri 1999), this new context offered an opportunity for APEC once again to play a positive role in moving global liberalization forward. This may yet prove to be the case. The negotiations leading to the failure of the Seattle Ministerial Meeting of the WTO in December 1999, however, highlighted a significant reason why it appears unlikely that APEC will play a prominent role in the new talks. The issues that were the major stumbling blocks at Seattle – agricultural protectionism, especially its new rationalization in arguments that agriculture plays a 'multifunctional' role in society and therefore should not be subject to the rules that govern trade in other products, and the attempt to attach labour and environmental conditionality to trade agreements – are ones that divide rather than unite APEC. APEC fell at the first hurdle on the lengthy path to a new WTO agreement: it was simply unable to reach a common position to take to the Seattle meeting.

In the meantime, the East Asian crises of 1997–98 provided a further unfavourable contextual development for APEC. Crises, as argued in Chapter 1, often provide an opening for new ideas and for coalitions aiming to change the status quo. Economic crises had previously opened the way for an increased pace of economic liberalization in the Asia-Pacific region. In some East Asian countries, the 1997–98 crises provided a dramatic example of this effect. The most notable case was Korea, where the newly elected Kim Dae-jung government embarked on a radical program of economic restructuring. Elsewhere, however, governments reacted to the crisis by slowing some elements of the liberalization program. Malaysia and Thailand both raised some of their tariffs in response to the balance-of-payments difficulties that were central to the crises. And the crises, and APEC's ineffective response to them, were to have a critical impact on identity issues, discussed in the next section.

APEC and Identities

Writers using constructivist perspectives have emphasized that interaction in international institutions can change the prospects for collaboration through its effects on actors' conception of their identity. Peter Katzenstein (1997: 5) provides a succinct summary of this reasoning:

> Strategic interactions in or through economic institutions can alter the views actors hold of what each can do separately and what both can accomplish jointly. Distinct identities thus can become blurred, leading to subsequent redefinitions of interests as actors discuss joint possibilities that may reflect a redefinition of identities, objectives, and strategies.

A study of APEC's first decade illustrates both the fluidity in the construction of identities in the region and changing ideas on the definition of region itself.

As discussed in Chapter 2, one of the intentions behind Australia's APEC initiative was to head off the possibility that an exclusive East Asian regional grouping would come into existence. Hawke's omission of Canada and the United States from his original list of potential members of the proposed grouping created ambiguity about whether it was to be a Western Pacific Rim (with Australia and New Zealand included) or an Asia-Pacific grouping. In the months leading up to the Canberra Ministerial Meeting, this ambiguity was resolved in favour of the latter definition. In its first couple of years, APEC triumphed over Prime Minister Mahathir's alternative conception of regionalism, the East Asian Economic Group, whose membership was to be confined to the states of

Northeast and Southeast Asia. Other Asian governments allowed Mahathir to save face by transforming the proposed group into a caucus within APEC itself (not one that had any obvious impact on policy outcomes before the financial crises of 1997). The caucus had a second incarnation in the Asian component of the Asia–Europe Meeting. But ASEM appeared to be little more than a loosely connected discussion forum that did little to reinforce the links between its East Asian members.[17] By the mid-point of its first decade, APEC appeared victorious in the contest for dominant regional definition.

Five years later, the situation is far more ambiguous. East Asian states have moved towards institutionalizing an exclusively Asian grouping in the ASEAN Plus Three meetings, a body that has adopted an increasingly ambitious agenda for regional economic cooperation.[18] In the meantime, some of APEC's 'Western' members have moved away from close identification with Asia.

APEC itself has had a significant impact on these trends. The behaviour of Western members in APEC, especially their hijacking of its agenda in the mid-1990s, their efforts to turn APEC into a negotiating rather than a discussion forum, and their apparent disregard for Asian members' insistence that the principle of consensus be observed (most notably in the EVSL fiasco), all increased the discomfiture many Asian governments felt with a regional grouping that extended beyond East Asia.[19] To be sure, some Asian governments (most consistently Singapore) were not unhappy at Western attempts to push the pace of trade liberalization in APEC, but they were very much in the minority. Attacks on Mahathir by some representatives of Western governments at the Kuala Lumpur meetings in 1998 further unsettled Asian governments. So did proposals (from William Perry and Paul Keating) that APEC should embrace a security agenda (see Bonnor 1996; Job and Langdon 1997; Smith 1997; Sopiee 1997) or a human rights agenda (the Canadian government at the Vancouver Leaders' Meeting).

The economic crises of 1997–98 reinforced the perceptions of many Asian governments that their economic priorities diverged from those of the West. They differed from most Western governments and the IMF in their views of the causes of the crises, putting more blame on flows of short-term speculative capital and less on the failings of domestic policies (see Noble and Ravenhill 2000). Consequently, their preferred policy prescriptions also differed from those of most Western governments and the international financial institutions, placing emphasis on a greater provision of rapidly disbursing international assistance, and on the need for curbs on short-term capital flows. But it was not just policy differences that helped consolidate perceptions of a separate Asian identity: it was also the behaviour of Western governments and Western-dominated international financial institutions during the crises. For many Asian governments, the financial response from their Western counterparts to the crisis was unsatisfactory and their policy prescriptions viewed as opportunistically capitalizing on Asian calamities to force through an unwelcome agenda. Nowhere was Western arrogance better symbolized than in the picture of IMF President Michel Camdessus standing with folded arms behind Indonesian President Soeharto while the latter signed a statement of intent with the Fund.

APEC's own ineffective response to the crisis further strengthened Asian views that an exclusively Asian association was required not only to address some of the problems that came to the fore in the crisis but also to improve the bargaining position of Asian countries in the global economy. Although US opposition quashed the proposal for an Asian monetary fund, when Japan and Taiwan originally put it forward during the crisis, the idea has subsequently resurfaced. And the ASEAN Plus Three meetings have institutionalized for the first time annual meetings of all East Asian heads of government – with the notable exception of Taiwan, which the grouping has excluded, at China's insistence. At the time of writing, the future of the ASEAN Plus Three group is far from certain. Some of the ideas put forward, such as a free-trade area for the whole of East Asia, or an Asian monetary fund, appear unlikely candidates for promoting better relations among governments of the region.[20] Nonetheless, ASEAN Plus Three is an important sign of a new sense of communal identity among Asian countries.

Closer collaboration and identity formation among East Asian states has not been prompted by a growth in interdependence. If anything, the opposite argument applies: collaboration has been stimulated by an interruption, caused by the financial crises, in a trend of growing interdependence among East Asian economies over the previous fifteen years. Intra-regional trade among East Asian states declined from the end of 1995 onwards, in marked contrast to the record within NAFTA (Figure 5.1).

Other factors are also contributing to identity change. Japan's involvement in the promotion of Asia-Pacific cooperation has long involved 'a psychologically deep process of reinterpretation regarding Japan and her place in the world' (Korhonen 1994: 6). Several factors have combined in recent years to cause Japanese governments to identify more closely with Asia. These include concerns about countering the ongoing US unilateral trade pressure against Japan, but also positive factors such as the growth of Japanese economic influence in other parts of Asia, which has occurred through the extension of the production networks of Japanese companies. Japan's willingness to provide substantial assistance to crisis-stricken Asian economies through its 'New Miyazawa Fund' was symbolic of its closer identification with and desire to provide economic leadership to the rest of Asia. Tokyo has also shown an increasing inter-

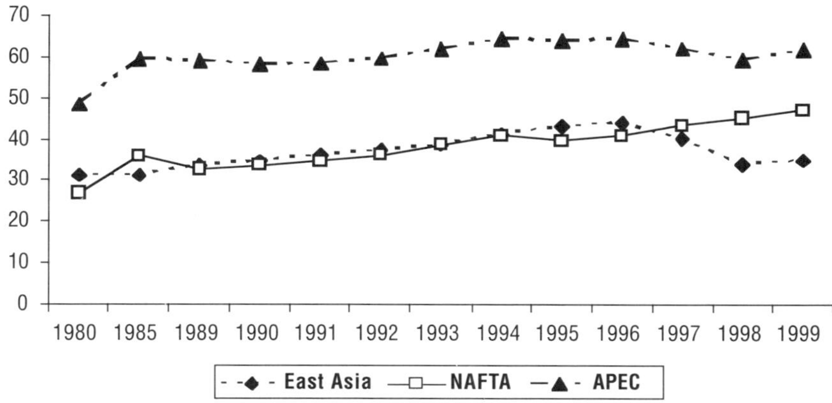

Figure 5.1 Intra-regional exports as a percentage of total exports

est in promoting greater use of the yen as an international currency (though whether it will be willing to undertake the necessary domestic reforms required to effect this remains to be seen).

Elsewhere in East Asia, some other governments increasingly appear willing to accept Japan's playing more of a role in leading a new Asian regionalism. The rapprochement between Korea and Japan, cemented by President Kim Dae-jung's visit to Tokyo in 1998, was a remarkable turning point in one of the most bitter relationships in Asia. It paved the way for the two governments' decision to investigate the possibility of establishing a bilateral free-trade area. It also liberalized access to the Korean market for various forms of Japanese popular culture. The increasing consumption of Japanese music and comics by the youth of Korea and Taiwan may be further evidence of the enhancement of Japan's 'soft power' (S. Shiraishi 1997).

Some of APEC's Western members in the meantime have moved away from the enthusiasm with which they embraced 'Asia' at the time of APEC's establishment. Again, disenchantment with APEC has contributed to this trend. The United States, in particular, has been disappointed at APEC's failure to produce concrete results. From the negotiation of the Non-Binding Investment Principles in 1994, it had been obvious that APEC in its current configuration will not deliver the results that Washington desires. The experience of negotiation within APEC has merely reinforced American perceptions about the unwillingness of Asian governments to enter meaningful agreements, and about the opacity of their institutions. Washington increasingly found that, despite disagreements over agriculture, it had more in common on international trade issues with Europe than with Asia. The establishment of the Transatlantic Partnership in 1998, building on the New Transatlantic

Agenda announced at the EU–US summit in Madrid in 1995, symbolized the new community of interests. Washington has also been preoccupied with a southwards extension of NAFTA, again signifying a shift in emphasis away from the Asian region.

A re-evaluation of relations with Asia also occurred in Australia, one of the most enthusiastic proponents of APEC, which it saw as the crown jewel in its policy of seeking closer engagement with Asia. The 1996 election brought to power a conservative government under John Howard that was determined to differentiate its foreign policy from that of its predecessor, and thereby to attempt to court support for a policy directed mainly at its populist conception of the national interest. The Howard government criticized the Labor governments of Hawke and Keating for their alleged fixation with Asia, declaring that henceforth the country would pursue 'an Asia first but not an Asia only' policy. One of the government's first foreign policy initiatives was to try to strengthen the defence alliance with the United States, a move that China criticized as part of efforts to encircle it. Inevitably, given Australia's location, Asia looms large in the country's foreign and defence policies. But Asian governments discerned the Howard government's attempts to distance itself from the foreign policies of its predecessors as also involving a distancing from Asia. The unwillingness of this government to attempt to provide leadership in APEC, and its decision to continue protection for sensitive sectors of Australian manufacturing industry, all seemed to point to a change in priorities away from Asia.

The interruption of the East Asian economic miracle by the crises of 1997–98 has further encouraged a re-examination of the assumption that the new millennium would herald the advent of the Pacific Century. The crises generated a new triumphalism in the West – whether over the alleged superiority of Western capitalism, financial systems, or the development and application of the information technology revolution – and this new confidence in the virtues of the Western model caused Western members of APEC to emphasize the factors that differentiated themselves from their Asian partners.

Rather than contributing to the reinforcement of an Asia-Pacific identity, APEC itself, perversely, and in conjunction with the Asian financial crises, has had the opposite effect. It has encouraged the Asian members to see their interests as distinct from those of the West, and its Western members to differentiate themselves from the East Asian.

APEC's diversity makes it a peculiar regional economic grouping. Indeed, it is more appropriate to conceive of APEC as a *trans*-regional than as a regional body. In its geographical scope and breadth of membership, it is more akin to the Asia-Europe Meeting and to the Transatlantic Economic Partnership (TEP) than to the longest established of the regional economic groupings, the European Union. And while APEC is more institutionalized than either ASEM or the TEP, it falls closer to their end of the institutionalization spectrum than to either the EU or NAFTA. The evolution of APEC during its first decade arguably saw its member governments themselves increasingly regarding it as a trans-regional grouping, rather than as 'the region'. Conceptualizing APEC in this manner inevitably had consequences for governments' commitments to the grouping, both ideational and material.

At the turn of the century, APEC was not where the action was in terms of regionalism in the Asia-Pacific. Its eighth Leaders' Meeting, staged in Brunei in November 2000, passed largely unnoticed by the world's media (and without making any significant advance on APEC's agenda). In contrast, the ASEAN Plus Three summits and the summit of Western Hemisphere leaders attracted a great deal of media interest. Equally importantly, it was on these meetings that governments appeared to be concentrating their bureaucratic and political resources.

Can APEC be Fixed?

Some of the problems that have beset APEC in its first decade might be overcome with a modest investment of resources. The Secretariat, for instance, has been unable to perform even the limited roles that the member states have approved for it because of a lack of staff resources. Greater continuity in personnel through the appointment of permanent staff rather than relying on officials seconded from national bureaucracies should also enhance its capacity. Similar modest measures could improve the effectiveness of APEC's ECOTECH activities if, for instance, members rationalized the number of projects and set a clear list of priorities, if better procedures for project evaluation were introduced, and if funding was increased through APEC improving its relations with other international organizations such as the multilateral development banks.[21] The recent introduction of electronic versions of individual action plans, sponsored by a grant from Microsoft, may make these documents more transparent and enable APEC to establish more of a case for its own contribution to the process of trade liberalization – if the 100-page forms are completed. But this is a very big 'if' given the lack of bureaucratic capacity in many APEC economies. The experience with ECOTECH self-assessment, noted above, does not inspire confidence.

Could the problems of APEC's diversity and numbers be overcome through improved institutional design, through a 'multi-speed' APEC operating according to an *N–x* formula (as appears to be increasingly common in the European Union; see Moravcsik and Nicolaidis 1998)? The Bogor Declaration allows for the possibility of subgroupings moving forward with proposals with the expectation that others will join them when ready. But the fragility of APEC as an institution makes such a procedure unlikely for any issue of significance. A multi-speed APEC would risk fragmentation of the whole enterprise.

The argument is not that only one form of institutional design is appropriate for international collaboration, a proposition that Kahler (1995b) persuasively demolishes. It is, rather, that the institutional design that member economies have been willing to adopt for APEC is simply not appropriate for the tasks that the forum sought to undertake. To return to the language of game theory, trade liberalization is a collaboration game, in which governments have mixed motives and incentives to cheat. Collaboration games require regimes that have clear rules and provisions for monitoring and that provide remedies for non-compliance. APEC fails on all three counts.

Two alternative courses of action are available to move APEC beyond the present credibility gap that exists between its commitments and its lack of relevant institutions for realizing these commitments. One would be to change the institutions. For a variety of reasons discussed throughout this book, such a course of action is unlikely. The alternative is to change the agenda to make it more consistent with the type of institutions that members are willing to sanction. APEC's institutional design is far more suited to addressing issues that fall into the category of coordination games, that is, structures of interaction where compliance is self-enforcing and where cheating does not become an issue. To some degree, such a change in APEC's agenda has occurred since the EVSL debacle, as APEC switched its efforts away from trade liberalization towards its trade facilitation and economic and technical cooperation agendas. Negotiation of uniform product standards, a significant focus of APEC discussions, would be a classic example of a coordination game. The final section of this chapter provides discussion of some of the implications of this change in emphasis in APEC's agenda.

APEC as a Stepping-Stone?

Since the advent of the 'new regionalism' in the second half of the 1980s, debate has raged on whether regionalism is a stepping-stone or a stumbling block in the path towards global trade liberalization. The debate is unresolved, not helped by the paucity of evidence because of the relatively short history of most integrative schemes. Nonetheless, with the successful conclusion of the Uruguay Round and subsequent sectoral agreements in information technology and financial services, no evidence exists that the growth in regionalism has interrupted the secular decline in trade barriers that has been under way since the establishment of GATT (World Bank 2000). Regional groupings have had exactly the effect predicted by some political scientists: they have contributed to a lowering of trade barriers because of the 'pull' effect they have exercised on neighbouring states. Fearing that they will suffer discrimination in what are often their most important markets, that potential investors will divert their funds to the new regional entity, that they will not share in the accelerated growth that regionalism generates, and/or that they will become victims of trade wars between emerging regional blocs, governments of countries bordering regional economic groupings have lined up for admission.[22]

APEC has been no exception to this trend, the grouping having experienced a 75 per cent growth in membership in its first decade. Other countries, including India, are clamouring for admission. In some ways, this desire for APEC membership poses a puzzle. If APEC's efforts at economic cooperation have been as ineffective as this book suggests, and if the trade liberalization undertaken by APEC members is applied in a non-discriminatory way so that it does not disadvantage non-members of APEC, what explains the desire to join the institution?

Several factors may have entered governments' considerations. They may have been concerned that although APEC had proclaimed 'open regionalism' as its modus operandi, the grouping might move towards a discriminatory approach in the future. US insistence on reciprocity, and the ambiguity in the EPG reports on how APEC should proceed on trade liberalization, would have heightened such concerns. A second factor may have been a desire on the part of governments – at least until the financial crises of 1997–98 – to be associated with an institution that brought together the world's fastest growing economies. Governments may also have seen value in APEC for its contributions in non-economic areas, particularly, the opportunity it provided for government leaders to meet regularly. More cynical suggestions include the proposition that 'no international institution exists that governments do not wish to be part of', and, noting the proliferation of meetings of officials from APEC countries in resorts throughout the region, bureaucratic interests in being part of this particular gravy train.[23] Whatever the reason for other governments' enthusiasm, the growth in APEC membership has been constrained only by the refusal of existing members to interpret 'open regionalism' as 'open membership', and their application, twice, of moratoriums on expansion.

To what extent has APEC served as a 'stepping-stone' for global liberalization? Previous chapters have noted the (disputed) claim that the staging of the first Leaders' Meeting in Seattle in 1993 was instrumental in bringing the Europeans back to the table in the Uruguay Round, and the often expressed desire of the Eminent Persons Group that APEC would play a role in 'ratcheting up' liberalization in the WTO. Claims that APEC had a positive role in bringing the Uruguay Round to a successful conclusion have some credibility, though the introduction of leaders' meetings in APEC in 1993 was but one of several factors that came together to induce the agreement that led to the successful conclusion of the round. Arguments that APEC has served to ratchet up the global liberalization process are far more tenuous. Governments are inevitably going to consider the implications of their actions within APEC for their positions in the WTO (where they may be negotiating simultaneously). Such considerations belie claims that APEC's unilateral process will lead governments away from the unhealthy attitude that liberalization involves the granting of concessions to trading partners.

Some commentators claimed that APEC's endorsement of the Information Technology Agreement at its Subic Bay meeting in November 1996 was evidence of the positive role that APEC could play in leading global liberalization. The reality of this episode is rather different. The Quadrilateral Group (Canada, the European Union, Japan and the United States) had previously reached agreement in principle on the liberalization of trade in information technology products at its meeting in Kobe, Japan, earlier that year. The European Union (and Japan) had been seeking to avoid any further renewal of the bilateral Semiconductor Trade Agreement between the United States and Japan, which was about to expire. A more encompassing liberalization of trade in information technology products offered a means to do so. With the three major players – the European Union, Japan and the United States – already having reached agreement in principle to a signature of an information technology agreement at the Singapore ministerial meeting of the WTO, the contribution of APEC to the successful conclusion of this global accord was minor.

APEC's subsequent efforts at ratcheting up sectoral liberalization through the EVSL program not only exposed the differences among members on trade liberalization issues and caused the grouping severe embarrassment. When APEC itself was unable to resolve the issue, it also caused an unwanted set of problems to be dumped in the lap of the WTO. Rather than enhancing the prospects for global negotiations, the failure of the EVSL arguably contributed to a poisoning of the atmosphere and a hardening of national positions in the run-up to the Seattle WTO Ministerial Meeting of December 1999.

APEC's non-discriminatory approach to liberalization based on the principle of open regionalism avoids the major negative features of regional free-trade areas that economists deplore. The most prominent of these are the possibility of the diversion of trade to higher cost sources, the installation of cumbersome rules of origin, and the entrenchment of groups with vested interests in the maintenance of protection. On the other hand, APEC's approach generates its own set of problems that might place stumbling blocks in the path to trade liberalization.

Among the most serious of these is the impact that a voluntary process of liberalization has on the structure of tariffs. As noted above, APEC's approach to freeing up trade contributes nothing towards resolving domestic political economy problems that governments face in liberalization. Governments will inevitably choose to leave the most difficult sectors to last or to insulate them altogether from the liberalization process. These tendencies were evident in the choice of products within sectors targeted under the abortive EVSL program; they were also apparent in members' individual action plans. A greater dispersion of tariff rates results from such a process of selective liberalization; the effective rate of protection for the most protected sectors therefore often increases. The effects on the political economy equation are disadvantageous. The industries most resistant to liberalization become further entrenched.

The other major negative effect of APEC on global liberalization is the diversion of scarce bureaucratic and leadership resources into negotiations that often generate inferior outcomes to those achieved in other forums. Too often, APEC seems to have ignored the question the Canadian Minister for International Trade, John C. Crosbie, posed at the first Ministerial Meeting in Canberra: 'What is it that nations of the Asia Pacific can do together that is not being done in other fora?' (DFAT 1989b: 277). Negotiations on various dimensions of trade liberalization have proliferated in international economic institutions at various levels: at the regional level, such as NAFTA; at the trans-regional level, such as the Transatlantic Partnership and ASEM; in the OECD and in global forums such as the WTO. This proliferation has occurred at a time when resources available to trade and foreign affairs bureaucracies have been shrinking in many countries. Bureaucratic capacity is increasingly overstretched. In Southeast Asia, ASEAN alone has more than 300 official meetings a year. APEC has more than thirty ministerial-level meetings annually plus numerous gatherings of officials.

Governments currently face negotiations on the same issues, such as harmonization of standards, or the treatment to be accorded foreign investment, at several different levels simultaneously. Optimizing the use of scarce bureaucratic resources would require picking 'horses for courses'. The experience in APEC's first decade showed that its voluntary, consensus-oriented approach is not the best means of delivering effective outcomes on issues of any significant political sensitivity. The Non-Binding Investment Principles were a classic illustration of the problems involved. Some issues are best left to the global institutions.

APEC as Process

Some commentators might argue that the evaluation of APEC presented above entirely misses the point. Their view is that what matters about APEC is not its substantive outcomes, or lack of them, but the opportunities APEC provides for confidence-building in a region where many governments have little experience of constructive interaction with one another. Hadi Soesastro (1994b: 48) provides a succinct statement of this argument. 'The development of regional economic co-operation in the Asia-Pacific region in general, and the APEC process in particular', he suggests, 'needs to be guided by the wisdom that processes are more important than structures'. Elsewhere he adds that 'APEC is not fundamentally about liberalising trade and investment. APEC is much more; it is first and foremost about community building' (Soesastro 1998b: 95).

Such views are commonly held in the PAFTAD and PECC communities, where economists dominate. Political scientists, on the other hand, frequently hold a more sceptical view of APEC. It is a matter of some irony that political scientists often base their judgements of APEC on analytical techniques borrowed from economics, especially game-theoretical analysis. The enthusiasm of economists for APEC, on the other hand, rests on approaches to integration borrowed from sociology and political science, approaches that place a great deal of faith in the socialization effects of institutions in changing the behaviours of member states.

Some wits have interpreted the APEC acronym as '*A Perfect Excuse to Chat*'. Chatting may be highly desirable in a region where legacies of the Second World War and the Cold War continue to cloud relations between states. The very existence of APEC, linking countries of enormous diversity, a grouping that spans Southeast and Northeast Asia and the Pacific Ocean, is itself an achievement. Its establishment helped popularize the concept of the 'Asia-Pacific' (though, as noted above, its subsequent evolution may have done little towards cementing this identity). Process in itself may be a positive contribution to the evolution of international collaboration through the effects it has on confidence-building. APEC may have played a role in making some countries more comfortable in dealing with one another.

If confidence-building was the name of the game, however, trade liberalization was an unlikely choice to be the centrepiece of APEC's agenda in its first decade. The long history of *concerted* liberalization in the global economy points to the importance of considerations of reciprocity, of reputation, and of enforcement in governments' decision-making, and to the difficult political economy issues they face in overcoming domestic resistance to liberalization. To suggest that the Asia-Pacific region would somehow be immune to such issues was scarcely credible. The increasingly tense trade relations across the Pacific in the 1980s flagged the difficulties that a liberalization process based on unilateralism would encounter. Many Asian governments had an approach to trade liberalization, grounded in particular patterns of state–business and state–society relations, which was at odds with that of their Western counterparts. A focus on trade liberalization was almost certain to reproduce within APEC the existing tensions in bilateral relationships, and to risk a souring of interstate relations.

Concerted unilateralism did not deliver the goods. The EVSL fiasco demonstrated that neither would negotiated liberalization within APEC. By the end of the first decade, the institution was retreating from its trade liberalization emphasis and giving greater attention to trade facilitation issues. In doing so, it had come full circle, back to the agenda originally proposed for an intergovernmental institution by the PAFTAD/PECC community, and restated in Bob Hawke's Seoul initiative. An agenda dominated by trade facilitation supported by economic and technical cooperation is very much in accord with the preferences of most of the Asian members of APEC. Nowhere was this more true than Japan. Given that the Japanese government over the years has been the major proponent of Asia-Pacific regionalism, it is perhaps appropriate that APEC is finally evolving into the type of organization Japan has always wanted.[24]

A renewed emphasis on trade facilitation and ECOTECH would be to move APEC back to its path dependency that had been interrupted by the EPG and the enthusiasm generated by the first two leaders' meetings, and to an agenda more suited to its institutional capacity. But it raises two significant questions. The first is whether APEC is really equipped to play a significant role on these agendas. If APEC is, in the words of Gary Hufbauer (1995: 91) to revert to being 'a sort of "OECD-minus" organization', the minus in the equation is a very large one: the weakness of the APEC Secretariat in contrast to that of the OECD.[25] The flaws in APEC's attempt to construct a 'virtual secretariat' by relying on the bureaucracies of its member states and the research capacity of PECC were very evident in the grouping's first decade. Collaboration suffered not only from inadequate research capacity but also from lack of coordination and lack of funding. A significantly strengthened Secretariat might alleviate some of the problems, but member economies have shown no inclination either to enlarge the Secretariat or to provide additional funding for collaborative activities.

The second issue that a reversion to a more modest agenda raises is its implications for what is arguably APEC's most significant achievement in its first decade: the staging of annual leaders' meetings. No other forum exists that brings together political leaders from both sides of the Pacific. The leaders' meetings have been a particularly important innovation in periods of tension between Washington and Beijing, when bilateral visits were off the agenda. But it was not just the major powers that benefited. Leaders of smaller countries gained an opportunity to talk to their counterparts from all countries, including the regional giants. And the agendas of the leaders' meetings, inevitably, have extended far beyond the official agenda of economic cooperation. The summits have undoubtedly played some role in confidence-building. They are not merely a photo op, contrary to the cynicism of the *Far Eastern Economic Review* expressed in one of the quotations at the head of this chapter.

They have suffered, however, from exaggerated expectations – that each meeting will produce a significant 'announceable': a new declaration, a substantially revised action package, and so on. Given the grouping's lack of substantive outputs, each new announcement has further enlarged the credibility gap between stated aspirations and achievements. The Auckland APEC Leaders' Meeting perhaps points the way for the future: the focus was less on APEC's economic agenda than on political and security issues in the region, and the meeting arguably made an important contribution to resolving the East Timor crisis. Whether an institution whose principal focus is the minutiae of trade facilitation and whose achievements remain modest will continue to attract participation at the highest political level remains to be seen. Therein lies APEC's most pressing dilemma.

APPENDIX 1

APEC Chronology

January 1989	Australian Prime Minister Bob Hawke proposes establishment of APEC in speech in Seoul.
November 1989	First APEC Ministerial Meeting, Canberra Announcement of 8 General Principles for Asia-Pacific Economic Cooperation Initiation of work program.
February 1990	ASEAN ministerial meeting in Kuching, Malaysia formulates conditions for ASEAN participation in APEC.
November 1990	Second Ministerial Meeting, Singapore APEC Declaration on the Uruguay Round Establishment of 7 Working Groups: Trade and Investment Data Review, Trade Promotion, Investment and Technology Transfer, Energy, Telecommunications, Marine Resource Conservation, Human Resource Development.[1]
November 1991	Third Ministerial Meeting, Seoul Seoul APEC Declaration: stipulates APEC's objectives, scope of activity, mode of operation, rules for participation, and organizational structure Admission of China, Hong Kong, and Taiwan Establishment of 3 Working Groups: Fishery; Transportation; Tourism Agreement to develop inventory of trade data.
September 1992	Fourth Ministerial Meeting, Bangkok Declaration on institutional arrangements of APEC Establishment of APEC Secretariat, APEC Central Fund Appointment of APEC Eminent Persons' Group.
November 1993	First Leaders' Meeting and Fifth Ministerial Meeting, Blake Island, Seattle Admission of Mexico and Papua New Guinea 1st report of Eminent Persons' Group Establishment of Committee on Trade and Investment

[1] For details of APEC's committee structure, see Appendix 2.

	Establishment of Pacific Business Forum Establishment of APEC Education Program Establishment of Ministerial committees on Finance, Small and Medium Enterprises, Environment, and Trade.
November 1994	Second Leaders Meeting and Sixth Ministerial Meeting, Bogor, Indonesia Admission of Chile Bogor Declaration of Common Resolve Adoption of APEC Non-Binding Investment Principles 2nd report of Eminent Persons' Group Establishment of Economic Committee; PLG on Small and Medium Enterprises; Ministerial committees on Telecommunications, Science and Technology, and Sustainable Development.
November 1995	Third Leaders' Meeting and Seventh Ministerial Meeting, Osaka Announcement of Osaka Action Agenda Three objectives of the Action Agenda – facilitation, liberalization and cooperation – declared to be the 'three pillars' of APEC Establishment of APEC Business Advisory Council Establishment of APEC Education Foundation 3rd report of Eminent Persons' Group.
November 1996	Fourth Leaders' Meeting and Eighth Ministerial Meeting, Subic Bay, Philippines Manila Plan of Action: Presentation and Review of Collective and Individual Action Programs Declaration on an APEC Framework for Strengthening Economic Cooperation and Development Commissioning of Study to identify sectors for Early Voluntary Sectoral Liberalization Leaders call for adoption of an Information Technology Agreement Partnership for Progress program to promote economic and technical cooperation.
November 1997	Fifth Leaders' Meeting and Ninth Ministerial Meeting, Vancouver Manila Framework for Financial Stability Endorsement of EVSL program Framework for Facilitating Private Sector Investment in Infrastructure in APEC Ministerial Meeting on Women.
November 1998	Sixth Leaders Meeting and Tenth Ministerial Meeting, Kuala Lumpur Admission of Peru, Russia and Vietnam Referral of EVSL to WTO Establishment of ECOTECH Subcommittee.
September 1999	Seventh Leaders Meeting and Eleventh Ministerial Meeting, Auckland Endorsement of APEC Principles to Enhance Competition and Regulatory Reform

	Endorsement of APEC Food System
	Establishment of ECOTECH Clearing House
	Adoption of *Framework for the Integration of Women in APEC.*
November 2000	Eighth Leaders Meeting and Twelfth Ministerial Meeting, Bandar Seri Begawan, Brunei Darussalam
	Adoption of Action Agenda for the New Economy
	Endorsement of APEC Tourism Charter.

APPENDIX 2

APEC Structure

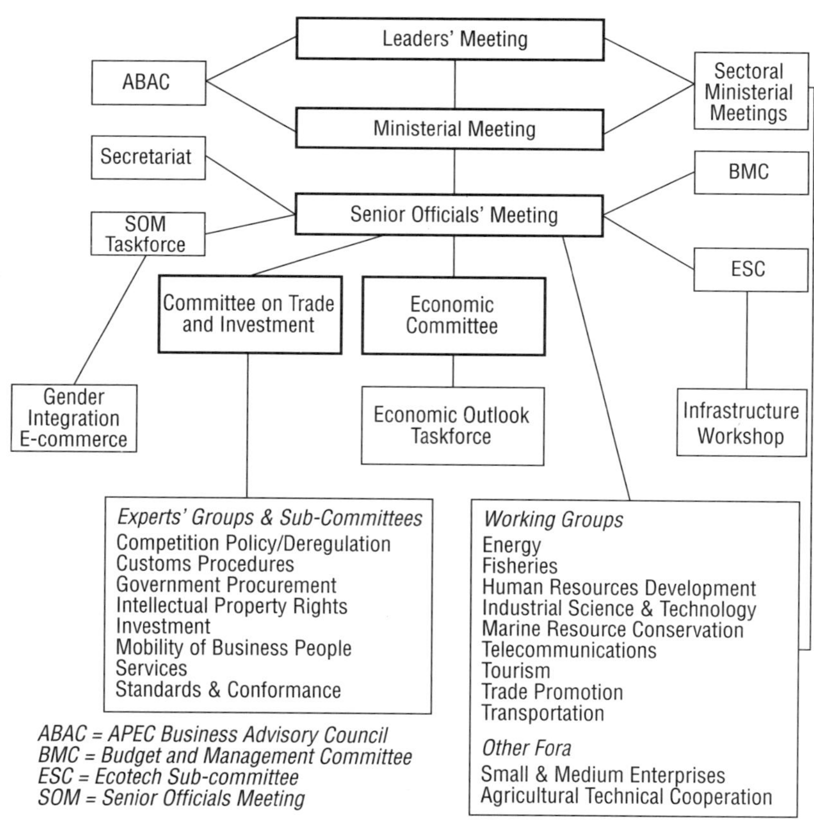

Source: Parliament of Australia (2000 p. 44)

APPENDIX 3

APEC Non-Binding Investment Principles

Jakarta, November 1994

In the spirit of APEC's underlying approach of open regionalism,

Recognising the importance of investment to economic development, the stimulation of growth, the creation of jobs and the flow of technology in the Asia-Pacific region,

Emphasising the importance of promoting domestic environments that are conducive to attracting foreign investment, such as stable growth with low inflation, adequate infrastructure, adequately developed human resources, and protection of intellectual property rights,

Reflecting that most APEC economies are both sources and recipients of foreign investment,

Aiming to increase investment, including investment in small and medium enterprises, and to develop supporting industries,

Acknowledging the diversity in the level and pace of development of member economies as may be reflected in their investment regimes, and committed to ongoing efforts towards the improvement and further liberalisation of their investment regimes,

Without prejudice to applicable bilateral and multilateral treaties and other international instruments,

Recognising the importance of fully implementing the Uruguay Round TRIMs Agreement,

APEC members aspire to the following non-binding principles:

Transparency

- Member economies will make all laws, regulations, administrative guidelines and policies pertaining to investment in their economies publicly available in a prompt, transparent and readily accessible manner.

Non-discrimination between Source Economies

- Member economies will extend to investors from any economy treatment in relation to the establishment, expansion and operation of their investments that is no less favourable than that accorded to investors from any other economy in like situations, without prejudice to relevant international obligations and principles.

National Treatment

- With exceptions as provided for in domestic laws, regulations and policies, member economies will accord to foreign investors in relation to the establishment, expansion, operation and protection of their investments, treatment no less favourable than that accorded in like situations to domestic investors.

Investment Incentives

- Member economies will not relax health, safety, and environmental regulations as an incentive to encourage foreign investment.

Performance Requirements

- Member economies will minimise the use of performance requirements that distort or limit expansion of trade and investment.

Expropriation and Compensation

- Member economies will not expropriate foreign investments or take measures that have a similar effect, except for a public purpose and on a non-discriminatory basis, in accordance with the laws of each economy and principles of international law and against the prompt payment of adequate and effective compensation.

Repatriation and Convertibility

- Member economies will further liberalise towards the goal of the free and prompt transfer of funds related to foreign investment, such as profits, dividends, royalties, loan payments and liquidations, in freely convertible currency.

Settlement of Disputes

- Member economies accept that disputes arising in connection with a foreign investment will be settled promptly through consultations and negotiations between the parties to the dispute or, failing this, through procedures for arbitration in accordance with members' international commitments or through other arbitration procedures acceptable to both parties.

Entry and Sojourn of Personnel

- Member economies will permit the temporary entry and sojourn of key foreign technical and managerial personnel for the purpose of engaging in activities connected with foreign investment, subject to relevant laws and regulations.

Avoidance of Double Taxation

- Member economies will endeavour to avoid double taxation related to foreign investment.

Investor Behaviour

- Acceptance of foreign investment is facilitated when foreign investors abide by the host economy's laws, regulations, administrative guidelines and policies, just as domestic investors should.

Removal of Barriers to Capital Exports

- Member economies accept that regulatory and institutional barriers to the outflow of investment will be minimised.

Notes

Introduction

1 The term 'Economic Leader' is a euphemism for head of state employed by APEC to cope with the membership of Hong Kong and Taiwan ('Chinese Taipei') as well as the People's Republic of China (PRC) in APEC. The PRC has succeeded in exercising an effective veto over the participation of the Taiwanese President in APEC Leaders' Meetings.

1 The Construction of Regional Intergovernmental Collaboration

1 Some may object that the United Nations' Economic and Social Commission for Asia and the Pacific (ESCAP), established in 1947 at the Economic Commission for Asia and the Far East, warrants the title of first trans-Pacific regional organization. ESCAP's membership, however, goes beyond the Pacific Rim to include Central and South Asian states, and European countries – France, the Netherlands, and the United Kingdom – that had colonies in Southeast Asia. On the politics surrounding the membership of ECAFE at the time of its establishment, see Singh (1966: ch. 3).

2 APEC members argue that because the grouping promotes trade liberalization on a non-discriminatory basis, its arrangements are compatible with the GATT/WTO Article I requirement that members offer MFN status to all other member governments. APEC, consequently, has not been notified to GATT as a regional grouping that complies with the Article XXIV provisions on regional preferential arrangements and which therefore is exempt from the provisions of Article I.

3 Of the 190 agreements notified under GATT Article XXIV, 109 were still in force at the turn of the century. Not all regional trade agreements (RTAs) are notified to the WTO, however. The WTO Secretariat estimated that 172 RTAs were in existence in July 2000 (WTO 2000: 4).

4 Following Lorenz (1991), I distinguish regionalism from regionalization, the process whereby interactions, such as trade, within a geographical area increase more rapidly than those between states within the area and those outside it (for further discussion, see Hurrell 1995: 38–45). It is common to confine discussions of regionalism to preferential trade agreements, as Mansfield

and Milner (1999) do. These agreements are, however, but one form of the phenomenon. Regionalism also encompasses functional cooperation on a geographically limited basis in a broad array of issue areas, such as meteorology, river basin management, etc. I emphasize the geographically limited scope of regional cooperation to distinguish it from other non-universal cooperative arrangements. To fail to do so gives rise to infelicitous terminology such as 'regional regionalism' (Ethier 1999: 135). To insist on a geographical criterion as a qualification if arrangements are to be classified as 'regional', however, calls into question the 'regional' status of APEC as we will see later in this book.

5 The membership of the ARF and APEC overlaps considerably but is not identical. Chile, Mexico, Peru, Hong Kong and Taiwan are members of APEC but not the ARF. Burma, Cambodia, Laos, India and the European Union are members of the ARF but not of APEC. Leifer (1996) provides the most comprehensive analysis to date of the ARF.

6 Compare Young (1998: xiii) on explanations for the formation of international regimes: 'simple generalizations spelling out necessary or sufficient conditions for regimes to form in international society are not likely to fare well when subjected to empirical testing'.

7 For the original formulation, see Johnson (1954); for an application to the hegemonic stability debate, see Conybeare (1987).

8 For early examples of what is now a huge literature, see Brander and Spencer (1981), Lipsey and Dobson (1987), Krugman (1986), Spencer and Brander (1983). For an argument that Northeast Asian states have followed the precepts of strategic trade theory, see Matthews and Ravenhill (1994). For suggestions that strategic trade literature provided reasons why the United States should be more concerned than in the past about free-riding by others, see Sandholtz et al. (1992), and Tyson (1993).

9 For an analysis that links declining hegemony to an increase in regionalism, see Mansfield (1998). But a conclusion along these lines may be an example of the dangers of extrapolating from a sample of one. The proliferation of regional arrangements in recent years that has coincided with 'declining hegemony' – itself a problematic proposition – has much to do with the expansion of the EU and the breakup of the former Soviet Union, neither development necessarily related to a relative weakening of US power.

10 Multivariate studies on the relationship between interdependence and conflict suggest that interdependence may simultaneously create collaboration *and* conflict. Much depends on the components of interdependence, and on the symmetry of the relationship. Confounding variables, for example the presence of a hegemon, make it unlikely that quantitative studies will establish the presence of a straightforward relationship between interdependence and collaboration. For a review of the empirical studies, see Stein (1993: 282–5).

11 Proponents of the 'interdependence builds community' arguments are sufficiently sophisticated analysts that they recognize that such a relationship is not inevitable. The adage that 'familiarity breeds contempt', and the evidence that most wars are fought between neighbouring states are well known to anyone working in the field.

12 The *Economist* (15–21 August 1998: 49) discusses one example of the growth in significance of a regional centre: it estimated that more than 13 000 lobbyists were working in Brussels.

13 For nuanced analyses of the relationship between interdependence, globalization and regionalism, see Hurrell (1995: 54–8), and Wyatt-Walter (1995).

14 Although often asymmetrical and favouring dominant economies, access to knowledge in a particular sector may change over time – as emphasized by the literature on obsolescing bargains in minerals industries (see e.g. Moran 1974; Tugwell 1975). I am grateful to Greg Noble for this point.

15 This definition is adapted from that provided by Levy (1994). See also Haas (1990).

16 Stein (1989a 243) summarizes the findings from case studies of pre-negotiation that find that ideational change is frequently associated with actual or anticipated crises. See also Adler (1991: 55).

17 Others dispute the significance of the independent role that secretariats play in regional institutions. See, particularly, Moravcsik (1999) but also Young's (1999) rejoinder.

18 On Canadian conceptions of middle power diplomacy, see Holmes (1982), Keating (1993), Nossal (1989), Neufeld (1995), Granatstein and Bothwell (1990). For a comparison of recent Australian and Canadian activism, see Cooper et al. (1993), and Ravenhill (1998c).

19 Although it is important to note here that it was not always the smaller of the two parties that had taken the initiative on promoting trade liberalization in North America: the United States had on several previous occasions sought to liberalize bilateral trade with Canada but Canadian governments had previously rejected these overtures (Baldwin 1997: 869).

20 For an early assessment of the Cairns Group, see Higgott and Cooper (1990); for a sceptical appraisal of the Group's impact on the Uruguay Round negotiations, see Paarlberg (1997).

21 For discussion of the Australian and Canadian experiences, see Ravenhill (1998c).

22 Land may not be under-represented in comparison with its share of the total workforce, however. In federal systems where upper houses provide for equal representation for each territorial unit, rural areas are often disproportionately over-represented.

23 For a useful review of what is now a huge literature, see Mackie (1992).

24 For an Australian case study see Ravenhill (1990).

25 On the gains from universal liberalization, see Samuelson (1939), and Kemp (1962). The case that any regional trading scheme can in principle be welfare enhancing is established by Kemp and Wan (1976). For a contemporary reaffirmation of the superiority of a global approach to economic cooperation, see Bergsten (1996), and Bhagwati and Panagariya (1996).

26 Static gains from European integration are estimated to be less than 5 per cent of the region's GDP, substantially below the estimated gains achieved through non-discriminatory liberalization.

27 For a theoretical statement of this case, see Grossman and Helpman (1995).

28 To argue that security considerations have influenced the construction of regional economic arrangements is straightforward. To hypothesize how security configurations will affect specific instances of regional economic collaboration is a much more difficult task. Because regionalism from an economic perspective is a second-best approach whose welfare effects are ambiguous, arguments that countries' concerns about the possible negative security externalities of economic integration will prevent them from collaborating with potential adversaries are less plausible for regional than for global integration (contrast Mansfield and Bronson 1997). To deduce how security considerations will affect states' propensity to enter regional collaboration requires once more a consideration of perceptions – the views that state elites hold of power relativities and of potential threats to their interests (Walt 1987).

29 The free-trade agreement between the European Union and its former colonies, first under the Treaty of Rome and then the Yaoundé Conventions, is an exception to this argument. The Lomé Convention arrangements, which succeeded the Yaoundé Conventions, however, did not establish a free-trade area among the signatories. The African, Caribbean and Pacific (ACP) group of countries, although obliged by the Convention to give the EU the most favoured tariff treatment they gave to any industrialized economy, were not required to provide reciprocal treatment to that given to them by the EU. Nor were they required to give any preferential status to other ACP economies. Rather than being justified under the GATT/WTO Article XXIV that allow approved regional arrangements to claim exemption from the MFN requirement, Lomé owed its justification to Part IV of the GATT, which allowed for non-reciprocal preferences to be given to less developed economies (Ravenhill 1985). The EU's most recent treaty with the ACP, the Cotonou Agreement, which succeeded the Lomé Convention in 2000, signals a commitment to return to bilateral free-trade areas between the parties. They are committed to negotiate these new arrangements between 2002 and 2007. The provisions of the Cotonou Agreement are accessible at: http://www. acpsec.org/gb/cotonou/accord1.htm.

30 For analysis of the Lomé relationship between the EU and the ACP Group from this perspective, see Ravenhill (1985).

2 The Construction of APEC

1 Some authors would argue that the history of regional collaboration is substantially longer and, in particular, that the inter-war Institute of Pacific Relations was a precursor to contemporary Asia-Pacific cooperation. See Woods (1993), and Akami (1995).

2 I will often use the Asia-Pacific region – or, in shorthand form, the Pacific – as synonymous with the contemporary membership of APEC. Although the decision at the Vancouver meeting of APEC leaders to admit Peru, Russia, and Vietnam gave the organization a more comprehensive coverage of the Pacific, APEC still excludes a number of states with a Pacific littoral. These include the Central American states of Guatemala, El Salvador, Honduras, Nicaragua, Costa Rica and Panama, the South American states of Colombia and Ecuador, all the island states of Polynesia and Melanesia apart from Papua New Guinea, as well as Cambodia (assuming the Gulf of Thailand is considered part of the Pacific) and North Korea.

3 Some East Asian supporters of 'Asian values' and of an East Asian Economic Grouping are as guilty as Western commentators of exaggerating the homogeneity of 'Asia'. I use East Asia as shorthand for both Northeast Asia (Hong Kong, Japan, the People's Republic of China, South Korea, and Taiwan) and Southeast Asia (the seven ASEAN states that are members of APEC – Brunei, Indonesia, Malaysia, the Philippines, Singapore, Thailand and Vietnam).

4 Although the focus in this chapter is on the agreement between the twelve founding members of APEC (Australia, Brunei, Canada, Indonesia, Japan, Malaysia, New Zealand, the Philippines, Singapore, South Korea, Thailand and the United States), to avoid unnecessary duplication of tables I have included data in this chapter on all 21 member economies.

5 The first year for which the Heritage Foundation constructed its index was 1995.

6 The members of SEATO, established by the Manila Treaty of September 1954 in the wake of the unsuccessful Geneva settlement of the Vietnam conflict,

were Australia, France, New Zealand, the Philippines, Pakistan, Thailand, the UK and the US. For a discussion of the reasons for SEATO's failure, see Buszynski (1983).

7 Wightman (1963: 344), in an early assessment of ECAFE, comments: 'The expectations Asian governments had entertained of the Commission were rudely disappointed. In the process they lost and have never fully recovered the belief that more could be obtained from the West by acting together rather than singly. The overwhelmingly bilateral character of the aid subsequently given by the West underlined this harsh lesson. The cause of regional cooperation had suffered its first major setback'.

8 The negotiation of the Treaty is testimony both to the relative autonomy of the Australian state, and to the influence on trade policy of agricultural and mining interests in a coalition government in which the Country Party held the Trade portfolio. As the specific factors (Ricardo-Viner) model of endogenous tariff theory would predict, relatively scarce factors of production – capital (represented by the Associated Chambers of Manufactures) and labour (represented by trade unions, and the opposition Labor Party) – opposed the trade agreement. The Secretary of the Department of Trade at the time of the signature of the Treaty, Sir John Crawford, was later to play a major role in the establishment of the Pacific Economic Cooperation Council. For a discussion of Australia–Japan relations in the period leading up to the Treaty, see Rix (1986).

9 Following the French veto of Britain's application for membership in the European Community, governments in Asia and Oceania had a new cause for concern: proposals for the establishment of a North Atlantic free-trade area with Britain, Canada, and the US at its core (see Maxwell Stamp Associates 1967).

10 Other governments believed that Japan would be the major beneficiary of PAFTA – as indeed the analysis in Kojima's early publications on the proposal suggested (see Korhonen 1994: 141). For an assessment of the proposal and the reasons for its likely failure, primarily but not exclusively from an Australian perspective, see Arndt (1967). Official Australian scepticism towards the concept appears in Australia (1973), especially Chapter 5.

11 The economists attending the first PAFTAD conference came from the five industrialized countries that Kojima had proposed for membership in PAFTA. Membership was later broadened not only to include economists from the developing market economies of Northeast and Southeast Asia, but also the Soviet Union (1974), China (1979), Vietnam and North Korea. PAFTAD was one of the few forums in which China and Taiwan, and North and South Korea were represented. For details on the development of PAFTAD, see Drysdale (1984), PAFTAD Secretariat (1989), Patrick (1996), and Woods (1993).

12 I use the term 'Western hemisphere' in the same way as the International Monetary Fund to refer to the countries of North, Central and South America.

13 The PAFTAD economists (even the Americans among them) generally were far more sympathetic to East Asian (especially Japanese) policies than to those of the United States. In making the argument for a new regional institution to manage the problems of interdependence, Drysdale (1988: 22) provides a list of protectionist actions in the region that includes US measures on steel, automobiles, electronics and textiles. Japan is mentioned only in the context of its agricultural policies. Patrick (1979: 20) concludes that 'Japanese government restrictions on imports of manufactures from the United States are, on balance, no more severe, and possibly less severe, than United States restrictions on imports from Japan.' At another PAFTAD conference, Kojima (1981a: 551) asserted that 'US trade policy has been irrational, highly

politicized and without any sound economic principle'. The unbalanced view of the problems of Asia-Pacific trade that PAFTAD participants often presented did little to enthuse Washington for their arguments about the desirability of creating a regional economic organization.

14 Given the unwillingness of governments to commit themselves to the proposal for an intergovernmental organization (OPTAD), government officials were to participate in PECC in a private capacity. This mechanism would avoid the implication that governments would be bound in any way by PECC's discussion of and decisions on issues. PECC was subsequently renamed the Pacific Economic Cooperation Council.

15 Australia, Canada, Fiji, Indonesia, Japan, Malaysia, New Zealand, Papua New Guinea, the Philippines, Singapore, South Korea, Thailand, Tonga, and the United States.

16 On uncertainty within Japan as to the optimal form for collaboration, see Morris-Suzuki (1981) and Kimura (1987).

17 Rostow (1986: 95) commented: 'rarely has a concept been so intensively and systematically studied with so little result. In the words of the old Chinese proverb, there has been a great deal of noise on the staircase, but no one has come into the room.' The final report of the Pacific Basin Cooperation Study Group to advise Prime Minister Ohira had concluded that intergovernmental collaboration in the Pacific would only be realized in the twenty-first century and that the way forward should be through more international conferences managed by a group of fifteen to twenty eminent persons (cited in Morley 1987: 27–8). Fraser (1984: 7) again provided an apposite comment: 'It is all very well and useful to support the study groups, to support the broad framework involving academics and business, but in itself it is not enough. There is a limit to how many times one can hold essentially the same conference or seminar – and if we transgress that limit, we shall begin to kill the idea with boredom rather than promote it.'

18 See also the subtitle of Soesastro's (1981) article on the Pacific Community: 'Much Ado About Nothing?'.

19 On Japan, see Yamakage (1990); on the United States, see Morrison (1981) and Borthwick (1987).

20 Sandhu (1981: 178) noted the 'confusion, uncertainty and perhaps even outright distrust that grow out of a flow of contradictory or ambivalent, vague statements signifying different things to different people'.

21 Soesastro (1983b: 44–5) quoted the *Far Eastern Economic Review* (26 September 1980) in noting: '"The cause of the Pacific Basin Community appears to be paying the price of the mistaken Japanese strategy in asking the [Australians] to undertake preliminary studies into the concept," in part because Australia is – in Southeast Asia's eyes – a country unwilling to adopt free trade policies or even to contemplate the regional restructuring of industry.'

22 Calculated from IMF Directions of Trade data, accessed through the International Economic Data Bank, Australian National University. See also the data presented in Webb and Krasner (1989).

23 These figures do not take into account the 'structural impediments' to imports in many East Asian economies, a form of NTB about which Washington frequently complained.

24 The dispute with Japan over the Kurile islands delayed the admission of the Soviet Union to full membership status in PECC. Eventually this membership was granted in September 1991, but with the breakup of the Soviet Union a few months later, Russia took over the membership.

25 As reflected in the writings of some US commentators: compare Harland (1996: xiii): 'America no longer needs Asian allies as it did during the Cold War ... because it sees no threat it cannot meet alone, or in some temporary coalition. So Americans feel free to pursue their own interests, as they see them'. Also Betts (1995: 43): 'The United States now has more leverage in more places on more issues than any other state, simply because there is no other comparable pole, as during the Cold War'.

26 Patrick (1996: 191) records that 'at least seven active PAFTAD participants are currently serving on the PECC Standing Committee or its Coordinating Group; six of the APEC Eminent Persons Group have been members of the PAFTAD International Steering Committee, and four of them have chaired host committees for PAFTAD conferences'.

The influence of the PAFTAD group was also felt in the business organization, PBEC. In the early 1970s, the PBEC International Steering Committee decided to strengthen relations with PAFTAD (Woods 1993: 83). Another dimension to the epistemic community was the 'Williamsburg Meetings', sponsored by the Asia Society of New York, which brought together government officials, business and media leaders, and academics (Morley 1987: 18–19).

27 Harris (1994) discusses the diversity of views in early PAFTAD meetings, noting not only the presence of development economists from less developed economies of the region, but also the divisions that existed among neo-classical economists over the desirability of a regional as opposed to a global approach to free trade.

28 As Harris (1994) records, however, the emphasis of some East Asian economists who participated in PAFTAD was on the liberalization of *export* rather than of domestic markets. PAFTAD may be seen as strengthening one strand of economic thinking among academics and officials in East Asian economies, but the enthusiasm for liberalization was by no means universal, as we will see in Chapter 4. One of the few surveys of opinion of academic economists in East Asia found that while these academics supported the abstract proposition that tariffs and non-tariff barriers are welfare-reducing, they gave much less support to the proposition that these barriers in their own economies should be reduced significantly by the year 2000. Japanese economists were the least disposed to the reduction of tariff and non-tariff protection for their domestic economy (Anderson et al. 1993).

29 On the rise of the Treasury view and of economic rationalism in Australia, see Pusey (1991), and Whitwell (1993). On New Zealand, see Boston et al. (1991), and the memoirs of the New Zealand Treasurer, Roger Douglas (1993).

30 On the Australian and Canadian experiences, see Cooper et al. (1993).

31 The Royal Commission on the Economic Union and Development Prospects for Canada produced more than forty volumes of research reports. In Australia, Garnaut's (1989) report on Australia's relations with Northeast Asia emphasized the need for domestic economic liberalization.

32 See, for instance, studies directed by Anne Krueger (1978) for the National Bureau of Economic Research. Garnaut (1989) reviews the implications for Australia of the growth of the Northeast Asian economies and reaches the same conclusion: that economic liberalization was the best option.

33 On the equivocal character of the response in Indonesia to the problems of the first half of the 1980s, see Hill (1996).

34 For a systematic evaluation of the relationship between economic crisis and liberalization in Southeast Asia, see Bowie and Unger (1997).

35 Grant (1996: 68), Hill (1996: 96), and Schwarz (1994: 72) reach similar conclusions.

36 Several studies of industry policy in Australia in the 1980s emphasize the autonomy enjoyed by the state (see e.g. Capling and Galligan 1992; Bell 1993).

37 The six ASEAN states plus Australia, Canada, New Zealand, the United States, Japan, South Korea, and the three Chinas – Hong Kong, the People's Republic, and Taiwan.

38 These figures are those officially recorded for Taiwanese investment. All the evidence points to these being only a small fraction of actual Taiwanese overseas investment. The World Bank (1989: 10) notes that Taiwan's balance of payments figures suggest that foreign investments are 25 times those actually recorded; data on inflows from Taiwan reported by host countries similarly reveal very large discrepancies from official Taiwanese data.

39 After 1985, Japan and the NICs also made large investments in China. Here accurate data are difficult to obtain owing to Korea and Taiwan's refusal until recently to acknowledge trade with China, and the frequent use of front companies in Hong Kong as a means of channelling funds. Japan's Ministry of Finance, however, estimates that total Japanese investment in manufacturing in China in 1990 amounted to $2.8 billion dollars, roughly 40 per cent of its manufacturing investment in the NICs and 30 per cent of that in ASEAN in that year. Again the electrical machinery sector was predominant, accounting for over one-third of the total value of all investments.

40 Economic growth and diversification had another important effect on domestic interests in protection: it significantly reduced the importance of trade taxes in overall government revenue. In Indonesia, Hill (1996: 113) documents, export taxes and import duties constituted 37 per cent of non-oil government revenue in 1970; by the early 1980s their contribution was less than 20 per cent, by the end of the 1980s only 10 per cent.

41 The trade intensity index is constructed by dividing the share of a country's exports going to a particular region by that region's share in overall world exports.

42 Compare Sudo (1988a: 131): 'Japan's slow and minimal response has failed to satisfy ASEAN'. He quotes Thai Prime Minister Prem's assessment that 'Japan's economic relationship with ASEAN has been an unequal one, something that has generated resentment against Tokyo'.

43 Trade shares calculated from IMF Directions of Trade data accessed through the International Economic Data Bank, Australian National University.

44 The share of EEC investors in the stock of FDI in ASEAN, Korea and China, which amounted to 16.4 per cent in 1980, fell to less than 13 per cent by the end of the decade (Dent 1997–98: 508, Fig. 1; see also Primo Braga and Bannister 1994).

45 On variants of strategic trade theory, see Krugman (1986); Lipsey and Dobson (1987); Cohen and Zysman (1987). For a discussion of US trade policy in this period, see Stern (1987, 1989); Bhagwati and Patrick (1990); Tyson (1993); Ryan (1995).

46 For the reaction of the Japanese government to these US moves, see Komiya (1999: 291).

47 None of these proposals was developed in any detail. Mark Borthwick, executive director of the US National Committee for Pacific Economic Cooperation, suggested, for example, that Shultz's speech 'created the illusion that the State Department had a plan', whereas it had yet to undertake any development of the proposal (quoted in Walsh 1993: 548). Non-government actors had also been advocating greater collaboration at the official level. In late 1987, the chairman of the AUSPECC, the Australian branch of the PECC,

Sir Russel Madigan, recommended to the PECC Standing Committee that a meeting of regional ministers should be held to discuss economic cooperation. A proposal for a regional governmental meeting was first discussed at PECC VI in May 1988, and raised by Madigan in talks with the Australian Minister for Foreign Affairs, Gareth Evans, in December 1988.

48 Terada (1999a) provides a comprehensive review of the process leading to Hawke's initiative.

49 It was surely no coincidence that Hawke's initiative occurred just a few days after the tenth Australia-Japan Ministerial Committee had met in Tokyo and agreed on a joint study of the effects on the region of the Canada-US Free Trade Agreement, and of the implementation of the Single Internal Market in the European Union. Hawke made reference to the ministerial meeting in his Seoul speech. Japanese government officials meanwhile continued to believe that Tokyo's capacity to take an initiative in the region was constrained by lingering resentment at Japan's wartime role (Terada 1999a).

50 Compare Mattli (1999) on the significance of poor economic performance relative to that of other countries as a factor in governments' demand for regionalism.

51 Funabashi (1995: 63–4) records the anti-US sentiments expressed by Australian ministers in conversations with their Japanese counterparts. Krauss (2000b: 479) notes that MITI officials not only believed that Australia proposed to exclude the United States from the grouping but that Tokyo had informed other potential Asian participants about this possibility.

52 MITI's Vice Minister for International Affairs, Shigeo Muraoka, reportedly told Southeast Asian ministers that the inclusion of the US in APEC would provide an opportunity for constraining US unilateralism (Funabashi 1995: 58).

53 See, for instance, Secretary of State James Baker's address to the Japan Society in New York, June 1989.

54 ASEAN Foreign Ministers at their twenty-second annual meeting in July 1989 did not endorse but merely 'noted the recent trends and developments in the Asia-Pacific region and in particular the proposals made by some of the Dialogue Countries for enhanced economic cooperation' (ASEAN Secretariat 1989; see also Crone 1992: 71).

55 For details of some of these initial conflicts, see Funabashi (1995, chapter 2). Both MITI and the Ministry of Foreign Affairs sent their ministers to the Canberra meeting.

56 These arguments, couched in terms of the transformation of domestic economic structures, the increasing linkage of economies through the growth of production networks, and the influence of prevailing liberal ideas, seem a better explanation for the evolution of official attitudes towards regional economic cooperation than those that focus on disparities in aggregate economic size (contrast Grieco 1997). It would be very difficult to present a credible argument that Southeast Asian governments were less inclined towards regional economic cooperation at the end of the 1980s than at the beginning of the decade. This positive change in their attitudes occurred even though the ratio of the Japanese GDP to total Southeast Asian GDP increased in this period.

57 For evidence that earlier US pressure on market access for agricultural products had aversely affected Australian exporters, see George (1983 and 1984).

3 The Evolution of APEC

1 Asia-Pacific Economic Cooperation, Second Ministerial Meeting (Singapore, 29–31 July 1990), 'Joint Statement', paragraph 26. The statements from all

APEC's ministerial meetings can be found on the website of the APEC Secretariat available at http://www.apecsec.org.sg/.

2 Discussion in this section of government interests inevitably is selective. I focus – at the risk of causing offence to citizens of other APEC countries such as Canada, Chile, Korea, Mexico and New Zealand – on those governments that I perceive to have been the main players in APEC: the United States, Japan, China, the ASEAN countries, and Australia.

3 A survey of business people in the APEC region by the Asia Pacific Foundation of Canada for the APEC Business Advisory Council in July 2000 on customs regulations, standards, and business mobility in the APEC region concluded that 'respondents were either unaware of APEC's efforts or they felt APEC's efforts were not effective'. Quoted in APIAN (2000: 25).

4 Baker suggested that APEC had the potential to be 'a new Bretton Woods agreement', and that it was the 'top item on our agenda' (Baker 1989 cited in Clarke 1995: 85).

5 Funabashi (1995: 107) cites the Australian and Korean leaders at the time, Paul Keating and Kim Young Sam, as believing that Seattle had brought the Europeans back to the Uruguay Round bargaining table. The Chair of the Eminent Persons Group, US economist C. Fred Bergsten, has consistently asserted this position (see, for instance, Bergsten 1997c). So, too, did the first Executive Director of the APEC Secretariat, William Bodde Jr., who commented that the Seattle meeting 'sent a very powerful message to the European Union' (Bodde 1994: 45). Compare the Thai economist, Medhi Krongkaew (1996: 95), who wrote that Seattle 'probably sent a strong signal to other countries particularly members of the European Community that if the Uruguay Round failed, the possible or impending trade war between Asia Pacific and Europe would be a messy one'. Drysdale (1997) presents a dissenting opinion on this issue.

6 In an address to the APEC senior officials meeting in Washington in December 1992, Acting Secretary of State, Lawrence Eagleburger asserted: 'We must now move beyond the phase of institutionalizing APEC to making it operational; we must move, in short, from rhetoric to results' (*United States Information Services Backgrounder*, 4 December 1992).

7 On the East Asian Economic Caucus, as it was later to be renamed, more generally, see Higgott and Stubbs (1995).

8 And, as discussed in Chapter 5, MITI's White Paper on International Trade in 1999 signalled a change in the Japanese government's attitude on free trade agreements, leading to the launch of negotiations with three other APEC members: Korea, Mexico, and Singapore.

9 Japan's turn to host the APEC meetings came at a particularly difficult time when the country was governed by a weak coalition led by Prime Minister Tomiichi Murayama (see Johnstone 1995).

10 Illustrative of the frustration of Western member governments with Japan's failure to agree to liberalization in forestry and fisheries in the sectoral trade liberalization program APEC pursued in the second half of the 1990s was the undiplomatic comment of Australia's Deputy Prime Minister, Tim Fischer, that he was 'mightily underwhelmed' by the Japanese government's stance (*Sydney Morning Herald* 13 November 1998).

11 The leader of the APEC Eminent Persons Group, Fred Bergsten, blamed the Japanese leadership style 'where bureaucrats make virtually all the decisions' for the lacklustre outcome of the Osaka Leaders' Meeting (quoted in *AFR* 1 November 1996: 25). Some business representatives also complained that the Japanese government had discouraged them from participating in the Osaka meetings (see Gadbaw 1997: 238).

12 For the report of Hashimoto's concerns, see *AFR* (29 April 1997).

13 Noting that fisheries and forests 'are politically sensitive sectors', Japan's foreign minister, Masahiko Komura, suggested that 'a further opening could shake the government's political base' (quoted in *Wall Street Journal* 16 November 1998).

14 For further discussion of the bureaucratic politics in Japan's preparations for the Osaka meetings, see Mori (1997).

15 A rare exception to Japan's lack of interest in trade liberalization in APEC was its support for APEC's endorsement of the removal of tariffs for trade in information technology products. The background to this sectoral agreement was unusual, however. APEC endorsed an agreement reached by the Quad Group (Canada, EU, Japan and the US) which supplanted the highly unequal bilateral semiconductor trade arrangement between the US and Japan.

16 Japan Forum on International Relations, *The Future of Regionalism and Japan*, quoted in Pyle (1995: 50). For further discussion of Japan's interests in APEC, see Akao (1995), Clark (1993), Deng (1997a), Doner (1997), Funabashi (1995), Hamashita (1997), Hirata et al. (1996), Johnstone (1995), Korhonen (1994), Matsunaga (1995), Mori (1997), Nukazawa (1995), Pempel (1997), Pyle (1995), Shibusawa et al. (1992), Terada (1999a, b), Watanabe (1995), Watanabe and Kikuchi (1995), Yamakage (1995, 1997 and 1990), Yamamoto and Kikuchi (1998), Yamazawa (1995a, b), and Yamazawa and Hirata (1996).

17 On the lack of unity in ASEAN's position on APEC, see *FEER* (10 November 1994: 29–32), Lee (1996), and Soesastro (1995c). On ASEAN relations with APEC more generally, see Acharya (1997), Akashi (1997), Alitas (1994), Ariff (1994a), Chia (1994b), Crone (1996), Dutta (1999), Gallant and Stubbs (1997), Khanna (1996), Kodama (1996), Lim (1995), MacIntyre (1997), Parrenas (1998), Plummer (1998), Rezasyah (1996), Rudner (1994, 1995), T. Shiraishi (1997), Soesastro (1994a, b, c, 1995a, 1996, 1997b, 1998b); Soesastro and Bergin (1996), Tan et al. (1992), Wesley (1997), and Zhang (1996).

18 See the remarks of former Australian Prime Minister Paul Keating: 'Suharto's pride in the Bogor agreement was always evident. He expressed intense irritation at some white-anting of Bogor that one of the other ASEAN members was reportedly engaged in' (2000: 119).

19 A certain irony was present in Mahathir's decision to launch the EAEG proposal without engaging in prior consultation with other ASEAN leaders. His failure to do so was perceived in the region as a direct snub to Indonesian President Soeharto.

20 See also the views expressed in Mahathir's co-authored work with Shintaro Ishihara (1995), published originally in Japanese with the title *'No' to ieru Ajia* ('The Asia that Can Say "No"').

21 Compare Trade Minister Rafidah Aziz: 'Kuala Lumpur will oppose attempts to give APEC a formal structure because it will weaken ASEAN ... The moment APEC is institutionalized, ASEAN will be submerged' (*Jakarta Post* 18 January 1994, quoted in Soesastro 1994b: 46).

22 Mahathir was not slow in using APEC's increasing ineffectiveness as an argument for establishing an East Asian Economic Group. In January 1999, for instance, he described APEC as a 'toothless talking shop' in calling for the institutionalization of the ASEAN Plus 3 summit (*Agence France Presse* 13 January 1999, cited in Leaver and Kelton 1999: 248).

23 On ASEM see Bobrow (1999), Bridges (1996), Dent (1997–98), Gilson (1999), Higgott (1998), Jung and Lehmann (1997), Lee Tsao Yuan (1997), Maull et al. (1998), Richards and Kirkpatrick (1999), Segal (1997), Stokhof and van der Velde (1999), Yeo Lay Hwee (2000).

24 For further discussion see Moore and Yang (1999), the most comprehensive English-language discussion of China's relations with APEC. Wu (1997) is also very useful on this relationship. See also Anderson (1997); Cai (1999); Cheung (1997); Deng (1997b); Dezhao and Mei (1996); Harris (1996, 1997); Klintworth (1995); Kueh (1997); Ramasamy (1997); Selden (1997); Shibusawa et al. (1992); Yunling (1998).

25 President Jiang Zemin, for instance, told the host of the 1999 annual meetings, New Zealand Prime Minister Jenny Shipley, that economic and technological cooperation, and trade and investment liberalization 'must be developed in a balanced manner' to achieve 'APEC's goal of narrowing the gaps between members and realizing common prosperity' (*China Daily* 20 July 1999). The Canadian government's report on the third Senior Officials Meeting in the run up to the Vancouver Leaders' Meeting of 1997 recorded that China had made 'an impassioned intervention' on the need for an Economic and Technical Cooperation Committee to manage APEC's ECOTECH agenda. The proposal received support from other developing members but was blocked by the developed economies, led by the United States, on the ground that the 'key issue was ensuring quality outputs rather than focus on bureaucratic process' ('APEC: SOM III – Canadian Delegation Report', distributed by aprenet@nautilus.org).

26 Australia's geographical location and its lack of alternatives should the Uruguay Round fail distinguish it from Canada, a country with which it is often compared in terms of 'middle powers'. Whereas Ottawa was usually a keen proponent of initiatives for international cooperation, its support for APEC has been decidedly lukewarm, a reflection of the greater priority given to building relations within NAFTA. Unlike Australia, Canada has a viable regional alternative to APEC. On this point, see Cooper et al. (1993). Given the unimportance of its trade with Asia relative to that with its southern neighbours, and the high domestic profile of non-governmental organizations, it is not surprising that Canada has focused within APEC on its economic and technical cooperation agenda. For an official Canadian viewpoint, see Lambert (1997).

27 In the lead-up to the decisions, the Australian financial press had emphasized the need to accelerate tariff cuts so that Australia could maintain its leadership and reputation in APEC. This argument was repeated in the comments of Bill Scales, of the Productivity Commission, made on ABC TV (19 December 1996).

28 For discussion in the context of the literature on middle powers, see Ravenhill (1998c).

29 The average level of tariffs in Japan has increased following the tariffication of agricultural protection, however. By 1996, Japan's unweighted average tariff had reached 9 per cent, higher than the figures for Korea and Taiwan, and very close to the (arbitrary) figure I have used to discriminate between low and high tariff economies.

30 On the prevalence of such barriers in Japan, see Lincoln (1990), and Lawrence (1987); on Korea, see Kwon (2000). PECC (1995) provides an initial survey of non-tariff barriers across APEC.

31 And here one should distinguish unicameral, unitary systems such as New Zealand, from the bicameral, federal system of Australia, the former in principle providing much greater decision-making autonomy to a government.
32 For discussion of the operations of Japanese companies in other parts of Asia, see Hatch and Yamamura (1996).
33 Members of the Group were: Narongchai Akrasanee (Thailand: academic, company director and government advisor); C. Fred Bergsten (United States: director of the Institute for International Economics, former government official and academic economist); Victor K. Fung (Hong Kong: company director and government advisor); Huang Wenjun (People's Republic of China: senior trade official); Mahn Je Kim (Korea: former minister of finance and academic economist); Hank Lim Giok Hay (Singapore: academic economist and first director-general of the PECC Secretariat); John S. MacDonald (Canada: consultant, government adviser and former academic scientist); Suhadi Mangkusuwondo (Indonesia: academic economist and former senior trade official); Neville Wran (Australia: company director and former state premier); Rong-I Wu (Taiwan: academic economist, government advisor and director-general of the Chinese Taipei PECC); Ippei Yamazawa (Japan: academic economist, government adviser and PECC member).
34 Whether the EPG should subsequently report to the ministerial meeting or to that of the leaders became a matter of dispute (see Soesastro 1996: 37).
35 Executive summaries of the reports are available on the APEC Secretariat website.
36 ASEAN was also concerned that implementation of the EPG Report would dilute its own free trade area or make it completely redundant (*FEER* 6 October 1994: 15; see also Linnan 1995: 830).
37 The former secretary of Australia's Department of Foreign Affairs and Trade, Stuart Harris (1989a: 66), noted that Australia had 'an influence in PECC that is probably greater than we would have in a permanent institution trying to emulate the OECD. [This] would not only raise the cost and influence agenda setting but would institutionalise and enhance US and Japanese dominance, something that would worry countries in the region, and we would not appreciate'.
38 The 1993 Seattle Leaders Meeting encouraged the foundation of APEC Study Centres as part of the APEC Education Initiative. By 2000, Centres had been created in universities in 18 member countries, sometimes with financial support from the national government. For information about the Study Centres see http://www.arts.monash.edu.au/ausapec/studylinks.htm.
39 By the end of the first decade, APEC's budget had tripled; For the 2001 financial year it was slightly over $7.5 million, still tiny by comparison with those of most international organizations.
40 At the 1989 Canberra ministerial meeting, APEC senior officials had nominated seven areas for which working groups would be established: trade and investment data, trade promotion, expansion of investment and technology transfer, human resource development, energy, marine resource conservation, and telecommunication. At the third APEC annual meeting in Seoul in November 1991, ministers added three more areas: fisheries, transportation, and tourism. As part of the Osaka Action Agenda, another three areas for economic and technical cooperation were added: small and medium enterprises, economic infrastructure, and agricultural technology. At the end of 1999, APEC had nine working groups in the ECOTECH area: energy, fisheries,

tourism, transportation, trade promotion, telecommunication, industrial science and technology, marine resources conservation, and human resource development. In addition, there was an Expert Group on Agricultural Technology Cooperation, and an 'Ad Hoc Policy Level Group on Small and Medium Enterprises'. For APEC's organizational structure see Appendix 2.

4 Does APEC make a Difference? Trade, Regimes, and Compliance

1 Rent in this context refers to the income enjoyed by a factor of production in excess of the earnings it would command in alternative employment.

2 Lipson's (1982: 426) comments on the GATT expand on Ruggie's argument: 'Its fundamental institutional logic – and a crucial source of its political stability – is that it facilitates openness without ignoring domestic aspects of trade policy. There is no commitment to free trade orthodoxy, and hence no falling away from it.'

3 'We have tariffs and other economic policy distortions because they are efficient – that is, they are politically efficient. Because they are politically optimal, they are not aberrations, but a necessary part of any reasonable political equilibrium' (Magee et al. 1989: xiii).

Australian public opinion, surely not unique in its attitudes towards protectionism, illustrates the incentive structure that governments face. In 1996, two decades after Australian governments began a policy of unilaterally lowering tariff barriers, 59 per cent of poll respondents either 'strongly agreed' or 'agreed' with the proposition that 'Australia should use tariffs to protect its industry'. Only 12 per cent of respondents either 'disagreed' or 'strongly disagreed' with the statement. And the public was not alone in these views. A survey of 615 members of the Australian Institute of Company Directors in 1998 found that although 70 per cent of directors voiced support for unilateral trade liberalization, more than half supported the continuation of protection for domestic industry. Public opinion data from *Australian Electoral Survey 1996* accessed through the Social Science Data Archives, Research School of Social Sciences, Australian National University; Company Directors' data from *AFR* (26 June 1998).

4 On the political importance of reciprocity, compare Robert Triffin (1954: 531): 'progress toward freedom of trade and payments can hardly be achieved, and particularly consolidated, by unilateral national action. This has long been recognized in the tariff field, and has prompted both bilateral and multilateral negotiation of tariff agreements, binding the partners to *simultaneous* and *reciprocal* commitments. We cannot rely on Platonic appeals to international cooperation to prevail upon the national interests which are necessarily the first preoccupation of national governments. Desirable tariff action can only be made attractive, and undesirable action unattractive, from the national point of view through a system of collective agreements making the benefits of trade liberalization for each country dependent on its own trade policy toward the others'.

5 In an econometric study of the effects of trade liberalization, McKibbin (1997: 216) found that 'in the medium to long term, substantial gains are realised from own liberalisation *and* additional gains emerge for all countries from other countries' liberalisation. Multilateral liberalisation leads to larger overall gains for each country' (emphasis in original). Studies that focus specifically on APEC economies similarly find that gains from liberalization

are maximized when this occurs globally rather than being confined to APEC members (see, for instance, APEC 1997; and Chan and Nugent 1999).

6 'Yet there is a dirty little secret in international trade analysis. The measurable costs of protectionist policies – the reductions in real income that can be attributed to tariffs and import quotas – are not all that large...These costs are very real, but when you try to add them up, they are usually much smaller than the rhetoric of free trade would suggest' (Krugman 1995: 31). Krugman notes that trade liberalization will seldom bring (one-off benefits) of more than five per cent of GDP, little more than half the *annual* rate of growth achieved by many East Asian economies in the 1980s and first half of the 1990s. Similarly, Whalley (1985: 261) concludes that the benefits of trade liberalization are likely in many economies to be outweighed by gains from the reform of other domestic policies that have introduced even larger distortions into the local economy. See also Rodrik (1992), and Rodriguez and Rodrik (2000).

7 In the real world, where interactions are repeated and where the spectrum of behaviours is more complex than a simple dichotomy of cooperate/defect, it is by no means the case that interactions in the trade field will always be characterized by a Prisoner's Dilemma structure. In the absence of reassurance mechanisms provided by international regimes, however, the possibility of opportunistic behaviour is much stronger. Uncertainty itself is a major factor inhibiting cooperative behaviour.

8 In APEC, the specific implications of 'open regionalism' have been a matter of controversy. Some participants, such as the leader of the Eminent Persons Group, Fred Bergsten, have asserted that regionalism will be open if the arrangements negotiated within the region are available for others to join so long as they are willing to provide reciprocity. Others argue that a full definition of open regionalism would require that membership in the grouping be open to all economies desiring to participate. The last of these definitions has been repeatedly rejected by APEC governments, which on two occasions have imposed moratoria on the expansion of membership.

Bergsten (1997c: 551–7) identifies five possible meanings for 'open regionalism': open membership, liberalization on an unconditional MFN basis, liberalization on a conditional MFN basis, a pledge to contribute to global liberalization while pursuing regional cooperation, and trade facilitation.

9 To these reasons, Drysdale, Vines and House (1998: 6) add another: open regionalism offers an opportunity for non-members to join the process by simultaneously liberalizing.

10 A view echoed by Peter Petri (1997: 43) who suggests that APEC's 'repeated game' in which member economies announce modest annual improvements to their tariffs is advantageous to the WTO's approach of large, 'lumpy' negotiations where participants tend to hoard concessions as bargaining chips. The credibility of this argument is questionable, however, because governments are often negotiating simultaneously within the WTO and within APEC. Because the WTO remains the 'main game' in international trade liberalization, considerations relating to strategy in that forum are likely to overshadow those pertaining to APEC.

11 Elsewhere in their individual and joint writings, Drysdale and Garnaut acknowledge the other barriers to trade cooperation, particularly the domestic political economy obstacles, that even pro-trade liberalization governments face:

> [T]he conventional wisdom in international trade theory ... suggests that it is an advantage to cooperate through pursuing a free trade strategy even when partners adopt policies that retreat from trade specialisation. But the fact is that only in the rarest circumstances can it be imagined that each partner will have identical interests in the retreat from trade specialisation, so that commonly the interest in non-cooperative strategies is strong unless agreements to secure trade cooperation are possible. (Drysdale 1988: 30)

And Garnaut (1995: 39) asserts that success in Asia-Pacific trade liberalization 'will depend, too, on each government realising that the implementation of non-binding commitments that together are of great value to it, depend on every country (including its own) pulling its weight; otherwise others will become disillusioned with the process and withdraw'.

12 Compare the distinction Haas (1990: 3) makes between adaptation and learning.

13 The classic study is Haas's work on the redirection of lobbying activity with the establishment of the European Community (Haas 1958; see also Camilleri and Falk 1992).

14 For an example from the security sphere, see Nye (1987: 400).

15 On governments' use of Tokyo Round obligations to achieve reforms in domestic trade policies that might otherwise have eluded them, see Winham (1986).

16 Bergsten (1996) examines the importance of international trade agreements in locking in domestic reforms.

17 Downs and colleagues do acknowledge that ideas and socialization, the motors in constructivist approaches to international cooperation, may in the medium to long term be more effective than sanctions in changing states' conceptions of their interests and thus their propensity to enter into and comply with international obligations (Downs et al. 1996: 398). But they suggest that a considerable period may elapse before states redefine their interests in response to these influences.

18 On the new WTO mechanisms, see Jackson (1998). The deepening of cooperation in the trade regime through the Uruguay Round negotiations in turn arguably owed much to the unilateral sanctions imposed by the US under section 301 and super 301 of the Trade Act. For a review of US unilateralism that asserts its importance for the integrity of the trade regime, see Hudec (1990).

19 A sceptic might observe that although APEC itself was formed only at the end of 1989, the process of economic cooperation in the Asia-Pacific dates back at least until the mid-1960s, as discussed in Chapter 2. Is the relevant period over which progress in Asia-Pacific economic cooperation should be assessed merely a decade or more than thirty years?

20 This interpretation is consistent with the understanding of DFAT at the time of APEC's founding as to how APEC would operate: 'There is a widespread regional agreement that the process of regional cooperation should avoid the type of policy co-ordination that imposes prescriptive conditions on participants' (DFAT 1989a: 11).

21 Many Asian officials would not have been reassured by Bergsten's argument in defence of APEC in the *Economist* (6 January 1996: 77) that 'despite some wistful chatter about "keeping APEC as a consultative forum", it has already undertaken serious and successful negotiations'. Bergsten pointed to the

Non-Binding Investment Principles, the Bogor Declaration, and the Osaka Action Agenda as APEC agreements that were the product of substantial negotiations.

22 President Soeharto rebuffed Korea's efforts to have an intermediate date of 2015 for liberalization by the grouping's newly industrializing countries.

23 In October 1999, ASEAN Economic Ministers brought forward to 2002 the deadline for the realization of this vision for the group's six original members. They further agreed that the ultimate target of AFTA will be zero customs duties, and announced a target date of 2015 to achieve this for the original six members, and 2018 for Cambodia, Laos, Myanmar and Vietnam.

24 To many observers, these statements further undermined the credibility of the Bogor goals. That free trade in the region would not in any event be achieved until 2020 had already generated considerable public scepticism. Guy de Jonquieres, *Financial Times* correspondent, wrote that by the 2020 deadline, 'most of the leaders who met in Jakarta will be out of office, forgotten or dead' (cited in Baldwin 1997: 873).

25 See also Bergsten's report of correspondence from Ippei Yamazawa conceding that APEC's unilateral liberalization would not produce results in agriculture, services and textiles (Bergsten 1997b, footnote 22: 98). Similarly, see the views of two economists generally supportive of APEC: 'While noble, and certainly grounded in solid economic theory, [concerted unilateralism] faces considerable political difficulties, such as strong lobby groups' (Bora and Graham 1997: 78).

26 A form of decentralized sanctions could, however, be seen to have been introduced by the back door in the form of governments seeking reciprocity before agreeing to further liberalization. The Liberal-National Party coalition government that was elected in Australia in 1996, for instance, asserted that it would not commit itself to further liberalization in sensitive sectors unless APEC partners made demonstrable progress in liberalization. Such an approach is, of course, totally contrary to the logic of APEC's unilateral liberalization.

27 See, for instance, 'China Pushes for Mediation Forum in APEC', *Agence France Presse* (24 May 1996). For a thoughtful discussion of the views of various APEC members on the dispute settlement issues see Green (1995).

28 If APEC is true to its intention of being a non-discriminatory grouping, the case is weak for establishing a separate dispute settlement mechanism beyond that of the WTO. Rather than creating a different set of preferential rules for behaviour towards fellow members, APEC aspires to WTO consistency through the application of the MFN principle. Since APEC members are supposed to give the same treatment to all trading partners it is logical for their behaviour to be subject to WTO disciplines rather than to a specific APEC dispute-settlement regime.

29 For an alternative perspective, critical of the ambiguities in APEC's approach, see Yuen (1999).

30 APEC's proponents have argued that the fear of 'free-riding' by non-members is unwarranted because of the high percentage of trade where APEC members are principal suppliers to one another (see Wonnacott 1995; Garnaut 1996, Tables 4.1 and 4.2: 76–9).

31 The relationship between the ABAC and PECC has on occasion been tense. For a number of business representatives, APEC would have been better served by building on the business component of PECC – and specifically on PBEC. See Gadbaw 1997 and Bodde 1997.

32 The first Executive Director of the APEC Secretariat, William Bodde (1994: 27) details the costs to APEC of having Senior Officials Meeting (SOMs) play such a prominent role in agenda-setting:

> Clearly, the SOMs are too large and cumbersome. There is a constantly changing cast of characters, which means that a certain amount of time is taken up at each meeting to bring the newcomers up to date. It is not that they have not read their briefs, but that they must learn the APEC corporate culture. It is not uncommon to see a SOM get bogged down by some minor, albeit symbolic, procedural issue that takes up a great deal of time. The result is that more important issues are sometimes given less attention than they deserve.

33 The literature on collaboration suggests that monitoring by individual states becomes more difficult as the number of participants increases.

34 The South Pacific Forum, renamed the Pacific Islands Forum in October 2000, was established in 1971 and represents all the independent island states of the Pacific. Its members are Australia, Cook Islands, Federated States of Micronesia, Fiji, Kiribati, Nauru, New Zealand, Niue, Palau, Papua New Guinea, Republic of the Marshall Islands, Samoa, Solomon Islands, Tonga, Tuvalu, and Vanuatu. Although South Pacific islands had participated in the discussions on Asia-Pacific regionalism in the 1980s, and the Forum has full membership in PECC, Pacific islands economies were excluded from the list of countries Australia proposed as candidates for APEC membership. Papua New Guinea was admitted to APEC at the first leaders' meeting but the other islands remain, in R. Gerald Ward's term, the 'hole in the doughnut' of the Pacific Rim (Ward 1989).

35 The previous year, NGOs found their hotel reservations cancelled in Jakarta by the Indonesian government (Wilkinson 1996: 8).

36 On Canadian government suppression of the demonstrations at the 1997 Vancouver meetings, see Ericson and Doyle (1999). Other articles that discuss NGOs' exclusion from APEC include Bowles (1998), and Delahunty (1999).

37 Haworth (1999) records that although Human Resource Development was one of the first areas identified for economic and technical cooperation, members have restricted discussions of this topic to 'technical' issues such as training and productivity, and have avoided 'political' issues such as labour standards. Recent American attempts to broaden APEC's human resource development agenda to include labour standards not surprisingly have gone nowhere.

38 Stephen Holloway, Acting National Manager, Executive Support Branch, Australian Customs Service, quoted in Australia, Parliament of the Commonwealth (2000: 149).

39 A PECC Study conducted for APEC identified the major foreign direct investment impediments within the then eighteen APEC economies as: restricted or closed sectors (all economies), screening or notification requirements (17 countries), taxation incentives (13), fiscal incentives (11), performance requirements (9), and exchange controls (5) (see PECC 1995; Pangestu 1999: 284–5).

40 The 'sectors' were defined narrowly at the two- or four-digit levels of the harmonized tariff code, with some products to be excluded defined at the six-digit level. This definition of a sector is much narrower than that for an 'industry', which is usually defined at the one- or two-digit level. Such a narrow definition has implications for the welfare effects of tariff removal,

especially since – as in the food sector proposal – numerous processed products were excluded. Where tariffs are removed on upstream producers yet retained on final products – as was proposed, for instance, in the chemicals and food sectors – the effect may be to raise the effective rates of protection of the downstream producers, thereby encouraging resources to move away from a welfare-optimizing distribution. Moreover, the sectors selected for liberalization were not those with the highest levels of tariffs: selective liberalization again promised to distort the allocation of resources away from that optimal for global welfare. A study by the Australian Productivity Commission (Dee et al. 1998) estimated, for instance, that implementation of the EVSL program's food proposal would cause a loss in allocative efficiency in several APEC economies, including Malaysia, Japan, and New Zealand, as resources shift out of the partially liberalized areas into those products that continued to enjoy high levels of tariff protection. The study concluded that 'it remains a real question, therefore, whether EVSL initiatives are likely to guarantee real income gains to a majority of APEC members'. See also Lloyd (1999b).

41 At the subsequent ministerial meeting in Kuala Lumpur, the Japanese Foreign Minister, Masahiko Komura, was reported to have asserted that 'Although I am not very familiar with the English language, I understand that the V in EVSL stands for voluntary, which means this is not a process for negotiation' (quoted in Boyd 1998).

42 For instance, an APEC Automotive Dialogue was established in 1999.

43 So sensitive is the fisheries sector for the Japanese government that it has refused even to participate in the economic and technical cooperation dimensions of APEC collaboration on this sector.

5 APEC Adrift

1 Attempts by the New Zealand government to revive the EVSL program went nowhere. Nonetheless, a palpable sense of relief characterized the Auckland meetings after the public relations disaster of APEC's previous Leaders' Meeting in Kuala Lumpur. That meeting had seen not only open dispute among members over the EVSL program, but also acrimony arising from thinly-veiled attacks by US Vice-President Al Gore and other Western representatives on the meeting's host, Prime Minister Mahathir, over his treatment of his former deputy, Anwar. For a positive interpretation of the Auckland meeting along these lines, see, for instance, comments by the President of the East-West Centre, Charles Morrison, 'Auckland, a New Lease of Life for APEC' (*Honolulu Advertiser* 19 September 1999). Rather than being able to report forward movement on its economic agenda, however, recent APEC meetings have been limited to proclaiming that members had reaffirmed existing commitments and, despite the economic crises in Asia in 1997–98, had not retreated from APEC's program.

2 Negotiations with Singapore have progressed most rapidly. The proposal, eschewing the phrase 'free-trade agreement', is for a 'Japan–Singapore Economic Agreement for a New Age Partnership' to be concluded before the end of 2001 (Ministry of Economy, Trade and Industry 2000). Cameron (1998) and Plummer (1998) discuss relations between APEC and the two most significant regional agreements currently nested within it, NAFTA and ASEAN.

3 A more cynical interpretation of the new interest in bilateralism, an interpretation consistent with views that regional arrangements can be stumbling blocks in the road of global trade liberalization, is that the free-trade agreements negotiated in bilateral or minilateral arrangements often lack comprehensiveness. Despite the WTO stricture that such agreements should cover 'substantially all trade', governments frequently exempt their most sensitive sectors from their coverage. Negotiating bilaterally may enable governments to avoid the hard political choices – and domestic political opposition – that arise from WTO negotiations (or from the 'comprehensive' sectoral coverage pledged for APEC). It was almost certainly no coincidence that the first negotiations that the Japanese government completed for a bilateral agreement were with Singapore. Few countries in the global economy pose less of a threat to Japan's sensitive domestic commodity producers than does Singapore. Nonetheless, perceiving that this agreement might be the thin end of an unattractive wedge, Japan's Ministry of Agriculture, Forestry and Fisheries opposed it.

4 At the time, six APEC economies – Brunei, Malaysia, Papua New Guinea, the Philippines, Singapore, and Vietnam – did not have laws on competition policy. On competition policy in APEC, see Lloyd (1998) and Choi (1999).

5 Information on APEC's ECOTECH activities is available on the APEC Secretariat's web site at http://203.127.220.68/Apecp1.nsf?OpenDatabase.

6 In Yamazawa's (1997: 143) words: 'A typical APEC ECOTECH activity is a pet project proposed and coordinated by a member, financed mainly by the sponsor, and partly supported by APEC.'

7 For other studies of APEC's projects in the environmental field, which note similar weaknesses, see Crowley and Findlay (1996), Zarsky and Hunter (1997), Rugman and Soloway (1997), Merson (1998), Wenjing and Yumin (1998), Zarsky (1998), and Dua and Esty (1997).

8 Broken down by type of activity, the 220 projects under way in 2000 consisted of: Survey/Study/Report (75); Workshop/Seminar (59); Training (38); Standard/Best Practice (4); Database/Website/Network (37); and APEC Centre/Exposition (7) (APEC 2000b).

9 With acknowledgement to the title of Thornton's (1988) delightful little book.

10 Details available on the WTO's dispute settlement mechanisms web pages at http://www.wto.org. The frequency with which APEC members have appeared at the WTO casts some doubt on arguments (e.g. Drysdale et al. 1998: 20) that APEC has a 'calming influence' on bilateral trade tensions.

11 I am grateful to Natasha Hamilton-Hart for this point.

12 Further evidence to support the argument of Smith (2000).

13 The comments by Australian Prime Minister Paul Keating (2000: 107–8) to the US ambassador in Canberra in the run-up to the debate on setting a target date for trade liberalization at Bogor are perceptive on the considerations of some Asian governments: 'it was not hyperbole to say we would never get a chance like this again. China was not quite confident enough to say no; the Japanese were not quite politically secure enough to say no; and we had this proposal for free trade before us from one of the leading developing countries'.

14 A similar pattern of bureaucratic capacity and/or commitment to APEC is evident in the EVSL program. Four economies – Chile, Korea, Mexico, and Papua New Guinea – did not nominate any of the sectors on the final list for the EVSL program. A review of later data (up until the end of 1999) on eco-

nomic and technical cooperation on the APEC Secretariat website shows Chile and Mexico taking responsibility for leading three ECOTECH projects each. The full list of APEC projects can be searched through the database accessible at: http://203.127.220.68/Apecp1.nsf?OpenDatabase.

15 The decision to admit Russia was another case where some smaller APEC members felt obliged to go along with the wishes of the major economies. Australia had opposed Russian entry to the institution but to no avail. Consensus, indeed, did not always require unanimity – smaller states felt compelled to refrain from using their unit veto when faced by a coalition of more powerful partners.

16 The magazine commented that the addition of Russia, Vietnam and Peru to APEC's membership in 1998 'makes the organisation seem all the odder'.

17 On ASEM, see the references in Chapter 3 note 23.

18 ASEAN Plus Three brings together the ten member states of ASEAN with China, Korea and Japan.

19 This is an appropriate point at which to remind readers that I use the term East Asia as shorthand for Northeast and Southeast Asia.

20 Moreover, the exclusion of Taiwan denies membership to one of Asia's largest, most wealthy, and technologically vibrant economies. Long-term cooperation within the group is also likely to be vulnerable to leadership rivalries between China and Japan. Meanwhile, ASEAN's determination to be the focal point of the grouping does not bode well for its chances of developing into something more than a discussion forum.

21 APIAN (2000) provides further modest suggestions for improving APEC's operations.

22 For historical examples, see Oye (1992); for discussion of more contemporary developments, see Baldwin (1997) and Mattli (1999).

23 The rapid growth of official meetings, and the rush by most government ministries to create a division or desk dealing with APEC, might appear to support the cynical interpretation of Hughes (1991).

24 'Japan Conquers APEC' was the *Economist*'s (11 November 1995: 31–2) reflection on the Japanese government's success in diluting the trade liberalization push at the Osaka meetings.

25 Sylvia Ostry (1998) provides further comparisons of the OECD and APEC.

References

Abbott, Kenneth W. 1985, 'The trading nation's dilemma: the functions of the law of international trade', *Harvard International Law Journal* 26(2): 501–32.

Acharya, Amitav 1997, 'Ideas, identity, and institution-building: from the "ASEAN way" to the "Asia-Pacific way"?' *Pacific Review* 10(3): 319–46.

Adler, Emanuel 1991, 'Cognitive evolution: a dynamic approach for the study of international relations and their progress'. In Adler and Crawford (eds), *Progress in Postwar International Relations,* 43–88.

Adler, Emanuel, and Beverly Crawford (eds) 1991, *Progress in Postwar International Relations,* New York: Columbia University Press.

Aggarwal, Vinod K. 1985, *Liberal Protectionism: The International Politics of Organized Textile Trade,* Berkeley, Cal.: University of California Press.

Aggarwal, Vinod K. 1993, 'Building international institutions in Asia-Pacific', *Asian Survey* 33(11): 1029–42.

Aggarwal, Vinod K. 1995, 'Comparing regional cooperation efforts in the Asia-Pacific and North America'. Mack and Ravenhill (eds), *Pacific Cooperation,* 40–65.

Aggarwal, Vinod K. 1996, *Debt Games: Strategic Interaction in International Debt Rescheduling,* Cambridge University Press.

Aggarwal, Vinod K., and Charles E. Morrison (eds) 1998, *Asia-Pacific Crossroads: Regime Creation and the Future of APEC,* New York: St Martin's.

Aggarwal, Vinod K., and Charles E. Morrison 1999, 'APEC as an international institution'. Paper presented at the 25th Pacific Trade and Development Conference, Kansai, 16–18 June.

Akami, Tomoko 1995, The liberal dilemma: internationalism and the Institute of Pacific Relations in the USA, Australia and Japan, 1919–1942. PhD thesis, ANU, Canberra.

Akao, Nobutoshi 1995, 'Strategy for APEC: a Japanese view', *Japan Review of International Affairs* 9(3): 169–77.

Akashi, Yoji 1997, 'An ASEAN perspective on APEC'. Working Paper No. 240. South Bend, In.: Helen Kellogg Institute for International Studies, University of Notre Dame.

Akrasanee, Narongchai 1981, 'ASEAN and Pacific economic co-operation: a survey of issues of interdependence'. In Crawford and Seow (eds), *Pacific Economic Co-operation*, 163–73.

Alesina, Alberto, and Romain Wacziarg 1998, 'Openness, country size and government', *Journal of Public Economics* 69(3): 305–22.

Alitas, Ali 1994, 'Basic principles, objectives and modalities of APEC'. In Hadi Soesastro (ed.), *Indonesian Perspectives on APEC and Regional Cooperation in Asia Pacific*, Jakarta: Centre for Strategic and International Studies.

Alt, James E., Jeffrey Frieden, Michael J. Gilligan, Dani Rodrik and Ronald Rogowski 1996, 'The political economy of international trade: enduring puzzles and an agenda for inquiry', *Comparative Political Studies* 29(6): 689–717.

Amsden, Alice H. 1989, *Asia's Next Giant: South Korea and Late Industrialization*, New York: Oxford University Press.

Anderson, Kym 1997, 'On the complexities of China's WTO accession', *World Economy* 20(6): 749–72.

Anderson, Malcolm, Richard Blandy and Sarah Carne 1993, 'Academic economic opinion in East Asia', *Australian Economic Review* 103 (July–September): 5–19.

APEC 1991, Asia-Pacific Economic Cooperation, Third Ministerial Meeting, Seoul 12–14 November, Annex B, 'Seoul APEC Declaration', Paragraph 7. Available on the APEC Secretariat website.

APEC 1993, *A Vision for APEC: Towards an Asia Pacific Economic Community, Report of the Eminent Persons Group to APEC Ministers, October 1993*, Singapore: APEC Secretariat.

APEC 1994a, *Achieving the APEC Vision: Free and Open Trade in the Asia Pacific: Second Report of the Eminent Persons Group*, Singapore: APEC Secretariat.

APEC 1994b, 'APEC economic leaders' Declaration of Common Resolve, Bogor, Indonesia, 15 November 1994', Singapore: APEC Secretariat. Available at http://www. http://www.apecsec.org.sg/virtualib/econlead/bogor.html.

APEC 1995a, *Implementing the APEC Vision, Third Report of the Eminent Persons Group*, Singapore: APEC Secretariat.

APEC 1995b, 'The Osaka Action Agenda: implementation of the Bogor Declaration', Singapore: APEC Secretariat. Available at http://www.apecsec.org.sg/virtualib/history/osaka/agenda.html.

APEC 1996, 'APEC economic leaders' Declaration, "From Vision to Action", Subic Bay, 25 November 1996', Singapore: APEC Secretariat. Available at http://www.apecsec.org.sg/virtualib/history/mapa/mapa.html.

APEC 1997, 'The impact of trade liberalization in APEC', Singapore: APEC Secretariat.

APEC 1998, 'APEC working groups and experts groups: research and analysis', Singapore: APEC Secretariat. Available at http://www.apecsec.org.sg/workgroup/research.html.

APEC 2000a, 'Open Economies Delivering to People: APEC's Decade of Progress'. Report prepared for the APEC Economic Leaders' Meeting, Brunei Darussalam 2000, Singapore: APEC Secretariat.

APEC 2000b, '2000 Report on Economic and Technical Cooperation', Singapore: APEC Secretariat, APEC #00-ES-01.1, November.

APIAN (APEC International Assessment Network) 2000, 'Learning from Experience: The first APIAN Policy Report', Singapore: Singapore APEC Study Center for APIAN.

Arase, David 1995, *Buying Power: The Political Economy of Japan's Foreign Aid*, Boulder, Co.: Lynne Rienner Publishers.

Ariff, Mohamed 1994a, 'APEC and ASEAN: complementing or competing?' In Chia Siow Yue (ed.), *APEC: Challenges and Opportunities*, 151–74.

Ariff, Mohamed 1994b, 'The role of APEC: an Asian perspective', *Journal of Japanese Trade and Industry* 13(1): 46–9.

Arndt, H. W. 1967, 'PAFTA: An Australian assessment', *Intereconomics* 10: 271–6.

ASEAN Secretariat 1989, 'Joint Communique of the Twenty-Second ASEAN Ministerial Meeting, Bandar Seri Begawan, 3–4 July 1989', Jakarta: ASEAN Secretariat, July. Available at http://www.asean.or.id/.

Australia, Parliament of the Commonwealth 1973, 'Japan: Report from the Senate Standing Committee on Foreign Affairs and Defence', Canberra: AGPS.

Australia, Parliament of the Commonwealth 2000, 'Australia and APEC: A Review of Asia Pacific Economic Cooperation', Canberra: Senate Foreign Affairs, Defence and Trade References Committee.

Axelrod, Robert M. 1984, *The Evolution of Cooperation*, New York: Basic Books.

Axline, W. Andrew 1977, 'Underdevelopment, dependence and integration: the politics of regionalism in the Third World', *International Organization* 31(1): 83–105.

Axline, W. Andrew 1994, 'Cross-regional comparisons and the theory of regional cooperation: lessons from Latin America, the Caribbean, South East Asia and the South Pacific'. In W. Andrew Axline (ed.), *The Political Economy of Regional Cooperation: Comparative Case Studies*, London: Pinter, 178–224.

Baker, James A. 1988, 'A new trade policy strategy for the United States, address before the Canadian Importers Association (June 22, 1988)', *World Economy* 11(2): 215–16.

Baker, Richard W. 1989, 'A new Pacific partnership', *Department of State Bulletin*, August.

Baker, Richard W. 1998, 'The United States and APEC regime building'. In Aggarwal and Morrison (eds), *Asia-Pacific Crossroads*, 165–89.

Baldwin, Richard E. 1997, 'The causes of regionalism', *World Economy* 20(7): 865–88.

Baldwin, Richard E., and Anthony J. Venables 1995, 'Regional economic integration'. In Gene Grossman and Kenneth Rogoff (eds), *Handbook of International Economics* vol. 3, New Holland: Elsevier, 1597–644.

Bandura, Y. 1980, 'The Pacific Community – a brain-child of imperialist diplomacy', *International Affairs* (Moscow) June: 63–70.

Barichello, Richard R., and Frank R. Flatters 1991, 'Trade policy reform in Indonesia'. In Dwight H. Perkins and Michael Roemer (eds), *Reforming Economic Systems in Developing Countries*, Cambridge, Ma.: Harvard Institute for International Development, 271–91.

Bates, Robert H. 1981, *Markets and States in Tropical Africa: The Political Basis of Agricultural Policies*, Berkeley, Cal.: University of California Press.

Bates, Robert H., and Anne O. Krueger (eds) 1993, *Political and Economic Interactions in Economic Policy Reform: Evidence from Eight Countries*, Oxford: Basil Blackwell.

Bates, Stephen Edward 1996, The new regionalism: comparing the development of the EC Single Integrated Market, NAFTA and APEC. PhD thesis, ANU, Canberra.

Bayard, Thomas O., and Kimberly Ann Elliott 1994, *Reciprocity and Retaliation in US Trade Policy*, Washington, D.C.: Institute for International Economics.

Bell, Stephen 1993, *Australian Manufacturing and the State: The Politics of Industry Policy in the Post-War Era*, Cambridge University Press.

Bergsten, C. Fred 1994, 'APEC and world trade: a force for worldwide liberalization', *Foreign Affairs* 73(3): 20–6.

Bergsten, C. Fred 1996, 'Globalizing free trade', *Foreign Affairs* 75(3): 105–21.

Bergsten, C. Fred 1997a, 'APEC in 1997: prospects and possible strategies'. In C. Fred Bergsten (ed.), *Whither APEC? The Progress to Date and Agenda for the Future*, Washington, D.C.: Institute for International Economics, 3–17.

Bergsten, C. Fred 1997b, 'Open regionalism'. In C. Fred Bergsten (ed.), *Whither APEC? The Progress to Date and Agenda for the Future*, Washington, D.C.: Institute for International Economics, 83–105.

Bergsten, C. Fred 1997c, 'Open regionalism', *World Economy* 20(5): 545–65.

Bergsten, C. Fred 2001, 'Alternative Trade Liberalization Strategies'. Speech presented at the 2001 PBEC Annual Policy Conference. Accessed 8 April 2001, http://www.pbec.org/speeches/2001/010205bergsten.htm.

Bernard, Mitchell, and John Ravenhill 1995, 'Beyond product cycles and flying geese: regionalization, hierarchy, and the industrialization of East Asia', *World Politics* 45(2): 179–210.

Betts, Richard K. 1995, 'Wealth, power and conflict: East Asia after the Cold War'. In Robert S. Ross (ed.), *East Asia in Transition: Toward a New Regional Order*, Armonk: M. E. Sharpe, 21–55.

Bhagwati, Jagdish, and Arvind Panagariya 1996a, 'Preferential trading areas and multilateralism – strangers, friends, or foes?' In Bhagwati and Panagariya (eds), *The Economics of Preferential Trade Agreements*, 1–78.

Bhagwati, Jagdish, and Arvind Panagariya (eds) 1996b, *The Economics of Preferential Trade Agreements*, Washington, D.C.: AEI Press.

Bhagwati, Jagdish, and Hugh T. Patrick (eds) 1990, *Aggressive Unilateralism: America's 301 Trade Policy and the World Trading System*, Ann Arbor: University of Michigan Press.

Biersteker, Thomas J. 1992, 'The "triumph" of neoclassical economics in the developing world: policy convergence and bases of governance in the international economic order'. In James N. Rosenau and Ernst-Otto Czempiel (eds), *Governance without Government: Order and Change in World Politics*, Cambridge University Press, 102–31.

Biersteker, Thomas J. 1995, 'The "triumph" of liberal economic ideas in the developing world'. In Barbara Stallings (ed.), *Global Change, Regional Response: The New International Context of Development*, Cambridge University Press, 174–96.

Bobrow, Davis B. 1999, 'The US and ASEM: why the hegemon didn't bark', *Pacific Review* 12(10): 103–28.

Bodde, William 1994, *View from the 19th Floor: Reflections of the First APEC Executive Director*, Singapore: ASEAN Economic Research Unit, Institute of Southeast Asian Studies.

Bodde, William 1997, 'Managing APEC'. In C. Fred Bergsten (ed.), *Whither APEC? The Progress to Date and Agenda for the Future*, Washington, D.C.: Institute for International Economics, 11–23.

Bonnor, Jenelle 1996, 'APEC's contribution to regional security'. In Soesastro and Bergin (eds), *The Role of Security and Economic Cooperation Structures in the Asia Pacific Region*, 45–56.

Bora, Bijit, and Christopher Findlay (eds) 1996, *Regional Integration in the Asia-Pacific*, Melbourne: Oxford University Press.

Bora, Bijit, and E. M. Graham 1997, 'Can APEC deliver on investment?' In C. Fred Bergsten (ed.), *Whither APEC? The Progress to Date and Agenda for the Future*, Washington, D.C.: Institute for International Economics, 69–82.

Borrus, Michael, Dieter Ernst and Stephan Haggard (eds) 2000, *International Production Networks in Asia: Rivalry or Riches?* London: Routledge.

Borthwick, Mark 1987, 'United States policies toward Pacific cooperation'. In Kim and Conroy (eds), *New Tides in the Pacific*, 125–42.

Boston, Jonathan, John Martin, June Pallot and Pat Walsh (eds) 1991, *Reshaping the State: New Zealand's Bureaucratic Revolution*, Auckland: Oxford University Press.

Bowie, Alasdair, and Danny Unger 1997, *The Politics of Open Economies: Indonesia, Malaysia, the Philippines, and Thailand*, Cambridge University Press.

Bowles, Paul 1997, 'APEC: progress based on the wrong model?' *Canadian Business Economics* 6(1): 48–64.

Bowles, Paul 1998, 'APEC: no place for labour', *Labour/Le Travail* 41 (Spring): 330–1.

Bowles, Paul, and Brian McLean 1996, 'Regional trading blocs: will East Asia be next?' *Cambridge Journal of Economics* 20(4): 393–412.

Brander, J., and B. Spencer 1981, 'Tariffs and the extraction of foreign monopoly rents under potential entry', *Canadian Journal of Economics* 14: 371–89.

Breslauer, George W. 1987, 'Ideology and learning in Soviet Third World policy', *World Politics* 39(3): 429–48.

Bridges, Brian 1996, 'Western Europe and Southeast Asia'. In David Wurfel and Bruce Burton (eds), *Southeast Asia in the New World Order: The Political Economy of a Dynamic Region*, New York: St Martin's, 204–18.

Bull, Hedley 1977, *The Anarchical Society: A Study of Order in World Politics*, London: Macmillan.

Bull, Hedley, and Adam Watson (eds) 1984, *The Expansion of International Society*, Oxford: Clarendon Press.

Buszynski, Leszek 1983, *SEATO: The Failure of an Alliance Strategy*, Singapore University Press.

Butterfield, Herbert, and Martin Wight (eds) 1966, *Diplomatic Investigations: Essays in the Theory of International Politics*, Cambridge, Ma.: Harvard University Press.

Buzan, Barry 1991, *People, States and Fear: An Agenda for International Security Studies in the Post-Cold War Era*, 2nd edn, Hemel Hempstead: Harvester Wheatsheaf.

Cai, Kevin G. 1999, 'The political economy of economic regionalism in Northeast Asia: a unique and dynamic pattern', *East Asia: An International Quarterly* 17(2): 6–46.

Calder, Kent E. 1988a, *Crisis and Compensation: Public Policy and Political Stability in Japan, 1949–1986*, Princeton University Press.

Calder, Kent E. 1988b, 'Japanese foreign economic policy formation: explaining the reactive state', *World Politics* 40(4): 517–41.

Callaghy, Thomas M., and John Ravenhill (eds) 1993, *Hemmed In: Responses to Africa's Economic Decline*, New York: Columbia University Press.

Cameron, Maxwell A. 1998, 'Nesting NAFTA in APEC: the political economy of open subregionalism'. In Aggarwal and Morrison (eds), *Asia-Pacific Crossroads*, 257–78.

Camilleri, Joseph A., and Jim Falk 1992, *End of Sovereignty?: The Politics of a Shrinking and Fragmenting World*, Aldershot, England: Edward Elgar.

Camroux, David 1994, 'The Asia Pacific policy community in Malaysia', *Pacific Review* 7(4): 421–34.

Capling, Ann, and Brian Galligan 1992, *Beyond the Protective State: The Political Economy of Australia's Manufacturing Industry Policy*, Cambridge University Press.

Caporaso, James A. 1992, 'International relations theory and multilateralism: the search for foundations', *International Organization* 46(3): 599–632.
Castles, Francis G. 1988, *Australian Public Policy and Economic Vulnerability: A Comparative and Historical Perspective*, Sydney: Allen & Unwin.
Castles, Francis G., Rolf Gerritsen and Jack Vowles (eds) 1996, *The Great Experiment: Labour Parties and Public Policy Transformation in Australia and New Zealand*, Sydney: Allen & Unwin.
Chai, Joseph C. H., Y. Y. Kueh and Clement A. Tisdell (eds) 1997, *China and the Asian Pacific Economy*, Commack: Nova Science Publishers.
Chan, Kitty K., and Jeffrey B. Nugent 1999, 'Factor endowments, trade liberalization, and the future of APEC trade patterns', *Contemporary Economic Policy* 17(4): 517–29.
Chayes, Abram, and Antonia Handler Chayes 1993, 'On compliance', *International Organization* 47(2): 175–205.
Chayes, Abram, and Antonia Handler Chayes 1995, *The New Sovereignty: Compliance with International Regulatory Arrangements*, Cambridge, Ma.: Harvard University Press.
Checkel, Jeffrey T. 1998, 'The constructivist turn in International Relations theory', *World Politics* 50(2): 324–48.
Cheung, Gordon C. K. 1997, 'APEC as a regime for Taiwan's interdependence with the United States and mainland China', *Issues and Studies* 33(2): 21–39.
Chia Siow Yue 1994a, 'Asia-Pacific foreign direct investment: an APEC investment code?' In Chia Siow Yue (ed.), *APEC: Challenges and Opportunities*, 113–50.
Chia Siow Yue (ed.) 1994b, *APEC: Challenges and Opportunities*, Singapore: Institute of Southeast Asian Studies.
Chia Siow Yue and Lee Tsao Yuan 1993, 'Subregional economic zones: a new motive force in Asia-Pacific development'. In C. Fred Bergsten and Marcus Noland (eds), *Pacific Dynamism and the International Economic System*, Washington, D.C.: Institute for International Economics, 225–69.
Choi, Byung-il 1999, 'Competition principles and policy in the APEC: how to proceed and link with WTO', *Global Economic Review* 28(3): 31–48.
Clad, James Clovis 1992, 'The half-empty basin', *Wilson Quarterly* 16(1): 76–88.
Clark, Greg 1993, 'APEC: cornucopia or cul-de-saki?' *21C* Winter: 58–9.
Clarke, Jonathan 1995, 'APEC as a semi-solution', *Orbis* 39(1): 81–95.
Clinton, Bill 1993, 'Building a New Pacific Community'. Address at Waseda University, Tokyo, Japan, 7 July, *U.S. Department of State Dispatch* 4(28): 485–8.
Cohen, Stephen S., and John Zysman 1987, *Manufacturing Matters: The Myth of the Post-Industrial Economy*, New York: Basic Books.
Coker, Christopher 1988, 'The myth or reality of the Pacific century', *Washington Quarterly* 11(3): 5–16.
Conybeare, John A. C. 1987, *Trade Wars: The Theory and Practice of International Commercial Rivalry*, New York: Columbia University Press.
Cooper, Andrew F., Richard A. Higgott and Kim Richard Nossal 1993, *Relocating Middle Powers: Australia and Canada in a Changing World Order*, Vancouver: University of British Columbia Press.
Cooper, Richard N. 1968, *The Economics of Interdependence: Economic Policy in the Atlantic Community*, New York: McGraw-Hill.
Cooper, Richard N., Barry Eichengreen, C. Randall Henning, Gerald Holtham and Robert D. Putnam (eds) 1989, *Can Nations Agree? Issues in International Economic Cooperation*, Washington, D.C.: Brookings Institution.
Corden, W. Max 1974, *Trade Policy and Economic Welfare*, Oxford: Clarendon Press.

Cortright, David, and George A. Lopez (eds) 1995, *Economic Sanctions: Panacea of Peacebuilding in a Post-Cold War World?* Boulder, Co.: Westview.

Cowhey, Peter F. 1993a, 'Domestic institutions and the credibility of international commitments: Japan and the United States', *International Organization* 47(2): 299–326.

Cowhey, Peter F. 1993b, 'Elect locally – order globally: domestic politics and multilateral cooperation'. In John Gerard Ruggie (ed.), *Multilateralism Matters: The Theory and Praxis of an Institutional Form*, New York: Columbia University Press, 157–200.

Cox, Robert W. 1969, 'The executive head: an essay on leadership in international organization', *International Organization* 23(2): 205–30.

Cox, Robert W. 1986, 'Social forces, states, and world orders: beyond International Relations theory'. In Robert O. Keohane (ed.), *Neorealism and its Critics*, New York: Columbia University Press, 204–55.

Cox, Robert W. 1987, *Production, Power, and World Order: Social Forces in the Making of History*, New York: Columbia University Press.

Cox, Robert W., and Harold K. Jacobson (eds) 1974, *The Anatomy of Influence*, New Haven, Ct.: Yale University Press.

Crawford, Sir John, and Saburo Okita (eds) 1976, *Australia, Japan, and Western Pacific Economic Relations: A Report to the Governments of Australia and Japan, presented by Sir John Crawford and Dr. Saburo Okita*, Canberra: AGPS.

Crawford, Sir John, and Greg Seow (eds) 1981, *Pacific Economic Co-operation: Suggestions for Action*, Selangor, Malaysia: Heinemann Asia.

Crawford, Sue E. S., and Elinor Ostrom 1995, 'A grammar of institutions', *American Political Science Review* 89(3): 582–600.

Crone, Donald 1992, 'The politics of emerging Pacific cooperation', *Pacific Affairs* 65(1): 68–83.

Crone, Donald 1993, 'Does hegemony matter? The reorganization of the Pacific political economy', *World Politics* 45(4): 501–25.

Crone, Donald 1996, 'New political roles for ASEAN'. In David Wurfel and Bruce Burton (eds), *Southeast Asia in the New World Order: The Political Economy of a Dynamic Region*, New York: St Martin's, 36–51.

Crowley, Peter, and Christopher Findlay 1996, 'Environmental issues'. In Bora and Findlay (eds), *Regional Integration in the Asia-Pacific*, 140–50.

Curtis, John M., and Dan Ciuriak 1999, 'APEC after ten years: performance and prospects'. Paper presented at APEC Study Centre Consortium Conference, Auckland, 31 May–2 June.

Davis, Brent 1997, Testimony before the Senate Foreign Affairs, Defence and Trade Reference Committee, Parliament of the Commonwealth of Australia, *Official Hansard Report*, 29 September.

de Melo, Jaime, and Arvind Panagariya (eds) 1993, *New Dimensions in Regional Integration*, Cambridge University Press.

Dee, P., A. Hardin and M. Schuele 1998, 'APEC Early Voluntary Sectoral Liberalisation'. Productivity Commission Staff Research Paper. Canberra: AusInfo.

Delahunty, Jim 1999, 'APEC at Auckland', *Monthly Review* 51(7): 15–23.

Deng, Yong 1997a, 'Japan in APEC: the problematic leadership role', *Asian Survey* 37(4): 353–67.

Deng, Yong 1997b, *Promoting Asia-Pacific Economic Cooperation: Perspectives from East Asia*, London: Macmillan.

Dent, Christopher M. 1997–98, 'The ASEM: managing the new framework of the EU's economic relations with East Asia', *Pacific Affairs* 70(4): 495–516.

Department of the Environment, Commonwealth of Australia 1998, 'Submission'. In Senate Standing Committee on Foreign Affairs Defence and Trade: References Committee (ed.), *APEC Inquiry Submissions*, vol. 7, Canberra: Parliament of Australia.

DFAT (Department of Foreign Affairs and Trade), Commonwealth of Australia 1989a, 'Asia Pacific Economic Co-operation: Preliminary submission to the Joint Committee on Foreign Affairs, Defence and Trade', Canberra: DFAT, October.

DFAT, Commonwealth of Australia 1989b, 'APEC Ministerial-Level Meeting Canberra, 6–7 November 1989: Documentation', Canberra: DFAT, November.

DFAT, Commonwealth of Australia 1989c, 'Asia Pacific Economic Cooperation: World and Regional Economic Developments: Background Information Paper by Australia'. In Commonwealth of Australia DFAT (ed.), *APEC Ministerial-Level Meeting Canberra, 6–7 November 1989: Documentation*, Canberra: DFAT, 62–83.

Deutsch, Karl W., Sidney A. Burrell, Robert A. Kann, Maurice Lee, Jr., Martin Lichterman, Raymond E. Lindgren, Francis L. Loewenheim and Richard W. Van Wagenen 1957, *Political Community and the North Atlantic Area*, Princeton University Press.

Deutsch, Karl W., et al. 1966, 'Political community and the North Atlantic Area'. In *International Political Communities: An Anthology*, New York: Anchor Books, 1–91.

Dezhao, Chen, and Kuang Mei 1996, 'APEC vs. China's reform and opening up'. In Yamazawa and Hirata (eds), *APEC: Cooperation from Diversity*, 53–9.

Doner, Richard 1993, 'Japanese foreign investment and the creation of a Pacific-Asian Region'. In Jeffrey A. Frankel and Miles Kahler (eds), *Regionalism and Rivalry: Japan and the United States in Pacific Asia*, University of Chicago Press, 159–215.

Doner, Richard F. 1997, 'Japan in East Asia: institutions and regional leadership'. In Katzenstein and Shiraishi (eds), *Network Power*, 197–233.

Doner, Richard F., and Ansil Ramsay 1993, 'Postimperialism and development in Thailand', *World Development* 21(5): 691–704.

Dosi, Giovanni, Keith Pavitt and Luc Soete 1990, *The Economics of Technical Change and International Trade*, New York: Harvester Wheatsheaf.

Douglas, Roger 1993, *Unfinished Business*, Auckland: Random House.

Downs, George W., and David M. Rocke 1995, *Optimal Imperfection? Domestic Uncertainty and Institutions in International Relations*, Princeton University Press.

Downs, George W., David M. Rocke and Peter N. Barsoom 1996, 'Is the good news about compliance good news about cooperation?' *International Organization* 50(3): 379–406.

Drysdale, Peter 1968, 'Pacific economic integration: an Australian view'. In Kiyoshi Kojima (ed.), *Pacific Trade and Development: Papers and Proceedings of a Conference held by the Japan Economic Research Center in January, 1968*, Tokyo: Nihon Keizai Kenkyu Senta.

Drysdale, Peter 1978, 'An organization for Pacific trade, aid and development: regional arrangements and the resource trade'. In Lawrence B. Krause and Hugh Patrick (eds), *Mineral Resources in the Pacific Area: Papers and Proceedings of the Ninth Pacific Trade and Development Conference*, San Francisco: Federal Reserve Bank of San Francisco, 611–48.

Drysdale, Peter 1984, 'The Pacific Trade and Development Conference: a brief history'. ANU Research Paper No. 112. Canberra: Australia–Japan Research Centre.

Drysdale, Peter 1988, *International Economic Pluralism: Economic Policy in East Asia and the Pacific,* Sydney: Allen & Unwin.

Drysdale, Peter 1996, 'The APEC initiative: maintaining the momentum in Manila', *Asia-Pacific Magazine* 2 (May): 44–6.

Drysdale, Peter 1997, 'APEC and the WTO: complementary or competing?' Paper presented to ISEAS APEC Roundtable, Singapore, 'APEC – Sustaining the Momentum', August.

Drysdale, Peter, and Ross Garnaut 1993, 'The Pacific: an application of a general theory of economic integration'. In C. Fred Bergsten and Marcus Noland (eds), *Pacific Dynamism and the International Economic System,* Washington, D.C.: Institute for International Economics, 183–223.

Drysdale, Peter, and Hugh Patrick 1981, 'An Asian-Pacific regional economic organisation: an exploratory concept paper'. In Crawford and Seow (eds), *Pacific Economic Co-operation,* 63–82.

Drysdale, Peter, David Vines and Brett House 1998, 'Europe and East Asia: a shared global agenda?' In Peter Drysdale and David Vines (eds), *Europe, East Asia, and APEC: A Shared Global Agenda?* Cambridge University Press, 3–30.

Dua, Andre, and Daniel C. Esty 1997, 'APEC and sustainable development'. In C. Fred Bergsten (ed.), *Whither APEC? The Progress to Date and Agenda for the Future,* Washington, D.C.: Institute for International Economics, 151–78.

Dunning, John H. 1977, 'Trade, location of economic activity and the MNE: a search for an eclectic approach'. In Bertil Gotthard Ohlin, Per-Ove Hesselborn and Magnus Per Wijkman (eds), *The International Allocation of Economic Activity,* London: Macmillan, 395–418.

Dunning, John H. 1988, *Explaining International Production,* London: Unwin Hyman.

Dupont, Alan 2001, *East Asia Imperilled: Transnational Challenges to Security,* Cambridge University Press.

Dutta, M. 1999, *Economic Regionalization in the Asia-Pacific: Challenges to Economic Cooperation,* Cheltenham, England: Edward Elgar.

Eichengreen, Barry 1989, 'Hegemonic stability theories of the international monetary system'. In Cooper et al. (eds), *Can Nations Agree?,* 255–98.

Eichengreen, Barry, and Peter B. Kenen 1994, 'Managing the world economy under the Bretton Woods system: an overview'. In Peter B. Kenen (ed.), *Managing the World Economy: Fifty Years After Bretton Woods,* Washington, D.C.: Institute for International Economics, 3–57.

Elek, Andrew 1992, 'Trade policy options for the Asia-Pacific region in the 1990s: the potential of open regionalism', *American Economic Review* 82(2): 74–8.

Elek, Andrew (ed.) 1997, *Building an Asia-Pacific Economic Community: Development Co-operation within APEC,* Brisbane: Foundation for Development Cooperation.

Elek, Andrew, and Hadi Soesastro 1999, 'ECOTECH at the heart of APEC: capacity-building in the Asia-Pacific'. Paper presented at the 25th Pacific Trade and Development Conference, Kansai, 16–18 June.

Elster, Jon 1976, 'Some conceptual problems in political theory'. In Brian Barry (ed.), *Power and Political Theory: Some European Perspectives,* London: John Wiley.

Encarnation, Dennis J., and Mark Mason 1990, 'Neither MITI nor America: the political economy of capital liberalization in Japan', *International Organization* 44(1): 25–54.

Ensign, Margee M. 1992, *Doing Good or Doing Well? Japan's Foreign Aid Program,* New York: Columbia University Press.

Ericson, Richard, and Aaron Doyle 1999, 'Globalization and the policing of protest: the case of APEC 1997', *British Journal of Sociology* 50(4): 589–608.

Ethier, Wilfred J. 1998, 'The new regionalism', *Economic Journal* 108(449): 1149–61.

Ethier, Wilfred J. 1999, 'Multilateral roads to regionalism'. In John Piggott and Alan Woodland (eds), *International Trade Policy and the Pacific Rim: Proceedings of the IEA Conference Held in Sydney, Australia*, London: Macmillan, 131–52.

Evans, Gareth 1995, 'APEC: a blueprint for Asia's long-term growth'. Address to World Economic Forum 1995, Europe–East Asia Economic Summit, Singapore.

Evans, Gareth, and Bruce Grant 1991, *Australia's Foreign Relations in the World of the 1990s*, Melbourne University Press.

Evans, Peter B. 1993, 'Building an integrative approach to international and domestic politics: reflections and projections'. In Evans et al. (eds), *Double-Edged Diplomacy*, 397–430.

Evans, Peter B., Harold K. Jacobson and Robert D. Putnam (eds) 1993, *Double-Edged Diplomacy: International Bargaining and Domestic Politics*, Berkeley, Cal.: University of California Press.

Fane, George 1995, 'APEC: Regionalism, Globalism, or Obfuscation?' *Agenda* 2(4): 399–409.

Fernandez, Raquel 1997, 'Returns to regionalism: an evaluation of nontraditional gains from regional trade agreements'. Working Paper No. 1816. Washington, D.C.: World Bank, Policy Research.

Fernandez, Raquel, and Jonathan Portes 1998, 'Returns to regionalism: an analysis of nontraditional gains from regional trade agreements', *World Bank Economic Review* 12(2): 197–220.

Finnemore, Martha 1996a, *National Interests in International Society*, Ithaca: Cornell University Press.

Finnemore, Martha 1996b, 'Norms, culture, and world politics: insights from sociology's institutionalism', *International Organization* 50(2): 325–47.

Fishlow, Albert, and Stephan Haggard 1992, *The United States and the Regionalisation of the World Economy*, Paris: OECD.

Flam, H. 1995, 'From EEA to EU: economic consequences for the EFTA countries', *European Economic Review* 39(3–4): 457–66.

Flamm, Kenneth, and Edward J. Lincoln 1997, 'Time to reinvent APEC', *Brookings Policy Brief* 26 (November).

Franck, Thomas M. 1990, *The Power of Legitimacy Among Nations*, Oxford: Oxford University Press.

Franck, Thomas M. 1995, *Fairness in International Law and Institutions*, Oxford: Clarendon Press.

Frankel, Jeffrey 1991, 'Is a yen bloc forming in Pacific Asia?' In Richard O'Brien (ed.), *Finance and the International Economy 5: The AMEX Bank Review Prize Essays*, Oxford: Oxford University Press, 5–20.

Frankel, Jeffrey A. 1993, 'Is Japan creating a yen bloc in East Asia and the Pacific?' In Jeffrey A. Frankel and Miles Kahler (eds), *Regionalism and Rivalry: Japan and the United States in Pacific Asia*, University of Chicago Press, 53–87.

Fraser, Malcolm 1984, 'Pacific community: further steps'. In Robert L. Downen and Bruce J. Dickson (eds), *The Emerging Pacific Community: A Regional Perspective*, Boulder, Co.: Westview, 3–11.

Freedom House n.d., 'Table of independent countries, comparative measures of freedom 1995–1996'. Available at http://www.freedomhouse.org.

Freeman, Michael 1996, 'Human rights, democracy and "Asian values"', *Pacific Review* 9(3): 352–66.

Frieden, Jeffry 1991, *Debt, Development, and Democracy: Modern Political Economy and Latin America, 1965–1985*, Princeton University Press.

Frieden, Jeffry A., and Ronald Rogowski 1996, 'The impact of the international economy on national policies: an analytical overview'. In Robert O. Keohane and Helen V. Milner (eds), *Internationalization and Domestic Politics*, Cambridge University Press, 25–47.

Funabashi, Yoichi 1995, *Asia Pacific Fusion: Japan's Role in APEC*, Washington, D.C.: Institute for International Economics.

Gadbaw, R. Michael 1997, 'A business perspective on APEC's progress'. In C. Fred Bergsten (ed.), *Whither APEC? The Progress to Date and Agenda for the Future*, Washington, D.C.: Institute for International Economics, 235–40.

Gallant, Nicole, and Richard Stubbs 1997, 'APEC's dilemmas: institution-building around the Pacific Rim', *Pacific Affairs* 70(2): 203–18.

Garnaut, Ross 1989, *Australia and the Northeast Asian Ascendancy*, Canberra: AGPS.

Garnaut, Ross 1995, 'The Bogor Declaration on Asia-Pacific trade liberalisation', *Australian Quarterly* 67(2): 28–42.

Garnaut, Ross 1996, *Open Regionalism and Trade Liberalization: An Asia-Pacific Contribution to the World Trade System*, Singapore: Institute of Southeast Asian Studies.

Garrett, Geoffrey, and Barry R. Weingast 1993, 'Ideas, interests, and institutions: constructing the European Community's internal market'. In Goldstein and Keohane (eds), *Ideas and Foreign Policy*, 173–206.

George, Alexander L. 1979, 'Case studies and theory development: the method of structured, focused comparison'. In Paul Gordon Lauren (ed.), *Diplomacy: New Approaches in History, Theory, and Policy*, New York: Free Press, 43–68.

George, Aurelia 1983, 'The changing patterns of Japan's agricultural import trade: implications for Australia'. Research Paper No. 100. Canberra: Australia–Japan Research Centre, ANU.

George, Aurelia 1984, 'Japan's beef import policies, 1978–84: the growth of bilateralism'. Pacific Economic Papers No. 113. Canberra: Australia–Japan Research Centre, ANU.

Gill, Stephen 1990, *American Hegemony and the Trilateral Commission*, Cambridge University Press.

Gilpin, Robert 1972, 'The politics of transnational economic relations'. In Keohane and Nye (eds), *Transnational Relations and World Politics*.

Gilpin, Robert 1981, *War and Change in World Politics*, Cambridge University Press.

Gilpin, Robert 1987, *The Political Economy of International Relations*, Princeton University Press.

Gilson, Julie 1999, 'Japan's role in the Asia–Europe Meeting: establishing an interregional or intraregional agenda?' *Asian Survey* 39(5): 736–52.

Goldstein, Judith 1988, 'Ideas, institutions, and American trade policy', *International Organization* 42(1): 179–217.

Goldstein, Judith 1993, *Ideas, Interests and American Trade Policy*, Ithaca: Cornell University Press.

Goldstein, Judith 1996, 'International law and domestic institutions: reconciling North American "unfair" trade laws', *International Organization* 50(4): 541–64.

Goldstein, Judith, and Robert O. Keohane (eds) 1993a, *Ideas and Foreign Policy: Beliefs, Institutions and Political Change*, Ithaca: Cornell University Press.

Goldstein, Judith, and Robert O. Keohane 1993b, 'Ideas and foreign policy: an analytical framework'. In Goldstein and Keohane (eds), *Ideas and Foreign Policy*, 3–30.

Gordon, Bernard K. 1983, 'Japan and the Pacific Basin proposal'. In Hadi Soesastro and Han Sung-Joo (eds), *Pacific Economic Cooperation: The Next Phase*, Jakarta: Centre for Strategic and International Studies, 246–53.

Gourevitch, Peter Alexis 1977, 'International trade, domestic coalitions, and liberty: comparative responses to the crisis of 1873–96', *Journal of Interdisciplinary History* 8: 281–313.

Gourevitch, Peter Alexis 1996, 'Squaring the circle: the domestic sources of international cooperation', *International Organization* 50(2): 349–73.

Graham, Edward M. 1994, 'Towards an Asia-Pacific investment code', *Transnational Corporations* 3(2): 1–27.

Granatstein, J. L., and Robert Bothwell 1990, *Pirouette: Pierre Trudeau and Canadian Foreign Policy*, University of Toronto Press.

Grant, Bruce 1996, *Indonesia*, 3rd edn, Melbourne University Press.

Green, Carl J. 1995, 'APEC and trans-Pacific dispute management', *Law and Policy in International Business* 26(3): 719–34.

Grieco, Joseph M. 1990, *Cooperation among Nations: Europe, America, and Non-Tariff Barriers to Trade*, Ithaca: Cornell University Press.

Grieco, Joseph M. 1993a, 'The relative-gains problem for international cooperation: comment', *American Political Science Review* 87(3): 729–35.

Grieco, Joseph M. 1993b, 'Understanding the problem of international cooperation: the limits of neoliberal institutionalism and the future of Realist theory'. In David A. Baldwin (ed.), *Neorealism and Neoliberalism: The Contemporary Debate*, New York: Columbia University Press, 301–338.

Grieco, Joseph M. 1997, 'Systemic sources of variation in regional institutionalization in Western Europe, East Asia, and the Americas'. In Mansfield and Milner (eds), *The Political Economy of Regionalism*, 164–87.

Grossman, Gene M., and Elhanan Helpman 1990, 'Trade, innovation and growth', *American Economic Review* 80(2): 86–91.

Grossman, Gene M., and Elhanan Helpman 1995, 'The politics of free trade agreements', *American Economic Review* 85(4): 667–90.

Guisinger, Stephen 1991, 'Foreign direct investment flows in East and Southeast Asia: policy issues', *ASEAN Economic Bulletin* 8(1): 29–46.

Guisinger, Stephen 1993, 'A Pacific Basin investment agreement', *ASEAN Economic Bulletin* 10(2): 176–83.

Haas, Ernst B. 1958, *The Uniting of Europe: Political, Social, and Economic Forces, 1950–1957*, Stanford University Press.

Haas, Ernst B. 1971, 'The study of regional integration: reflections on the joy and anguish of pretheorizing'. In Lindberg and Scheingold (eds), *Regional Integration*, 3–42.

Haas, Ernst B. 1975, *The Obsolescence of Regional Integration Theory*, Berkeley, Cal.: Institute of International Studies, University of California.

Haas, Ernst B. 1990, *When Knowledge is Power: Three Models of Change in International Organizations*, Berkeley, Cal.: University of California Press.

Haas, Ernst B., and Philippe C. Schmitter 1966, 'Economics and differential patterns of political integration: projections about Latin America'. In *International Political Communities: An Anthology*, New York: Anchor Books, 259–99.

Haas, Peter M. 1992, 'Introduction: epistemic communities and international policy coordination', *International Organization* 46(1): 1–35.

Haas, Peter M. 1998, 'Compliance with EU directives: insights from international relations and comparative politics', *Journal of European Public Policy* 5(1): 17–37.

Haas, Peter M. 2000, 'Choosing to comply: theorizing from international relations and comparative politics'. In Dinah Shelton (ed.), *Commitment and Compliance: The Role of Non-Binding Norms in the International Legal System*, New York: Oxford University Press.

Haas, Peter M. (ed.) 1992, *Knowledge, Power, and International Policy Coordination, International Organization* 46(1), special edition.

Haas, Peter M., Robert O. Keohane and Marc A. Levy (eds) 1993, *Institutions for the Earth: Sources of Effective International Environmental Protection*, Cambridge, Ma.: MIT Press.

Haggard, Stephan 1988, 'The politics of industrialization in the Republic of Korea and Taiwan'. In Helen Hughes (ed.), *Achieving Industrialization in East Asia*, Cambridge University Press, 260–82.

Haggard, Stephan 1990a, *Pathways from the Periphery*, Ithaca: Cornell University Press.

Haggard, Stephan 1990b, 'The political economy of the Philippine debt crisis'. In Joan M. Nelson (ed.), *Economic Crisis and Policy Choice: The Politics of Adjustment in the Third World*, Princeton University Press, 215–55.

Haggard, Stephan 1991, 'Structuralism and its critics: recent progress in International Relations theory'. In Adler and Crawford (eds), *Progress in Postwar International Relations*, 403–37.

Haggard, Stephan 1995, *Developing Nations and the Politics of Global Integration*, Washington, D.C.: Brookings Institution.

Haggard, Stephan 1997, 'Regionalism in Asia and the Americas'. In Mansfield and Milner (eds), *The Political Economy of Regionalism*, 20–49.

Haggard, Stephan, and Beth A. Simmons 1987, 'Theories of International Regimes', *International Organization* 41(3): 491–517.

Hall, Peter A. (ed.) 1989, *The Political Power of Economic Ideas*, Princeton University Press.

Hamashita, Takeshi 1997, 'The intra-regional system in East Asia in modern times'. In Katzenstein and Shiraishi (eds), *Network Power*, 113–35.

Hamilton-Hart, Natasha 1999, Asia: the origins of uneven regionalism. Mimeo, May, Canberra: Australian National University.

Harland, Bryce 1996, *Collision Course: America and East Asia in the Past and the Future*, Singapore: Institute of Southeast Asian Studies.

Harris, Stuart 1989a, 'Economic cooperation and trading blocs', *Australian Foreign Affairs and Trade: The Monthly Record* 60(3): 63–6.

Harris, Stuart 1989b, 'Regional economic cooperation, trading blocs and Australian interests', *Australian Outlook: The Australian Journal of International Affairs* 43(2): 16–24.

Harris, Stuart 1994, 'Policy networks and economic cooperation: policy coordination in the Asia-Pacific region', *Pacific Review* 7(4): 381–96.

Harris, Stuart 1996, 'China in the WTO and APEC'. In David S. G. Goodman and Gerald Segal (eds), *China Rising: Nationalism and Interdependence*, London: Routledge, 134–55.

Harris, Stuart 1997, 'China, economics and regional security'. In Chai et al. (eds), *China and the Asian Pacific Economy*, 1–9.

Harris, Stuart 2000a, 'Asian multilateral institutions and their response to the Asian economic crisis: the regional and global implications', *Pacific Review* 13(3): 495–516.

Harris, Stuart 2000b, 'Ellis Krauss on APEC origins', *Pacific Review* 13(3): 521–3.

Hasenclever, Andreas, Peter Mayer and Volker Rittberger 1996, 'Interests, power, knowledge: the study of international regimes', *Mershon International Studies Review* 40, Supplement 2 (October): 177–228.

Hasenclever, Andreas, Peter Mayer and Volker Rittberger 1997, *Theories of International Regimes*, Cambridge University Press.

Hatch, Walter, and Kozo Yamamura 1996, *Asia in Japan's Embrace: Building a Regional Production Alliance*, Cambridge University Press.

Haworth, Nigel 1999, 'Setting the standard: APEC and the US Government's campaign for international labour standards'. Paper presented at the APEC Study Centre Consortium Conference, 'Towards APEC's Second Decade: Challenges Opportunities and Priorities', Auckland, 31 May–2 June.

Helleiner, Gerald K. 1981, *Intra-Firm Trade and the Developing Countries*, London: Macmillan.

Helleiner, G. K. 1996, 'Why small countries worry: neglected issues in current analyses of the benefits and costs for small countries of integrating with large ones', *World Economy* 19(6): 759–63.

Hellmann, Donald C. 1988, 'Japanese politics and foreign policy: elitist democracy within an American greenhouse'. In Takashi Inoguchi and Daniel Okimoto (eds), *The Political Economy of Japan*, vol. 2, Stanford University Press, 345–78.

Henkin, Louis 1979, *How Nations Behave: Law and Foreign Policy*, 2nd edn, New York: Columbia University Press for the Council on Foreign Relations.

Higgott, Richard 1991, 'The politics of Australia's international economic relations: adjustment and two-level games', *Australian Journal of Political Science* 26(1): 2–28.

Higgott, Richard 1995, 'APEC – a sceptical view'. In Mack and Ravenhill (eds), *Pacific Cooperation*, 66–97.

Higgott, Richard 1998, 'The Pacific and beyond: APEC, ASEM and regional economic management'. In Grahame Thompson (ed.), *Economic Dynamism in the Asia-Pacific: The Growth of Integration and Competitiveness*, London: Routledge, 335–55.

Higgott, Richard, and Andrew Fenton Cooper 1990, 'Middle power leadership and coalition building: Australia, the Cairns Group and the Uruguay Round of trade negotiations', *International Organization* 44(4): 589–632.

Higgott, Richard, and Richard Stubbs 1995, 'Competing conceptions of economic regionalism: APEC versus EAEC in the Asia Pacific', *Review of International Political Economy* 2(3): 516–35.

Hill, Hal 1996, *The Indonesian Economy Since 1966: Southeast Asia's Emerging Giant*, Cambridge University Press.

Hirata, Akira, Jiro Okamoto and Tatsushi Ogita 1996, 'Strategy toward APEC: the case of Japan'. In Yamazawa and Hirata (eds), *APEC: Cooperation from Diversity*, 29–42.

Hirschman, Albert O. 1945, *National Power and the Structure of Foreign Trade*, Berkeley, Cal.: University of California Press.

Holmes, John W. 1982, *The Shaping of Peace: Canada and the Search for World Order 1943–1957*, vol. 2, University of Toronto Press.

Holsti, K. J. 1992, 'Governance without government: polyarchy in nineteenth-century European international politics'. In James N. Rosenau and Ernst-Otto Czempiel (eds), *Governance without Government: Order and Change in World Politics*, Cambridge University Press, 30–57.

Hudec, Robert E. 1990, 'Thinking about the new Section 301: beyond good and evil'. In Bhagwati and Patrick (eds), *Aggressive Unilateralism*, 113–59.

Hufbauer, Gary Clyde 1995, 'Whither APEC?' *Journal of Asian Economics* 6(1): 89–94.

Hufbauer, Gary Clyde, Jeffrey J. Schott and Kimberly Ann Elliott 1985, *Economic Sanctions Reconsidered: History and Current Policy*, Washington, D.C.: Institute for International Economics.

Hughes, Helen 1991, 'Does APEC make sense?' *ASEAN Economic Bulletin* 8(2): 125–36.

Hurrell, Andrew 1993, 'International society and the study of regimes: a reflective approach'. In Rittberger (ed.), *Regime Theory and International Relations*, 49–72.

Hurrell, Andrew 1995, 'Regionalism in theoretical perspective'. In Louise Fawcett and Andrew Hurrell (eds), *Regionalism in World Politics: Regional Organization and International Order*, Oxford: Oxford University Press, 37–73.

Ikenberry, G. John 1992, 'A world economy restored: expert consensus and the Anglo-American postwar settlement', *International Organization* 46(1): 289–321.

Ikenberry, G. John 1993, 'Creating yesterday's new world order: Keynesian "new thinking" and the Anglo-American postwar settlement'. In Goldstein and Keohane (eds), *Ideas and Foreign Policy*, 57–86.

Ikenberry, G. John, and Charles A. Kupchan 1990, 'Socialization and hegemonic power', *International Organization* 44(3): 283–315.

Jackson, John H. 1998, 'Designing and implementing effective dispute settlement procedures: WTO dispute settlement, appraisal and prospects'. In Anne O. Krueger (ed.) with the assistance of Chonira Aturupane, *The WTO as an International Organization*, University of Chicago Press, 161–80.

Jacobsen, John Kurt 1995, 'Much ado about ideas: the cognitive factor in economic policy', *World Politics* 47(2): 283–310.

Jayasuriya, Kanishka 1994, 'Singapore: the politics of regional definition', *Pacific Review* 7(4): 411–20.

JNCPEC (Japanese National Committee for Pacific Economic Cooperation) 1988, *Review on Pacific Economic Cooperation Activities*, Tokyo: Japan Institute of International Affairs.

Job, Brian L., and Frank Langdon 1997, 'APEC beyond economics: the politics of APEC'. Working Paper No. 243. South Bend, In.: Helen Kellogg Institute for International Studies, University of Notre Dame.

Johnson, Chalmers 1982, *MITI and the Japanese Miracle: The Growth of Industrial Policy, 1925–1975*, Stanford University Press.

Johnson, Chalmers 1987, 'Political institutions and economic performance: the government–business relationship in Japan, South Korea, and Taiwan'. In Frederick C. Deyo (ed.), *The Political Economy of the New Asian Industrialism*, Ithaca: Cornell University Press, 136–64.

Johnson, Harry G. 1954, 'Optimum tariffs and retaliation', *Review of Economic Studies*, 21(2): 142–53.

Johnstone, Christopher B. 1995, 'An awkward dance: the Osaka Summit, Japanese leadership and the future of APEC', *JEI Report* 39A (20 October).

Jomo, K. S. (ed.) 1993, *Industrialising Malaysia: Policy, Performance, Prospects*, London: Routledge.

Jomo, K. S. (ed.) 1995, *Privatizing Malaysia: Rents, Rhetoric, Realities*, Boulder, Co.: Westview.

Jung, Ku-Hyun, and Jean-Pierre Lehmann 1997, Report on Asia–Europe economic and business relations in the ASEM framework. Submitted to the Third Plenary Session of the Council for Asia Europe Cooperation held in Tokyo in November 1997.

Kahler, Miles 1988, 'Organizing the Pacific'. In Robert Scalapino, Seizaburo Sato, Jusuf Wanandi and Sung-joo Han (eds), *Pacific-Asian Economic Policies and Regional Interdependence,* Berkeley, Cal.: Institute of East Asian Studies, University of California.

Kahler, Miles 1992, 'Multilateralism with small and large numbers', *International Organization* 46(3): 681–708.

Kahler, Miles 1993, 'Bargaining with the IMF: two-level strategies and developing countries'. In Evans et al. (eds), *Double-Edged Diplomacy,* 363–94.

Kahler, Miles 1995a, 'Institution-building in the Pacific'. In Mack and Ravenhill (eds), *Pacific Cooperation,* 16–39.

Kahler, Miles 1995b, *International Institutions and the Political Economy of Integration,* Washington, D.C.: Brookings Institution.

Katzenstein, Peter J. 1985, *Small States in World Markets: Industrial Policy in Europe,* Ithaca: Cornell University Press.

Katzenstein, Peter J. (ed.) 1996, *The Culture of National Security: Norms and Identity in World Politics,* New York: Columbia University Press.

Katzenstein, Peter J. 1997, 'Asian regionalism in comparative perspective'. In Katzenstein and Shiraishi (eds), *Network Power: Japan and Asia,* 1–44.

Katzenstein, Peter J., and Takashi Shiraishi (eds) 1997, *Network Power: Japan and Asia,* Ithaca: Cornell University Press.

Keating, Paul 2000, *Engagement: Australia Faces the Asia-Pacific,* Sydney: Pan Macmillan Australia.

Keating, Tom 1993, *Canada and World Order: The Multilateralist Tradition in Canadian Foreign Policy,* Toronto: McClelland & Stewart.

Kelly, Paul 1992, *The End of Certainty: The Story of the 1980s,* Sydney: Allen & Unwin.

Kemp, Murray C. 1962, 'The gains from international trade', *Economic Journal* 72(288): 803–19.

Kemp, Murray C., and Henry Y. Wan, Jr. 1976, 'An elementary proposition concerning the formation of customs unions', *Journal of International Economics* 6 (February): 95–8.

Keohane, Robert O. 1980, 'The theory of hegemonic stability and changes in international economic regimes'. In Ole R. Holsti, Randolph M. Siverson and Alexander L. George (eds), *Change in the International System,* Boulder, Co.: Westview.

Keohane, Robert O. 1984, *After Hegemony: Cooperation and Discord in the World Political Economy,* Princeton University Press.

Keohane, Robert O. 1986, 'Reciprocity in international relations', *International Organization* 40(1): 1–28.

Keohane, Robert O. 1989, *International Institutions and State Power: Essays in International Relations Theory,* Boulder, Co.: Westview.

Keohane, Robert O. 1990, 'International liberalism reconsidered'. In John Dunn (ed.), *The Economic Limits to Modern Politics,* Cambridge University Press, 165–94.

Keohane, Robert O. 1993a, 'The analysis of international regimes: towards a European–American research programme'. In Rittberger (ed.), *Regime Theory and International Relations,* 23–48.

Keohane, Robert O. 1993b, 'Institutional theory and the Realist challenge after the Cold War'. In David A. Baldwin (ed.), *Neorealism and Neoliberalism: The Contemporary Debate,* New York: Columbia University Press, 269–300.

Keohane, Robert O. 1997, 'Problematic lucidity: Stephen Krasner's "State power and the structure of international trade"', *World Politics* 50(1): 150–70.

Keohane, Robert O., and Joseph S. Nye (eds) 1972, *Transnational Relations and World Politics,* Cambridge, Ma.: Harvard University Press.

Kerr, Pauline, Andrew Mack and Paul Evans 1995, 'The evolving security discourse in the Asia-Pacific'. In Mack and Ravenhill (eds), *Pacific Cooperation*, 233–55.

Khanna, Jane 1996, 'Asia-Pacific economic cooperation and challenges for political leadership', *Washington Quarterly* 19(1): 255–74.

Khong, Yuen Foong 1992, *Analogies at War: Korea, Munich, Dien Bien Phu, and the Vietnam Decisions of 1965*, Princeton University Press.

Kim, Roy and Hilary Conroy (eds) 1987, *New Tides in the Pacific: Pacific Basin Cooperation and the Big Four (Japan, PRC, USA, USSR)*, New York: Greenwood Press.

Kimura, Hiroshi 1987, 'The Japanese concept of "Pacific Basin Cooperation" from the Soviet perspective'. In Kim and Conroy (eds), *New Tides in the Pacific*, 49–68.

Kindleberger, Charles P. 1973, *The World in Depression, 1929–39*, Berkeley, Cal.: University of California Press.

Kindleberger, Charles P. 1986, 'International public goods without international government', *American Economic Review* 76(1): 1–13.

King, Gary, Robert O. Keohane, and Sidney Verba 1994, *Designing Social Inquiry: Scientific Inference in Qualitative Research*, Princeton University Press.

Klintworth, Gary 1995, 'China's evolving relationship with APEC', *International Journal* 50(3): 488–515.

Klotz, Audie 1995a, *Norms in International Relations: The Struggle Against Apartheid*, Ithaca: Cornell University Press.

Klotz, Audie 1995b, 'Norms reconstituting interests: global racial equality and U.S. sanctions against South Africa', *International Organization* 49(3): 451–78.

Kocs, Stephen A. 1994, 'Explaining the strategic behavior of states: international law as system structure', *International Studies Quarterly* 38(4): 535–56.

Kodama, Yoshi 1996, 'Asia-Pacific region: APEC and ASEAN', *International Lawyer* 30(2): 367–89.

Koh, Harold Hongju 1997, 'Why do nations obey international law?' *Yale Law Journal* 106(8): 2599–659.

Kohona, Palitha T. B. 1986, 'The evolving concept of a Pacific Basin community', *Asian Survey* 26(4): 399–419.

Kojima, Kiyoshi 1966, 'A Pacific economic community and Asian developing countries', *Hitotsubashi Journal of Economics* 7(1): 17–37.

Kojima, Kiyoshi 1968, 'Japan's interest in Pacific trade expansion'. In Kiyoshi Kojima (ed.), *Pacific Trade and Development: Papers and Proceedings of a Conference held by the Japan Economic Research Center in January, 1968*, Tokyo: Nihon Keizai Kenkyu Senta.

Kojima, Kiyoshi 1971, *Japan and a Pacific Free Trade Area*, London: Macmillan.

Kojima, Kiyoshi 1981, 'Comment'. In Wontack Hong and Lawrence B. Krause (eds), *Trade and Growth of the Advanced Developing Countries in the Pacific Basin: Papers and Proceedings of the Eleventh Pacific Trade and Development Conference*, Seoul: Korea Development Institute, 551–3.

Kojima, Kiyoshi 1983, 'How to strengthen economic cooperation in the Asia-Pacific region?' In Hadi Soesastro and Sung-joo Han (eds), *Pacific Economic Cooperation: The Next Phase*, Jakarta: Centre for Strategic and International Studies, 116–26.

Komiya, Ryutaro 1999, 'APEC as seen through the eyes of a Japanese economist'. In John Piggott and Alan Woodland (eds), *International Trade Policy and the Pacific Rim: Proceedings of the IEA Conference Held in Sydney, Australia*, London: Macmillan, 289–301.

Kono, Yohei 1995, 'Japan's Position: Remarks by Minister Yohei Kono, Minister for Foreign Affairs of Japan', Tokyo: Ministry of Foreign Affairs, Japan, APEC 1995 Osaka Official Information. Available at http://apec.tokio.co.jp/osaka/info/j_position.html.

Koppel, Bruce M., and Robert M. Orr, Jr. (eds) 1993, *Japan's Foreign Aid: Power and Policy in a New Era*, Boulder, Co.: Westview.

Korhonen, Pekka 1994, *Japan and the Pacific Free Trade Area*, London: Routledge.

Krasner, Stephen D. 1976, 'State power and the structure of international trade', *World Politics* 28(3): 317–47.

Krasner, Stephen D. 1982, 'Structural causes and regime consequences: regimes as intervening variables', *International Organization* 36(2): 185–205.

Krasner, Stephen D. 1987, *Asymmetries in Japanese–American Trade: The Case for Specific Reciprocity*, Berkeley, Cal.: Institute of International Studies, University of California.

Krasner, Stephen D. 1991, 'Global communications and national power: life on the Pareto frontier', *World Politics* 43(3): 336–66.

Kratochwil, Friedrich V. 1989, *Rules, Norms and Decisions: On the Conditions of Practical and Legal Reasoning in International Relations and Domestic Affairs*, Cambridge University Press.

Kratochwil, Friedrich, and John Gerard Ruggie 1986, 'International organization: a state of the art on an art of the state', *International Organization* 40(4): 753–75.

Krause, Lawrence B. 1997, 'The progress to date and agenda for the future: a summary'. In C. Fred Bergsten (ed.), *Whither APEC? The Progress to Date and Agenda for the Future*, Washington, D.C.: Institute for International Economics, 241–6.

Krause, Lawrence B., and Sueo Sekiguchi 1981, 'Economic interaction in the Pacific Basin: dealing with change'. In Crawford and Seow (eds), *Pacific Economic Co-operation*, 138–53.

Krauss, Ellis S. 2000a, 'Commentary on Stuart Harris's "Asian multilateral institutions and their response to the Asian economic crisis"', *Pacific Review* 13(30): 517–19.

Krauss, Ellis S. 2000b, 'Japan, the US, and the emergence of multilateralism in Asia', *Pacific Review* 13(3): 473–94.

Kroll, John A. 1993, 'The complexity of interdependence', *International Studies Quarterly* 37(3): 321–48.

Krongkaew, Medhi 1996, 'Problems and prospects of APEC: a view from Thailand'. In Yamazawa and Hirata (eds), *APEC*, 89–103.

Krueger, Anne O. 1978, *Foreign Trade Regimes and Economic Development: Liberalization Attempts and Consequences*, New York: National Bureau of Economic Research.

Krueger, Anne O. 1997, 'Free trade areas versus customs unions', *Journal of Development Economics* 54(1): 169–87.

Krueger, Anne O. 1999, 'Are preferential trading arrangements trade-liberalizing or protectionist?' *Journal of Economic Perspectives* 13(4): 105–24.

Krugman, Paul 1986, 'Introduction: new thinking about trade policy'. In Paul Krugman, *Strategic Trade Policy and the New International Economics*, Cambridge, Ma.: MIT Press, 1–22.

Krugman, Paul 1990, *Rethinking International Trade*, Cambridge, Ma.: MIT Press.

Krugman, Paul 1992, 'Does the new trade theory require a new trade policy?' *World Economy* 15(4): 423–43.

Krugman, Paul 1993, 'Regionalism versus multilateralism: analytical notes'. In de Melo and Panagariya (eds), *New Dimensions in Regional Integration*, 58–79.

Krugman, Paul 1995, 'Dutch tulips and emerging markets', *Foreign Affairs* 74(4): 28–44.

Kueh, Y. Y. 1997, 'China and the prospects for economic integration within APEC'. In Chai et al. (eds), *China and the Asian Pacific Economy*, 10–28.

Kupchan, Charles A. 1997, 'Regionalizing Europe's security: the case for a new Mitteleuropa'. In Mansfield and Milner (eds), *The Political Economy of Regionalism*, 209–38.

Kwon, O. Yul 2000, 'The Korean financial crisis: implications for international business', *Asian Studies Review* 24(1): 25–50.

Lake, David A. 1988, *Power, Protection, and Free Trade: International Sources of U.S. Commercial Strategy, 1887–1939*, Ithaca: Cornell University Press.

Lake, David A. 1993, 'Leadership, hegemony, and the international economy: naked emperor or tattered monarch with potential?' *International Studies Quarterly* 37(4): 459–89.

Lambert, James M. 1997, 'Institution-building in the Pacific – Canada in APEC', *Pacific Affairs* 70(2): 195–202.

Langdon, Steven, and Lynn K. Mytelka 1979, 'Africa in the changing world economy'. In Colin Legum, I. William Zartman, Steven Langdon and Lynn K. Mytelka (eds), *Africa in the 1980s: A Continent in Crisis*, New York: McGraw-Hill, 179–88.

Langhammer, Rolf J. 1998, 'Europe's trade, investment and strategic policy interests in Asia and APEC'. In Peter Drysdale and David Vines (eds), *Europe, East Asia, and APEC: A Shared Global Agenda?* Cambridge University Press, 223–53.

Laothamatas, Anek 1988, 'Business and politics in Thailand', *Asian Survey* 28(4): 451–70.

Lawrence, Robert Z. 1987, 'Imports in Japan: closed markets or minds?' *Brookings Papers on Economic Activity* 2: 517–48.

Lawrence, Robert Z. 1991, 'Emerging regional arrangements: building blocks or stumbling blocks?' In Richard O'Brien (ed.), *Finance and the International Economy 5: The AMEX Bank Review Prize Essays*, Oxford: Oxford University Press, 23–35.

Lawrence, Robert Z. 1996, *Regionalism, Multilateralism, and Deeper Integration*, Washington, D.C.: Brookings Institution.

Leaver, Richard, and Maryanne Kelton 1999, 'Issues in Australian foreign policy: July to December 1998', *Australian Journal of Politics and History* 45(2): 239–53.

Lee Tsao Yuan 1996, 'APEC 1996: an ASEAN perspective', *Journal of Asian Economics* 7(2): 217–36.

Lee Tsao Yuan 1997, 'APEC and ASEM in comparative perspective'. Paper presented to ISEAS APEC Roundtable, APEC – Sustaining the Momentum, Singapore, August.

Lee Tsao Yuan (ed.) 1991, *Growth Triangle: The Johor-Singapore-Riau Experience*, Singapore: Institute of Southeast Asian Studies.

Leifer, Michael 1996, *The ASEAN Regional Forum*. Adelphi Paper No. 302. Oxford: Oxford University Press.

Levy, Jack S. 1994, 'Learning and foreign policy: sweeping a conceptual minefield', *International Organization* 48(2): 279–312.

Levy, Marc A., Oran R. Young and Michael Zürn 1995, 'The study of international regimes', *European Journal of International Relations* 1(3): 267–330.

Liddle, R. William 1987, 'Indonesia in 1986: contending with scarcity', *Asian Survey* 27(2): 206–18.

Lim, Linda Y. C. 1995, 'Southeast Asia: success through international openness'. In Barbara Stallings (ed.), *Global Change, Regional Response: The New International Context of Development*, Cambridge University Press, 238–71.

Lincoln, Edward J. 1990, *Japan's Unequal Trade*, Washington, D.C.: Brookings Institution.

Lindberg, Leon N., and Stuart A. Scheingold (eds) 1971, *Regional Integration: Theory and Research*, Cambridge, Ma.: Harvard University Press.

Linder, Staffan Burenstam 1986, *The Pacific Century: Economic and Political Consequences of Asian-Pacific Dynamism*, Stanford University Press.

Linnan, David K. 1995, 'APEC quo vadis?' *American Journal of International Law* 89(4): 824–34.

Lipsey, Richard G., and Wendy Dobson (eds) 1987, *Shaping Comparative Advantage*, Toronto: C. D. Howe Institute.

Lipson, Charles 1982, 'The transformation of trade: the sources and effects of regime change', *International Organization* 36(2): 417–55.

Lipton, Michael 1977, *Why Poor People Stay Poor: A Study of Urban Bias in World Development*, London: Temple Smith.

Lloyd, P. J. 1995, 'An APEC or multilateral investment code?' *Journal of Asian Economics* 6(1): 53–70.

Lloyd, P. J. 1998, 'Competition policy in APEC: principles of harmonisation'. In Rong-I Wu and Yun-Peng Chu (eds), *Business, Markets and Government in the Asia Pacific*, London: Routledge, 157–77.

Lloyd, P. J. 1999a, 'APEC and the WTO'. Paper presented at the Pacific Economic Cooperation Council Trade Policy Forum, Auckland, 3–4 June.

Lloyd, P. J. 1999b, 'EVSL and sector-based negotiations'. Paper presented at the APEC Study Centre Consortium Conference, 'Towards APEC's Second Decade: Challenges, Opportunities and Priorities', Auckland, 31 May–2 June.

Lorenz, Detlef 1991, 'Regionalization versus regionalism: problems of change in the world economy', *Intereconomics* 26(1): 3–10.

MacIntyre, Andrew 1991, *Business and Politics in Indonesia*, Sydney: Allen & Unwin.

MacIntyre, Andrew 1997, 'South-East Asia and the political economy of APEC'. In Garry Rodan, Kevin Hewison and Richard Robison (eds), *The Political Economy of South-East Asia: An Introduction*, Oxford: Oxford University Press, 225–47.

MacIntyre, Andrew (ed.) 1994, *Business and Government in Industrializing East Asia*, Ithaca: Cornell University Press.

Mack, Andrew, and John Ravenhill (eds) 1995, *Pacific Cooperation: Building Economic and Security Regimes in the Asia-Pacific Region*, Boulder, Co.: Westview.

Mackie, Jamie 1992, 'Overseas Chinese entrepreneurship', *Asian-Pacific Economic Literature* 6(1): 41–64.

Mackie, Jamie, and Andrew MacIntyre 1994, 'Politics'. In Hal Hill, *Indonesia's New Order: The Dynamics of Socio-economic Transformation*, Sydney: Allen & Unwin, 1–53.

Magee, Stephen P., William A. Brock, and Leslie Young 1989, *Black Hole Tariffs and Endogenous Policy Theory: Political Economy in General Equilibrium*, Cambridge University Press.

Mahathir bin Mohamad 1994, 'Regional groupings in the Pacific Rim: an East Asian perspective'. In Barbara K. Bundy, Stephen D. Burns and Kimberly V. Weichel (eds), *The Future of the Pacific Rim: Scenarios for Regional Cooperation*, Westport, Ct.: Praeger, 94–9.

Mahathir bin Mohamad, and Shintaro Ishihara 1995, *The Voice of Asia: Two Leaders Discuss the Coming Century*, New York: Kodansha International.

Mahbubani, Kishore 1992, 'The West and the rest', *National Interest* 28 (Summer): 3–12.

Mahbubani, Kishore 1993, 'The dangers of decadence: what the rest can teach the West', *Foreign Affairs* 72(4): 10–14.

Mahbubani, Kishore 1995, 'The Pacific way', *Foreign Affairs* 74(1): 100–11.

Mansfield, Edward D. 1998, 'The proliferation of preferential trade arrangements', *Journal of Conflict Resolution* 42(5): 523–43.

Mansfield, Edward D., and Rachel Bronson 1997, 'Alliances, preferential trade arrangements, and international trade', *American Political Science Review* 91(1): 94–107.

Mansfield, Edward D., and Helen V. Milner 1999, 'The new wave of regionalism', *International Organization* 53(3): 589–627.

Mansfield, Edward D., and Helen V. Milner (eds) 1997, *The Political Economy of Regionalism*, New York: Columbia University Press.

March, James G., and Johan P. Olsen 1989, *Rediscovering Institutions: The Organizational Basis of Politics*, New York: Free Press.

Martin, Lisa L. 1992, 'Interests, power, and multilateralism', *International Organization* 46(4): 765–92.

Matsunaga, Nobuo 1995, 'APEC and PECC', *Japan Review of International Affairs* 9(3): 195–8.

Matthews, Trevor, and John Ravenhill 1994, 'Strategic trade policy: the East Asian experience'. In MacIntyre (ed.), *Business and Government in Industrializing East Asia*, 29–90.

Mattli, Walter 1999, *The Logic of Regional Integration: Europe and Beyond*, Cambridge University Press.

Maull, Hanns, Gerald Segal and Jusuf Wanandi (eds) 1998, *Europe and the Asia Pacific*, London: Routledge.

Mauzy, Diane 1997, 'The human rights and "Asian values" debate in Southeast Asia: trying to clarify the issues', *Pacific Review* 10(2): 210–36.

Maxwell Stamp Associates 1967, *The Free Trade Area Option: Opportunity for Britain*, London: The Atlantic Trade Study.

McKeown, Timothy J. 1983, 'Hegemonic stability theory and nineteenth century tariff levels in Europe', *International Organization* 37(1): 73–91.

McKibbin, Warwick 1997, 'Regional and multilateral trade liberalization: the effects on trade, investment and welfare'. Brookings Discussion Paper in International Economics No. 134. Washington, D.C.: Brookings Institution.

Merson, John 1998, 'Asia's environmental crisis: innovation, sustainable development, and the future of APEC', *Asian Perspective* 22(2): 79–103.

Messing, Joel W. 1995, 'Toward a modern APEC investment policy', *NBR Analysis* 6(1): 55–61.

Millett, Michael 1998, 'APEC's slowing bicycle in danger of falling over', *Sydney Morning Herald* 19 November.

Milner, Anthony 1997, 'The rhetoric of Asia'. In James Cotton and John Ravenhill (eds), *Seeking Asian Engagement: Australia in World Affairs, 1991–95*, Melbourne: Oxford University Press, 32–45.

Milner, Helen V. 1988, *Resisting Protectionism: Global Industries and the Politics of International Trade*, Princeton University Press.

Milner, Helen V. 1992, 'International theories of cooperation among nations', *World Politics* 44(3): 466–96.

Milner, Helen V. 1997, *Interests, Institutions, and Information: Domestic Politics and International Relations*, Princeton University Press.

Miyagawa, Makio 1992, *Do Economic Sanctions Work?* New York: St Martin's.

Ministry of Economy, Trade and Industry, Government of Japan 2000, 'Report of the Japan–Singapore Free Trade Agreement (JSFTA) Joint Study Group', September, Tokyo: Ministry of Economy, Trade and Industry.

Moore, Thomas G., and Dixia Yang 1999, 'China, APEC and economic regionalism in the Asia-Pacific', *Journal of East Asian Affairs* 13(2): 361–411.

Moran, Theodore H. 1974, *Multinational Corporations and the Politics of Dependence: Copper in Chile*, Princeton University Press.

Moravcsik, Andrew 1993, 'Preferences and power in the European Community: a liberal intergovernmentalist approach', *Journal of Common Market Studies* 31(4): 473–524.

Moravcsik, Andrew 1997, 'Taking preferences seriously: a liberal theory of international politics', *International Organization* 51(4): 513–54.

Moravcsik, Andrew 1998, *The Choice for Europe: Social Purpose and State Power from Messina to Maastricht*, Ithaca: Cornell University Press.

Moravcsik, Andrew 1999, 'A new statecraft? Supranational entrepreneurs and international cooperation', *International Organization* 53(2): 267–306.

Moravcsik, Andrew, and Kalypso Nicolaidis 1998, 'Keynote article: federal ideals and constitutional realities in the Treaty of Amsterdam', *Journal of Common Market Studies* 36, Annual Review (September): 13–38.

Mori, Katsuhiko 1997, 'New regionalism or Asian ambiguity? Japan and the 1995 APEC Action Agenda'. In Karen Mingst and Katsuhiko Mori (eds), *Teaching International Affairs with Cases: Cross-National Perspectives*, Boulder, Co.: Westview, 81–101.

Morley, James William 1987, 'The genesis of the Pacific Basin Movement and Japan'. In Kim and Conroy (eds), *New Tides in the Pacific*, 11–34.

Morrison, Charles E. 1981, 'American interests in the concept of a Pacific Basin Community'. In Crawford and Seow (eds), *Pacific Economic Co-operation*, 114–17.

Morrison, Charles E. 1996, 'Comments'. In Yamazawa and Hirata (eds), *APEC: Cooperation from Diversity*, 162–6.

Morrison, Charles E. 1997, 'Development cooperation in the 21st century: implications for APEC', *Asian Perspective* 21(2): 37–56.

Morrison, Charles E. 1998, 'APEC: the evolution of an institution'. In Aggarwal and Morrison (eds), *Asia-Pacific Crossroads*, 1–22.

Morris-Suzuki, Tessa 1981, 'Japan and the Pacific Basin community', *World Today* 37 (December): 454–61.

Murofushi, Minoru 1996, 'A business agenda for APEC', *Asia-Pacific Review* 3(2): 21–36.

Muzaffar, Chandra 1993, *Human Rights and the New World Order*, Penang: Just World Trust.

Mytelka, Lynn Krieger 1979, *Regional Development in a Global Economy: The Multinational Corporation, Technology, and Andean Integration*, New Haven, Ct.: Yale University Press.

Nelson, Douglas 1988, 'Endogenous tariff theory: a critical survey', *American Journal of Political Science* 32(3): 796–837.

Nesadurai, Helen E. S. 1996, 'APEC – a tool for US regional domination?' *Pacific Review* 9(1): 31–57.

Neufeld, Mark 1995, 'Hegemony and foreign policy analysis: the case of Canada as middle power', *Studies in Political Economy* 48(1): 7–29.

Noble, Greg, and John Ravenhill 2000, 'The Asian financial crisis: causes and responses'. In Greg Noble and John Ravenhill (eds), *The Asian Financial Crises and the Global Financial Architecture*, Cambridge University Press.

Nogues, Julio J., Andrzej Olechowski and L. Alan Winters 1986, 'The extent of nontariff barriers to imports of industrial countries'. Staff Working Paper No. 789. Washington, D.C.: World Bank.

Noland, Marcus 1995, 'The United States and APEC'. In Woo Sik Kee, In-Taek Hyun and Kisoo Kim (eds), *APEC and a New Pacific Community: Issues and Prospects*, Seoul: Sejong Institute, 69–99.

Nossal, Kim Richard 1989, *The Politics of Canadian Foreign Policy*, 2nd edn, Scarborough, Ontario: Prentice-Hall Canada.

Nukazawa, Kazuo 1995, 'APEC: A a body in search of a spirit', *Japan Review of International Affairs* 9(3): 212–16.

Nye, Joseph S. 1987, 'Nuclear learning and U.S.–Soviet security regimes', *International Organization* 41(3): 372–402.

Nye, Joseph S. 1990, *Bound to Lead: The Changing Nature of American Power*, New York: Basic Books.

Olson, Mancur 1965, *The Logic of Collective Action: Public Goods and the Theory of Groups*, Cambridge, Ma.: Harvard University Press.

Onuf, Nicholas Greenwood 1989, *World of Our Making: Rules and Rule in Social Theory and International Relations*, Columbia, S.C.: University of South Carolina Press.

Osherenko, Gail, and Oran R. Young 1993, 'The formation of international regimes: hypotheses and cases'. In Young and Osherenko (eds), *Polar Politics*, 1–21.

Ostrom, Elinor 1990, *Governing the Commons: The Evolution of Institutions for Collective Action*, Cambridge University Press.

Ostry, Sylvia 1998, 'APEC and regime creation in the Asia-Pacific: the OECD model?' In Aggarwal and Morrison (eds), *Asia-Pacific Crossroads*, 317–50.

Oye, Kenneth A. 1985, 'Explaining cooperation under anarchy: hypotheses and strategies', *World Politics* 28(1): 1–24.

Oye, Kenneth A. 1992, *Economic Discrimination and Political Exchange: World Political Economy in the 1930s and 1980s*, Princeton University Press.

Paarlberg, Robert 1997, 'Agricultural policy reform and the Uruguay Round: synergistic linkage in a two-level game', *International Organization* 51(3): 413–44.

Pacific Basin Co-operation Study Group 1981, 'Report on the Pacific Basin operation concept'. In Crawford and Seow (eds), *Pacific Economic Co-operation*, 183–204.

PAFTAD Secretariat 1989, *The Pacific Trade and Development Conference: The First Twenty Years*, Canberra: PAFTAD Secretariat, ANU.

Pangestu, Mari 1994, 'APEC and investment facilitation'. In Hadi Soesastro (ed.), *Indonesian Perspectives on APEC and Regional Cooperation in Asia Pacific*, Jakarta: Centre for Strategic and International Studies, 69–89.

Pangestu, Mari 1999, 'APEC leadership in liberalization: an untested experiment'. In John Piggott and Alan Woodland (eds), *International Trade Policy and the Pacific Rim: Proceedings of the IEA Conference Held in Sydney, Australia*, London: Macmillan, 274–88.

Park, Ungsuh K. 1995, 'The impact of APEC: a private sector view', *Korea and World Affairs* 19(4): 632–45.

Parrenas, Julius Caesar 1998, 'ASEAN and Asia-Pacific economic cooperation', *Pacific Review* 11(2): 233–48.

Patrick, Hugh 1975, 'United States foreign economic policy towards Japan and the Pacific'. Australia–Japan Economic Relations Research Project Research Paper, November. Canberra: ANU.

Patrick, Hugh 1979, 'United States–Japan political economy: is the partnership in jeopardy?' Australia–Japan Economic Relations Research Project Research Paper No. 59. Canberra: ANU.

Patrick, Hugh 1996, 'From PAFTAD to APEC: homage to Professor Kiyoshi Kojima', *Surugadai Economic Studies* 5(2): 183–216.

Patrick, Hugh, and Peter Drysdale 1979, 'An Asian-Pacific regional economic organization: an exploratory concept paper'. Prepared for the Senate Committee on Foreign Relations by the Congressional Research Service, Library of Congress, July. Washington, D.C.: US Government Printing Office.

PECC (Pacific Economic Cooperation Council) 1995, *Survey of Impediments to Trade and Investment in the APEC Region: A Report by the Pacific Economic Cooperation Council for APEC*, Singapore: Pacific Economic Cooperation Council.

PECC 1996, 'Perspectives on the Manila Action Plan for APEC', Manila: 2nd edn, December.

PECC 1999, 'Progress towards Bogor Goals not reflected in IAPs', 10 September.

Pempel, T. J. 1997, 'Transpacific Torii: Japan and the emerging Asian regionalism'. In Katzenstein and Shiraishi (eds), *Network Power*, 47–82.

Perroni, Carlo, and John Whalley 1994, 'The new regionalism: trade liberalization or insurance?' Working Paper No. 4626. Cambridge, Ma.: National Bureau of Economic Research.

Petri, Peter A. 1993, 'The East Asian trading bloc: an analytical history'. In Jeffrey A. Frankel and Miles Kahler (eds), *Regionalism and Rivalry: Japan and the United States in Pacific Asia*, University of Chicago Press, 21–48.

Petri, Peter A. 1997, 'Measuring and comparing progress in APEC', *ASEAN Economic Bulletin* 14(1): 1–13.

Petri, Peter A. 1999, 'APEC and the millennium round'. Paper presented at the 25th Pacific Trade and Development Conference, Kansai, 16–18 June.

Phongpaichit, Pasuk 1992, 'Technocrats, businessmen, and generals: democracy and economic policy-making in Thailand'. In Andrew J. MacIntyre and Kanishka Jayasuriya (eds), *The Dynamics of Economic Policy Reform in South-East Asia and the South-West Pacific*, Singapore: Oxford University Press, 10–30.

Pillai, M. G. G. 1994, 'APEC and the Mahathir conundrum', *Economic and Political Weekly* 29, 10 December: 3135.

Plummer, Michael G. 1998, 'ASEAN and institutional nesting in the Asia-Pacific: leading from behind in APEC'. In Aggarwal and Morrison (eds), *Asia-Pacific Crossroads*, 279–314.

Pomfret, Richard 1996, 'Sub-regional economic zones'. In Bora and Findlay (eds), *Regional Integration in the Asia-Pacific*, 207–22.

Powell, Robert 1991, 'Absolute and relative gains in international relations theory', *American Political Science Review* 85(4): 1303–20.

Powell, Robert 1993, 'The relative-gains problem for international cooperation: response', *American Political Science Review* 87(3): 735–7.

Powell, Robert 1994, 'Anarchy in international relations theory: the neorealist–neoliberal debate', *International Organization* 48(2): 313–44.

Prestowitz, Clyde V., Jr. 1988, *Trading Places: How We Allowed Japan to Take the Lead*, New York: Basic Books.

Primakov, Yevgeny M. 1987, 'Problems of peace and security in Asia'. In Kim and Conroy (eds), *New Tides in the Pacific*, 35–48.

Primo Braga, Carlos A., and Geoffrey Bannister 1994, 'East Asian investment and trade: prospects for growing regionalization in the 1990s', *Transnational Corporations* 3(1): 97–136.

Pusey, Michael 1991, *Economic Rationalism in Canberra: A Nation-building State Changes its Mind*, Cambridge University Press.

Putnam, Robert D. 1988, 'Diplomacy and domestic politics: the logic of two-level games', *International Organization* 42(3): 427–60.

Putnam, Robert D., and Nicholas Bayne 1987, *Hanging Together: Cooperation and Conflict in the Seven-Power Summits*, rev. and enl. edn, London: Sage.

Putnam, Robert D., and C. Randall Henning 1989, 'The Bonn Summit of 1978: a case study in coordination'. In Cooper et al. (eds), *Can Nations Agree?*, 12–140.

Putnam, Robert D., with Robert Leonardi and Raffaella Y. Nanetti 1993, *Making Democracy Work: Civic Traditions in Modern Italy*, Princeton University Press.

Pyle, Kenneth B. 1995, 'The context of APEC: U.S.–Japan relations', *NBR Analysis* 6(3): 37–53.

Ramasamy, Bala 1997, 'The importance of APEC to China'. In Chai et al. (eds), *China and the Asian Pacific Economy*, 29–43.

Ravenhill, John 1979, 'Regional integration and development in Africa: lessons from the East African Community', *Journal of Commonwealth and Comparative Politics* 17(3): 227–46.

Ravenhill, John 1985, *Collective Clientelism: The Lomé Conventions and North–South Relations*, New York: Columbia University Press.

Ravenhill, John 1990, 'Australia'. In Hans J. Michelmann and Panyotis Soldatos (eds), *Federated States in International Relations*, Oxford: Oxford University Press, 76–123.

Ravenhill, John 1993, 'The "Japan problem" in Pacific trade'. In Richard Higgott, Richard Leaver and John Ravenhill (eds), *Pacific Economic Relations in the 1990s: Cooperation or Conflict?* Boulder, Co.: Lynne Rienner, 106–32.

Ravenhill, John 1995a, 'Competing logics of regionalism in the Asia-Pacific', *Journal of European Integration* 18(2–3): 179–99.

Ravenhill, John 1995b, 'Economic cooperation in Southeast Asia: changing incentives', *Asian Survey* 35(9): 850–66.

Ravenhill, John 1998a, 'Adjusting to the ASEAN Way: thirty years of Australia's relations with ASEAN', *Pacific Review* 11(2): 267–89.

Ravenhill, John 1998b, 'Australia and APEC'. In Aggarwal and Morrison (eds), *Asia-Pacific Crossroads*, 143–64.

Ravenhill, John 1998c, 'Cycles of middle power activism: constraint and choice in Australian and Canadian foreign policies', *Australian Journal of International Affairs* 52(3): 309–27.

Ravenhill, John 2000, 'Aiming to secure a piece of the action: interests, ideas, institutions and individuals in Australian integration into the global economy'. In Aseem Prakesh and Jeffrey A. Hart (eds), *Responding to Globalization*, London: Routledge, 118–48.

Raymond, Gregory A. 1997, 'Problems and prospects in the study of international norms', *Mershon International Studies Review* 41, Supplement 2 (November): 205–45.

Rezasyah, Teuku 1996, 'The long path towards APEC: where do Indonesia, Australia and Japan stand?' *Indonesian Quarterly* 24(2): 181–94.

Richards, Gareth A., and Colin Kirkpatrick 1999, 'Reorienting interregional cooperation in the global political economy: Europe's East Asian policy', *Journal of Common Market Studies* 37(4): 683–710.

Riedel, James 1991, 'Intra-Asian trade and foreign direct investment', *Asian Development Review* 9(1): 111–46.

Rittberger, Volker (ed.) with the assistance of Peter Mayer 1993, *Regime Theory and International Relations*, Oxford: Clarendon Press.

Rix, Alan 1986, *Coming to Terms: The Politics of Australia's Trade with Japan 1945–1957*, Sydney: Allen & Unwin.

Rix, Alan 1993, 'Japan and the region: leading from behind'. In Richard Higgott, Richard Leaver and John Ravenhill (eds), *Pacific Economic Relations in the 1990s: Cooperation or Conflict?* Boulder, Co.: Lynne Rienner, 62–82.

Robison, Richard 1988, 'Authoritarian states, capital-owning classes and the politics of newly industrializing countries: the case of Indonesia', *World Politics* 41(1): 52–74.

Rodan, Garry 1996, 'The internationalization of ideological conflict: Asia's new significance', *Pacific Review* 9(3): 328–51.

Rodriguez, Francisco, and Dani Rodrik 2000, Trade policy and economic growth: a skeptic's guide to the cross-national evidence. Mimeo, May. Cambridge, Ma.: John F. Kennedy School of Government.

Rodrik, Dani 1989, 'Promises, promises: credible policy reform via signalling', *Economic Journal* 99(397): 756–72.

Rodrik, Dani 1992, 'The limits of trade policy reform in developing countries', *Journal of Economic Perspectives* 6(1): 87–105.

Rodrik, Dani 1995, 'Political economy of trade policy'. In Gene M. Grossman and Kenneth Rogoff (eds), *Handbook of International Economics*, vol. 3, Amsterdam: Elsevier, 1457–95.

Rogowski, Ronald L. 1989, *Commerce and Coalitions: How Trade Affects Domestic Political Alignments*, Princeton University Press.

Romer, Paul M. 1986, 'Increasing returns and long-run growth', *Journal of Political Economy* 94(5): 1002–37.

Romer, Paul M. 1987, 'Growth based on increasing returns due to specialization', *American Economic Review* 77(2): 56–62.

Root, Hilton L. 1996, *Small Countries, Big Lessons: Governance and the Rise of East Asia*, Hong Kong: Oxford University Press.

Rostow, W. W. 1986, *The United States and the Regional Organization of Asia and the Pacific, 1965–1985*, Austin, Texas: University of Texas Press.

Rothstein, Robert L. 1979, *Global Bargaining: UNCTAD and the Quest for a New International Economic Order*, Princeton University Press.

Rudner, Martin 1994, 'Institutional approaches to regional trade and cooperation in the Asia Pacific area', *Transnational Law and Contemporary Problems* 4(1): 159–86.

Rudner, Martin 1995, 'APEC: the challenges of Asia Pacific economic cooperation', *Journal of Modern Asian Studies* 29(2): 403–37.

Ruffin, Roy J. 1999, 'The nature and significance of intra-industry trade', *Federal Reserve Bank of Dallas Economic and Financial Review*, Fourth Quarter: 2–8.

Ruggie, John Gerard 1982, 'International regimes, transactions, and change: embedded liberalism in the postwar economic order', *International Organization* 36(2): 379–416.

Ruggie, John Gerard 1983, 'Continuity and transformation in the world polity: toward a neorealist synthesis', *World Politics* 35(2): 261–85.

Ruggie, John Gerard 1998, 'What makes the world hang together? neo-utilitarianism and the social constructivist challenge', *International Organization* 52(4): 855–85.

Rugman, Alan M., and Julie A. Soloway 1997, 'An environmental agenda for APEC: lessons from NAFTA', *International Executive* 39(6): 735–44.

Russett, Bruce 1967, *International Regions and the International System: A Study in Political Ecology*, Chicago, Ill.: Rand-McNally.

Ryan, Michael P. 1995, *Playing by the Rules: American Trade Power and Diplomacy in the Pacific*, Washington, D.C.: Georgetown University Press.

Saeki, Kiichi (ed.) 1981, 'The search for Japan's comprehensive policy guideline in the changing world: national priorities for the 21st century'. In Crawford and Seow (eds), *Pacific Economic Co-operation*, 207–13.

Samuelson, Paul A. 1939, 'The gains from international trade', *Canadian Journal of Economics and Political Science* 5(2): 195–205.

Sandholtz, Wayne, Michael Borrus and John Zysman (eds) 1992, *The Highest Stakes*, New York: Oxford University Press.

Sandhu, Kernial 1981, 'The Pacific Basin concept: a view from ASEAN'. In Crawford and Seow (eds), *Pacific Economic Co-operation*, 176–80.

Sapir, Andre 1993, 'Discussion of Chapter 7'. In de Melo and Panagariya (eds), *New Dimensions in Regional Integration*, 1491–506.

Saxonhouse, Gary R. 1986, 'What's wrong with Japanese trade structure?' Research Paper No. 137. Canberra: Australia–Japan Research Centre, ANU.

Saxonhouse, Gary R. 1996, 'Regionalism and U.S. trade policy in Asia'. In Bhagwati and Panagariya (eds), *The Economics of Preferential Trade Agreements*, 108–35.

Saxonhouse, Gary R., and Robert M. Stern 1989, 'An analytical survey of formal and informal barriers to international trade and investment in the United States, Canada, and Japan'. In Stern (ed.), *Trade and Investment Relations among the United States, Canada, and Japan*, 293–361.

Schwarz, Adam 1994, *A Nation in Waiting: Indonesia in the 1990s*, Sydney: Allen & Unwin.

Segal, Gerald 1990, *Rethinking the Pacific*, Oxford: Clarendon Press.

Segal, Gerald 1997, 'Thinking strategically about ASEM: the subsidiarity question', *Pacific Review* 10(1): 124–34.

Selden, Mark 1997, 'China, Japan and the regional political economy of East Asia, 1945–1995'. In Katzenstein and Shiraishi (eds), *Network Power*, 306–40.

Shibusawa, Masahide, Zakaria Haji Ahmad and Brian Bridges 1992, *Pacific Asia in the 1990s*, London: Routledge for the Royal Institute of International Affairs.

Shinohara, Miyohei 1982, *Industrial Growth, Trade, and Dynamic Patterns in the Japanese Economy*, University of Tokyo Press.

Shiraishi, Saya S. 1997, 'Japan's soft power: Doraemon goes overseas'. In Katzenstein and Shiraishi (eds), *Network Power*, 234–72.

Shiraishi, Takashi 1997, 'Japan and Southeast Asia'. In Katzenstein and Shiraishi (eds), *Network Power*, 169–94.

Sikkink, Kathryn 1991, *Ideas and Institutions: Developmentalism in Brazil and Argentina*, Ithaca: Cornell University Press.

Singh, Lalita Prasad 1966, *The Politics of Economic Cooperation in Asia: A Study of Asian International Organizations*, Columbia, Miss.: University of Missouri Press.

Skelton, Russell 1998, 'US, Japan push rival aid plans', *Sydney Morning Herald* 14 November.

Smith, Gary J. 1997, 'Multilateralism and regional security in Asia: the ASEAN Regional Forum (ARF) and APEC's geopolitical value'. Paper No. 97-2. Cambridge, Ma.: Weatherhead Center for International Affairs, Harvard University.

Smith, James McCall 2000, 'The politics of dispute settlement design: explaining legalism in regional trade pacts', *International Organization* 54(1): 137–80.

Snape, Richard H. 1986, 'Should Australia seek a trade agreement with the United States?' EPAC Discussion Paper No. 86/01. Canberra: EPAC.

Snape, Richard H. 1989, 'A free trade agreement with Australia?' In Jeffrey J. Schott (ed.), *Free Trade Areas and U.S. Trade Policy*, Washington D.C.: Institute for International Economics, 167–96.

Snape, Richard H. 1996, 'Which regional trade agreement?' In Bora and Findlay (eds), *Regional Integration in the Asia-Pacific*, 49–63.

Snidal, Duncan 1985, 'The limits of hegemonic stability theory', *International Organization* 39(4): 579–614.

Snidal, Duncan 1991, 'Relative gains and the pattern of international cooperation', *American Political Science Review* 85(3): 701–26.

Snidal, Duncan 1993, 'The relative-gains problem for international cooperation: response', *American Political Science Review* 87(3): 738–42.

Snyder, Scott 1999, 'Constructing a global architecture with an American blueprint: the ambivalent U.S. attitude toward Asian regional cooperation', *Global Economic Review* 28(3): 76–89.

Soesastro, Hadi 1981, 'The Pacific community idea: much ado about nothing?' *Asian Perspective* 5(1): 1–14.

Soesastro, Hadi 1983a, 'ASEAN and the political economy of Pacific cooperation', *Asian Survey* 23(12): 1255–70.

Soesastro, Hadi 1983b, 'Institutional aspects of Pacific economic cooperation'. In Hadi Soesastro and Han Sung-Joo (eds), *Pacific Economic Cooperation: The Next Phase*, Jakarta: Centre for Strategic and International Studies, 3–52.

Soesastro, Hadi 1989, 'The political economy of deregulation in Indonesia', *Asian Survey* 29(9): 853–69.

Soesastro, Hadi 1994a, 'APEC's institutional development from an ASEAN perspective'. In Hadi Soesastro (ed.), *Indonesian Perspectives on APEC and Regional Cooperation in Asia Pacific*, Jakarta: Centre for Strategic and International Studies, 149–70.

Soesastro, Hadi 1994b, 'The institutional framework for APEC: an ASEAN perspective'. In Chia (ed.), *APEC: Challenges and Opportunities*, 36–53.

Soesastro, Hadi 1995a, 'APEC after the Bogor Declaration', *Sydney Papers* 7(4): 79–85.

Soesastro, Hadi 1995b, 'The APEC Nonbinding Investment Principles', *NBR Analysis* 6(1): 62–9.

Soesastro, Hadi 1995c, 'ASEAN and APEC: do concentric circles work?' *Pacific Review* 8(3): 475–93.

Soesastro, Hadi 1996, 'APEC's contribution to regional security: ASEAN and the APEC processes'. In Soesastro and Bergin (eds), *The Role of Security and Economic Cooperation Structures in the Asia Pacific Region*, 21–44.

Soesastro, Hadi 1997a, 'The APEC approach to trade liberalisation commitments', Canberra: National Centre for Development Studies, ANU, 24 October. Available at http://ncds.anu.edu.au/online/conference/cf97–3.htm.

Soesastro, Hadi 1997b, 'APEC: an ASEAN perspective'. In Donald C. Hellmann and Kenneth B. Pyle (eds), *From APEC to Xanadu: Creating a Viable Community in the Post-Cold War Pacific*, Armonk: M.E. Sharpe, 174–94.

Soesastro, Hadi 1998a, 'APEC and the future of the Asia Pacific region'. In Senate Standing Committee on Foreign Affairs Defence and Trade: References Committee (ed.), *APEC Inquiry Submissions*, Canberra: Parliament of Australia, 7–17.

Soesastro, Hadi 1998b, 'Open regionalism'. In Maull et al. (eds), *Europe and the Asia Pacific*, 84–96.

Soesastro, Hadi 1999, 'APEC after ten years', *Indonesian Quarterly* 27(2): 146–70.

Soesastro, Hadi, and Anthony Bergin (eds) 1996, *The Role of Security and Economic Cooperation Structures in the Asia Pacific Region: Indonesian and Australian Views*, Jakarta: Centre for Strategic and International Studies in cooperation with Australian Defence Studies Centre, Canberra.

Sohmen, Helmut 1998, 'PBEC's role in APEC'. Accessed 5 April 2001. Available at http://www.pbec.org/speeches/1998/helmutapec.htm.

Sopiee, Dato Dr Noordin 1997, 'Should APEC address security issues?' In C. Fred Bergsten (ed.), *Whither APEC? The Progress to Date and Agenda for the Future*, Washington, D.C.: Institute for International Economics, 207–10.

Spencer, Barbara J., and James A. Brander 1983, 'International R & D rivalry and industrial strategy', *Review of Economic Studies* 50: 707–22.

Spero, Joan 1995, 'The Future of Asia-Pacific Economic Cooperation'. Testimony, 18 July. Washington, D.C.: US Congress House of Representatives, Committee on International Relations, Subcommittee on Asia and Pacific Affairs and International Economic Policy and Trade.

Srinivasan, T. N. 1995, 'APEC and open regionalism', Washington, D.C.: World Bank, Economic Development Institute, November.

Stein, Arthur A. 1982, 'Coordination and collaboration: regimes in an anarchic world', *International Organization* 36(2): 294–324.

Stein, Arthur A. 1984, 'The hegemon's dilemma: Great Britain, the United States, and the international economic order', *International Organization* 38(2): 355–86.

Stein, Arthur A. 1990, *Why Nations Cooperate: Circumstance and Choice in International Relations*, Ithaca: Cornell University Press.

Stein, Arthur A. 1993, 'Governments, economic interdependence, and international cooperation'. In Philip E. Tetlock, Jo L. Husbands, Robert Jervis, Paul C. Stern and Charles Tilly (eds), *Behavior, Society, and International Conflict*, New York: Oxford University Press, 241–324.

Stein, Janice Gross 1989a, 'Getting to the table: the triggers, stages, functions, and consequences of prenegotiation'. In Stein (ed.) , *Getting to the Table*, 239–68.

Stein, Janice Gross (ed.) 1989b, *Getting to the Table: The Processes of International Prenegotiation*, Baltimore: Johns Hopkins University Press.

Stern, Robert M. (ed.) 1987, *U.S. Trade Policies in a Changing World Economy*, Cambridge, Ma.: MIT Press.

Stern, Robert M. (ed.) 1989, *Trade and Investment Relations among the United States, Canada, and Japan*, University of Chicago Press.

Stokhof, Wim, and Paul van der Velde (eds) 1999, *ASEM: The Asia–Europe Meeting – A Window of Opportunity*, London: Kegan Paul in association with the International Institute for Asian Studies.

Stone Sweet, Alec, and Thomas L. Brunell 1998, 'Constructing a supranational constitution: dispute resolution and governance in the European Community', *American Political Science Review* 92(1): 63–81.

Stone Sweet, Alec, and Wayne Sandholtz 1997, 'European integration and supranational governance', *Journal of European Public Policy* 4(3): 297–317.

Strange, Susan 1982, '*Cave! Hic Dragones*: a critique of regime analysis', *International Organization* 36(2): 479–96.

Strange, Susan 1987, 'The persistent myth of lost hegemony', *International Organization* 41(4): 551–74.

Strange, Susan 1988, *States and Markets*, London: Pinter.

Sudo, Sueo 1988, 'From Fukuda to Takeshita: a decade of Japan–ASEAN relations', *Contemporary Southeast Asia* 10(2): 119–43.

Tan Kong Yam, Toh Mun Heng and Linda Low 1992, 'ASEAN and Pacific economic cooperation', *ASEAN Economic Bulletin* 8(3): 309–32.

Terada, Takashi 1998, 'The origins of Japan's APEC Policy – Foreign Minister Miki Takeo's Asia-Pacific policy and current implications', *Pacific Review* 11(3): 337–63.

Terada, Takashi 1999a, Creating an Asia Pacific economic community: the roles of Australia and Japan in regional institution-building. PhD thesis, ANU, Canberra.

Terada, Takashi 1999b, 'The Japanese origins of PAFTAD: the beginning of an Asian Pacific economic community'. Pacific Economic Papers No. 292. Canberra: Australia–Japan Research Centre, ANU.

Thelen, Kathleen, and Sven Steinmo 1992, 'Historical institutionalism in comparative politics'. In Sven Steinmo, Kathleen Thelen and Frank Longstreth (eds), *Structuring Politics: Historical Institutionalism in Comparative Analysis*, Cambridge University Press, 1–32.

Thornton, Robert 1988, *Lexicon of Intentionally Ambiguous Recommendations*, Deephaven, Mn: Meadowbrook.

Toh Mun Heng and Linda Low (eds) 1993, *Regional Cooperation and Growth Triangles in ASEAN*, Singapore: Times Academic Press.

Triffin, Robert 1954, 'Economic integration: institutions, theories, and policies', *World Politics* 6(4): 526–37.

Tugwell, Franklin 1975, *The Politics of Oil in Venezuela*, Stanford University Press.

Tyson, Laura D'Andrea 1993, *Who's Bashing Whom? Trade Conflicts in High-Technology Industries*, Washington, D.C.: Institute for International Economics.

Van Wolferen, Karel 1989, *The Enigma of Japanese Power: People and Politics in a Stateless Nation*, London: Macmillan.

Venables, Anthony J. 1999, 'Regional integration agreements: a force for convergence or divergence?' Working Paper Series No. 2260. Washington, D.C.: World Bank.

Venables, Anthony J., and Alasdair Smith 1986, 'Trade and industrial policy under imperfect competition', *Economic Policy* 3(1): 621–72.

Verdier, Daniel 1994, *Democracy and International Trade: Britain, France, and the United States, 1860–1990*, Princeton University Press.

Vernon, Raymond 1996, 'Passing through regionalism: the transition to global markets', *World Economy* 19(6): 621–33.

Vousden, Neil 1990, *The Economics of Trade Protection*, Cambridge University Press.

Wade, Robert 1990, *Governing the Market: Economic Theory and the Role of Government in East Asian Industrialization*, Princeton University Press.

Wallis, W. Allen 1984, 'The Near West: America and the Pacific', *Department of State Bulletin* 84(2089): 50–53.

Wallis, W. Allen 1988, 'The U.S. and the Pacific Basin: trade and adjustment issues', *Department of State Bulletin* 88(2135): 23–6.

Walsh, J. Richard 1993, 'A pillar of the community: the role of APEC in US policy', *Journal of East Asian Affairs* 7(2): 545–62.

Walt, Steven M. 1987, *The Origins of Alliances*, Ithaca: Cornell University Press.

Waltz, Kenneth N. 1970, 'The myth of national interdependence'. In Charles P. Kindleberger (ed.), *The International Corporation*, Cambridge, Ma.: MIT Press.

Waltz, Kenneth N. 1979, *Theory of International Politics*, Reading, Ma.: Addison-Wesley.

Ward, R. G. 1989, 'Earth's empty quarter? The Pacific Islands in a Pacific century', *The Geographical Journal* 155(2): 235–46.

Watanabe, Akio 1995, 'What is Asia-Pacific regionalism?' *Japan Review of International Affairs* 9(3): 189–94.

Watanabe, Akio, and Tsutomu Kikuchi 1995, 'Japan's perspective on APEC: community or association', *NBR Analysis* 6(3): 23–36.

Weatherbee, Donald E. 1989, 'ASEAN and Pacific regionalism'. Institute of Security and International Studies Paper No. 4. Bangkok: Chulalongkorn University.

Webb, Michael C., and Stephen D. Krasner 1989, 'Hegemonic stability theory: an empirical assessment', *Review of International Studies* 15(2): 183–98.

Weber, Steve 1992, 'Shaping the postwar balance of power: multilateralism in NATO', *International Organization* 46(3): 633–80.

Wendt, Alexander 1987, 'The agent-structure problem', *International Organization* 41(3): 335–70.

Wendt, Alexander 1992, 'Anarchy is what states make of it: the social construction of power politics', *International Organization* 46(2): 391–425.

Wendt, Alexander 1994, 'Collective identity formation and the international state', *American Political Science Review* 88(2): 384–96.

Wendt, Alexander 1995, 'Constructing international politics', *International Security* 20(1): 71–81.

Wendt, Alexander, and Raymond Duvall 1989, 'Institutions and international order'. In Ernst-Otto Czempiel and James N. Rosenau (eds), *Global Changes and Theoretical Challenges*, Lexington, Ma.: Lexington Books, 51–74.

Wendt, Alexander, and Danield Friedheim 1995, 'Hierarchy under anarchy: informal empire and the East German state', *International Organization* 49(4): 689–721.

Wenjing, Chen, and Zhao Yumin 1998, 'Promoting sustainable development of the Asia-Pacific region through the APEC approach: challenges and opportunities', *Asian Perspective* 22(2): 105–31.

Wesley, Michael 1997, 'The politics of exclusion: Australia, Turkey and definitions of regionalism', *Pacific Review* 10(4): 523–55.

Whalley, John 1985, *Trade Liberalization among Major World Trading Areas*, Cambridge, Ma.: MIT Press.

Whitwell, Greg 1993, 'Economic ideas and economic policy: the rise of economic rationalism in Australia', *Australian Economic History Review* 33(2): 8–28.

Wight, Martin 1991, *International Theory: The Three Traditions*, ed. Gabriele Wight and Brian Porter, Leicester University Press, a division of Pinter Publishers.

Wightman, David 1963, *Toward Economic Cooperation in Asia: The United Nations Economic Commission for Asia and the Far East*, New Haven, Ct.: Yale University Press.

Wilkinson, Jens 1996, 'Dealing with a fiction: the NGO conference on APEC', *AMPO Japan-Asia Quarterly Review* 26(4): 6–9.

Williamson, John (ed.) 1990, *Latin American Adjustment: How Much Has Happened?* Washington, D.C.: Institute for International Economics.

Wilson, Dick 1985, 'The Pacific Basin is coming together', *Asia Pacific Community* 30 (Fall): 1–12.

Winham, Gilbert R. 1986, *International Trade and the Tokyo Round Negotiation*, Princeton University Press.

Winham, Gilbert R. 1988, 'Why Canada acted'. In William Diebold, Jr (ed.), *Bilateralism, Multilateralism and Canada in U.S. Trade Policy*, Cambridge, Ma.: Ballinger Publishing Co., 37–54.

Winham, Gilbert R. 1992, *The Evolution of the International Trade Agreements*, University of Toronto Press.

Winters, L. Alan 1996, 'Regionalism versus multilateralism'. Policy Research Working Paper No. 1687. Washington, D.C.: World Bank.

Wonnacott, Paul 1995, 'Merchandise trade in the APEC region: is there scope for liberalisation on an MFN basis?' *World Economy*, Global Trade Policy Supplement: 33–51.

Woo, Jung-en 1991, *Race to the Swift: State and Finance in Korean Industrialization*, New York: Columbia University Press.

Woods, Lawrence T. 1993, *Asia-Pacific Diplomacy: Nongovernmental Organizations and International Relations*, Vancouver: University of British Columbia Press.

Woods, Ngaire 1995, 'Economic ideas and international relations: beyond rational neglect', *International Studies Quarterly* 39(2): 161–80.

Woolcott, Richard 1989, 'Australia's regional economic initiative: status as at June 1989', Canberra: DFAT, June.

World Bank n.d., *World Development Indicators*. Available at http://www.worldbank.org.

World Bank 1989, 'Foreign direct investment from the newly industrialized economies'. Industry Series Paper No. 22. Washington, D.C.: World Bank Industry and Energy Department.

World Bank 1990, 'The long-term perspective study of sub-Saharan Africa: Background Papers Volume 4', Washington, D.C.: World Bank.

World Bank 1993, *The East Asian Miracle: Economic Growth and Public Policy*, New York: Oxford University Press.

World Bank 2000, *Trade Blocs*, New York: Oxford University Press.

WTO (World Trade Organization) 1999, 'Annual Report 1999', Geneva: WTO. Available at http://www.wto.org/english/res_e/anrep_e/anre99_e.pdf.

WTO 2000, 'Report (2000) of the Committee on Regional Trade Agreements to the General Council', Geneva: WTO, 22 November.

WTO 2001, 'Regionalism: Facts and Figures'. Accessed 4 April 2001. Available at http://www.wto.org/english/tratop_e/region_e/regfac_e.htm.

WTO Secretariat 1995, 'Regionalism and the World Trading System', Geneva: WTO, April.

'WTO Ministerial Conference Highlights' 1996, *Sustainable Developments* (electronic bulletin list) 3(2) 10 December.

Wu, Linjun 1997, 'The PRC and APEC: a planned excursion for conciliation', *Issues and Studies* 33(11): 95–111.

Wyatt-Walter, Andrew 1995, 'Regionalism, globalization, and world economic order'. In Louise Fawcett and Andrew Hurrell (eds), *Regionalism in World Politics: Regional Organization and International Order*, Oxford: Oxford University Press, 74–121.

Yamakage, Susumu 1990, 'Will Japan seek regionalism?' In Michael S. Steinberg (ed.), *The Technical Challenges and Opportunities of a United Europe*, Savage, Md.: Barnes & Noble, 147–63.

Yamakage, Susumu 1995, 'Plotting APEC's future: a case for holding the ASEAN course', *Japan Review of International Affairs* 9(3): 199–205.

Yamakage, Susumu 1997, 'Japan's national security and Asia-Pacific's regional institutions in the post-Cold War era'. In Katzenstein and Shiraishi (eds), *Network Power*, 275–305.

Yamamoto, Yoshinobu, and Tsutomu Kikuchi 1998, 'Japan's approach to APEC and regime creation in the Asia-Pacific'. In Aggarwal and Morrison (eds), *Asia-Pacific Crossroads*, 191–211.

Yamamura, Kozo 1986, 'Caveat emptor: the industrial policy of Japan'. In Krugman (ed.), *Strategic Trade Policy and the New International Economics*, 169–209.

Yamazawa, Ippei 1995a, 'Implementing the APEC Bogor Declaration', *Japan Review of International Affairs* 9(3): 178–88.

Yamazawa, Ippei 1995b, 'What the Osaka Action Agenda should look like', *NBR Analysis* 6(1): 73–7.

Yamazawa, Ippei 1997, 'APEC's economic and technical cooperation: evolution and tasks ahead'. In C. Fred Bergsten (ed.), *Whither APEC? The Progress to Date and Agenda for the Future*, Washington, D.C.: Institute for International Economics, 135–78.

Yamazawa, Ippei 1998, 'Economic integration in the Asia-Pacific region'. In Grahame Thompson (ed.), *Economic Dynamism in the Asia-Pacific: The Growth of Integration and Competitiveness*, London: Routledge, 163–84.

Yamazawa, Ippei, and Akira Hirata (eds) 1996, *APEC: Cooperation from Diversity*, Tokyo: Institute of Developing Economies.

Yamazawa, Ippei, and Shujiro Urata 1999, 'APEC's progress toward the Bogor targets in trade and investment liberalization and facilitation: a quantitative assessment'. Paper presented at the 25th Pacific Trade and Development Conference, Kansai, 16–18 June.

Yarbrough, Beth V., and Robert M. Yarbrough 1992, *Cooperation and Governance in International Trade: The Strategic Organizational Approach*, Princeton University Press.

Yee, Albert S. 1996, 'The causal effects of ideas on policies', *International Organization* 50(1): 69–108.

Yeo Lay Hwee 2000, 'ASEM: looking back, looking forward', *Contemporary Southeast Asia* 22(1): 113–44.

Yoffie, David B., and Robert O. Keohane 1981, 'Responding to the "new protectionism": strategies for the advanced developing countries in the Pacific Basin'. In Wontack Hong and Lawrence B. Krause (eds), *Trade and Growth of the Advanced Developing Countries in the Pacific Basin: Papers and Proceedings of the Eleventh Pacific Trade and Development Conference*, Seoul: Korea Development Institute, 560–94.

Yoshimatsu, Hidetaka 1996, The internationalisation of Japanese corporations and its impact on Japan's commercial policy. PhD thesis, ANU, Canberra.

Young, Oran R. 1979, *Compliance and Public Authority*, Baltimore: Johns Hopkins University Press for Resources for the Future.

Young, Oran R. 1989, *International Cooperation: Building Regimes for Natural Resources and the Environment*, Ithaca: Cornell University Press.

Young, Oran R. 1991, 'Political leadership and regime formation: on the development of institutions in international society', *International Organization* 45(3): 281–308.

Young, Oran R. 1998, *Creating Regimes: Arctic Accords and International Governance*, Ithaca: Cornell University Press.

Young, Oran R. 1999, 'Comment on Andrew Moravcsik, "A New Statecraft? Supranational Entrepreneurs and International Cooperation"', *International Organization* 53(4): 805–9.

Young, Oran R., and Gail Osherenko 1993a, 'International regime formation: findings, research priorities, and applications'. In Young and Osherenko (eds), *Polar Politics*, 223–61.

Young, Oran R., and Gail Osherenko (eds) 1993b, *Polar Politics: Creating International Environmental Regimes*, Ithaca: Cornell University Press

Yuen Pau Woo 1999, 'APEC after ten years: what's left of open regionalism'. Paper presented at the APEC Study Centre Consortium Conference, 'Towards APEC's Second Decade: Challenges, Opportunities and Priorities', Auckland, 31 May–2 June.

Yunling, Zhang 1998, 'China and APEC'. In Aggarwal and Morrison (eds), *Asia-Pacific Crossroads*, 213–32.

Zacher, Mark W., with Brent A. Sutton 1996, *Governing Global Networks: International Regimes for Transportation and Communication*, Cambridge University Press.

Zarsky, Lyuba 1998, 'APEC, globalization, and the "sustainable development" agenda', *Asian Perspective* 22(2): 133–68.

Zarsky, Lyuba, and Jason Hunter 1997, 'Environmental cooperation at APEC: the first five years', *Journal of Environment and Development* 6(3): 222–51.

Zhang, Zhaoyong 1996, 'AFTA and APEC, with policy implications for Vietnam's trade and FDI', *Development Policy Review* 14(3): 273–97.

Index